Table of Con

INTRODUCTION

It doesn't matter what instruments on the kitchen you have if you don't have detailed directions and well prepared recipes to cook something super delicious! This is first and main law of each professional chef. Air Fryer – cooker machine of the third generation that can help you to cook easier, better and more delicious without butter and oil. However, to use Air Fryer most effectively, you need to know what to cook. Dear friend, I have prepared this great book of recipes for Air Fryer to make cooking sessions for your easier! I have created the most delicious 600 recipes for Air Fryer. This is the fullest book of Air Fryer you may find! On the following pages you will see: recipes of national Indian cuisine dishes, national Italian cuisine dishes recipes, examples of Spanish soups, French traditional desserts and authentic recipes. You will never have to look for the new ideas – this book will become your best friends and will be saving you for years! Cooking with this book you may eat different dishes all the day during 5 seasons! Can you imagine what an interesting life is waiting for you? Try new tastes every day and enjoy new dishes from day to day! Get as much creativity and energy as possible! Let this book become your source of inspiration. Apart from the great variety of the recipes, you will be pleased with the quality of dishes you may cook following further presented directions! I have written recipes, checked by the professional chefs! Each recipe in this book is a kind of unique. You will find in the recipes presented above small secrets of cooking, just like secret ingredients and additional steps! You will never have questions about the next step in cooking session or feeling you forgot something. Just follow the steps I have described in this book – and cooking will seem as easy as never before!

Good news for you it is easy navigation in the book. I have made ten paragraphs in this book for you to be able to find the recipe you need quickly and easily. Each category contains 60 checked, detailed and delicious recipes. What was the idea? If earlier you had to google for hours looking for the checked, proved and detailed recipes, now everything you need to do is to open this great book of recipes and to find a page in the needed category. Moreover, my recipes contain all the necessary information for the easy cooking. In the very beginning of the recipe, you will be able to see time frames needed to finish cooking session. I have included time needed to prepare products (wash, peel and cut them into slices) and time needed to cook products in the Air Fryer. Knowing this data, you will not only understand how much time you need to finish cooking session, amount of consumed electricity. Moreover, in the end of each recipe you will be able to find nutritional data. I have included calories, fats, carbohydrates and proteins contained in the certain dish. This information will help you to keep healthy lifestyle and choose recipes you want!

Now let's turn to the advantages of cooking with Air Fryer. This is cooing machine small enough not to take much space on the kitchen and the same time powerful enough to cook anything you need: from desserts and birthday cakes and up to light and delicious salads. You can cook even full size chicken in the Air Fryer. Apart from the size and power of this cooker, there are many other advantages. You don't need oil and butter to cook. It is not only great economy for you, but also avoid of heart diseases caused by the high cholesterol level. Many restaurants already started cooking French fries and other types of dishes with Air Fryer to get both healthy and crispy dishes. Another profit of the cooking with Air Fryer – it is consumed electricity. Cooking appliance of the third generation requires three times less electricity, than ordinary machines. What is the secret? Air Fryer consists of three basic parts^ bottom with hot spiral and fans for the circulation of air flows; cooking lid and third part on the top of the appliance with fans. In the bottom of the machine or main block, in the other words, we can see fans and spiral. When you are turning Air Fryer on, spiral is getting hotter and hotter (up to the set temperature). That is why you need to preheat Air Fryer. Ordinary, it takes from 5 to 10 minutes to preheat Air Fryer. While preheating, spiral made of metal gathers electricity and starts producing hot air. After the spiral is hot enough, fans are turning on and starting to spread hot air all over the cooking lid. Fans on the bottom of the appliance are placed below the spiral to spread air flows quickly. On the bottom of the cooking lid you can find small holes where air is going from the first block. This is the way, how air gets in the cooking lid and starting to circulate over the products. Fans direct air in the one or another side to cover all the sides of the ingredients. Moreover, the form of the cooking appliance helps air flows to circulate as long as it is needed. Appliance is made of the special material what makes air circulation easier and longer. Apart from the fans on the bottom of the Air Fryer, there is also one bid fan on the top of the cooking lid. That is how air produced by the spiral, circulates during all the cooking session in the cooking lid. This technology has many advantages. One of the most important is ability to get meat or poultry, vegetables or dessert cooked equally from all the sides. Just place products in the cooking lid and have rest, while Air Fryer is working. Air Fryer it is absolutely ecological cooking appliance that is working according to the system of the low electricity consuming. Even if cooking session will last for hours, Air Fryer will consume the same amount of electricity, as coffee machine to make one cup of Americano. Cooking in Air Fryer is better than cooking in oven or microwave: you almost don't need oil and butter; there is no harmful influence on the food (like waves in microwave); it is quicker; you are eating healthy, fresh and delicious food!

One of the most important steps while cooking with Air Fryer is to set right temperature and time of cooking session. In each recipe you will find information about the time needed for the Air Fryer preheating, temperature regime and time needed to get well-cooked and crispy dishes. I have made super detail recipes for you not to miss a step and to feel confident while cooking new dish for the first time. Let me help you and economy your time! One more advantage of the book you are reading right now: products we have chosen for each recipe. Sometimes it happens, when we have delicious recipe, but the list of ingredients is that long, that we just can't find half of them or can't even buy them in the nearest shops. I have included only recipes with plus minus standard set of the needed ingredients – all of them are cheap and you will be able to buy them on any market!

Dear friend, you are not just reading a book of recipes you are holding a guide to the life of delicious dishes and healthy lifestyle! With this book it will be super easy to cook and you will get only positive emotions from the cooking sessions! I hope, you will like recipes presented on the further pages and you will find this book quite useful and helpful!

BREAKFAST

Scrumptious Potatoes

It is not difficult and flavorsome for breakfast. The delicious meal with crispy skin.

Prep time:5 minutes | **Cooking time**:30 minutes | **Servings**:4

Ingredients:
- 9 oz of potatoes
- ½ teaspoon of salt
- 1 teaspoon of pepper
- 1 teaspoon of cumin
- ½ teaspoon of oregano
- ½ teaspoon of chili pepper
- ½ tablespoon of dry herbs

Directions:
1. Rinse and clean potatoes.
2. Slice them in the pieces.
3. Take the container and blend salt, pepper, cumin, oregano, chili pepper and dry herbs there.
4. Then rub potatoes with these seasonings.
5. Preheat the Air Fryer to 320F.
6. Sprinkle the Air Fryer with oil.
7. Place potatoes and cook for 25 minutes at 320F.
8. Then shake it and cook for 5 minutes at 350F.
9. Serve hot with sauce or vegetables.

Nutrition:
- Calories: 192
- Fat: 9,8g
- Carbohydrates: 23,4g
- Protein: 2,8g

Grilled and Appetizing Tomatoes

This meal is delectable and mouthwatering. Prepare these flavorsome tomatoes for breakfast.

Prep time:5 minutes | **Cooking time**:20 minutes | **Servings**:2

Ingredients:
- 2 tomatoes
- ½ teaspoon of salt
- ½ teaspoon of pepper
- ½ teaspoon of garlic
- ½ teaspoon of cumin
- ½ teaspoon of oregano
- 2 tablespoons of oil

Directions:
1. Rinse and clean tomatoes.
2. Slice them in two pieces.
3. Grease them with the tablespoon of oil.
4. Then blend salt, pepper, oregano, cumin with garlic.
5. Rub potatoes with this combination of flavors.
6. Preheat the Air Fryer to 320F for 20 minutes.
7. Cook tomatoes in the Air Fryer for 10 minutes.
8. Shake them well.
9. Cook the meal for 10 minutes.
10. Serve the hot meal. Decorate it with parsley or basil.

Nutrition:
- Calories: 56,5
- Fat: 3,9g
- Carbohydrates: 4,23g
- Protein: 1,1g

Potato Hash

Do you want something new and delicious for breakfast? Try this potato hash. It is flavorsome and great.

Prep time:15 minutes	**Cooking time**:40 minutes	**Servings**:4

Ingredients:
- 2 eggs
- 1 teaspoon of salt
- ½ teaspoon of pepper
- ½ green pepper
- ½ teaspoon of thyme
- ½ teaspoon of paprika
- 2 tablespoons of oil
- 1 onion

Directions:
1. Sprinkle the frying basket with oil. Preheat the Air Fryer for 2 minutes to 350F.
2. Cut onion in the pieces, place in the Air Fryer. Cook for 2 minutes.
3. Then chop pepper, add in the Air Fryer to onion, blend everything and cook for 5 minutes more. After that wash and clean potatoes.
4. Cut them in the pieces. Blend salt, pepper, thyme and paprika in the bowl.
5. Add these seasonings to potatoes and blend them.
6. Then place potatoes in the Air Fryer and cook for 30 minutes at 350F.
7. Beat eggs in the bowl.
8. Then pour potatoes with eggs, add pepper and onion and cook for 5 minutes at the same temperature.

Nutrition:
- Calories: 213
- Fat: 8,6g
- Carbohydrates: 6,7g
- Protein: 2,9g

Sweet Polenta Bites

These sweet bites will be great for morning tea or coffee. They are easy in preparing and very delicious.

Prep time:10 minutes	**Cooking time**:16 minutes	**Servings**:4

Ingredients:
- 2 tablespoons of oil
- 1 tablespoon of coconut oil
- ¼ cup of flour
- 1 cup of cornmeal
- 2 cups of water
- 1 tablespoon of butter
- ½ teaspoon of salt

Toppings:
- Powdered sugar
- Jam
- Maple syrup

Directions:
1. Boil water with salt.
2. Then add cornmeal. Mix everything well and cook.
3. Then add the tablespoon of butter.
4. Put the mixture in the fridge for 20 minutes. It should not be hot.
5. Then add coconut oil to the dough.
6. Make the balls from this mixture. Cover them with flour.
7. Then preheat the Air Fryer to 320F. Cook them for 8 minutes.

Nutrition:
- Calories: 360
- Fat: 9,8g
- Carbohydrates: 8,7g
- Protein: 3,5g

Scrumptious and Crispy Potatoes

This tempting recipe is for you. Cook and try. The meal is really flavorsome.

Prep time:30 minutes | **Cooking time**:35 minutes | **Servings**:4

Ingredients:

- 1 teaspoon of onion powder
- 1 teaspoon of pepper

- 1 teaspoon of garlic powder
- 2 teaspoons of salt
- 2 tablespoons of oil

- 1 red pepper
- 1 onion
- 6 big potatoes

Directions:

1. Rinse and clean potatoes.
2. Cut and place potatoes in the container.
3. Rub with pepper, garlic powder, salt
4. Sprinkle the Air Fryer with oil.
5. After that place potatoes in the Air Fryer.
6. Cook for 20 minutes at 350F.
7. Then slice onion in the pieces.
8. Cut pepper in the small parts and blend them with onion.
9. Add to potatoes and cook at the same temperature for 10 minutes.
10. Then blend and cook for 5 minutes.
11. Serve hot food with parsley or ketchup.

Nutrition:

- Calories: 280
- Fat: 9,3g

- Carbohydrates: 8,2g
- Protein: 3,1g

Toasted Bagels

It will be your favorite meal for breakfast. There is nothing difficult in preparing and after eating this delicious breakfast you will have a lot of energy.

Prep time:2 minutes | **Cooking time**:6 minutes | **Servings**:2

Ingredients:

- 2 bagels
- 1 tablespoon of jam

- 1 tablespoon of chocolate
- 1 teaspoon of icing sugar

- 1 tablespoon of butter

Directions:

1. Sprinkle the Air Fryer with oil.
2. Preheat it to 350F.
3. Cut bagels in 2 pieces.
4. Put them in the Air Fryer and cook for 3 minutes.
5. Then cover bagels with butter and cook for 3 minutes more.
6. Take out of Air Fryer and put on the plate.
7. They should not be very hot. It is possible to put them in the fridge.
8. Cover with the icing sugar, jam and melted chocolate.
9. Eat with tea, coffee, juice or milk.

Nutrition:

- Calories: 270
- Fat: 7,5g

- Carbohydrates: 7,5g
- Protein: 1,1g

Scrumptious Cinnamon Toast

This toast is really perfect. It will take only 5 minutes for cooking. Breakfast will be appetizing.

Prep time:5 minutes	**Cooking time:**5 minutes	**Servings:**4

Ingredients:

- 1 tablespoon of vanilla
- 1 teaspoon of ground cinnamon
- ½ cup of sugar
- 1 stick salted butter
- 12 pieces of bread
- 2 tablespoon of oil

Directions:
1. Take the container and put butter there.
2. Then add sugar, cinnamon and vanilla.
3. Blend the components.
4. Take the pieces of bread and cover one side with this mixture.
5. Sprinkle the Air Fryer basket with oil.
6. Place the pieces of bread with the combination in the Air Fryer and cook for 5 minutes at 390F.
7. Place on the dish and cut in 2 pieces.
8. Serve warm with different toppings or ice cream.
9. Enjoy with this perfect meal.

Nutrition:
- Calories: 157
- Fat: 6,2g
- Carbohydrates: 2,3g
- Protein: 1,2g

Delectable and Peppery Frittata

It is something wonderful and flavorsome. Then cook this appetizing frittata.

Prep time:5 minutes	**Cooking time:**5 minutes	**Servings:**4

Ingredients:

- ½ teaspoon of salt
- ½ teaspoon of pepper
- 1 tablespoon of oil
- 1 tablespoon of parsley
- 4 small tomatoes
- ½ of Italian sausage
- 3 eggs
- ½ teaspoon of dry herbs
- ½ teaspoon of paprika

Directions:
1. Preheat the Air Fryer to 380F.
2. Sprinkle the basket with oil.
3. Cut sausage in the pieces.
4. Rub them with salt, pepper, parsley, dry herbs and paprika.
5. Slice tomatoes in 4-6 pieces and blend with sausage.
6. Place in the Air Fryer and cook for 5 minutes at 380F.
7. Then beat 3 eggs, add to the combination.
8. Cook them for 5 minutes.
9. Serve hot with fresh vegetables or basil leaves.

Nutrition:
- Calories: 330
- Fat: 9,5g
- Carbohydrates: 8,7g
- Protein: 3,2g

Breakfast Potatoes

If you have some doubts about what prepare for breakfast – choose potatoes. You will like this meal because of crispy skin and also it is very tasty.

Prep time: 10 minutes	**Cooking time:** 20-22 minutes	**Servings:** 4

Ingredients:

- ¼ cup of onion
- 1 small red pepper
- ½ teaspoon of salt
- ½ teaspoon of pepper
- 2 tablespoon of oil
- 4 big potatoes
- ½ teaspoon of dry herbs

Directions:

1. Wash and chop potatoes in the pieces.
2. Then add salt, pepper and dry herbs to the bowl with potatoes and blend everything well.
3. Preheat the Air Fryer to 380F.
4. Sprinkle the frying basket with oil.
5. Place potatoes in the Air Fryer and cook for 15 minutes at 380F.
6. Then chop pepper in the strings.
7. Chop onion in the pieces and blend with pepper.
8. Add this combination to potatoes and cook for 5-7 minutes more at 320F.
9. Serve hot with sauces.

Nutrition:

- Calories: 190
- Fat: 6,7g
- Carbohydrates: 5,3g
- Protein: 2,3g

Fried English Breakfast

Do you want to prepare real English breakfast at home? There is nothing easier then to prepare it. You will like it, be sure.

Prep time: 10 minutes	**Cooking time:** 16 minutes	**Servings:** 4

Ingredients:

- 8 pieces of toast
- 1 can backed beans
- 4 eggs
- 8 pieces of bacon
- 8 medium sausages
- 2 tablespoons of oil

Directions:

1. Preheat the Air Fryer to 320F.
2. Sprinkle the frying basket with oil.
3. Then put sausages in the Air Fryer and cook for 5 minutes.
4. After that cook bacon for 5 minutes at the same temperature.
5. Then cook some part of sausages and bacon for 5 minutes at 300F.
6. The second part of bacon and sausages should be cooked with egg for 6 minutes at 300F.
7. Serve hot with sauce and vegetables.
8. You can enjoy with this meal with your friends.

Nutrition:

- Calories: 287
- Fat: 4,9g
- Carbohydrates: 4,9g
- Protein: 1,7

Eggs with Bacon and Buns

It is possible to prepare delicious buns for breakfast. They need only a few minutes of your time and your breakfast is ready.

| **Prep time**:10 minutes | **Cooking time**: 7 minutes | **Servings**:4 |

Ingredients:
- 4 cooked eggs
- 8 pieces of bacon
- ½ teaspoon of salt
- ½ teaspoon of pepper
- 4 buns
- 2 tablespoons of butter
- 2 tablespoons of ketchup
- ½ teaspoon of dry herbs
- 2 tablespoons of mustard

Directions:
1. Preheat the Air Fryer to 320F.
2. Sprinkle the Air Fryer basket with oil.
3. Then cut buns in 2 parts.
4. Cover them with butter and cook in the Air Fryer at 320F for 2 minutes.
5. Then mix sauce, mustard, salt, pepper, dry herbs in the bowl.
6. Cover buns with this mixture.
7. Put the piece of bacon and egg on buns.
8. Then cook them in the Air Fryer at 320F for 5 minutes.
9. Serve hot and enjoy with your breakfast.

Nutrition:
- Calories: 213
- Fat: 5,7g
- Carbohydrates: 4,6g
- Protein: 1,2g

Scrumptious and Sharp Burrito

Try to prepare this dish for your family. Very appetizing and satisfying! Remember this recipe!

| **Prep time**:10 minutes | **Cooking time**: 25 minutes | **Servings**:4 |

Ingredients:
- 1 tortilla
- ½ teaspoon of salt
- ½ teaspoon of pepper
- ¼ cup of cheese
- ¼ avocado
- 1/3 big red pepper
- 2 eggs
- 3-4 piece of chicken fillets
- 2 tablespoons of oil

Directions:
1. Beat 2 eggs in the bowl.
2. Then add salt and pepper and mix everything.
3. Sprinkle the Air Fryer basket with oil.
4. Place eggs in the Air Fryer and cook for 5 minutes at 290F.
5. Slice fillets in the pieces.
6. Then cut avocado and red pepper and blend together.
7. Blend all ingredients and add to eggs.
8. Cook for 15 minutes at 330F.
9. Then cover with cheese and cook for 5 minutes more at 300F.
10. Serve hot and enjoy with your meal.

Nutrition:
- Calories: 187
- Fat: 5,4g
- Carbohydrates: 4,2g
- Protein: 3,8g

Scrumptious Sausage with Cheese

Delicious and appetizing dish in a short time. When you prepare it, you will see that it is ideal meal for breakfast.

Prep time:10 minutes	**Cooking time**: 16 minutes	**Servings**:4

Ingredients:
- 5 tablespoons of ketchup or sauces
- 8 wooden skewers
- 1 can of roll dough
- 1 cup of cheese
- 8 sausages
- ½ teaspoon of salt
- ½ teaspoon of pepper

Directions:
1. Preheat the Air Fryer to 340F. Sprinkle the basket with oil.
2. Then cut sausages in the pieces and mix them with salt and pepper.
3. Place them in the Air Fryer and cook for 3 minutes.
4. Then put on another side and cook for 3 minutes more at the same temperature.
5. Cut the dough in the pieces. Blend sausages with ketchup.
6. Then put them on the pieces of dough. Cover with cheese and make rolls.
7. Put in the Air Fryer and cook for 5 minutes at 300F.
8. Then place on the other side and cook for 5 minutes more.
9. The temperature should be the same.

Nutrition:
- Calories: 210
- Fat: 5,9g
- Carbohydrates: 4,6g
- Protein: 3,9g

French Toasts Sticks

Such a bright, interesting toast is an excellent choice for breakfast. Also, it is wonderful and easy in preparing.

Prep time:10 minutes	**Cooking time**: 8 minutes	**Servings**:2

Ingredients:
- 2 teaspoons of icing sugar
- 2 teaspoons of maple syrup
- ½ teaspoon of cinnamon
- ½ teaspoon of nutmeg
- ½ teaspoon of salt
- 2 eggs
- 2 tablespoons of butter
- 4 pieces of bread
- 2 tablespoons of oil

Directions:
1. Sprinkle the frying basket with oil.
2. Then preheat the Air Fryer for 5 minutes to 340F.
3. Beat 2 eggs in the bowl.
4. Put salt, cinnamon and nutmeg there and blend everything well. Cut bread in the strings.
5. Cover them with butter on 2 sides. Place every bread string in egg.
6. Check if they are completely covered with egg.
7. Then place the strings in the Air Fryer and cook for 4 minutes.
8. Shake them well and cook for 4 minutes more at the same temperature.

Nutrition:
- Calories: 156
- Fat: 2,3g
- Carbohydrates: 3,2g
- Protein: 2,2g

Souffle for Breakfast

You can think that it is ordinary recipe, but when you try it, you will change your mind. You will remember this breakfast forever, because it is really delicious.

Prep time:15 minutes	**Cooking time**: 8 minutes	**Servings**:2

Ingredients:
- ½ teaspoon of parsley
- 2 tablespoons of cream
- 1 teaspoon of red pepper
- 2 eggs
- 2 tablespoons of oil

Directions:
1. Sprinkle the Air Fryer basket with oil.
2. Preheat it for 5 minutes to 300F.
3. Chop parsley and pepper in small pieces.
4. Beat eggs and mix them with parsley, cream and pepper.
5. Then put the mixture in the special forms for baking.
6. Cook for 8 minutes at 300F.
7. When they are ready, put them on the plate and leave for 10 minutes.
8. Serve warm with juice or tea.
9. Enjoy with this perfect breakfast.

Nutrition:
- Calories: 123
- Fat: 2,1g
- Carbohydrates: 3,2g
- Protein: 2,1g

Peppery Bacon with Mushrooms

This breakfast is wonderful. Just include this flavorsome meal in breakfast.

Prep time:15 minutes	**Cooking time**: 18 minutes	**Servings**:2

Ingredients:
- 4 eggs
- 6 oz of spinach
- 4 pieces of bacon
- 1 teaspoon of garlic powder
- ½ teaspoon of salt
- ½ teaspoon of paprika
- ½ teaspoon of pepper
- 8 tomatoes
- 8 mushrooms
- 2 tablespoons of oil

Directions:
1. Sprinkle the frying basket with oil.
2. Preheat the Air Fryer to 350F.
3. Blend salt, pepper, paprika and garlic in the bowl.
4. Then rub the pieces of bacon with this mixture.
5. After that place bacon in the Air Fryer.
6. Slice tomatoes and add them to bacon.
7. Then chop mushrooms and blend them with the products in the Air Fryer.
8. Then add boiled spinach and blend.
9. Cook for 13 minutes at 350F.
10. Then beat eggs, add them to the Air Fryer. Cook for 5 minutes at the same temperature.
11. Serve hot with sauces.

Nutrition:
- Calories: 178
- Fat: 4,9g
- Carbohydrates: 3,6g
- Protein: 2,8g

Flavorsome Avocado

It is delicious meal and also, it will be great breakfast for your family. If you prepare it one time, it will be your favorite one for the rest of life.

Prep time: 10 minutes | **Cooking time:** 15 minutes | **Servings:** 2

Ingredients:
- ½ teaspoon of salt
- ½ teaspoon of pepper
- 1 cup of bread crumbs
- 1 big avocado
- 2 oz of aquafaba
- 2 teaspoons of oil
- ½ teaspoon of dry herbs

Directions:
1. Take the bowl and mix salt, pepper, bread crumbs with dry herbs.
2. Put aquafaba in the second bowl.
3. Wash and clean avocado. Cut it in the small pieces.
4. Put every piece of avocado in aquafaba and then in bread crumbs.
5. They should be completely covered with bread crumbs.
6. Sprinkle the Air Fryer with oil. Preheat it to 300F for 2 minutes.
7. Then put the pieces of avocado in the Air Fryer.
8. Cook them for 10 minutes. Then shake them well and cook for 5 minutes more.
9. It is possible to decorate with parsley or basil leaves.

Nutrition:
- Calories: 141
- Fat: 3,8g
- Carbohydrates: 3,1g
- Protein: 2,7g

Flavorsome Avocado

It is delicious meal and also, it will be great breakfast for your family. If you prepare it one time, it will be your favorite one for the rest of life.

Prep time: 10 minutes | **Cooking time:** 15 minutes | **Servings:** 2

Ingredients:
- ½ teaspoon of salt
- ½ teaspoon of pepper
- 1 cup of bread crumbs
- 1 big avocado
- 2 oz of aquafaba
- 2 teaspoons of oil
- ½ teaspoon of dry herbs

Directions:
1. Take the bowl and mix salt, pepper, bread crumbs with dry herbs.
2. Put aquafaba in the second bowl.
3. Wash and clean avocado. Cut it in the small pieces.
4. Put every piece of avocado in aquafaba and then in bread crumbs.
5. They should be completely covered with bread crumbs.
6. Sprinkle the Air Fryer with oil. Preheat it to 300F for 2 minutes.
7. Then put the pieces of avocado in the Air Fryer. Cook them for 10 minutes.
8. Then shake them well and cook for 5 minutes more. It is possible to decorate with parsley or basil leaves.

Nutrition:
- Calories: 141
- Fat: 3,8g
- Carbohydrates: 3,1g
- Protein: 2,7g

Flavorsome Avocado

It is delicious meal and also, it will be great breakfast for your family. If you prepare it one time, it will be your favorite one for the rest of life.

Prep time: 10 minutes	**Cooking time:** 15 minutes	**Servings:** 2

Ingredients:
- ½ teaspoon of salt
- ½ teaspoon of pepper
- 1 cup of bread crumbs
- 1 big avocado
- 2 oz of aquafaba
- 2 teaspoons of oil
- ½ teaspoon of dry herbs

Directions:
1. Take the bowl and mix salt, pepper, bread crumbs with dry herbs.
2. Put aquafaba in the second bowl.
3. Wash and clean avocado. Cut it in the small pieces.
4. Put every piece of avocado in aquafaba and then in bread crumbs.
5. They should be completely covered with bread crumbs.
6. Sprinkle the Air Fryer with oil. Preheat it to 300F for 2 minutes.
7. Then put the pieces of avocado in the Air Fryer. Cook them for 10 minutes.
8. Then shake them well and cook for 5 minutes more.
9. It is possible to decorate with parsley or basil leaves.

Nutrition:
- Calories: 141
- Fat: 3,8g
- Carbohydrates: 3,1g
- Protein: 2,7g

Flavorsome Avocado

It is delicious meal and also, it will be great breakfast for your family. If you prepare it one time, it will be your favorite one for the rest of life.

Prep time: 10 minutes	**Cooking time:** 15 minutes	**Servings:** 2

Ingredients:
- ½ teaspoon of salt
- ½ teaspoon of pepper
- 1 cup of bread crumbs
- 1 big avocado
- 2 oz of aquafaba
- 2 teaspoons of oil
- ½ teaspoon of dry herbs

Directions:
1. Take the bowl and mix salt, pepper, bread crumbs with dry herbs.
2. Put aquafaba in the second bowl.
3. Wash and clean avocado. Cut it in the small pieces.
4. Put every piece of avocado in aquafaba and then in bread crumbs.
5. They should be completely covered with bread crumbs.
6. Sprinkle the Air Fryer with oil.
7. Preheat it to 300F for 2 minutes. Then put the pieces of avocado in the Air Fryer.
8. Cook them for 10 minutes. Then shake them well and cook for 5 minutes more.
9. It is possible to decorate with parsley or basil leaves.

Nutrition:
- Calories: 141
- Fat: 3,8g
- Carbohydrates: 3,1g
- Protein: 2,7g

Scrumptious, Sharp Chicken with Marinade

It is appetizing chicken with flavors. Easy and flavorsome.

| **Prep time:** 30 minutes | **Cooking time:** 20 minutes | **Servings:** 4 |

Ingredients:
- 4 chicken fillets
- 1 teaspoon of chili powder
- 1 teaspoon of pepper
- 1 teaspoon of salt
- 2 tablespoons of oil
- ½ tablespoon of mustard
- 1 teaspoon of garlic powder

Directions:
1. Cook up the Air Fryer to 390F.
2. Then prepare marinade.
3. Blend chili powder, pepper, salt, 1 tablespoon of oil, garlic powder and mustard.
4. Then slice meat in the pieces.
5. Cover the pieces of chicken with flavors and leave for 20 minutes.
6. Then blend the components again.
7. Grease the Air Fryer with oil.
8. Cook for 10 minutes at 390F.
9. Then change the temperature to 300F. Cook for 10 minutes more.

Nutrition:
- Calories: 320
- Fat: 9,5g
- Carbohydrates: 7,8g
- Protein: 8,3g

Tacos with Fish

You are waiting for the guests or you just do not have time for preparing breakfast? This delicious and quick recipe is exactly for you.

| **Prep time:** 15 minutes | **Cooking time:** 15 minutes | **Servings:** 4 |

Ingredients:
- 1 lemon
- 1 tablespoons of chopped cilantro
- 1 teaspoon of white pepper
- 1 teaspoon of black pepper
- ½ teaspoon of salt
- 1 cup of flour
- 1 cup of tempura butter
- 6 flour tortillas
- 10 oz of cod fillet
- 1 tablespoon of corn starch
- 1 cup of bread crumbs

Directions:
1. Take the bowl and mix 1 cup of flour, corn starch and add ½ cup of water.
2. Make the dough.
3. Add salt and mix everything.
4. After that, cut cod into the pieces.
5. Mix cilantro, white pepper, black pepper, tempura butter together and rub fish with it.
6. Then put fish in the pieces of dough and after that in bread crumbs.
7. Cook them in the Air Fryer for 10 minutes at 340F.
8. Then put them on other side and cook for 5 minutes.
9. After that put the pieces of fish on tortillas and sprinkle with lemon juice.
10. Serve hot with salad.

Nutrition:
- Calories: 198
- Fat: 6,3g
- Carbohydrates: 6,2g
- Protein: 5,7g

Delightful and Hot Onion Rings

Prepare this flavorsome rings with onion. This meal is appetizing.

| Prep time:15 minutes | Cooking time: 20 minutes | Servings:4 |

Ingredients:
- 4 oz of onion
- ½ teaspoon of salt
- ½ teaspoon of pepper
- ½ teaspoon of dry herbs
- ½ teaspoon of chili pepper
- ½ teaspoon of oregano
- ½ teaspoon of cumin
- 2 tablespoons of oil
- 2 eggs
- 1 cup of bread crumbs

Directions:
1. Cut onion in the pieces.
2. Take the container and blend salt, pepper, cumin, oregano, chili pepper and dry herbs there.
3. Beat eggs in the container.
4. Take onion ring, place it in beaten eggs and then in bread crumbs.
5. Preheat the Air Fryer to 350F.
6. Sprinkle the frying basket with oil.
7. Then cook onion rings for 10 minutes.
8. Shake them and cook for 10 minutes.
9. Serve hot with pasta.

Nutrition:
- Calories: 79
- Fat: 2,3g
- Carbohydrates: 5,1g
- Protein: 1,2g

Scrumptious Cheese with Macaroni

It is wonderful meal. This breakfast does not need a lot of time.

| Prep time:15 minutes | Cooking time: 20 minutes | Servings:4 |

Ingredients:
- 2 cups of whipped cream
- ½ teaspoon of salt
- ½ teaspoon of pepper
- 1 teaspoon of corn starch
- 2 cups of cheese
- 2 cups of ready macaroni
- 2 tablespoons of oil

Directions:
1. Preheat the Air Fryer to 300F.
2. Sprinkle the Air Fryer with oil.
3. Blend salt, pepper and corn starch in the bowl.
4. Then place macaroni there and mix everything well.
5. After that put the ingredients in the Air Fryer and cook for 15 minutes.
6. Then cover the meal with cheese. Cook for 5 minutes at 280F.
7. Serve hot with ketchup or different vegetables.
8. After that decorate with fresh parsley.

Nutrition:
- Calories: 167
- Fat: 2,5g
- Carbohydrates: 4,7g
- Protein: 1,5g

Appetizing Lamb with Lime

You should cook this lamb. It is scrumptious and peppery.

Prep time:10 minutes	Cooking time: 10 minutes	Servings:4

Ingredients:

- 1 teaspoon of salt
- 1 teaspoon of pepper
- 2 tablespoons of lime juice
- 1 teaspoon of cumin seeds
- 2 teaspoons of garam masala
- 1 teaspoon of coriander seeds
- ½ teaspoon of chili pepper
- 1 tablespoon of yogurt
- 2 tablespoons of oil

Directions:

1. Rinse meat.
2. Chop it in the pieces.
3. Take the container and blend pepper, cumin seeds, garam masala, coriander seeds, chili pepper and rub lamb with these spices.
4. After that blend yogurt and lime juice.
5. Then cover lamb with this combination.
6. Leave meat for 1 hour.
7. Sprinkle the Air Fryer with oil.
8. Cook meat in the Air Fryer for 10 minutes at 390F.
9. Serve the meal with basil leaves or parsley.

Nutrition:

- Calories: 314
- Fat: 10,2g
- Carbohydrates: 8,2g
- Protein: 15,8g

Flavorsome Spinach with Cheese

You will get the meal with crispy skin. Just try! It is appetizing.

Prep time:10 minutes	Cooking time: 5 minutes	Servings:4

Ingredients:

- 1 oz of nuts
- 1 lemon
- 1 egg
- ½ teaspoon of pepper
- ½ teaspoon of salt
- 1 teaspoon of dry herbs
- 1 lb of spinach
- 2 tablespoons of oil
- 4 pieces of filo pastry
- 7 oz of cheese

Directions:

1. Place spinach in the boiled water for 1 minutes.
2. Then take and cut spinach in the small pieces.
3. Take dry herbs, salt and pepper and blend everything with spinach well.
4. After that chop cheese in small pieces and add to the combination.
5. Beat egg and cover the products with it.
6. Blend the products in the bowl.
7. Sprinkle the Air Fryer with oil.
8. Cook breakfast for 5 minutes at 390F.
9. Then sprinkle it with lemon juice.

Nutrition:

- Calories: 89
- Fat: 2,1g
- Carbohydrates: 5,7g
- Protein: 2,2g

Scrumptious and Piquant Cheese Sticks

Amazing and unique cheese sticks. Breakfast is flavorsome.

Prep time: 10 minutes	**Cooking time:** 12 minutes	**Servings:** 4

Ingredients:
- 2 teaspoons of oil
- 1 cup of bread crumbs
- 3 tablespoons of nonfat milk
- ¼ cup of water
- 1 lb of cheese blocks
- ½ teaspoon of salt
- ½ teaspoon of pepper
- ½ teaspoon of paprika
- ¼ teaspoon of red chili pepper powder
- 2 eggs
- 1 cup of flour.

Directions:
1. Create the sticks from cheese.
2. Place bread crumbs with flour on the separate plates.
3. Blend eggs with milk in the bowl.
4. Rub cheese sticks with salt, pepper, paprika and red chili pepper powder.
5. After that place the sticks in flour, then in beaten eggs and in bread crumbs.
6. Sprinkle the Air Fryer with oil.
7. Cook them for 6 minutes at 390F.
8. Then shake well and cook for 6 minutes at the same temperature.
9. Serve hot with sauces.

Nutrition:
- Calories: 177
- Fat: 5,2g
- Carbohydrates: 6,4g
- Protein: 4,9g

Flavorsome Pork with Spices

This pork is delectable. It is great with piquant pepper.

Prep time: 10 minutes	**Cooking time:** 15 minutes	**Servings:** 4

Ingredients:
- ½ tablespoon of mustard
- 9 oz of pork
- 1 teaspoon of pepper
- 1 teaspoon of salt
- ½ teaspoon of dry herbs
- 1 onion
- 2 tablespoons of oil
- 1 big green pepper

Directions:
1. Chop pork in the pieces.
2. Then blend salt, pepper, dry herbs in the bowl and rub pork with spices.
3. Chop onion in the rings and add to meat.
4. Then cut pepper in the pieces and add to pork.
5. After that add mustard and blend everything.
6. Sprinkle the Air Fryer basket with oil.
7. Cook meat for 15 minutes at 390F.
8. Then decorate the meal with fresh basil leaves.
9. Serve hot with different sauces.

Nutrition:
- Calories: 315
- Fat: 13,8g
- Carbohydrates: 7,9g
- Protein: 19,8g

Backed Eggs with Spinach

If you wish to prepare something simple and easy for breakfast – these eggs are exactly for you. Delicious and not difficult.

Prep time: 10 minutes	**Cooking time:** 20 minutes	**Servings:** 4

Ingredients:
- ½ teaspoon of salt
- ½ teaspoon of pepper
- 2 tablespoons of oil
- 1 teaspoon of butter
- 4 eggs
- 1 lb of spinach
- 7 oz of ham
- ½ teaspoon of dry herbs

Directions:
1. Preheat the Air Fryer to 340F.
2. Cook spinach in the boiled water and chop it in the pieces when it is ready.
3. Then add salt, pepper, oil, butter and dry herbs there.
4. Blend everything well.
5. Chop ham in the pieces.
6. Mix all ingredients in the bowl.
7. Then cook in the Air Fryer for 15 minutes.
8. After that shake well and cook for 5 minutes more.
9. Serve hot with salad or different vegetables.

Nutrition:
- Calories: 160
- Fat: 7,8g
- Carbohydrates: 8,5g
- Protein: 10,3g

Flavorsome Rolls with Eggs

The rolls are basically and delightful. Cook and try.

Prep time: 10 minutes	**Cooking time:** 20-25 minutes	**Servings:** 4

Ingredients:
- 1 cup of cheese
- 1 teaspoon of pepper
- 1 teaspoon of salt
- 4 tablespoons of cream
- 1 tablespoon of dry herbs
- 1 tablespoons of chives
- 1 tablespoon of parsley
- 1 tablespoon of tarragon
- 4 big eggs
- 4 dinner rolls

Directions:
1. Chop the top of every roll and remove some bread. You need to have some place for the mixture of the products.
2. Then beat eggs in the bowl.
3. Add salt, dry herbs, chives, parsley and tarragon in the bowl.
4. Blend the whole things well.
5. Then add cream and cheese.
6. Blend the ingredients in the bowl.
7. Divide the combination in 4 parts and place it in the rolls.
8. Sprinkle the frying basket with oil.
9. Cook rolls for 20-25 minutes at 350F.

Nutrition:
- Calories: 147
- Fat: 3,2g
- Carbohydrates: 6,1g
- Protein: 2,3g

Scrumptious Egg Soufflé

Interesting combination of the products. This breakfast is easy in preparing.

Prep time: 10 minutes	**Cooking time:** 8 minutes	**Servings:**4

Ingredients:
- 4 eggs
- ½ teaspoon of salt
- ½ teaspoon of pepper
- ½ teaspoon of dry herbs
- 4 tablespoons of cream
- ½ teaspoon of red chili pepper
- ½ tablespoon of parsley
- 1 red pepper
- 2 teaspoons of oil

Directions:
1. Chop parsley in the small pieces and put in the bowl.
2. Then cut pepper and add to parsley.
3. Blend them together well.
4. Then beat eggs and mix with parsley and pepper.
5. Add cream.
6. Blend all components in the bowl.
7. Then add salt, pepper, fry herbs and red chili pepper.
8. Blend everything again.
9. Sprinkle the frying basket with oil.
10. Cook for 8 minutes at 390F.

Nutrition:
- Calories: 112
- Fat: 2,1g
- Carbohydrates: 3,6g
- Protein: 2,2g

Breakfast Sandwich

Another recipe for delicious breakfast. You can prepare it fast and it will be tasty. It is possible to prepare them when your children are going to school.

Prep time: 10 minutes	**Cooking time:** 6 minutes	**Servings:**4

Ingredients:
- 4 eggs
- 4 buns
- ½ teaspoon of salt
- ½ teaspoon of pepper
- ½ teaspoon of paprika
- ½ teaspoon of oregano
- 4 pieces of English bacon
- ¼ teaspoon of dry herbs
- 2 teaspoons of oil

Directions:
1. Beat eggs in the bowl.
2. Add salt, pepper, oregano, paprika and dry herbs.
3. Blend everything well.
4. Sprinkle the Air Fryer basket with oil.
5. Then preheat it to 390F.
6. Place eggs, bacon and buns in the Air Fryer.
7. Cook for 6 minutes at 390F.
8. Decorate them with basil leaves or you can sprinkle with lemon juice.

Nutrition:
- Calories: 190
- Fat: 5,9g
- Carbohydrates: 7,7g
- Protein: 4,8g

Full English Breakfast

You will get delicious breakfast in a few minutes. Just try and your breakfast will be the best in the world. It is very easy in preparing and you will be delighted to see the result.

Prep time: 10 minutes	**Cooking time:** 15 minutes	**Servings:** 4

Ingredients:

- 4 eggs
- 7 oz of spinach
- 1 onion
- 4 pieces of bacon

- 1 teaspoon of garlic powder
- 8 small tomatoes
- 8 white mushrooms
- ½ teaspoon of salt

- ½ teaspoon of pepper
- ½ teaspoon of paprika
- 2 teaspoons of oil

Directions:

1. Sprinkle the Air Fryer with oil.
2. Then preheat it to 390F.
3. Chop tomatoes and mushrooms in the pieces.
4. Put spinach in the boiled water for 2 minutes.
5. Then chop it in the pieces and mix with tomatoes and mushrooms.
6. Cut onion in the rings and add to the mixture.
7. Then add garlic powder, salt, pepper and paprika to the products.
8. Mix everything well.
9. Add bacon and put everything in the Air Fryer.
10. Cover with beaten eggs, mix everything again and cook for 15 minutes.

Nutrition:

- Calories: 65
- Fat: 4,3g

- Carbohydrates: 5,7g
- Protein: 3,5g

Enticing Buns with Cheese

Prepare these appetizing buns. They are delectable and scrumptious.

Prep time: 15 minutes	**Cooking time:** 15 minutes	**Servings:** 4

Ingredients:

- ½ teaspoon of pepper
- ½ teaspoon of salt
- 1 tablespoon of sauce
- 1 cup of cheese

- 1 tablespoon of baking powder
- 1 teaspoon of mustard
- 3 oz of flour
- 1/3 cup of milk

- 1 egg
- 2 tablespoons of oil
- 8 paper cake forms

Directions:

1. Grease the frying basket with oil.
2. Cook up the Air Fryer to 390F.
3. Beat egg. Then add butter with milk and blend.
4. After that add baking powder, flour, mustard.
5. Blend the components in the deep bowl. Then add sauce and cut cheese.
6. After that blend them.
7. Place the combination in the forms for muffins. Cook in the Air Fryer for 15 minutes.

Nutrition:

- Calories: 106
- Fat: 3,5g

- Carbohydrates: 5,2g
- Protein: 2,2g

Appetizing Tomato and Onion Quiche

It does not need a lot of your efforts to prepare breakfast. This tomato meal is flavorsome and great.

| **Prep time:** 15 minutes | **Cooking time:** 15 minutes | **Servings:** 2 |

Ingredients:

- 2 tablespoons of oil
- ½ teaspoon of salt
- ½ teaspoon of pepper
- ¼ cup of tomatoes
- 1 onion
- 1 cup of cheese
- ¼ cup of milk
- 2 eggs

Directions:

1. Chop onion in the pieces and put in the bowl.
2. Then cut tomatoes in the small pieces and add to onion.
3. Add salt, pepper and mix everything well.
4. Then put milk and beat eggs.
5. Blend all ingredients together.
6. Cover with cheese, blend everything again.
7. Sprinkle the Air Fryer basket with oil.
8. Cook for 20 minutes at 250F.
9. Serve hot with sauce.

Nutrition:

- Calories: 133
- Fat: 3,6g
- Carbohydrates: 4,8g
- Protein: 1,7g

Mouthwatering Hash Brown Potatoes

It is wonderful and scrumptious meal. Attempt and check it. It is not problematic in preparing.

| **Prep time:** 40 minutes | **Cooking time:** 15 minutes | **Servings:** 3 |

Ingredients:

- 1 teaspoon of butter
- ½ teaspoon of salt
- ½ teaspoon of pepper
- 7-8 big potatoes
- 4 tablespoons of flour
- ½ teaspoon of ginger powder
- ½ teaspoon of the cumin powder
- ½ teaspoon of oregano
- 3 tablespoons of oil

Directions:

1. Wash and clean potatoes.
2. Leave potatoes in cold water for 20 minutes.
3. Then chop it in the pieces and boil.
4. After that, blend it with salt, pepper, cumin powder, flour, oregano and butter.
5. Create the dough with the potato.
6. Add 1,5 tablespoon of oil to the dough and blend it.
7. Then divide the dough in the parts.
8. Sprinkle the Air Fryer with the rest of oil.
9. Preheat it to 350F for 5 minutes.
10. Cook potatoes for 15 minutes.

Nutrition:

- Calories: 113
- Fat: 1,3g
- Carbohydrates: 3,9g
- Protein: 1,2g

Flavorsome Eggs with Cheese and Tomatoes

The delicious eggs with tomatoes are scrumptious. Cheese gives the note and it is really enjoyable.

Prep time: 15 minutes | **Cooking time:** 9 minutes | **Servings:**4

Ingredients:
- 2 teaspoons of oil
- ½ teaspoon of salt
- ½ teaspoon of pepper
- 8 tomatoes
- 1 cup of milk
- 2 oz of cheese
- 1/3 teaspoon of garlic powder
- ¼ teaspoon of onion powder

Directions:
1. Sprinkle the Air Fryer with oil.
2. Then preheat it for 5 minutes to 360F.
3. Beat eggs in the bowl.
4. Then add milk to eggs and blend the components.
5. Add salt, onion powder, pepper and garlic powder in the bowl.
6. After that blend all components.
7. Then place the combination in the Air Fryer and cook for 6 minutes.
8. Blend eggs and add chopped tomatoes and cheese.
9. Cook them for 3 minutes more.

Nutrition:
- Calories: 145
- Fat: 2,7g
- Carbohydrates: 7,6g
- Protein: 2,1g

Tasty and Pepper Frittata

It is not too complicated in the preparing. This meal is really tasty, delicious and fantastic.

Prep time: 15 minutes | **Cooking time:** 16 minutes | **Servings:**3

Ingredients:
- 3 eggs
- ½ teaspoon of salt
- 1/3 teaspoon of pepper
- 2 pieces of bacon
- 6-8 tomatoes
- ¼ cup of sweat pepper
- ¼ cup of cheese
- ¼ cup of spinach

Directions:
1. Sprinkle the Air Fryer with oil.
2. Then preheat it to 360F for 3 minutes.
3. Chop bacon and tomatoes in the pieces.
4. Then cut pepper and add to tomatoes and bacon.
5. Mix all components well.
6. Place the products in the Air Fryer and cook for 8minutes.
7. Then mix beaten eggs with cheese and spinach.
8. Add them to the rest products in the Air Fryer.
9. Cook everything for 8 minutes more.
10. Serve hot with sauces.

Nutrition:
- Calories: 176
- Fat: 2,9g
- Carbohydrates: 7,9g
- Protein: 1,8g

Scrumptious Browned Ravioli

If you wish to cook something extravagant, then cook ravioli. Simple, pleasant and flavorsome meal.

Prep time: 30 minutes	**Cooking time:** 10 minutes	**Servings:**4

Ingredients:

- 1 cup of buttermilk
- 1/3 cup of cheese
- ½ teaspoon of pepper
- ¼ teaspoon of red chili pepper

- 1/5 teaspoon of salt
- 2 tablespoons of oil
- 1 cup of bread crumbs
- 1 box of ravioli
- 1 cup of sauce

- 1/3 teaspoon of garlic powder

Directions:

1. Place ravioli in buttermilk.
2. Leave them for 20 minutes.
3. Add one teaspoon of oil to bread crumbs and blend them.
4. After that cover ravioli with bread crumbs and oil.
5. Sprinkle the Air Fryer with the rest of oil.
6. After that preheat it to 380F for 3 minutes.
7. Place ravioli in the Air Fryer. Cook them for 10 minutes.

Nutrition:

- Calories: 389
- Fat: 6,8g

- Carbohydrates: 8,4g
- Protein: 9,8g

Fried Sausages with Spicy Sauce

If you wish to prepare something tasty for your family for breakfast, this recipe will be the best. Cook and check it.

Prep time: 20 minutes	**Cooking time:** 40 minutes	**Servings:**4

Ingredients:

- 1 big pepper
- ½ teaspoon of salt
- ½ teaspoon of pepper
- 2 onions
- 1 eggplant

- 3 tablespoons of olive oil
- 1 lb of beans
- 1 lb of tomatoes
- 2 cloves of garlic

- ½ teaspoon of red chili pepper
- 1 lb of mince
- ½ teaspoon of paprika

Directions:

1. Sprinkle the Air Fryer with oil.
2. Then preheat it to 300F for 2 minutes.
3. Chop onions and pepper with tomatoes in the pieces.
4. Put mince in the bowl and mix with salt, pepper, garlic, red chili pepper and paprika.
5. Chop eggplant in the pieces.
6. Mix mince with eggplant, tomatoes, onions together.
7. Then add beans.
8. Cook in the Air Fryer for 20 minutes.
9. Add ½ cup of water.
10. Cook for 20 minutes more.

Nutrition:

- Calories: 198
- Fat: 7,5g

- Carbohydrates: 8,7g
- Protein: 9,2g

Crispy Chicken

It is very easy for preparing. Also, this meal is very tasty and delicious.

Prep time: 20 minutes | **Cooking time:** 20 minutes | **Servings:** 4

Ingredients:
- 2 cups of buttermilk
- ½ teaspoon of pepper
- ½ teaspoon of salt
- 1 lb of chicken fillet
- 1 teaspoon of garlic powder
- 1 egg
- 1 cup of bread crumbs
- ½ teaspoon of oregano
- 4 tablespoons of flour
- 2 tablespoons of oil

Directions:
1. Wash and clean chicken.
2. Then cut it in the pieces.
3. Rub meat with salt, pepper, garlic, oregano.
4. Then place meat in flour and in buttermilk.
5. After that put it in egg and in bread crumbs.
6. Sprinkle the Air Fryer with oil.
7. Preheat for 5 minutes to 300F.
8. Cook chicken for 10 minutes.
9. Then shake meat well and cook for 10 minutes more.
10. Serve hot with sauce and mint.

Nutrition:
- Calories: 147
- Fat: 5,9g
- Carbohydrates: 7,5g
- Protein: 7,9g

Appetizing Salmon with Cream

This breakfast if very healthy, because fish has a lot of vitamins and minerals. It is not complicated to prepare this breakfast.

Prep time: 15 minutes | **Cooking time:** 30 minutes | **Servings:** 4

Ingredients:
- 1 lb of salmon fillet
- ½ teaspoon of salt
- ½ teaspoon of pepper
- 1 tablespoon of oil
- 1 teaspoon of parsley
- ½ teaspoon of dry herbs
- 1 avocado
- ½ teaspoon of paprika
- 1 teaspoon of garlic powder

Directions:
1. Chop salmon in the pieces.
2. Then rub fish with salt, pepper, parsley, dry herbs, paprika and garlic powder.
3. Sprinkle the Air Fryer with oil.
4. Preheat it for 5 minutes to 300F.
5. Then cook fish in the Air Fryer for 15 minutes.
6. Then place it on the other side and add chopped avocado.
7. Cook for 15 minutes more.
8. Serve hot with sauce.

Nutrition:
- Calories: 136
- Fat: 5,3g
- Carbohydrates: 7,2g
- Protein: 5,6g

Soft Lamb with Pumpkin

This meal is appetizing and wonderful. Cook and you will be surprised.

Prep time: 20 minutes | **Cooking time:** 30 minutes | **Servings:** 2

Ingredients:
- 1 rack of lamb
- ½ teaspoon of pepper
- ½ teaspoon of salt
- 2 tablespoons of oil
- 1 tablespoon of parsley
- 1 tablespoon of mustard
- 2 oz of bread crumbs
- 1 oz of cheese
- ½ teaspoon of paprika

Directions:
1. Sprinkle the Air Fryer with oil.
2. Preheat the Air Fryer to 350F for 3 minutes.
3. Rub meat with pepper, salt, parsley, mustard and paprika.
4. Cook in the Air Fryer for 15 minutes.
5. Then place in bread crumbs. Then cover the meal with cheese.
6. Cook this meal for 15 minutes more.
7. Serve hot with vegetables and sauce.
8. Decorate appetizing meal with parsley.
9. Enjoy with the great and appetizing meal.

Nutrition:
- Calories: 146
- Fat: 5,2g
- Carbohydrates: 5,7g
- Protein: 7,3g

Chicken with Paprika and Potato

It is ideal combination for breakfast. Your family will be glad to eat delicious and tasty meal.

Prep time: 20 minutes | **Cooking time:** 35 minutes | **Servings:**2

Ingredients:
- 2 chicken legs
- ½ teaspoon of pepper
- ½ teaspoon of salt
- 3 tablespoon of oil
- 2 teaspoons of paprika
- 1 teaspoon of honey
- 1 teaspoon of garlic powder
- 4 potatoes
- 1 teaspoon of parsley
- 1 cup of cabbage

Directions:
1. Sprinkle the Air Fryer with oil.
2. Preheat it for 5 minutes to 350F.
3. Mix pepper, salt, paprika, honey, garlic powder and parsley in the bowl.
4. Rub chicken legs with them.
5. Cook them in the Air Fryer for 15 minutes.
6. Then wash and clean potatoes in the pieces.
7. Mix with chopped cabbage and put in the Air Fryer.
8. Cook everything for 20 minutes more.
9. Serve hot with sauces.

Nutrition:
- Calories: 198
- Fat: 8,3g
- Carbohydrates: 7,2g
- Protein: 8,1g

Fried Bacon with Mushrooms

This breakfast meal is very easy for preparing. Just cook and enjoy with your family.

Prep time: 15 minutes | **Cooking time:** 15 minutes | **Servings:** 2

Ingredients:
- 8 mushrooms
- 5 tomatoes
- 2 cloves of garlic
- 4 pieces of bacon
- 6 oz of spinach
- 4 eggs
- ½ teaspoon of salt
- ½ teaspoon of pepper
- ½ teaspoon of dry herbs
- ½ teaspoon of paprika

Directions:
1. Chop tomatoes in the pieces.
2. Then chop mushrooms and mix them with tomatoes.
3. Rub bacon with garlic, salt, pepper, dry herbs and paprika.
4. Blend the ingredients well.
5. Then beat eggs and cover the products.
6. Sprinkle the Air Fryer with oil.
7. Preheat the Air Fryer to 350F.
8. Cook the meal for 15 minutes.
9. Then blend these components.
10. Serve hot with sauce.

Nutrition:
- Calories: 154
- Fat: 6,8g
- Carbohydrates: 6,7g
- Protein: 5,8g

Delicious Toast with Yogurt and Berries

It is incredibly delicious breakfast. Easy and fast, you will like it.

Prep time: 15 minutes | **Cooking time:** 8-9 minutes | **Servings:** 2

Ingredients:
- 2 big eggs
- 1 teaspoon of vanilla
- 2 pieces of bread
- 2 teaspoons of oil
- 2 tablespoons of frozen berries
- 1 tablespoon of honey
- ½ cup of yogurt

Directions:
1. Sprinkle the Air Fryer with oil.
2. Preheat it for 5 minutes to 350F.
3. Beat eggs and mix with vanilla.
4. Then place bread in the mixture.
5. Cook bread in the Air Fryer for 3 minutes.
6. Then place bread on the other side and cook for 3 minutes more.
7. After that place berries and honey on bread.
8. Cook for 2-3 minutes in the Air Fryer.
9. Pour with yogurt and serve hot.
10. Do not forget about juice or tea.

Nutrition:
- Calories: 135
- Fat: 2,1g
- Carbohydrates: 6,9g
- Protein: 1,1g

Sharp Chicken Wings with Yummy Soy Sauce and Sesame

These chicken wings are tempting and peppery. You will have energy and power for full day.

Prep time: 15 minutes | **Cooking time:** 8-9 minutes | **Servings:** 4

Ingredients:
- ½ teaspoon of pepper
- ½ teaspoon of salt
- 2 tablespoons of oil
- 8 chicken wings
- 2 tablespoons of soy sauce
- 1 teaspoon of sesame seeds
- ½ teaspoon of garlic powder
- ½ teaspoon of red chili pepper

Directions:
1. Sprinkle the Air Fryer with oil.
2. Then preheat the Air Fryer to 350F for 2-3 minutes.
3. Blend pepper, salt, soy sauce, sesame seeds, garlic powder and red chili pepper in the bowl.
4. Rub chicken wings with them.
5. After that place the wings in the Air Fryer.
6. Cook for 15 minutes.
7. Then shake them. Cook meat for 10 minutes more.
8. Serve hot with parsley and sauces.
9. Enjoy with flavorsome meat.

Nutrition:
- Calories: 188
- Fat: 6,3g
- Carbohydrates: 5,8g
- Protein: 6,2g

Wonderful Chili Squash with Cumin

You cannot imagine how it is flavorsome and great. It is fantastic meal.

Prep time: 15 minutes | **Cooking time:** 20 minutes | **Servings:** 4

Ingredients:
- ½ teaspoon of pepper
- ½ teaspoon of salt
- 2 tablespoons of oil
- 1 butternut squash
- 2 teaspoons of cumin seeds
- 1 teaspoon of chili flakes
- 5 oz of yogurt
- 1 teaspoon of coriander
- 1 oz of nuts

Directions:
1. Sprinkle the Air Fryer with oil.
2. Preheat it to 340F for 3 minutes.
3. Wash and slice squash in the pieces.
4. Then rub it with salt, pepper, chili flakes, cumin seeds and coriander.
5. After that add the nuts and blend everything well.
6. Cook it in the Air Fryer for 10 minutes.
7. Then cover with yogurt and cook for 10 minutes more.
8. Serve hot and decorate meal with parsley or dill.

Nutrition:
- Calories: 147
- Fat: 3,5g
- Carbohydrates: 5,1g
- Protein: 1,3g

Appetizing Backed Apple

It is tempting and sweat meal for breakfast. Everyone can cook it.

Prep time: 10 minutes | **Cooking time:** 20 minutes | **Servings:** 4

Ingredients:
- 2 teaspoons of oil
- 4 big apples
- 1 oz of butter
- 1 tablespoon of sugar
- 1 oz of bread crumbs
- 1 oz of orange juice
- 1 teaspoon of cinnamon

Directions:
1. Wash and cut apples in two parts.
2. Sprinkle the Air Fryer with oil.
3. Preheat it for 5 minutes to 350F.
4. Then cover with bread crumbs.
5. Cook in the Air Fryer for 10 minutes.
6. Then blend butter, sugar, orange juice and cinnamon.
7. Cover apples with this combination.
8. Cook apples in the Air Fryer for 10 minutes more.
9. Then serve hot with tea or juice.
10. It is possible to prepare coffee too for this meal.

Nutrition:
- Calories: 67
- Fat: 2,1g
- Carbohydrates: 5,7g
- Protein: 1,1g

Delicious Figs with Mascarpone and Honey

This breakfast is very delicious and tasty at the same time. Cook and you will like it.

Prep time: 15 minutes | **Cooking time:** 10-15 minutes | **Servings:** 4

Ingredients:
- 2 tablespoons of butter
- 8 figs
- 1 oz of butter
- 5 oz of mascarpone
- 1 teaspoon of water
- 3 tablespoons of almonds
- 3 tablespoons of jam

Directions:
1. Sprinkle the Air Fryer with oil.
2. Preheat the Air Fryer to 340F for 3 minutes.
3. Take figs and put butter on them.
4. Then mix mascarpone with almonds and water.
5. Put the mixture on the figs.
6. Cook it in the Air Fryer for 10-15 minutes.
7. Then take and decorate meal with jam.
8. Serve this delicious meal hot with juice, tea, milk or coffee.
9. Help yourself and enjoy with flavorsome breakfast with your family.

Nutrition:
- Calories: 168
- Fat: 6,2g
- Carbohydrates: 9,2g
- Protein: 1,6g

Cod with Tomato and Basil

It is very good to eat fish for breakfast. Also, it is really delicious and tasty. You will like it forever.

Prep time: 15 minutes | **Cooking time:** 30 minutes | **Servings:** 4

Ingredients:
- 4 cods
- 8 tomatoes
- 8 olives
- 1/3 cup of lemon juice
- 1 bunch of basil
- 2 teaspoons of oil
- ½ teaspoon of salt
- ½ teaspoon of pepper

Directions:
1. Sprinkle the Air Fryer with oil.
2. Preheat it to 360F for 3 minutes.
3. Wash and cut fish in the pieces.
4. After that rub them with lemon juice, salt and pepper.
5. Cook in the Air Fryer for 15 minutes.
6. Then chop tomatoes and add to fish.
7. Chop olives and add to the meal.
8. Mix everything well.
9. Cook for 15 minutes more.
10. Serve meal hot with soy sauce and decorate with basil leaves.

Nutrition:
- Calories: 147
- Fat: 3,4g
- Carbohydrates: 6,2g
- Protein: 2,3g

Flavorsome and Peppery Chicken Escalopes

Your family will like this delicious breakfast. If you wish to prepare something interesting and appetizing, you should choose this recipe.

Prep time: 15 minutes | **Cooking time:** 25 minutes | **Servings:** 4

Ingredients:
- 4 skinless chicken breasts
- ½ teaspoon of pepper
- ½ teaspoon of salt
- 3 teaspoons of oil
- 1 oz of cheese
- 2 oz of bread crumbs
- 2 eggs
- ½ teaspoon of red chili pepper
- ½ teaspoon of garlic powder

Directions:
1. Wash and cut chicken in the pieces.
2. Take the bowl and blend salt, pepper, garlic powder, red chili pepper there.
3. Then rub chicken with spices.
4. Beat eggs in the bowl.
5. Then cover chicken with eggs.
6. Then place them in bread crumbs.
7. Sprinkle the Air Fryer with oil.
8. Preheat it to 350F for 3 minutes.
9. Cook chicken for 10 minutes.
10. After that place meat on the other side and cook for 15 minutes more.

Nutrition:
- Calories: 196
- Fat: 5,8g
- Carbohydrates: 6,8g
- Protein: 5,2g

Fiery Lamb with Coriander

Unbelievably tempting recipe of meat and cucumber. The meal is undoubtedly flavorsome.

Prep time: 15 minutes | **Cooking time:** 25 minutes | **Servings:** 4

Ingredients:

- 4 tablespoons of yogurt
- ½ teaspoon of pepper
- ½ teaspoon of salt
- 3 teaspoon of oil
- 1 teaspoon of cumin
- 1 teaspoon of coriander
- 2 teaspoons of garam masala
- ½ teaspoon of red chili pepper
- 2 teaspoons of lime juice
- 1 lb of lamb

Directions:

1. Sprinkle the Air Fryer with oil.
2. Preheat it to 350F for 2 minutes.
3. Wash and slice lamb in the pieces.
4. Then blend pepper, salt, cumin, coriander, garam masala, red chili pepper and lime juice.
5. Rub lamb with these spices.
6. After that place meat in the Air Fryer and cook for 10 minutes.
7. Then place meat on the other side. Cook it for 15 minutes more.
8. Serve hot with basil leaves and ketchup.

Nutrition:

- Calories: 186
- Fat: 5,3g
- Carbohydrates: 6,5g
- Protein: 5,6g

Fantastic Rolls with Prawns

It is uncomplicated and delicious meal for breakfast. Just make and you will get tasty prawns.

Prep time: 15 minutes | **Cooking time:** 20 minutes | **Servings:** 4

Ingredients:

- 1 tablespoon of oil
- 1 tablespoon of soy sauce
- 1 teaspoon of ginger
- 1 oz of mushrooms
- 1 teaspoon of dry herbs
- 1 carrot
- 1 spring onion
- 8 spring rolls
- 6 oz of cooked prawns
- 1 egg

Directions:

1. Sprinkle the Air Fryer with oil.
2. Then preheat it for 5 minutes to 300F.
3. Chop carrot and spring onion in the pieces.
4. Then add cooked and chopped prawns
5. Blend everything with soy sauce, ginger, dry herbs.
6. Then chop mushrooms and add there.
7. Beat egg and cover the combination with it.
8. Cook the meal in the Air Fryer for 15 minutes.
9. Then blend everything well and cook for 5 minutes more.
10. Serve hot with salad.

Nutrition:

- Calories: 152
- Fat: 5,6g
- Carbohydrates: 8,9g
- Protein: 7,2g

Appetizing Backed Potatoes with Cheese

It is flavorsome and piquant potato. This meal is covered with cheese.

Prep time: 15 minutes	**Cooking time:** 20 minutes	**Servings:** 4

Ingredients:
- 1 lb of potatoes
- ½ teaspoon of pepper
- ½ teaspoon of salt
- ½ teaspoon of garlic powder
- ½ teaspoon of red chili pepper
- ½ teaspoon of cumin
- ½ teaspoon of paprika
- 2 tablespoons of oil
- ½ teaspoon of dry herbs
- 2 oz of cheese

Directions:
1. Sprinkle the Air Fryer with oil.
2. Preheat it to 380F.
3. Wash and clean potatoes.
4. Cut them in the pieces.
5. Then rub potatoes with pepper, salt, garlic powder, red chili pepper, cumin, paprika and dry herbs.
6. Place in the Air Fryer and cook for 20 minutes.
7. Then cover everything with cheese and cook for 10 minutes more.
8. Serve hot with parsley, onion and sauce.

Nutrition:
- Calories: 139
- Fat: 3,2g
- Carbohydrates: 8,4g
- Protein: 1,1g

Scrumptious Potato with Garlic and Bacon

It is vigorous and tempting breakfast. If you wish to prepare something not complicated and appetizing – you should choose this recipe.

Prep time: 15 minutes	**Cooking time:** 30 minutes	**Servings:** 4

Ingredients:
- 4 potatoes
- 6 cloves of garlic
- ½ teaspoon of pepper
- ½ teaspoon of salt
- 4 pieces of bacon
- ½ teaspoon of red chili pepper
- ½ teaspoon of rosemary
- ½ teaspoon of cumin powder
- ½ teaspoon of paprika

Directions:
1. Wash and clean potatoes.
2. Then chop potatoes in the pieces.
3. Blend pepper, salt, red chili pepper, rosemary, cumin powder and paprika in the bowl.
4. Rub potatoes with spices.
5. Sprinkle the Air Fryer with oil.
6. Then preheat it to 350F for 5 minutes.
7. Cook potatoes for 10 minutes.
8. Then add bacon and cook for 15 minutes more.
9. Serve hot with onion and sauce.

Nutrition:
- Calories: 149
- Fat: 3,8g
- Carbohydrates: 8,2g
- Protein: 3,6g

Fried Carrot with Cumin and Spices

This meal is very good for your eyes. It is flavorsome and wonderful.

Prep time: 15 minutes | **Cooking time:** 25 minutes | **Servings:** 4

Ingredients:

- 2 lbs of carrot
- 2 tablespoons of oil
- ½ teaspoon of red paprika
- 1 teaspoon of cumin
- ½ teaspoon of salt
- 4 cloves of garlic
- ½ teaspoon of red chili pepper
- 1/3 teaspoon of paprika
- ½ teaspoon of onion powder

Directions:

1. Sprinkle the Air Fryer with oil.
2. Then preheat it to 300F.
3. After that wash and clean carrot.
4. Cut it in the tiny pieces.
5. Blend onion powder, paprika, red chili pepper, garlic, salt, red paprika and cumin in the bowl.
6. Cover every piece of carrot with spices.
7. Cook them in the Air Fryer for 10 minutes.
8. Then blend everything well and cook for 15 minutes more.
9. Serve hot with salad and ketchup.

Nutrition:

- Calories: 57
- Fat: 1g
- Carbohydrates: 4,3g
- Protein: 1g

Yummy Salmon with Herbs

This fish is very appetizing and delicious. Flavors create unusual aroma to the meal.

Prep time: 15 minutes | **Cooking time:** 30 minutes | **Servings:** 4

Ingredients:

- 6 oz of salmon fillet
- ½ teaspoon of pepper
- ½ teaspoon of salt
- 2 teaspoon of oil
- 1 teaspoon of dry herbs
- ½ teaspoon of dry basil
- 3 tablespoon of honey mustard
- ¼ cup of bread crumbs
- ½ teaspoon of oregano

Directions:

1. Wash and clean salmon.
2. Cut it in the pieces.
3. Then rub with pepper, salt, dry herbs, basil, mustard and oregano.
4. Sprinkle the Air Fryer with oil.
5. Preheat it for 5 minutes to 350F.
6. Place salmon in bread crumbs and cover with them.
7. Cook fish for 15 minutes
8. Then place on the other side and cook for 10 minutes more.
9. Serve hot with fish sauce and parsley.

Nutrition:

- Calories: 147
- Fat: 5,2g
- Carbohydrates: 6,8g
- Protein: 3,9g

Peppery and Delicious Vegetables

It seems that fried vegetables can be always the great choice. Cook and check it.

| **Prep time:** 15 minutes | **Cooking time:** 30 minutes | **Servings:** 4 |

Ingredients:

- 1 red pepper
- 3 cloves of garlic
- ½ teaspoon of pepper
- ½ teaspoon of salt
- 2 teaspoons of oil
- 1 yellow summer squash
- 8 oz of mushrooms
- ½ teaspoon of thyme
- ½ teaspoon of tarragon
- 1/3 teaspoon of red chili pepper
- ½ teaspoon of dry herbs

Directions:

1. Chop pepper in the pieces.
2. Then chop mushrooms and mix them with pepper.
3. Place pepper, salt, thyme, tarragon, red chili pepper and dry herbs in the bowl.
4. Blend them with pepper and mushrooms.
5. Wash and clean squash.
6. Blend everything well.
7. Sprinkle the Air Fryer with oil.
8. Preheat it to 350F for 2 minutes.
9. Cook the meal for 15 minutes.
10. Then mix everything well and cook for 5 minutes more.

Nutrition:

- Calories: 126
- Fat: 2,1g
- Carbohydrates: 6,3g
- Protein: 1,1g

Scrumptious Salad with Appetizing Potato

This salad is fantastic and wonderful. You have never tried this unassuming and appetizing salad.

| **Prep time:** 15 minutes | **Cooking time:** 30 minutes | **Servings:** 4 |

Ingredients:

- 2 tablespoons of oil
- ½ teaspoon of pepper
- ½ teaspoon of salt
- 2 lbs of potatoes
- ½ teaspoon of red pepper
- ½ teaspoon of rosemary
- 4 cloves of garlic
- ½ teaspoon of dry herbs
- 1/3 teaspoon of cumin
- 1 red pepper
- 1 onion
- 1 tablespoon of mustard
- 2 teaspoons of lemon juice

Directions:

1. Sprinkle the Air Fryer with oil.
2. Cut pepper and onion in the pieces.
3. Wash and clean potatoes.
4. Then cut potatoes in the pieces and blend with onion and pepper.
5. Add lemon juice, mustard, cumin, dry herbs, rosemary, salt and pepper to the products.
6. Blend everything well.
7. Preheat the Air Fryer for 340F for 5 minutes.
8. Cook salad for 10 minutes.
9. Then blend and cook for 15 minutes more.

Nutrition:

- Calories: 113
- Fat: 1,4g
- Carbohydrates: 6,8g
- Protein: 1,1g

LUNCH

Salad with Cucumber and Potato

Incredibly delicious salad, which can be great for lunch. The combination of cucumber and potato is very tasty.

Prep time: 10 minutes	**Cooking time:** 25 minutes	**Servings:** 4

Ingredients:

- 1 tablespoon of oil
- 2 tablespoons of white wine vinegar
- 1 lb of potatoes

- 1 big cucumber
- 1/3 teaspoon of salt
- 1 big onion
- ½ teaspoon of pepper

- ½ teaspoon of cumin powder

Directions:

1. Wash and clean potatoes.
2. Then chop in the small pieces.
3. Sprinkle the Air Fryer with oil.
4. Preheat it to 350F for 2 minutes.
5. Place potatoes in the Air Fryer and cook for 20 minutes.
6. After that mix potatoes and cook for 5 minutes more.
7. Cut cucumber in the pieces. Chop onion in the rings.
8. Add salt, pepper, cumin powder and vinegar.
9. Mix salad well.

Nutrition:

- Calories: 127
- Fat: 2,2g

- Carbohydrates: 6,9g
- Protein: 2,1g

Pepper Rice

This rice with spices is exactly for lunch. It is uncomplicated and flavorsome. Cook and see.

Prep time: 20 minutes	**Cooking time:** 25 minutes	**Servings:** 4

Ingredients:

- 2 cups of rice
- 3 cups of water
- ½ teaspoon of salt
- ½ teaspoon of pepper

- ½ teaspoon of garlic powder
- 1/3 teaspoon of onion powder
- 1/3 teaspoon of ginger

- 1/5 teaspoon of oregano
- 1/3 teaspoon of red chili pepper
- 2 tablespoons of oil

Directions:

1. Sprinkle the Air Fryer with oil.
2. Preheat it to 350F. Put rice and water in the Air Fryer.
3. Add pepper, garlic powder, salt, onion powder, oregano and red chili pepper and blend everything well with rice. Cook rice for 20 minutes.
4. After that blend it well and cook for 5 minutes. Leave it for 20 minutes.
5. Serve hot with vegetables or meat.

Nutrition:

- Calories: 49
- Fat: 1,1g

- Carbohydrates: 3,9g
- Protein: 2,1g

Rice with Pepper

It will be tasty lunch. The red and green peppers will add special aroma to rice.

Prep time: 10 minutes	Cooking time: 25 minutes	Servings: 4

Ingredients:

- 1 lb of rice
- ½ teaspoon of pepper
- ½ teaspoon of salt
- 1/3 teaspoon of oregano
- 1/3 teaspoon of red chili pepper
- 1 big sweat red pepper
- 1 big green pepper
- 2 tablespoons of oil

Directions:

1. Wash rice under cold water.
2. Then grease the Air Fryer with oil.
3. Preheat it to 300F for 5 minutes.
4. After that place rice with water in the Air Fryer.
5. Cook it for 10 minutes.
6. Then add oregano, red chili pepper, salt and pepper and blend everything well.
7. Cook for 5 minutes.
8. Chop green and red peppers in the pieces.
9. Add them to rice and mix all components.
10. Cook the meal for 10 minutes.
11. Serve hot with sauces.

Nutrition:

- Calories: 89
- Fat: 1,3g
- Carbohydrates: 7,5g
- Protein: 2,4g

Piquant Fried Pumpkin

It is forceful and appetizing meal. Just prepare and try. This meal is really flavorsome.

Prep time: 15 minutes	Cooking time: 20 minutes	Servings: 4

Ingredients:

- 2 tablespoons of olive oil
- ½ teaspoon of pepper
- ½ teaspoon of salt
- 2 teaspoons of oregano
- 2 teaspoons of garlic powder
- ½ lb of pumpkin

Directions:

1. Sprinkle the Air Fryer with 1 tablespoon of oil.
2. Preheat it to 350F for 5 minutes.
3. Wash and clean pumpkin.
4. Then chop it in the slices.
5. Take the container and blend pepper, salt, oregano, garlic powder with oil there.
6. Then rub pumpkin with seasonings.
7. Cook for 10 minutes.
8. Then blend everything well. Cook for 10 minutes again.
9. Serve hot with parsley or with different sauces.
10. Enjoy with appetizing meal.

Nutrition:

- Calories: 76
- Fat: 3,6g
- Carbohydrates: 5,2g
- Protein: 1,4g

Fried Zucchini with Almonds

It is appetizing meal, which you will like. Uncomplicated and fast – just cook and check it.

Prep time: 10 minutes | **Cooking time:** 5 minutes | **Servings:** 4

Ingredients:
- ½ teaspoon of salt
- ½ teaspoon of pepper
- ½ lb of zucchini
- 2 tablespoons of silvered almonds
- 2 tablespoons of oil
- 1/3 teaspoon of garlic powder
- ¼ teaspoon of oregano

Directions:
1. Sprinkle the Air Fryer with 1 tablespoon of oil.
2. Preheat it to 280F for 5 minutes.
3. Place almonds with the rest of oil in the bowl.
4. Chop zucchini in the pieces.
5. Add salt, pepper, garlic powder and oregano in the bowl.
6. Blend all components.
7. Place the mixture in the Air Fryer.
8. Cook this meal for 5 minutes.
9. Serve hot meal decorated with fresh basil leaves.
10. Eat appetizing meal!

Nutrition:
- Calories: 98
- Fat: 3,2g
- Carbohydrates: 5,4g
- Protein: 1,3g

Flavorsome Spaghetti with Backed Corn

It is incredible mixture, which everyone will like. Easy and simple.

Prep time: 10 minutes | **Cooking time:** 25 minutes | **Servings:** 4

Ingredients:
- ¼ cup of margarine
- 1 ln of cream-style corn
- 1 cup of cheese
- 1 lb of whole kernel corn
- 1 cup of spaghetti
- ½ teaspoon of salt
- ½ teaspoon of pepper
- ½ teaspoon of oregano
- 2 teaspoons of oil

Directions:
1. Sprinkle the Air Fryer with oil.
2. Preheat it to 390F for 5 minutes.
3. Take the deep bowl.
4. Place spaghetti, cream-style corn and whole kernel corn there.
5. Blend everything well.
6. Then place the combination in the Air Fryer and cook for 15 minutes.
7. Grate cheese and add to the meal.
8. Cook for 10 minutes more.
9. Serve hot with sauces.
10. Enjoy with the appetizing and peppery meal.

Nutrition:
- Calories: 189
- Fat: 4,1g
- Carbohydrates: 8,9g
- Protein: 1,7g

Backed Cabbage

This lunch is really healthy. Also, cabbage is flavorsome and wonderful.

Prep time: 5 minutes	Cooking time: 40 minutes	Servings: 4

Ingredients:

- ½ teaspoon of salt
- ½ teaspoon of pepper
- 1 big cabbage

- 3 tablespoons of balsamic vinegar
- 2 tablespoons of oil
- 1 green or red cabbage

- 1/3 teaspoon of cumin powder
- 2 tablespoons of olive oil

Directions:

1. Grease the Air Fryer with oil.
2. Then preheat it to 350F for 2 minutes.
3. Cut cabbage in the pieces.
4. Then grease with olive oil and add salt, pepper and cumin powder.
5. Blend the components well.
6. Put cabbage in the Air Fryer.
7. Cover with the foil.
8. Cook for 20 minutes.
9. Then add balsamic vinegar, blend cabbage well and cover with the foil again.
10. Cook for 20 minutes more.
11. Serve hot with meat and parsley or dill.
12. Enjoy with the appetizing meal.

Nutrition:

- Calories: 67
- Fat: 1,8g

- Carbohydrates: 6,5g
- Protein: 1,2g

Scrumptious Sour Pickled Mustard Greens

It is surely uncomplicated and yummy lunch. This method is unusual and does not need a lot of time to be cooked.

Prep time: 5 minutes	Cooking time: 6-10 minutes	Servings: 4

Ingredients:

- ½ teaspoon of salt
- ½ teaspoon of pepper
- 1/3 cup of water
- 2 tablespoons of oil

- 6 oz of bean sprouts
- 8 oz of sour pickled mustard greens
- 4 small onions

- 2 teaspoons of fish sauce

Directions:

1. Sprinkle the Air Fryer with oil.
2. Preheat it for 3 minutes to 360F.
3. Put bean sprouts in the Air Fryer and cook for 1-2 minutes.
4. Then chop onions and cook them with mustard in the Air Fryer for 3-4 minutes.
5. After that add salt and pepper.
6. Then mix the ingredients, add water and cook for 2-3 minutes more.
7. Serve hot with basil leaves and lemon.

Nutrition:

- Calories: 112
- Fat: 2,1g

- Carbohydrates: 7,2g
- Protein: 1,4g

Fried Kimchi and Bean Sprouts

It is healthy and peppery food. You will like it because it has incredibly tasty ingredients.

Prep time: 10 minutes | **Cooking time:** 5 minutes | **Servings:** 2

Ingredients:
- 1 teaspoon of oil
- 7 oz of bean sprouts
- 4-5 pieces of the kimchi
- 4 tablespoons of oil
- 4 onions
- ½ teaspoon of salt
- ½ teaspoon of oil
- 1 teaspoon of sesame oil

Directions:
1. Sprinkle the Air Fryer with oil.
2. Preheat it to 350F for 2-3 minutes.
3. Cook bean sprouts for 1-2 minutes in the Air Fryer.
4. Chop onions and kimchi in the pieces.
5. After that add them to bean sprouts.
6. Then blend all ingredients and add salt, sesame oil and pepper.
7. Add water and cook the products in the Air Fryer for 3-4 minutes.
8. Serve hot with meat or sauces.
9. Enjoy with tasty meal with your friends.

Nutrition:
- Calories: 99
- Fat: 2,2g
- Carbohydrates: 7g
- Protein: 1,3g

Spring Onion for Barbecue

Even if this is for the picnic, you can prepare it for lunch at home. It is appetizing, fast and delicious.

Prep time: 40 minutes | **Cooking time:** 10 minutes | **Servings:** 4

Ingredients:
- 1-2 lemons
- ½ teaspoon of salt
- ½ teaspoon of pepper
- 3 tablespoons of olive oil
- 1 bunch of spring onion

Directions:
1. Wash spring onion.
2. Then cut it in the pieces.
3. Put in the bowl.
4. After that rub it with oil, salt and pepper.
5. Leave for 30 minutes.
6. Sprinkle the Air Fryer with oil.
7. Preheat it for 3 minutes to 350F.
8. Then sprinkle onion with juice of lemon.
9. Put in the Air Fryer and cook for 10 minutes.
10. Serve hot with potatoes or meat.
11. Decorate with basil leaves or mint.
12. It is possible to serve with sauce or ketchup.
13. Eat appetizing meal and enjoy.

Nutrition:
- Calories: 46
- Fat: 1,1g
- Carbohydrates: 2,7g
- Protein: 0,5g

Fried Rice with Pasta

It is the great and healthy meal. Enjoy with this tasty rice.

Prep time: 5 minutes	**Cooking time:** 30 minutes	**Servings:** 4

Ingredients:
- ½ teaspoon of salt
- ½ teaspoon of pepper
- 4 chicken stock cubes
- 2 cups of chicken stock
- 3 cups of rice
- 1 cup of spaghetti
- 3 oz of butter
- 2 teaspoons of oil
- ½ teaspoon of oregano

Directions:
1. Sprinkle the Air Fryer with oil.
2. Then preheat it to 350F for 3 minutes.
3. Put butter with spaghetti in the Air Fryer.
4. Add rice and chicken stock.
5. Then add chicken stock cubes and blend everything well.
6. Add salt, pepper and oregano.
7. Cook for 15 minutes.
8. Then blend everything well and cook for 15 minutes more.
9. Serve hot with sauces.
10. Decorate with vegetables or basil leaves.
11. Enjoy with the tasty meal.

Nutrition:
- Calories: 148
- Fat: 1,9g
- Carbohydrates: 3,1g
- Protein: 1g

Tasty and Pepper Pea Sprouts

This meal is fantastic. You will feel it from the first piece of the food. Cook and enjoy!

Prep time: 5 minutes	**Cooking time:** 10 minutes	**Servings:** 4

Ingredients:
- 1 teaspoon of sesame oil
- ½ teaspoon of salt
- ½ teaspoon of oil
- 1 teaspoon of sauce
- 5 cloves of garlic
- 2 teaspoons of oil
- 1 bag of pea sprouts

Directions:
1. Wash and clean pea sprouts.
2. Then dry them and leave aside.
3. Sprinkle the Air Fryer with oil
4. Then preheat it to 350F.
5. After that put pea sprouts and chopped garlic.
6. Add salt, pepper and mix everything.
7. Then add sesame oil and sauce.
8. Mix all ingredients completely.
9. Put everything in the Air Fryer and cook for 10 minutes.
10. Serve hot with vegetables or with different kinds of sauces.

Nutrition:
- Calories: 98
- Fat: 2,1g
- Carbohydrates: 3,5g
- Protein: 1,1g

Puree with Pumpkin

It can be as your lunch as your breakfast. Easy, healthy and very delicious.

Prep time: 10 minutes

Cooking time: 1 hour and 10 minutes

Servings: 4

Ingredients:
- ½ teaspoon of pepper
- ½ teaspoon of salt
- ½ teaspoon of cumin powder
- 1 tablespoon of oil
- 2 small pumpkins
- 6-8 bay leaves
- ½ teaspoon of coriander
- 1-2 tablespoons of maple syrup

Directions:
1. Grease the Air Fryer with oil.
2. Preheat the Air Fryer to 300F for 2 minutes.
3. Wash and clean pumpkins.
4. After that set pumpkin in the Air Fryer.
5. Cook this meal for 1 hour.
6. Then add butter and bay leaves to pumpkin and cook for 10 minutes more.
7. Add salt and black pepper.
8. Pour pumpkin with maple syrup.
9. Serve hot with the orange or apple juice.

Nutrition:
- Calories: 89
- Fat: 1,3g
- Carbohydrates: 6,8g
- Protein: 1,1g

Tasty Fried Celeriac

Just prepare this meal one time. Tasty, delicious and not complicated for cooking. This meal is simply and fantastic.

Prep time: 15 minutes

Cooking time: 25 minutes

Servings: 4

Ingredients:
- ½ teaspoon of pepper
- ½ teaspoon of salt
- 1 teaspoon of parsley
- 1 bunch of spring onion
- 2 celeriac roots
- 2 tablespoon of oil
- 1 teaspoon of onion powder
- ½ teaspoon of garlic powder

Directions:
1. Sprinkle the Air Fryer with oil.
2. Preheat it to 350F.
3. Chop celeriac roots in the pieces.
4. Cook in the Air Fryer for 10 minutes.
5. Then cut spring onion in the pieces and add to celeriac roots.
6. Add salt and pepper and blend everything very well.
7. Cook for 15 minutes more.
8. After that decorate the meal with parsley or basil leaves.

Nutrition:
- Calories: 99
- Fat: 1,2g
- Carbohydrates: 6,6g
- Protein: 1g

Courgette With Lemon and Butter

It is interesting and appetizing meal. The ingredients are very simple and it is easy for preparing.

Prep time: 5 minutes | **Cooking time:** 15 minutes | **Servings:** 4

Ingredients:
- ½ teaspoon of salt
- ½ teaspoon of pepper
- ½ lemon
- 2 oz of butter
- 2 tablespoons of oil
- 4-6 courgettes
- ½ teaspoon of onion powder

Directions:
1. Rinse and clean courgettes.
2. Chop them in the food processor.
3. Then sprinkle the Air Fryer with oil.
4. Preheat it to 300F.
5. Then place courgettes in the Air Fryer.
6. Cook for 5 minutes.
7. Then add onion powder, salt, pepper and then blend the products well.
8. Sprinkle the meal with juice of lemon and cook for 10 minutes more.
9. Serve it hot with fresh basil leaves or with parsley.

Nutrition:
- Calories: 138
- Fat: 1,2g
- Carbohydrates: 5,3g
- Protein: 1,3g

Fried Vegetarian Patties

This meal is really fantastic. You even cannot imagine how tasty it is. Just cook it and you will see how incredibly delicious it is.

Prep time: 20 minutes | **Cooking time:** 10 minutes | **Servings:** 4

Ingredients:
- 1 teaspoon of flour
- 1 egg
- ½ teaspoon of salt
- ½ teaspoon of pepper
- ½ teaspoon of oregano
- ½ green capsicum
- ½ onion
- 2-3 teaspoons of spices for vegetables
- ½ red capsicum
- 1 lb of chickpeas
- ½ backed avocado
- 2 teaspoons of oil

Directions:
1. Put chickpeas in the food processor and chop.
2. Then put chickpeas in the deep bowl.
3. Add salt, egg, pepper, flour, oregano and mix everything.
4. Cut capsicums in the tiny pieces and add there.
5. Then add chopped onion and avocado with vegetable spices.
6. Mix the ingredients in the bowl.
7. Create little cutlets from it.
8. Sprinkle the Air Fryer with oil.
9. Preheat it to 300F.
10. Put cutlets in the Air Fryer and cook for 10 minutes.

Nutrition:
- Calories: 142
- Fat: 1,5g
- Carbohydrates: 5,2g
- Protein: 1,2g

Appetizing Curry

This curry will be great for lunch. It is easy in preparing and truly tempting.

Prep time: 10 minutes | **Cooking time:** 14-15 minutes | **Servings:** 4

Ingredients:
- 1 teaspoon of butter
- ½ teaspoon of salt
- ½ teaspoon of pepper
- 3 oz of spinach
- 2 tomatoes
- 2 lbs of brown lentils
- 2 spring onions
- 1 teaspoon of ginger
- 1 teaspoon of garlic
- 1 teaspoon of mustard
- 1 teaspoon of cumin seeds
- 1 teaspoon of oil

Directions:
1. Grease the Air Fryer with oil.
2. Preheat it to 350F.
3. Then cook butter with cumin seeds, mustard for 2 minutes.
4. Then add garlic, ginger, chopped spring onion and cook for 3-4 minutes.
5. The next step is adding lentils.
6. Cook for 5 minutes.
7. Blend everything.
8. After that add sliced spinach and chopped tomatoes.
9. Blend the products well and cook for 5 minutes.
10. Serve hot with rice.

Nutrition:
- Calories: 135
- Fat: 1,3g
- Carbohydrates: 6,4g
- Protein: 1,1g

Flavorsome Rice with Bacon

It is the great combination of rice with bacon. You will see that you will get the appetizing and great meal for lunch.

Prep time: 15 minutes | **Cooking time:** 15 minutes | **Servings:** 4

Ingredients:
- 4 pieces of bacon
- ½ teaspoon of salt
- ½ teaspoon of pepper
- ½ teaspoon of oregano
- 4 tablespoons of soy sauce
- 2 teaspoons of oil
- 3 eggs
- 3 cups of cooked rice

Directions:
1. Sprinkle the Air Fryer with oil.
2. Preheat it to 300F for 3 minutes.
3. Chop bacon and cook it for 5 minutes.
4. Then add bacon to rice and mix them.
5. Add salt, pepper, oregano, eggs and mix the products well.
6. Cook for 10 minutes in the Air Fryer at 350F.
7. Then add soy sauce and blend rice again.
8. Serve hot with meat or vegetables.

Nutrition:
- Calories: 127
- Fat: 1,5g
- Carbohydrates: 5,2g
- Protein: 1,2g

Backed Potato with Bacon

It is incredibly delicious potato with flavorsome bacon. The perfect meal for lunch.

Prep time: 20 minutes | **Cooking time:** 1 hour 10 minutes | **Servings:** 4

Ingredients:
- 1 lb of cream
- ½ teaspoon of salt
- ½ teaspoon of pepper
- 1 tablespoon of spices for vegetables
- 8 oz of cheese
- 6 oz of bacon
- ½ teaspoon of pepper
- ½ teaspoon of red chili pepper
- 2 teaspoons of oil

Directions:
1. Wash and clean potatoes.
2. Then cut it in the slices.
3. Add salt, pepper and red chili pepper.
4. Blend spices with potatoes.
5. Add vegetable spices.
6. Blend potatoes well.
7. Sprinkle the Air Fryer with oil.
8. Then preheat it to 350F for 3 minutes.
9. Place potatoes in the Air Fryer. Cook for 30 minutes.
10. Then add cream, bacon and cheese and cover with foil.
11. Cook for 40 minutes at 300F.

Nutrition:
- Calories: 156
- Fat: 3,5g
- Carbohydrates: 6,9g
- Protein: 5,3g

Appetizing Salad with Bacon, Spring Onion and Potato

This salad is incredibly tasty. You will be pleased with this tempting salad for lunch.

Prep time: 10 minutes | **Cooking time:** 20 minutes | **Servings:** 4

Ingredients:
- 1 teaspoon of parsley
- ½ leaspoon of pepper
- ½ teaspoon of salt
- 1 teaspoon of white vinegar
- 3 spring onions
- ½ green capsicum
- ½ cucumber
- 1 lb of potatoes
- ½ teaspoon of cumin powder
- ½ teaspoon of chili pepper

Directions:
1. Cook potatoes and place in the bowl. Then chop potatoes in the pieces.
2. Add salt, pepper, cumin powder and chili pepper.
3. Blend the products in the bowl.
4. Then chop cucumber, bacon, capsicum and onions.
5. Add them to the bowl. Blend all products.
6. Sprinkle the combination with vinegar. Put in the Air Fryer and cook for 10 minutes at 350F.
7. Put the combination on the other side and cook for 10 minutes more.

Nutrition:
- Calories: 127
- Fat: 3,2g
- Carbohydrates: 6,8g
- Protein: 5,1g

Appetizing Potatoes with Sour Cream

This lunch is mouthwatering. Scrumptious potatoes meal is flavorsome.

Prep time: 15 minutes	**Cooking time:** 1 hour 30 minutes	**Servings:** 4

Ingredients:
- 6 potatoes
- 1 lb of chicken cream soup
- 6 oz of butter
- 1 lb of sour cream
- 1/3 cup of onion
- 1 cup of cheese
- ½ teaspoon of salt
- ½ teaspoon of pepper
- ½ teaspoon of garlic powder
- ½ teaspoon of cumin powder
- 2 teaspoons of oil

Directions:
1. Sprinkle the Air Fryer with oil.
2. Then preheat the Air Fryer to 300F.
3. Wash and clean potatoes.
4. Cut potatoes in the pieces and cook for 50 minutes.
5. After that place potatoes in the container.
6. Add chicken cream soup, salt, pepper, garlic powder and cumin powder.
7. Blend everything.
8. Then cut onion and add it with sour cream to potatoes.
9. Cover everything with cheese and cook for 40 minutes.
10. After that serve hot with basil leaves or mint.

Nutrition:
- Calories: 156
- Fat: 2,8g
- Carbohydrates: 7,5g
- Protein: 3,1g

Piquant French Carrots

This lunch is healthy and flavorsome. You can prepare scrumptious carrot meal and your children will be glad to eat this meal.

Prep time: 10 minutes	**Cooking time:** 20 minutes	**Servings:** 4

Ingredients:
- ½ teaspoon of salt
- ½ teaspoon of pepper
- 1 tablespoon of oil
- 2 teaspoons of lemon juice
- Fresh tarragon
- 1 lb of green beans
- 1 big carrot
- 1 tablespoon of honey

Directions:
1. Sprinkle the Air Fryer with oil.
2. Preheat it to 300F for 3 minutes.
3. Wash and clean carrot and beans.
4. Cut them in the small pieces.
5. After that place them in the bowl.
6. Then add salt, pepper, lemon juice, honey and blend everything.
7. Cook the products for 10 minutes.
8. Then blend them and cook for 10 minutes more.

Nutrition:
- Calories: 105
- Fat: 2,3g
- Carbohydrates: 7,9g
- Protein: 1,3g

Scrumptious and Pepper Coconut Rise

This rice is fantastic. The herbs give some unusual note. Rice is so delightful.

Prep time: 5 minutes | **Cooking time:** 20 minutes | **Servings:** 4

Ingredients:

- 2 cups of rice
- ½ teaspoon of pepper
- ½ teaspoon of salt
- 1 teaspoon of dry herbs
- 1/3 teaspoon of cumin
- ¼ teaspoon of oregano
- 1/3 teaspoon of red chili pepper
- 3 cups of coconut milk
- 2 tablespoons of oil

Directions:

1. Sprinkle the Air Fryer with oil.
2. Then preheat it to 350F.
3. Wash and clean rice.
4. Blend it with the coconut milk.
5. Add salt, pepper, herbs, oregano, cumin and red chili pepper there.
6. Blend spices with rice.
7. Cook this meal for 30 minutes in the Air Fryer.
8. After that serve it hot with basil leaves or 2-3 sprigs of fresh mint.
9. Enjoy with the coconut rice.

Nutrition:

- Calories: 98
- Fat: 1,2g
- Carbohydrates: 5,4g
- Protein: 1,2g

Fried Salad with Potato

This salad for lunch is very tasty. Prepare it only one time and it will be always on your table.

Prep time: 10 minutes | **Cooking time:** 50 minutes | **Servings:** 4

Ingredients:

- 2 lbs of potato
- 3 tablespoons of basil pesto
- 2 tablespoons of oil
- ½ teaspoon of pepper
- ½ teaspoon of salt
- 2 cups of spring onions
- 1 cup of tomatoes
- ¼ cup of nuts
- 5 tablespoons of mayonnaise

Directions:

1. Wash and clean potatoes.
2. Then cut potatoes in the pieces.
3. Sprinkle the Air Fryer with oil.
4. Preheat it for 3 minutes to 350F.
5. Cook potatoes for 40 minutes.
6. Then put potatoes in the bowl.
7. Add pepper, basil pesto, salt and mayonnaise and mix everything.
8. Chop tomatoes, nuts and onions.
9. Mix all products together.
10. After that cook everything for 10 minutes more.
11. Serve hot with parsley and sauce.

Nutrition:

- Calories: 135
- Fat: 1,6g
- Carbohydrates: 5,8g
- Protein: 1,1g

Tasty Backed Vegetables

You can find the diversity of vegetables in this recipe. This meal is very tasty and cool.

Prep time: 15 minutes | **Cooking time:** 30 minutes | **Servings:** 3

Ingredients:
- 2 teaspoons of oil
- ½ teaspoon of salt
- ½ teaspoon of pepper
- 2 large zucchinis
- 2-3 onions
- ½ cup of feta
- ½ cup of cheese
- 3 big potatoes
- 3 sweet potatoes

Directions:
1. Sprinkle the Air Fryer with oil.
2. Preheat it to 300F.
3. Wash and clean potatoes.
4. Then chop them in the pieces.
5. Then cut zucchinis and onions in the pieces.
6. Mix everything well.
7. Add salt, pepper, chopped feta and mix everything again.
8. Cover the meal with potatoes.
9. Then cook it in the Air Fryer for 30 minutes.
10. Serve hot with vegetables and with your favorite sauces.
11. Eat and enjoy with this meal.

Nutrition:
- Calories: 126
- Fat: 1,7g
- Carbohydrates: 5,3g
- Protein: 1,2g

Flavorsome Fried Pepper with Eggs

It is easy for preparing. This meal is yummy and great.

Prep time: 15 minutes | **Cooking time:** 30 minutes | **Servings:** 3

Ingredients:
- 2 teaspoons of oil
- ½ teaspoon of salt
- ½ teaspoon of pepper
- 1/3 teaspoon of dry herbs
- 1/3 teaspoon of oregano
- 1/3 teaspoon of red chili pepper
- 1 onion
- 3 eggs
- 2 big red peppers

Directions:
1. Wash and cut peppers in the strings.
2. Then chop onion in the rings.
3. Add red chili pepper, oregano, dry herbs, pepper and salt.
4. Then blend everything in the bowl.
5. After that beat eggs and add them to the combination.
6. Sprinkle the Air Fryer with oil.
7. Preheat it to 300F for 2 minutes.
8. Cook everything for 15 minutes.
9. Then blend the components well and cook for 30 minutes more.
10. Serve hot with sauce.

Nutrition:
- Calories: 146
- Fat: 2,3g
- Carbohydrates: 7,2g
- Protein: 1,3g

Appetizing Broccoli with Salad with Olives

This lunch is completely delicious and tasty. Also, it is vigorous.

| Prep time: 10 minutes | Cooking time: 15 minutes | Servings: 3 |

Ingredients:
- 1/2 teaspoon of salt
- ½ teaspoon of pepper
- 1 tablespoon of oil
- 2-3 spring onions
- 4 celery stalks
- 6-10 olives
- 1/3 cup of olive oil
- 1 tablespoon of capers
- 1 clove of garlic
- 2 tablespoons of vinegar
- 1/3 teaspoon of cumin
- 1 head of broccoli

Directions:
1. Slice broccoli in the pieces.
2. Sprinkle the Air Fryer with oil.
3. Then preheat it to 350F.
4. After that add pepper, 1 tablespoon of oil, salt vinegar, cumin and chopped garlic.
5. Blend everything well.
6. Slice onions, olives, capers in the pieces.
7. Blend all components well.
8. Place the meal in the Air Fryer and cook for 15 minutes.
9. Serve hot with sauces.

Nutrition:
- Calories: 126
- Fat: 1,5g
- Carbohydrates: 6,8g
- Protein: 1,1g

Tasty Cooked Eggplant with Flavors

This meal for lunch is scrumptious and peppery. It will be your favorite lunch for the whole life.

| Prep time: 10 minutes | Cooking time: 12 minutes | Servings: 4 |

Ingredients:
- ½ teaspoon of salt
- ½ teaspoon of pepper
- 2 tablespoons of oil
- 2 teaspoons of dark soy sauce
- 1 teaspoon of light soy sauce
- 1 oz of ginger
- 1 tablespoon of sugar
- ½ teaspoon of red chili pepper
- 1 lb of eggplants

Directions:
1. Sprinkle the Air Fryer with oil.
2. Then preheat it to 300F for 5 minutes.
3. Wash and clean eggplants.
4. Cut them in the pieces.
5. Then mix salt, pepper, dark soy sauce, chopped ginger, sugar, red chili pepper and light soy sauce in the bowl.
6. Rub eggplants with spices.
7. Then place them in the Air Fryer.
8. Cook for 6 minutes at 300F.
9. Then shake them well. Cook for 6 minutes more.

Nutrition:
- Calories: 103
- Fat: 1,7g
- Carbohydrates: 6,3g
- Protein: 1,2g

Fried Cucumbers

It is really unusual and interesting lunch. Prepare this unique and tasty meal.

Prep time: 10 minutes | **Cooking time:** 15 minutes | **Servings:** 4

Ingredients:
- 3 tablespoons of oil
- ½ lb of cucumbers
- ½ teaspoon of salt
- ½ teaspoon of pepper
- 1 tablespoon of hot chili oil
- ½ teaspoon of red chili pepper
- 1 tablespoon of soy sauce

Directions:
1. Wash and clean cucumbers.
2. Cut them in the pieces.
3. Take the bowl and blend salt, pepper, red chili pepper, soy sauce and hot chili oil there.
4. Rub cucumbers with these spices.
5. Then sprinkle the Air Fryer with oil
6. Preheat it for 3 minutes to 350F.
7. Place cucumbers in the Air Fryer and cook them for 15-16 minutes.
8. Serve warm with basil leaves and fresh parsley.
9. Enjoy with unique and appetizing lunch.

Nutrition:
- Calories: 46
- Fat: 1,1g
- Carbohydrates: 4,1g
- Protein: 1,1g

Fried Broccoli with Oyster Sauce

It is easy for preparing and flavorsome at the same time. Cook and taste it. You will be surprised a lot.

Prep time: 5 minutes | **Cooking time:** 15 minutes | **Servings:** 4

Ingredients:
- 2 tablespoons of oil
- ½ teaspoon of pepper
- ½ teaspoon of salt
- 1 cup of chicken stock
- ¼ cup of oyster sauce
- 2 teaspoons of sesame oil
- 2 lbs of broccoli

Directions:
1. Sprinkle the Air Fryer with oil.
2. Preheat it for 5 minutes to 320F.
3. Wash and cut broccoli in the pieces.
4. Then add pepper, salt and sesame oil and mix the products.
5. After that add cup of chicken stock and oyster sauce.
6. Mix the components well.
7. Put the mixture in the Air Fryer and cook for 15 minutes.
8. Serve hot with parsley or with basil leaves.
9. Enjoy with this tasty and delicious meal.

Nutrition:
- Calories: 167
- Fat: 3,4g
- Carbohydrates: 5,8g
- Protein: 2,3g

Warm and Peppery Soup

This soup is appetizing. Cook and like.

Prep time: 10 minutes | **Cooking time:** 15 minutes | **Servings:** 4

Ingredients:

- 3 cups of chicken
- ½ teaspoon of salt
- ½ teaspoon of pepper
- 2 tablespoons of oil
- 1 tablespoon of pasta
- 1 teaspoon of garlic powder
- 2 leaves of lime
- 1 tablespoon of fish sauce
- 3 oz of mushrooms
- 1 teaspoon of green chili
- 1 teaspoon of basil leaves
- 1 teaspoon of coriander

Directions:

1. Sprinkle the Air Fryer with oil.
2. Preheat it for 3 minutes to 350F.
3. Rinse, chop chicken in the pieces.
4. Then rub meat with salt, pepper, pasta, garlic powder, fish sauce, green chili and coriander.
5. Chop mushrooms in the pieces.
6. Blend with the products.
7. Cook for 15 minutes in the Air Fryer.

Nutrition:

- Calories: 146
- Fat: 3,7g
- Carbohydrates: 8,3g
- Protein: 9,1g

Curry with Chicken

This meal will be your favorite one. It is scrumptious and delicious. Cook it and you will see.

Prep time: 10 minutes | **Cooking time:** 25 minutes | **Servings:** 4

Ingredients:

- ½ teaspoon of pepper
- ½ teaspoon of salt
- 2 tablespoons of oil
- 1 cup of yogurt
- ¾ cup of coconut milk
- 1 chicken breast
- 1 tablespoon of tomato pasta
- 1 teaspoon of paprika
- 1 teaspoon of red chili pepper
- 2 tablespoons of curry
- 1 teaspoon of sugar
- 1 teaspoon of ginger
- 1 onion

Directions:

1. Sprinkle the Air Fryer with oil.
2. Preheat the Air Fryer to 300F for 5 minutes.
3. Slice chicken in the pieces.
4. Put salt, pepper, tomato pasta, paprika, red chili pepper, curry, sugar and ginger in the bowl with chicken.
5. Mix everything well.
6. After that cut onion and add to chicken.
7. Mix the components well.
8. Cook in the Air Fryer for 15 minutes,
9. Then cover everything with yogurt and cook for 10 minutes more.

Nutrition:

- Calories: 165
- Fat: 3,9g
- Carbohydrates: 8,2g
- Protein: 9,3g

Tasty Capsicum Beans and Rice

Prepare something special and extravagant. Cook rice and check the outcome.

Prep time: 10 minutes | **Cooking time:** 50 minutes | **Servings:** 4

Ingredients:
- 3 teaspoon of salt
- ½ teaspoon of pepper
- ½ teaspoon of salt
- 1 cup of rice
- 1 cup of beans
- 3 tablespoon of tomato pasta
- 2 cloves of garlic
- 1 onion
- 1 green paprika

Directions:
1. Sprinkle the Air Fryer with oil.
2. Preheat the Air Fryer to 350F for 3 minutes.
3. Cut onion and put it in the bowl.
4. Then add rice and beans. Blend everything well.
5. After that add chopped paprika, salt, pepper, garlic and tomato pasta.
6. Blend all ingredients well.
7. Add water and place in the aid fryer.
8. Cook for 40 minutes and mix everything.
9. Then cook for 10 minutes more.
10. Serve it hot with parsley and basil leaves.

Nutrition:
- Calories: 112
- Fat: 1,5g
- Carbohydrates: 8,5g
- Protein: 1,2g

Flavorsome Bean Soup with Spinach and Leek

Peppery soup will be great for lunch. You will be happy with the outcome.

Prep time: 10 minutes | **Cooking time:** 15 minutes | **Servings:** 4

Ingredients:
- 2 teaspoon of oil
- ½ teaspoon of pepper
- ½ teaspoon of salt
- 1 bunch of spinach
- ½ cup of couscous
- 2 bay leaves
- 2 teaspoons of cumin
- 1 lb of beans
- 1 cup of vegetable stick
- 2 cloves of garlic
- 4 onions

Directions:
1. Sprinkle the Air Fryer with oil.
2. Then preheat it to 300F for 3 minutes.
3. Chop spinach in the pieces.
4. Then add salt, pepper, couscous, cumin, bay leaves, garlic and mix everything.
5. Chop onions and add there.
6. Then pour everything with the cup of vegetable stock.
7. Blend everything well.
8. Cook in the Air Fryer for 15 minutes.
9. Serve hot with parsley or basil leaves.

Nutrition:
- Calories: 107
- Fat: 1,3g
- Carbohydrates: 8,6g
- Protein: 1,3g

Sharp Chicken with Garlic and Lemon

This lunch is scrumptious. It is easy and does not need a lot of your efforts.

Prep time: 10 minutes	**Cooking time:** 35 minutes	**Servings:** 4

Ingredients:

- 1 teaspoon of oregano
- ½ teaspoon of salt
- ½ teaspoon of pepper
- 1 lb of chicken fillet
- 3 tablespoons of water

- 1 tablespoon of butter
- 1 cloves of garlic
- 3 tablespoons of lemon juice

- 1 teaspoon of chicken stock powder
- 1 teaspoon of chopped parsley

Directions:

1. Sprinkle the Air Fryer with oil.
2. Preheat it for 5 minutes to 350F.
3. Then wash chicken fillet
4. Mix salt, pepper, oregano, water, butter, garlic, lemon juice and parsley in the bowl.
5. Rub chopped chicken fillet with spices.
6. After that cook it in the Air Fryer for 20 minutes.
7. Then blend everything. Cook for 15 minutes more.

Nutrition:

- Calories: 135
- Fat: 3,2g

- Carbohydrates: 8,7g
- Protein: 3,1g

Tasty Spag Bol Sauce

This sauce can be great for every meal. Just cook and you will see it. This sauce is spicy and tasty. You should cook it.

Prep time: 15 minutes	**Cooking time:** 50 minutes	**Servings:** 4

Ingredients:

- 2 bay leaves
- ½ teaspoon of pepper
- 2 tablespoons of oil
- 1 teaspoon of basil
- 1 teaspoon of oregano

- 1 red capsicum
- 1 celery stalk
- 1 cup of red wine
- 1 cup of tomato pasta
- 2 cups of tomatoes

- 1 cup of meat
- 3 onions
- 3 cloves of garlic
- 1 lb of mince

Directions:

1. Chop onions and garlic in the pieces.
2. Then add mince and mix everything.
3. Chop meat in the small pieces and add to mince.
4. Mix them well.
5. Then put bay leaves, pepper, basil, oregano, chopped capsicum, red wine, tomato pasta and mix everything.
6. Sprinkle the Air Fryer with oil.
7. Then preheat it to 350F.
8. Cook for 30 minutes.
9. Then mix everything and cook for 20 minutes more.

Nutrition:

- Calories: 189
- Fat: 8,2g

- Carbohydrates: 9,7g
- Protein: 5,6g

Garlic Rice with Mushrooms

It is the great combination of mushrooms and rice. You will get the delicious and flavorsome lunch.

| **Prep time:** 10 minutes | **Cooking time:** 25 minutes | **Servings:** 4 |

Ingredients:

- ½ teaspoon of pepper
- ½ teaspoon of salt
- 3 tablespoons of oil
- 1 cup of rice
- 1 tablespoon of chopped parsley
- 2 cups of chicken fillet
- 1 spring onion
- 1 tablespoon of butter
- 6 big mushrooms
- 1 clove of garlic

Directions:

1. Melt butter with salt, pepper, chopped parsley and garlic in the bowl.
2. Then add rice and mix everything.
3. Chop chicken fillet in the pieces.
4. Chop mushrooms and spring onion.
5. Blend everything in the bowl.
6. Sprinkle the Air Fryer with oil.
7. Preheat it to 360F for 3 minutes.
8. Then place the products in the Air Fryer, add water and cook for 20 minutes.
9. Then blend everything and cook for 5 minutes more.
10. Serve hot with basil leaves or sauces.

Nutrition:

- Calories: 178
- Fat: 8,3g
- Carbohydrates: 9,8g
- Protein: 5,3g

Flavorsome and Fiery Lamb

This meat is appetizing and if you cook it for lunch, it will be great. You will not spend a lot of your time. Easy, simple and wonderful.

| **Prep time:** 8 minutes | **Cooking time:** 50 minutes | **Servings:** 4 |

Ingredients:

- 1/2 teaspoon of pepper
- ½ teaspoon of salt
- 3 tablespoons of oil
- 2 lb of lamb neck
- ¼ cup of flour
- 3 onions
- 2 carrots
- 1 lb of potatoes
- ½ cup of chicken fillet
- 3 tablespoons of sauce

Directions:

1. Chop onions and carrots in the pieces.
2. Then wash and clean potatoes and chop them in the pieces.
3. Sprinkle the Air Fryer with oil.
4. Then preheat the Air Fryer with oil.
5. Rub potatoes and onions and carrot with pepper, salt, flour and sauce.
6. Then chop meat and add to the mixture.
7. Cook everything in the Air Fryer for 30 minutes.
8. Then blend the components and cook for 20 minutes more.
9. Serve hot with parsley and mint leaves.

Nutrition:

- Calories: 176
- Fat: 9,2g
- Carbohydrates: 9,7g
- Protein: 5,5g

Appetizing Varied Vegetables

If you like fresh vegetables, then this recipe is accurately for you.

Prep time: 15 minutes	**Cooking time:** 30 minutes	**Servings:** 4

Ingredients:

- 1 onion
- ½ teaspoon of pepper
- ½ teaspoon of salt
- 3 tablespoons of oil
- 1 green chili pepper
- 2 cloves of garlic
- 1 eggplant
- 2 tablespoons of water
- 1 teaspoon of curry
- 1 teaspoon of cumin
- 2 teaspoons of mustard
- 3 cups of vegetable stock
- 1 zucchinih
- 1 tomato
- 1 teaspoons of coriander

Directions:

1. Chop onion, tomato and zucchini in the pieces.
2. Then add pepper, salt, chopped chili pepper, garlic, chopped eggplant, water, curry, cumin, mustard and coriander and cook everything well.
3. Sprinkle the Air Fryer with oil.
4. Preheat it to 290F for 4 minutes.
5. Then place the products in the Air Fryer and pour with vegetable stock.
6. Cook in the Air Fryer for 20 minutes.
7. Then blend everything well and cook for 10 minutes more.

Nutrition:

- Calories: 123
- Fat: 4,3g
- Carbohydrates: 7,4g
- Protein: 1,3g

Spicy Mince

It you like meat then this recipe is exactly for you. Only here you can find the tasty lunch, which everyone will like.

Prep time: 10 minutes	**Cooking time:** 35 minutes	**Servings:** 4

Ingredients:

- ¾ cup of parsley
- ½ teaspoon of salt
- ½ teaspoon of pepper
- 3 tablespoons of oil
- ½ cup of sour cream
- 1 teaspoon of sherry
- 1 beef stock cube
- 1 cup of pasta
- 1 teaspoon of celery
- 1 cup of water
- 1 tablespoon of sauce
- 1 onion
- 1 cup of tomato pasta
- 1 lb of mince

Directions:

1. Sprinkle the Air Fryer with oil.
2. Then preheat the Air Fryer to 350F.
3. Cook pasta with water.
4. Then put it in the bowl.
5. Add salt, pepper, parsley, sherry, celery, chopped onion and mix everything well.
6. Then cook mince in the Air Fryer for 20 minutes.
7. Then mix with the rest of the ingredients from the bowl.
8. Cover everything with pasta, cream and add 1 cube of beef stock and sauce.
9. Mix everything well and cook for 15 minutes.

Nutrition:

- Calories: 189
- Fat: 8,6g
- Carbohydrates: 8,6g
- Protein: 5,2g

Incredibly Tasty Asparagus with Spices

This meal is original and very interesting. Cook and enjoy.

Prep time: 5 minutes | **Cooking time:** 40 minutes | **Servings:** 4

Ingredients:

- 4 tablespoons of lemon juice
- ½ teaspoon of salt
- 2 tablespoons of oil
- ½ teaspoon of pepper
- 5 oz of rocket leaves
- 8 oz of asparagus
- 2 cloves of garlic
- 6 pieces of bacon
- 3 tablespoons of olive oil
- 1 lb of linguine

Directions:

1. Sprinkle the Air Fryer with oil.
2. Then preheat it to 300F for 3 minutes.
3. Cook linguine in salt water and put in the bowl. Cook for 10 minutes.
4. Then add olive oil, pepper, salt, chopped garlic, lemon juice and blend everything well.
5. Cook for 5 minutes.
6. Then add bacon, rocket leaves and asparagus.
7. Cook for 15 minutes more.
8. Then blend everything well and cook for 10 minutes.
9. Serve hot with sauce.

Nutrition:

- Calories: 136
- Fat: 2,1g
- Carbohydrates: 5,4g
- Protein: 1,4g

Tasty Chickpeas with Tomato

This meal is really delicious and tomato can add the special flavor. Just cook and you will like it.

Prep time: 10 minutes | **Cooking time:** 20 minutes | **Servings:** 4

Ingredients:

- 1 onion
- ½ teaspoon of pepper
- 3 teaspoons of oil
- ½ teaspoon of salt
- 1 teaspoon of lemon juice
- 2 tomatoes
- 1 lb of canned chickpeas
- 1 teaspoon of cumin seeds
- ½ teaspoon of red chili pepper

Directions:

1. Sprinkle the Air Fryer with oil.
2. Preheat it to 280F for 3 minutes.
3. Chop onion in the rings and put in the bowl.
4. Then chop tomatoes and mix with onion.
5. After that add the chickpeas.
6. Mix the ingredients well.
7. Add pepper, salt, lemon juice, red chili pepper and cumin seeds.
8. Mix everything well.
9. Cook in the Air Fryer for 10 minutes.
10. Then mix everything and cook for 10 minutes more.

Nutrition:

- Calories: 112
- Fat: 2,2g
- Carbohydrates: 6,7g
- Protein: 1,2g

Spicy Chili

If you like too spicy food, this recipe is for you. Lunch fill be perfect and you will be satisfied with the result.

Prep time: 10 minutes | **Cooking time:** 25 minutes | **Servings:** 4

Ingredients:
- 1 cup of water
- 1 cup of onion
- ½ teaspoon of pepper
- ½ teaspoon of salt
- 2 cups of sauce
- ½ tablespoon of dry herbs
- 1 lb of tomatoes
- 1 lb of canned red beans
- ½ lb of turkey
- ½ teaspoon of oregano
- 2 tablespoons of oil

Directions:
1. Wash and cut turkey in the pieces.
2. Put them in the bowl.
3. Mix meat with salt, pepper, dry herbs and oregano.
4. Chop onion and tomatoes in the pieces and mix with turkey.
5. Add red beans.
6. Sprinkle the Air Fryer with oil.
7. Then preheat it to 250F for 5 minutes.
8. Cook the food for 10 minutes.
9. Then mix everything well, cover with sauce, change the temperature to 300F and cook for 15 minutes more.

Nutrition:
- Calories: 178
- Fat: 4,2g
- Carbohydrates: 8,9g
- Protein: 8,9g

Delicious Risotto with Mushrooms

If you prepare this lunch, all your family will be happy. This meal is very delicious, tasty and fantastic.

Prep time: 10 minutes | **Cooking time:** 25 minutes | **Servings:** 4

Ingredients:
- ½ teaspoon of salt
- ½ teaspoon of pepper
- 2 tablespoons of oil
- 1 lb of cooked rice
- 7 oz of cooked chicken
- 1,5 lb of mushrooms
- ¼ cup of olive oil
- 1 onion
- 1 oz of walnuts

Directions:
1. Chop chicken in the pieces and mix with rice.
2. Sprinkle the Air Fryer with oil.
3. Preheat it to 300F for 2 minutes.
4. Then cook walnuts for 5 minutes.
5. Then add them to rice.
6. Chop onion and mushrooms.
7. Mix everything with salt and pepper.
8. Cook lunch in the Air Fryer for 15 minutes.
9. Then mix everything well and cook for 10 minutes more.

Nutrition:
- Calories: 165
- Fat: 5,3g
- Carbohydrates: 6,9g
- Protein: 6,8g

Tasty Potatoes with Onion and Mushrooms

Prepare something not difficult for lunch. Easy, simple and really flavorsome.

Prep time: 10 minutes | **Cooking time:** 25 minutes | **Servings:** 4

Ingredients:

- ½ teaspoon of pepper
- ½ teaspoon of salt
- 2 teaspoon of oil
- 1 lb of potatoes
- 2 onions
- ½ lb of mushrooms
- ½ teaspoon of oregano
- 1 teaspoon of dry herbs
- ½ teaspoon of garlic powder
- ½ teaspoon of cumin

Directions:

1. Sprinkle the Air Fryer with oil.
2. Then preheat it for 3 minutes to 350F.
3. Wash and clean potatoes.
4. Then chop potatoes in the pieces.
5. Rub with pepper, salt, oregano, dry herbs, garlic powder and cumin.
6. Then cook in the Air Fryer for 10 minutes.
7. Add mushrooms and cook for 15 minutes.
8. After that chop onions in the rings and cook everything for 15 minutes more.
9. Decorate with basil leaves and parsley.
10. Serve hot with sauce.

Nutrition:

- Calories: 123
- Fat: 1,6g
- Carbohydrates: 4,3g
- Protein: 1,2g

Appetizing Watermelon with Salad

Try this salad. It is flavorsome and delicious.

Prep time: 40 minutes | **Cooking time:** 10 minutes | **Servings:** 4

Ingredients:

- ½ teaspoon of salt
- ½ teaspoon of pepper
- 2 tablespoons of oil
- 1 teaspoon of brown sugar
- 2 tablespoons of parsley
- 2 tablespoons of chopped coriander
- 20 olives
- 5 oz of feta
- 2 limes
- ½ watermelon
- 1 red onion

Directions:

1. Sprinkle the Air Fryer with oil.
2. Preheat it to 300F for 4 minutes.
3. Mix chopped onion with limes and place them in the fridge for 30 minutes.
4. Chop parsley, coriander, watermelon, feta and olives.
5. Blend everything well.
6. Then add onion with limes.
7. Blend the ingredients with salt and pepper.
8. Place them in the Air Fryer 10 minutes.
9. Serve and enjoy with scrumptious lunch.

Nutrition:

- Calories: 113
- Fat: 1,7g
- Carbohydrates: 6,2g
- Protein: 1,2g

Fried Piquant Mushrooms

They are delectable and wonderful. Cook and enjoy! It is truly flavorsome.

Prep time: 10 minutes	**Cooking time:** 20 minutes	**Servings:** 2

Ingredients:
- 1 teaspoon of sesame oil
- 1 teaspoon of sugar
- ½ teaspoon of salt
- ½ teaspoon of pepper
- ½ lb of mushrooms
- 1 tablespoon of soy sauce
- 1 tablespoon of oil
- ½ teaspoon of red chili pepper
- 1 teaspoon of dry herbs
- 1 teaspoon of corn flour

Directions:
1. Sprinkle the Air Fryer with oil.
2. Preheat it to 350F for 5 minutes.
3. Cook mushrooms in the Air Fryer for 10 minutes.
4. Then add sugar, salt, pepper, sesame oil, soy sauce, red chili pepper, flour and dry herbs.
5. Mix all products together.
6. Then set mushrooms in the Air Fryer.
7. Cook meal for 10 minutes.
8. Serve hot with parsley or fresh vegetables.
9. Enjoy with your lunch.

Nutrition:
- Calories: 78
- Fat: 1,5g
- Carbohydrates: 3,2g
- Protein: 1g

Fried Vegetables with Spicy Bacon

This combination of bacon and vegetables is really tasty. Just cook and you will like it very much.

Prep time: 10 minutes	**Cooking time:** 50 minutes	**Servings:** 2

Ingredients:
- 1/2 teaspoon of pepper
- ½ teaspoon of salt
- 2 tablespoons of oil
- 2 springs onions
- 2 brussels sprouts
- 5-6 pieces of bacon
- 2 cups of mushrooms
- ½ eggplant
- 2 potatoes

Directions:
1. Sprinkle the Air Fryer with oil.
2. Preheat it to 350F for 3 minutes.
3. Wash and clean potatoes.
4. Cut them in the pieces.
5. Cook in the Air Fryer for 30 minutes.
6. Then chop mushrooms and bacon in the pieces.
7. Add them to potatoes.
8. Chop brussels sprouts and spring onions with eggplant.
9. Mix them with salt and pepper and add to the rest of the products.
10. Cook everything for 20 minutes in the Air Fryer.
11. Serve with sauces and parsley.

Nutrition:
- Calories: 167
- Fat: 2,3g
- Carbohydrates: 5,6g
- Protein: 1,3g

Warm and Flavorsome Salad

It is the appetizing salad for lunch. Cook and check.

Prep time: 15 minutes | **Cooking time:** 15 minutes | **Servings:** 2

Ingredients:

- 1 cup of ham
- ½ teaspoon of salt
- ½ teaspoon of pepper
- 1/3 teaspoon of oregano
- ½ teaspoon of red chili pepper
- ½ cup of sauce
- ¼ cup of corn
- ¼ cup of peas
- 1 cup of pasta
- 2 teaspoons of oil

Directions:

1. Cook pasta in the boiled water and place in the container.
2. Cook peas in water for 10 minutes.
3. Then blend the peas with pasta in the bowl.
4. Cut ham and add to the products.
5. After that blend the products with salt, pepper, oregano, red chili pepper.
6. Sprinkle the Air Fryer with oil.
7. Preheat it to 350F.
8. Cook the food for 10 minutes.
9. Then cover meal with sauce. Cook for 5 minutes more.
10. Serve hot with onion rings.

Nutrition:

- Calories: 146
- Fat: 2,9g
- Carbohydrates: 8,4g
- Protein: 2,3g

Salad with Potato and Coriander

The simple and easy salad for lunch. It will be your best choice, because this salad is really tasty.

Prep time: 15 minutes | **Cooking time:** 25 minutes | **Servings:** 4

Ingredients:

- 2 tablespoons of oil
- ½ teaspoon of pepper
- ½ teaspoon of salt
- 1 lb of potatoes
- 3 oz of coriander
- 1 onion
- 2 gloves of garlic
- 1 teaspoon of sesame oil
- 1 teaspoon of ginger
- 1 teaspoon of vinegar

Directions:

1. Sprinkle the Air Fryer with oil.
2. Preheat it to 350F for 5 minutes.
3. Wash and clean potatoes.
4. After that chop potatoes in the pieces.
5. Create sauce with pepper, salt, coriander, chopped onion, garlic, sesame oil, ginger and vinegar.
6. Leave sauce aside.
7. Cook potatoes in the Air Fryer for 15 minutes.
8. Then cover with sauce and mix well.
9. Cook for 10 minutes more.

Nutrition:

- Calories: 128
- Fat: 2,6g
- Carbohydrates: 7,8g
- Protein: 1,2g

Scrumptious and Piquant Asparagus

This lunch will be vigorous. It is tasty.

Prep time: 15 minutes | **Cooking time:** 15 minutes | **Servings:** 4

Ingredients:
- ½ cup of sauce
- ½ teaspoon of salt
- ½ teaspoon of pepper
- 2 teaspoons of oil
- 1 cup of mayonnaise
- 2 cups of bread crumbs
- 2 eggs
- ½ cup of flour
- 2 asparagus spears

Directions:
1. Blend sauce with the mayonnaise.
2. Leave it aside.
3. Chop asparagus in the pieces.
4. Add salt, pepper and rub asparagus with them.
5. Then beat eggs in the bowl.
6. Set asparagus in flour, then in eggs and then in bread crumbs.
7. Sprinkle the Air Fryer with oil.
8. Preheat it to 350F.
9. Then cook asparagus for 10 minutes.
10. Add pasta. Cook for 5 minutes more.
11. Serve hot.
12. Decorate with basil leaves and parsley.
13. Eat and enjoy with this flavorsome meal.

Nutrition:
- Calories: 135
- Fat: 2,3g
- Carbohydrates: 6,9g
- Protein: 1,1g

Salad with Chicken and Tarragon

This salad will be your best choice for lunch. It is healthy, interesting and delicious.

Prep time: 20 minutes | **Cooking time:** 20 minutes | **Servings:** 4

Ingredients:
- ½ teaspoon of pepper
- 2 teaspoons of oil
- ½ teaspoon of salt
- ½ cup of almonds
- 2 oranges
- 5 oz of spinach
- 2 tablespoons of tahini
- 2 sprigs of tarragon
- 2 cups of chicken stock
- ½ lb of chicken

Directions:
1. Wash and cut chicken.
2. Sprinkle the Air Fryer with oil.
3. Preheat it to 300F for 5 minutes.
4. Then blend chicken with salt, almonds, tahini, tarragon and chicken stock.
5. Chop oranges in the small pieces and add them to the products.
6. Then chop spinach.
7. Blend everything well and cook in the Air Fryer for 20 minutes.

Nutrition:
- Calories: 187
- Fat: 5,3g
- Carbohydrates: 7,8g
- Protein: 3,5g

Salad with Apple and Chicken

It is very easy and simple recipe for your lunch. Just keep it in mind and enjoy with it.

Prep time: 20 minutes | **Cooking time:** 20 minutes | **Servings:** 4

Ingredients:
- 4 chicken breasts
- 4 green onions
- 1 celery stalk
- 1/3 cup of currants
- 1 apple
- 2 oz of green grapes
- ½ teaspoon of curry
- 1/8 teaspoon of pepper
- 2 tablespoons of oil

Directions:
1. Sprinkle the Air Fryer with oil.
2. Preheat it to 290F.
3. Chop chicken breasts in the pieces.
4. Cook them in the Air Fryer for 15 minutes.
5. Then chop celery, apple, onions and add them to chicken.
6. After that blend everything well.
7. Add pepper, curry, green grapes, currants and blend all ingredients again.
8. Cook in the Air Fryer for 5 minutes.
9. Serve hot and enjoy with unusual and tasty salad.

Nutrition:
- Calories: 134
- Fat: 3,2g
- Carbohydrates: 9,8g
- Protein: 2,1g

Sharp Chicken and Capsicum with Tasty Feta Salad

The ingredients are flavorsome and you will have the appetizing salad. It will not take too much time to prepare this lunch.

Prep time: 10 minutes | **Cooking time:** 10 minutes | **Servings:** 4

Ingredients:
- 1 oz of feta
- ½ teaspoon of salt
- ½ teaspoon of pepper
- 2 teaspoons of oil
- 1 red capsicum
- 1 lb of chicken fillet
- ¼ cup of fresh dill
- 2 tablespoons of vinegar
- 2 cloves of garlic
- ½ cup of mayonnaise

Directions:
1. Wash and chop chicken in the pieces.
2. Rub meat with salt and pepper.
3. Then add mayonnaise, garlic, vinegar, dill, chopped capsicum and feta.
4. Blend the components well.
5. Sprinkle the Air Fryer with oil.
6. Preheat it to 350F.
7. Cook salad in the Air Fryer for 10 minutes.
8. Serve warm with parsley or basil leaves.

Nutrition:
- Calories: 156
- Fat: 3,6g
- Carbohydrates: 8,9g
- Protein: 2,5g

Salad with Bacon and Chicken

This salad with meat will be your favorite lunch. It is very easy in preparing and also it is very tasty.

Prep time: 15 minutes	**Cooking time:** 30 minutes	**Servings:** 4

Ingredients:
- 1/3 cup of cheese
- ½ teaspoon of pepper
- ½ teaspoon of salt
- 2 teaspoons of oil
- ½ cup of Cesare salad
- 3 pieces of croutons
- 1 cos lettuce
- 1 chicken breast
- 8 oz of bacon

Directions:
1. Wash chicken and cut it in the pieces.
2. Sprinkle the Air Fryer with oil.
3. Preheat it to 350F.
4. Then cook the pieces of chicken for 10 minutes.
5. Then chop bacon and cook for 5 minutes more.
6. After that add salt, pepper, Cesare salad, croutons, lettuce.
7. Mix all components well.
8. Cook for 15 minutes more.
9. Decorate salad with parsley and vegetables.
10. Serve hot with sauces.

Nutrition:
- Calories: 167
- Fat: 3,8g
- Carbohydrates: 8,2g
- Protein: 2,4g

Scrumptious Basil Chicken Salad

This salad is not only vigorous but also flavorsome and delicious.

Prep time: 10 minutes	**Cooking time:** 30 minutes	**Servings:** 4

Ingredients:
- 1/2 teaspoon of pepper
- ½ teaspoon of salt
- 2 teaspoons of oil
- 4 tablespoons of cheese
- 2 celery stalks
- 2 cloves of garlic
- 2 tablespoons of basil leaves
- 1 cup of mayonnaise
- 2 pieces of chicken fillet

Directions:
1. Sprinkle the Air Fryer with oil.
2. Preheat it to 360F for 3 minutes.
3. Then was and chop chicken fillet.
4. Rub meat with salt, pepper, mayonnaise and garlic.
5. Then place meat in the Air Fryer.
6. Cook it for 15 minutes.
7. Then add chopped celery stalks and basil leaves.
8. Mix everything and cook for 15 minutes more.
9. Serve hot with the fresh parsley.
10. Eat this meal with your family.

Nutrition:
- Calories: 146
- Fat: 3,4g
- Carbohydrates: 8,6g
- Protein: 2,8g

Peppery Curry with Cauliflower

This meal is very yummy and spices create the special aroma. Cook and taste – you will like it forever.

Prep time: 15 minutes | **Cooking time:** 40 minutes | **Servings:** 4

Ingredients:

- 2 tablespoons of oil
- ½ teaspoon of salt
- ½ teaspoon of pepper
- 1 onion
- 1 clove of garlic
- 2 teaspoons of ginger
- 2 teaspoons of cumin
- 2 teaspoons of coriander
- ½ teaspoon of turmeric
- 1/3 cup of red lentils
- ½ cup of vegetable stock
- 1 head of cauliflower
- 1 carrot
- 1 cup of coconut milk
- ¾ cup of green beans
- 1 tablespoon of lemon juice
- 1 tablespoon of coriander leaves

Directions:

1. Sprinkle the Air Fryer with oil.
2. Preheat the Air Fryer to 350F for 3 minutes.
3. Chop onion, lentils, carrot, cauliflower and green beans in the pieces.
4. Then add salt, pepper, garlic, cumin, coriander, turmeric and lemon juice to the ingredients and mix them. Then add coconut milk and vegetable stock.
5. Mix everything again and cook in the Air Fryer for 30 minutes.
6. Then mix everything again. Cook the meal for 10 minutes more.

Nutrition:

- Calories: 178
- Fat: 5,6g
- Carbohydrates: 8,3g
- Protein: 4,1g

The Spicy Chicken with Butter

Chicken meal is really delicious and unusual. If you try it, you will see that it is fantastic.

Prep time: 15 minutes | **Cooking time:** 35 minutes | **Servings:** 4

Ingredients:

- 1-2 potatoes
- ½ teaspoon of pepper
- ½ teaspoon of salt
- 2 teaspoons of oil
- 2 cups of green peas
- 1 teaspoon of parsley
- 1 teaspoon of dill
- 1 teaspoon of turmeric
- 1/3 teaspoon of red chili pepper
- 1 teaspoon of garam masala
- 2-3 teaspoons of curry
- 1-2 teaspoons of paprika
- ½ cup of tomato sauce
- 1 onion
- 1 chicken fillet
- 2 cloves of garlic
- 2 oz of butter

Directions:

1. Wash and clean chicken fillet. Cut chicken fillet in the pieces.
2. Sprinkle the Air Fryer with oil. Preheat it to 360F.
3. After that cook chicken fillet for 15 minutes. Then cut potatoes and onion.
4. Add pepper, salt, parsley, dill, red chili pepper, turmeric, curry, garam masala, paprika and mix the ingredients.
5. Then add chopped garlic and butter. Cook everything for 15 minutes more.
6. Then cover the products with sauce and cook for 5 minutes.

Nutrition:

- Calories: 134
- Fat: 4,6g
- Carbohydrates: 5,3g
- Protein: 4,5g

Spicy Collard Greens

This meal is really soft and delicious. Cook and you will see how tasty it is.

Prep time: 10 minutes	**Cooking time:** 20 minutes	**Servings:** 4

Ingredients:
- ½ teaspoon of pepper
- ½ teaspoon of salt
- 2 teaspoon of oil
- 6 cups of water
- 2 lbs of ham
- 2 lbs of collard greens
- ¼ cup of olive oil
- ½ teaspoon of cumin powder
- ½ teaspoon of red chili pepper

Directions:
1. Sprinkle the Air Fryer with oil.
2. Then preheat it to 300F.
3. After that cook collard greens in water till it is soft. (10 minutes)
4. Then add pepper, salt, olive oil, cumin powder and red chili pepper.
5. Mix everything well.
6. Chop ham in the pieces.
7. Add to the rest of products.
8. Mix all components.
9. Then cook for 20 minutes.
10. Serve hot with basil leaves or with mint.

Nutrition:
- Calories: 123
- Fat: 4,7g
- Carbohydrates: 5,3g
- Protein: 4,2g

Prawns with garlic

This meal is delightful and peppery. The prawns are flavorsome.

Prep time: 15 minutes	**Cooking time:** 8 minutes	**Servings:** 4

Ingredients:
- 1 tablespoon of parsley
- ½ teaspoon of pepper
- ½ teaspoon of salt
- 2 tablespoons of oil
- ½ teaspoon of red chili pepper
- 2 lbs of prawns
- 1 clove of garlic

Directions:
1. Sprinkle the Air Fryer with oil.
2. Preheat it to 350F.
3. Then clean mint.
4. Mix them with pepper, salt, garlic and red chili pepper.
5. Then place the products in the Air Fryer.
6. Cook for 4 minutes.
7. At that moment shake them and cook for 4 minutes more.
8. Serve meal with parsley or choose chopped basil leaves. Also, it is possible to serve with fresh vegetables.

Nutrition:
- Calories: 124
- Fat: 2,2g
- Carbohydrates: 8,4g
- Protein: 9,6g

SIDE DISHES

Peppery Bacon with Appetizing Brussels Sprouts and Sweat Cream

This method in uncommon and wonderful. Make this flavorsome meal

Prep time: 10 minutes | **Cooking time**: 50 minutes | **Servings**:4

Ingredients:

- 1 tablespoon of thyme leaves
- ½ teaspoon of pepper
- ½ teaspoon of salt
- 2 teaspoons of oil

- 1 cup of milk
- 2 cups of cream
- 4 tablespoons of butter
- 4 tablespoons of flour
- 4 shallots

- 1 lb of bacon
- 1 lb of brussels sprouts

Directions:

1. Sprinkle the Air Fryer with oil.
2. Preheat to 400F.
3. Then place brussels sprouts in the Air Fryer and cook for 20 minutes.
4. Chop meat in the pieces and add to brussels sprouts. Cook them for 20 minutes more.
5. Blend cream, pepper, salt, milk, butter, flour, shallots in the bowl.
6. Cover bacon with brussels sprouts with this combination. Cook for 10 minutes more.

Nutrition:

- Calories: 137
- Fat: 2,2g

- Carbohydrates: 7,3g
- Protein: 1,1g

Browned Pasta Salad with Vegetables

It is really scrumptious and uncomplicated salad. Just prepare and you will like it forever.

Prep time: 10 minutes | **Cooking time**: 25 minutes | **Servings**:4

Ingredients:

- ¼ cup of oil
- 1 teaspoon of fresh basil
- 3 tablespoons of vinegar
- 1 teaspoon of dry herbs
- 1 cup of tomatoes

- 1 onion
- 4 oz of mushrooms
- 1 zucchini
- 1 yellow squash
- 1 red pepper

- 1 green pepper
- 1 yellow pepper
- ½ teaspoon of red chili pepper

Directions:

1. Chop yellow, red and green peppers in the pieces.
2. Then slice onion and add there.
3. After that cut tomatoes in the pieces. Blend the ingredients.
4. After that chop zucchini and mushrooms. Then blend everything well.
5. Add red chili pepper, salt, chopped squash, dry herbs, vinegar and basil.
6. Blend salad. Sprinkle the Air Fryer with oil.
7. Preheat to 350F. Cook salad for 15 minutes.
8. Then blend everything well and cook for 10 minutes more.

Nutrition:

- Calories: 79
- Fat: 1,1g

- Carbohydrates: 8,4g
- Protein: 1g

Potato Chips with Cream and Onion

It is easy and wonderful meal. You can make it any time you wish, because it does not require a lot of your efforts.

| **Prep time**: 10 minutes | **Cooking time**: 15 minutes | **Servings**:4 |

Ingredients:
- 2 big potatoes
- 3 tablespoons of oil
- ½ teaspoon of salt
- ½ teaspoon of pepper
- ½ cup of sour cream
- 1 teaspoon of lemon juice
- 1/3 teaspoon of red chili pepper
- 1/3 teaspoon of paprika
- ½ onion

Directions:
1. Rinse and clean potatoes.
2. Then chop potatoes in the small pieces.
3. Rub potatoes with salt, pepper, red chili pepper and paprika.
4. Sprinkle the Air Fryer with oil.
5. Preheat it to 350F.
6. Cook chips for 5 minute.
7. Then shake them well and cook for 10 minutes more.
8. Then blend sour cream with lemon juice.
9. Chop onion in small pieces and add to sour cream.
10. Blend everything well.
11. Place chips in sour cream and eat.

Nutrition:
- Calories: 123
- Fat: 1,6g
- Carbohydrates: 4,3g
- Protein: 1,1g

The Biscuits with Cheese

These biscuits are appetizing. Do not miss your chance to cook them.

| **Prep time**: 10 minutes | **Cooking time**: 20 minutes | **Servings**:4 |

Ingredients:
- 1 cup of flour
- 1 tablespoon of butter
- 3 tablespoons of oil
- 1 cup of buttermilk
- ½ cup of butter
- ½ cup of cheese
- 2 cups of self-rising flour
- 2 tablespoons of sugar

Directions:
1. Blend flour with butter.
2. Then add buttermilk and blend everything.
3. Add sugar, self-rising flour and butter to the ingredients.
4. Blend the components well.
5. Then chop cheese in the small pieces and add to the mixture.
6. Sprinkle the Air Fryer with oil.
7. Preheat it to 350F.
8. Make the balls and cook them in the Air Fryer for 10 minutes.
9. Then shake them well and cook for 10 minutes more.

Nutrition:
- Calories: 114
- Fat: 2,3g
- Carbohydrates: 4,6g
- Protein: 1,2g

Browned Zucchini

This meal is flavorsome and wonderful. Just cook and try it.

Prep time: 10 minutes | **Cooking time**: 20 minutes | **Servings**:4

Ingredients:
- 1 big zucchini
- ½ teaspoon of salt
- ½ teaspoon of pepper
- 2 eggs
- ½ cup of bread crumbs
- ½ cup of flour
- ½ cup of mayonnaise
- 1 teaspoon of lemon juice
- 1 teaspoon of garlic powder

Directions:
1. Rinse and chop zucchini in the pieces.
2. Beat eggs in the bowl.
3. Then add salt, pepper, lemon juice and garlic powder to eggs and blend them.
4. Take zucchini and place in flour.
5. Then place in eggs and in mayonnaise.
6. After that cover with bread crumbs
7. Sprinkle the Air Fryer with oil.
8. Preheat it to 300F for 3 minutes.
9. Cook zucchini for 10 minutes.
10. Then shake them. Cook for 10 minutes more.
11. Serve hot with pasta.
12. Decorate with parsley.

Nutrition:
- Calories: 103
- Fat: 2,2g
- Carbohydrates: 4,2g
- Protein: 1,1g

Appetizing Tomatoes with Garlic

If you like something peppery, choose this recipe. You will be delighted with the result.

Prep time: 10 minutes | **Cooking time**: 15 minutes | **Servings**:4

Ingredients:
- ½ teaspoon of pepper
- ½ teaspoon of salt
- 2 teaspoons of oil
- 4 tomatoes
- ½ teaspoon of dry herbs
- ½ teaspoon of dried thyme
- 1 onion
- ½ teaspoon of oregano
- ½ teaspoon of red chili pepper
- 1/3 teaspoon of parsley

Directions:
1. Sprinkle the Air Fryer with oil.
2. Preheat to 350F.
3. Wash and chop tomatoes.
4. Then slice onion in the rings.
5. Rub tomatoes with salt, pepper, dry herbs, thyme, oregano, red chili pepper and parsley.
6. Place the rings of onion on tomatoes.
7. Cook them for 15 minutes in the Air Fryer.
8. Serve hot with parsley or basil leaves.

Nutrition:
- Calories: 89
- Fat: 1,1g
- Carbohydrates: 4,2g
- Protein: 1g

Appetizing Potatoes

If you like crispy and flavorsome potatoes – then this technique is for you. Cook and enjoy with the fiery meal.

Prep time: 10 minutes	**Cooking time**: 25 minutes	**Servings**:4

Ingredients:
- 4 potatoes
- ½ teaspoon of salt
- ½ teaspoon of pepper
- 2 tablespoons of oil
- ½ teaspoon of rosemary
- 2 basil leaves
- ½ teaspoon of dry herbs
- 1/3 teaspoon of cumin
- ½ teaspoon of red chili pepper

Directions:
1. Rinse and clean potatoes
2. Cut potatoes in the strings.
3. Then rub them with pepper, rosemary, dry herbs, cumin and red chili pepper.
4. Sprinkle the Air Fryer with oil.
5. Preheat it to 360F.
6. Place potatoes in the Air Fryer and cook for 10 minutes.
7. Then shake well and cook for 15 minutes more.
8. Serve hot with sauces and vegetables.
9. Eat and enjoy with your family.

Nutrition:
- Calories: 114
- Fat: 1,2g
- Carbohydrates: 2,4g
- Protein: 1g

Fried Scrumptious Snow Pea

It is easy and lovely meal. Cook and enjoy.

Prep time: 5 minutes	**Cooking time**: 23 minutes	**Servings**:4

Ingredients:
- 1 lb of snow peas
- ½ teaspoon of pepper
- ½ teaspoon of salt
- 2 tablespoons of oil
- ½ teaspoon of dry herbs
- ½ teaspoon of rosemary
- 3 cloves of garlic
- ½ teaspoon of paprika
- 1/3 oregano
- 1 teaspoon of dill
- 1 teaspoon of parsley

Directions:
1. Wash and clean snow peas.
2. Then rub them with pepper, salt, dry herbs, rosemary, dill, parsley and paprika.
3. Chop garlic in the pieces and add there.
4. Blend everything well.
5. Sprinkle the Air Fryer with oil.
6. Preheat to 300F.
7. Cook the meal for 10 minutes.
8. Then blend everything again and cook for 13 minutes more.
9. Serve hot meal with fresh parsley.
10. Eat the appetizing food.

Nutrition:
- Calories: 98
- Fat: 1,3g
- Carbohydrates: 2,7g
- Protein: 1,1g

Tempting Smished Potatoes

Uncomplicated, easy and flavorsome. You should prepare this meal because of the yummy aroma.

Prep time: 5 minutes | **Cooking time**: 25 minutes | **Servings**:4

Ingredients:
- 1 teaspoon of pepper
- ½ teaspoon of salt
- 6 potatoes
- 1 green pepper
- ½ teaspoon of dry herbs
- ½ teaspoon of cumin
- 1/3 teaspoon of paprika
- 1/3 teaspoon of red chili pepper
- 3 cloves of garlic

Directions.
1. Wash and clean potatoes.
2. Slice potatoes in the pieces.
3. Blend pepper, salt, dry herbs, cumin, paprika, red chili pepper and garlic in the bowl.
4. Rub potatoes with these spices.
5. Then chop pepper in the strings.
6. Sprinkle the Air Fryer with oil.
7. Preheat it to 300F.
8. Cook potatoes for 15 minutes.
9. Then shake well, add pepper and cook for 10 minutes more.

Nutrition:
- Calories: 114
- Fat: 1,2g
- Carbohydrates: 2,8g
- Protein: 1g

Flavorsome Potatoes Pesto

If you are looking for something original and simple, this meal is exactly for you. It will not take too much of your time for preparing.

Prep time: 10 minutes | **Cooking time**: 25 minutes | **Servings**:4

Ingredients:
- 4 potatoes
- ½ teaspoon of pepper
- ½ teaspoon of salt
- 2 teaspoons of oil
- 1 tablespoon of pesto
- ½ teaspoon of garlic powder
- ½ teaspoon of onion powder
- ¼ cup of milk

Directions:
1. Wash and clean potatoes.
2. Cut potatoes in the pieces.
3. Rub them with salt, pepper, garlic powder and onion powder.
4. Sprinkle the Air Fryer with oil.
5. Then preheat the Air Fryer to 350F.
6. Blend potatoes with milk and pesto.
7. Cook in the Air Fryer for 10 minutes.
8. Then blend everything well and cook for 15 minutes more.

Nutrition:
- Calories: 106
- Fat: 1,2g
- Carbohydrates: 2,7g
- Protein: 1g

Appetizing Salad with Warm Cabbage and Pasta

It is easy and pleasant meal. You can prepare it as for the holiday as for supper.

| **Prep time**: 15 minutes | **Cooking time**: 25 minutes | **Servings**:4 |

Ingredients:
- 4 oz of cooked pasta
- ½ teaspoon of salt
- ½ teaspoon of pepper
- 2 tablespoons of oil
- ½ teaspoon of dry herbs
- ½ teaspoon of paprika
- 1/3 teaspoon of red chili pepper
- 1/3 teaspoon of cumin
- 3 cloves of garlic
- ½ teaspoon of onion powder
- ½ cabbage
- 1 onion

Directions:
1. Boil pasta for 10 minutes.
2. Then place pasta in the bowl.
3. Add onion powder, chopped garlic, paprika, red chili pepper, salt, pepper, dry herbs and blend everything.
4. Then chop onion in the rings.
5. Add them to pasta.
6. Cut cabbage in the strings and blend everything.
7. Preheat the Air Fryer to 350F.
8. Place pasta in the Air Fryer and cook for 15 minutes.
9. Then blend everything and cook for 5 minutes more.

Nutrition:
- Calories: 156
- Fat: 1,3g
- Carbohydrates: 3,3g
- Protein: 1g

Backed Chips with Zucchini

It is fantastic and easy meal. Just cook and you will be delighted.

| **Prep time**: 10 minutes | **Cooking time**: 20 minutes | **Servings**:4 |

Ingredients:
- ½ cup of bread crumbs
- ½ teaspoon of salt
- ½ teaspoon of pepper
- 2 tablespoons of oil
- 3 tablespoons of grated cheese
- ½ teaspoon of dry herbs
- 1/3 teaspoon of red chili pepper
- 1/3 teaspoon of paprika
- 2 eggs
- 2 big zucchinis

Directions:
1. Cut zucchinis in the pieces.
2. Then rub them with salt, pepper, dry herbs, red chili pepper and paprika.
3. Sprinkle the Air Fryer with oil.
4. Preheat it to 300F.
5. Then beat eggs.
6. Place zucchinis in eggs and after that in bread crumbs.
7. Cook them in the Air Fryer for 10 minutes.
8. Then shake them well and cook for 10 minutes more.

Nutrition:
- Calories: 121
- Fat: 1,2g
- Carbohydrates: 3,2g
- Protein: 1g

Appetizing Fried Sweat Carrot

If you need to make something easy and pleasant, cook this carrot. The meal is scrumptious and fantastic.

Prep time: 10 minutes | **Cooking time**: 20 minutes | **Servings**:4

Ingredients:

- 1 lb of carrot
- ½ teaspoon of pepper
- ½ teaspoon of salt
- 2 tablespoons of oil
- ½ teaspoon of dry herbs
- ½ teaspoon of cumin
- 1/3 teaspoon of red chili pepper
- ½ teaspoon of rosemary
- ½ teaspoon of paprika
- 1 tablespoon of butter
- 1 teaspoon of parsley

Directions:

1. Sprinkle the Air Fryer with oil.
2. Then preheat it for 5 minutes to 320F.
3. Wash and clean carrot.
4. Then chop it in the strings.
5. Blend the herbs, salt, pepper, cumin, red chili pepper, paprika, rosemary and parsley in the bowl.
6. Rub carrot with these spices.
7. Then place carrot in the Air Fryer and cook for 10 minutes.
8. Shake and cook the food for 10 minutes more.
9. Serve hot with sauces.

Nutrition:

- Calories: 89
- Fat: 1,3g
- Carbohydrates: 3,5g
- Protein: 1g

Peppery Rice with Herbs

This rice will be great with meat. It is very flavorsome, piquant and delicious.

Prep time: 10 minutes | **Cooking time**: 30 minutes | **Servings**:4

Ingredients:

- 1 cup of rice
- ½ teaspoon of pepper
- ½ teaspoon of salt
- 2 tablespoons of oil
- 2 cups of water
- 1 onion
- ½ teaspoon of red chili pepper
- ½ teaspoon of paprika
- ½ teaspoon of dry herbs
- ¼ tablespoon of parsley

Directions:

1. Sprinkle the Air Fryer with oil.
2. Preheat it to 350F.
3. Blend rice with pepper, salt, paprika, red chili pepper, dry herbs and parsley.
4. Then add water.
5. Cook it in the Air Fryer for 15 minutes.
6. Then chop onion in the pieces.
7. Add to rice and blend everything well.
8. Cook for 15 minutes more.
9. Serve hot with vegetables.

Nutrition:

- Calories: 68
- Fat: 1,1g
- Carbohydrates: 2,3g
- Protein: 1g

Flavorsome Tomatoes with Cheese

It is very easy for the preparing. Also, it is scrumptious. Cook and you will get the great result.

Prep time: 10 minutes | **Cooking time**: 10 minutes | **Servings**:4

Ingredients:
- 10 tomatoes
- ½ teaspoon of pepper
- ½ teaspoon of salt
- 3 tablespoons of oil
- 1/3 teaspoon of red chili pepper
- ½ tablespoon of dill
- 1/3 tablespoon of parsley
- ½ teaspoon of cumin
- ½ teaspoon of oregano
- 3 cloves of garlic
- 3 tablespoons of grated cheese

Directions:
1. Wash and chop tomatoes in the pieces.
2. Then blend pepper, salt, dill, red chili pepper, parsley, oregano, cumin and chopped garlic in the bowl.
3. Rub tomatoes with this mixture.
4. Sprinkle the Air Fryer with oil.
5. Preheat it to 300F.
6. Cook tomatoes for 5 minutes.
7. Then cover them with cheese and cook for 5 minutes more.

Nutrition:
- Calories: 71
- Fat: 1,1g
- Carbohydrates: 3,5g
- Protein: 1g

Appetizing Spinach

It is unusual meal. Spinach is certainly flavorsome.

Prep time: 10 minutes | **Cooking time:** 15 minutes | **Servings**:4

Ingredients:
- 1 lb of spinach
- ½ teaspoon of pepper
- 1 tablespoon of oil
- ½ teaspoon of salt
- 2 teaspoons of garlic powder
- 1 tablespoon of soy sauce
- ½ teaspoon of red chili pepper
- ½ teaspoon of sesame seeds
- ½ teaspoon of sesame oil
- 3 spring onions

Directions:
1. Wash spinach.
2. Chop it in the pieces.
3. Then rub spinach with pepper, salt, garlic powder, soy sauce, red chili pepper, sesame oil and sesame seeds.
4. Sprinkle the Air Fryer with oil.
5. After that, preheat the Air Fryer to 350F.
6. Cook spinach for 10 minutes.
7. Cut spring onions in the pieces. Then add sliced onions to spinach.
8. Blend the products.
9. Cook the meal for 5 minutes more.

Nutrition:
- Calories: 82
- Fat: 1,2g
- Carbohydrates: 2,8g
- Protein: 1g

Vegetables with Coriander and Couscous

It is unique meal and you will be glad with the result. It is peppery and delicious.

Prep time: 25 minutes	**Cooking time:** 15 minutes	**Servings:**4

Ingredients:
- ¼ cup of parsley
- 2 tablespoons of vinegar
- 1 lb of cooked vegetables (carrot, cauliflower, pepper, zucchini)
- 2 cups of tomatoes
- ½ teaspoon of pepper
- 1 teaspoon of sugar
- ½ teaspoon of salt
- ½ teaspoon of dry herbs
- ½ teaspoon of onion powder
- ½ teaspoon of red chili pepper
- 1/3 teaspoon of paprika

Directions:
1. Sprinkle the Air Fryer with oil. Preheat it for 5 minutes to 350F.
2. Blend vegetables with pepper, sugar, salt, dry herbs, onion powder, red chili pepper and paprika.
3. Cook in the Air Fryer for 5 minutes. Then chop tomatoes in the pieces.
4. Blend with the rest of components and cook for 10 minutes more.
5. Sprinkle with vinegar and decorate with parsley.

Nutrition:
- Calories: 145
- Fat: 1,5g
- Carbohydrates: 3,2g
- Protein: 1g

Backed Fiery Potato

This meal will be great for dinner. You should not spend a lot of your time. Just cook and see.

Prep time: 25 minutes	**Cooking time:** 50 minutes	**Servings:**4

Ingredients:
- 8 big potatoes
- 1 lb of cream
- 1 lb of grated cheese
- 6 oz of bacon
- 2 onions
- ½ teaspoon of pepper
- ½ teaspoon of salt
- 2 tablespoons of oil
- ½ teaspoon of dry herbs
- ½ teaspoon of parsley
- 1/3 teaspoon of red chili pepper
- ½ teaspoon of paprika

Directions:
1. Sprinkle the Air Fryer with oil.
2. Preheat it to 350F for 2-3 minutes.
3. Wash and clean potatoes.
4. Chop in the pieces.
5. Rub with pepper, salt, dry herbs, parsley, paprika and red chili pepper.
6. Cook in the Air Fryer for 20 minutes.
7. Then blend everything and add bacon. Cook for 20 minutes more.
8. Chop onions and blend with cream. Add the combination to potatoes.
9. Cover with cheese. Cook for 10 minutes.

Nutrition:
- Calories: 139
- Fat: 5,4g
- Carbohydrates: 5,2g
- Protein: 4,2g

Crispy Asparagus with Cream

It is very soft and delicious meal. You will like it because of the aroma.

Prep time: 10 minutes | **Cooking time:** 10 minutes | **Servings:**4

Ingredients:

- ½ teaspoon of salt
- ½ teaspoon of pepper
- 2 teaspoons of oil
- ¼ cup of cheese
- ¼ cup of cream
- 2 teaspoons of butter
- 1 lb or asparagus
- ½ teaspoon of cumin
- 3 cloves of garlic
- ½ teaspoon of red chili pepper
- ½ teaspoon of paprika

Directions:

1. Wash and chop asparagus in the pieces.
2. Rub with salt, pepper, butter, cumin, chopped garlic, paprika and red chili pepper.
3. After that sprinkle the Air Fryer with oil.
4. Preheat it to 300F.
5. Then cook asparagus for 5 minutes.
6. Cover with cream and cheese.
7. Blend everything well.
8. Cook for 5 minutes more.
9. Serve hot with parsley.

Nutrition:

- Calories: 146
- Fat: 3,8g
- Carbohydrates: 3,2g
- Protein: 1,3g

Browned Broccoli with Peppery Sauce

This meal is flavorsome and wonderful. Attempt and prepare it.

Prep time: 10 minutes | **Cooking time:** 20 minutes | **Servings:**4

Ingredients:

- 1 lb of broccoli
- ½ teaspoon of red chili pepper
- 3 tablespoons of grated cheese
- 1 cup of sauce
- ½ teaspoon of pepper
- ½ teaspoon of salt
- ½ teaspoon of dry herbs
- ½ teaspoon of rosemary
- 1 onion
- 2 tablespoons of oil

Directions:

1. Sprinkle the Air Fryer with oil.
2. Preheat it to 350F.
3. Wash and cut broccoli in the pieces.
4. Rub them with pepper, salt, herbs and rosemary.
5. Chop onion in the pieces.
6. Blend onion with broccoli.
7. Cook for 10 minutes in the Air Fryer.
8. Then cover the meal with sauce and cheese.
9. Cook for 10 minutes more.
10. Serve hot with parsley.

Nutrition:

- Calories: 124
- Fat: 2,1g
- Carbohydrates: 4,7g
- Protein: 1,1g

Backed Vegetables

It is vigorous and wonderful meal. You will prepare it very quickly.

Prep time: 10 minutes	**Cooking time:** 30 minutes	**Servings:**4

Ingredients:
- 1 cauliflower
- 1 broccoli
- 4 potatoes
- 3 carrots
- 4 oz of mushrooms
- ½ teaspoon of salt
- ½ teaspoon of pepper
- 1/3 teaspoon of dry herbs
- 2 tablespoons of oil
- 2 oz of flour
- 2 oz of butter
- 1 lb of milk
- 5 oz of cheese
- ½ teaspoon of red chili pepper
- 2 cloves of garlic

Directions:
1. Cut cauliflower, broccoli, potatoes and carrots in the pieces.
2. Rub them with salt, pepper, dry herbs, red chili pepper and chopped garlic.
3. Sprinkle the Air Fryer with oil. Preheat for 2-3 minutes to 300F.
4. Place the combination in the Air Fryer and cook for 10 minutes.
5. Blend everything well and add mushrooms.
6. Cook for 10 minutes more. Then blend milk, cheese, butter and flour.
7. Cover the meal with the combination and cook for 10 minutes.

Nutrition:
- Calories: 139
- Fat: 1,5g
- Carbohydrates: 4,8g
- Protein: 1,1g

Peppery Potato Gratin with Bacon

It is easy and delicious meal. Cook and you will see how scrumptious it is.

Prep time: 20 minutes	**Cooking time:** 45 minutes	**Servings:**4

Ingredients:
- 2 tablespoons of oil
- 1 onion
- 2 cloves of garlic
- 1 lb of potatoes
- 4 pieces of bacon
- ½ teaspoon of salt
- ½ teaspoon of pepper
- 1/3 teaspoon of red chili pepper
- ½ teaspoon of dry herbs
- ½ teaspoon of cumin
- 2 oz of cheese
- ½ lb of milk
- 3 oz of cream

Directions:
1. Sprinkle the Air Fryer with oil.
2. Preheat it to 300F.
3. Wash and clean potatoes. Chop in the pieces.
4. Blend chopped garlic, salt, pepper, herbs, red chili pepper and cumin in the bowl.
5. Add potatoes and blend everything. Then cook potatoes for 25 minutes.
6. Chop onion, bacon and add to potatoes. Them cover the meal with cream and milk.
7. Decorate with cheese and cook for 20 minutes more.

Nutrition:
- Calories: 167
- Fat: 3,4g
- Carbohydrates: 5,7g
- Protein: 3,1g

Zucchini and Backed Herbs

It is unusual and unique recipe. Your relatives will be happy to eat this meal.

Prep time: 15 minutes	Cooking time: 40 minutes	Servings:4

Ingredients:

- ½ teaspoon of pepper
- ½ teaspoon of salt
- 3 tablespoons of olive oil
- ¼ cup of cheese

- ¼ cup of bread crumbs
- 1 teaspoon of salt
- ½ teaspoon of herbs

- ½ teaspoon of red chili pepper
- 1 teaspoon of paprika
- 3 big zucchinis

Directions:

1. Cut zucchinis in the pieces.
2. Rub them with salt, pepper, dry herbs, paprika and red chili pepper.
3. Sprinkle the Air Fryer with oil.
4. Then preheat it for 5 minutes to 290F.
5. Cook zucchinis in the Air Fryer for 20 minutes.
6. Then blend them with bread crumbs and cover with cheese.
7. Cook for 20 minutes more.
8. Serve hot with sauce.
9. Enjoy with delicious and tasty meal.

Nutrition:

- Calories: 121
- Fat: 2,1g

- Carbohydrates: 4,2g
- Protein: 1,1g

Fresh Asparagus with Butter and Sauce

Prepare asparagus with wonderful sauce.

Prep time: 10 minutes	Cooking time: 10 minutes	Servings:4

Ingredients:

- ½ teaspoon of pepper
- ½ teaspoon of salt
- 2 tablespoons of oil
- 20 asparagus
- 1 oz of butter

- 2 tablespoons of soy sauce
- 2 tablespoons of ketchup
- 1 tablespoon of vinegar.
- 1 teaspoon of dry herbs

- ½ teaspoon of chili pepper
- ½ teaspoon of cumin

Directions:

1. Sprinkle the Air Fryer with oil.
2. Preheat to 300F for 2 minutes.
3. Chop asparagus in the pieces.
4. Blend them with salt, pepper, soy sauce, ketchup, vinegar, dry herbs, chili pepper and cumin.
5. Cook them in the Air Fryer for 5 minutes.
6. Then add butter and cook 5 minutes more.
7. Serve hot with vegetables.
8. Enjoy with the scrumptious and great meal.

Nutrition:

- Calories: 101
- Fat: 1,3g

- Carbohydrates: 2,8g
- Protein: 1,1g

Fried Potatoes with Meat

Easy, scrumptious and delicious. Cook and check it on your end.

Prep time: 5 minutes | **Cooking time:** 35 minutes | **Servings:** 4

Ingredients:

- 1 lb of potatoes
- ½ teaspoon of salt
- ½ teaspoon of pepper
- 3 tablespoons of oil
- 2 onions
- 1 oz of butter
- 2 oz of bacon
- 1/3 teaspoon of paprika
- 1/3 teaspoon of onion powder
- ½ teaspoon of red chili pepper

Directions:

1. Wash and clean potatoes.
2. Chop them in the pieces.
3. Blend salt, pepper, butter, paprika, onion powder and red chili pepper in the bowl.
4. Place potatoes there and mix everything well.
5. Sprinkle the Air Fryer with oil.
6. Preheat it to 330F for 2 minutes.
7. Cook potatoes for 20 minutes.
8. Then chop onion and bacon in the pieces.
9. Blend with potatoes.
10. Cook for 15 minutes more.

Nutrition:

- Calories: 176
- Fat: 5,3g
- Carbohydrates: 4,2g
- Protein: 4,1g

Delicious Savory Cabbage

Prepare this easy and flavorsome cabbage. It is truthfully appetizing.

Prep time: 10 minutes | **Cooking time:** 35 minutes | **Servings:** 4

Ingredients:

- 1 lb of cabbage
- ½ teaspoon of pepper
- ½ teaspoon of salt
- 1 tablespoon of oil
- 5 pieces of bacon
- 2 oz pf cream
- 2 oz of butter
- ½ teaspoon of cumin
- 3 cloves of garlic
- ½ teaspoon of paprika
- ¼ tablespoon of dry herbs

Directions:

1. Wash and cut cabbage in the pieces.
2. Then chop bacon and blend with cabbage.
3. Rub them with pepper, salt, oil, cumin, garlic, paprika and dry herbs.
4. Sprinkle the Air Fryer with oil.
5. Then preheat it to 350F for 1-2 minutes.
6. Cook cabbage with bacon for 20 minutes.
7. Then add butter and cream.
8. Blend everything well.
9. Cook for 15 minutes more.

Nutrition:

- Calories: 138
- Fat: 2,6g
- Carbohydrates: 3,8g
- Protein: 2,6g

Brussels Sprouts with Fried Mushrooms

Appetizing and pleasant meal. Just attempt and enjoy with it.

Prep time: 15 minutes	**Cooking time:** 25 minutes	**Servings:**4

Ingredients:

- ½ teaspoon of salt
- ½ teaspoon of pepper
- 2 tablespoons of oil
- 4 cups of brussels sprouts.
- 2 cups of mushrooms
- ½ teaspoon of parsley
- 5 tablespoons of butter
- 1 teaspoon of lemon juice
- ½ teaspoon of garlic powder
- ½ teaspoon of paprika

Directions:

1. Sprinkle the Air Fryer with oil.
2. Preheat it to 350F.
3. Wash and chop brussels sprouts in the pieces.
4. Chop mushrooms in the pieces.
5. Blend them with brussels sprouts.
6. Add salt, pepper, parsley, butter, lemon juice, garlic powder and paprika.
7. Blend everything.
8. After that cook for 15 minutes.
9. Then shake the components well and cook 10 minutes more.
10. Serve hot with sauce.

Nutrition:

- Calories: 98
- Fat: 2,2g
- Carbohydrates: 4,5g
- Protein: 1,1g

Sweet Fried Carrot with Balsamic Vinegar

It is surely unassuming and wonderful. This meal is just fantastic.

Prep time: 5 minutes	**Cooking time:** 10 minutes	**Servings:**4

Ingredients:

- 3 cups of carrots
- ½ teaspoon of salt
- ½ teaspoon of pepper
- 2 tablespoons of oil
- 1 teaspoon of sugar
- 1 tablespoon of balsamic vinegar
- ½ teaspoon of dry herbs
- ½ teaspoon of turmeric
- ½ teaspoon of paprika

Directions:

1. Rinse and clean carrots.
2. Chop them in the strings.
3. Sprinkle the Air Fryer with oil.
4. Preheat it to 350F for 2 minutes.
5. Rub carrots with pepper, salt, sugar, dry herbs, paprika and turmeric.
6. Cook for 10 minutes in the Air Fryer.
7. Sprinkle the ready meal with balsamic vinegar.
8. Serve hot with the dill or fresh parsley.
9. Eat with your family or friends.

Nutrition:

- Calories: 56
- Fat: 1,2g
- Carbohydrates: 4,2g
- Protein: 1g

Spiced Vegetables with Honey

It is very vigorous and flavorsome meal. Also, you will not spend a lot of time and efforts on it.

Prep time: 15 minutes | **Cooking time:** 30 minutes | **Servings:**4

Ingredients:
- 1 big potato
- 1 bit carrot
- 3 oz of mushrooms
- 2 oz of beans
- 4 oz of spinach
- 1 teaspoon of cumin
- ½ teaspoon of pepper
- ½ teaspoon of salt
- 2 tablespoons of oil
- 1 teaspoon of rosemary
- 1 teaspoon of paprika
- 2 tablespoons of lemon juice
- 2 tablespoons of honey
- ½ cup of butter
- 2 cloves of garlic

Directions:
1. Chop the potato, carrot, mushrooms, beans and spinach in the pieces.
2. Then blend them with pepper, salt, cumin, rosemary, paprika, lemon juice, butter and honey.
3. Sprinkle the Air Fryer with oil.
4. Preheat it to 350F.
5. Cook the meal for 20 minutes.
6. Then blend everything well.
7. Cook for 10 minutes more.
8. Serve hot with parsley.

Nutrition:
- Calories: 124
- Fat: 1,5g
- Carbohydrates: 4,8g
- Protein: 1,3g

Fiery and Appetizing Potatoes

This potato meal is tempting, it is not challenging for preparing. It is scrumptious and wonderful.

Prep time: 15 minutes | **Cooking time:** 30 minutes | **Servings:**4

Ingredients:
- 4 big potatoes
- 1 tablespoon of olive oil
- 1 teaspoon of salt
- ½ teaspoon of pepper
- 1 teaspoon of cumin
- 1 teaspoon of rosemary
- ½ teaspoon of paprika
- ½ teaspoon of red chili pepper

Directions:
1. Sprinkle the Air Fryer with oil.
2. Preheat the Air Fryer to 340F for 3 minutes.
3. Wash and clean potatoes.
4. Cut them in the pieces.
5. Blend salt, pepper, cumin, rosemary, paprika and red chili pepper in the container.
6. Rub potatoes with spices.
7. Cook potatoes in the Air Fryer for 15 minutes.
8. Then combine the products and cook for 15 minutes.
9. Serve it hot with ketchup.

Nutrition:
- Calories: 112
- Fat: 1,3g
- Carbohydrates: 3,5g
- Protein: 1g

Warm Salad with Cucumber and Feta

It is the great combination of the products. You will see that the meal is delicious and appetizing.

Prep time: 20 minutes | **Cooking time:** 5 minutes | **Servings:**4

Ingredients:
- 1 big cucumber
- 1 big pepper
- 4-5 tomatoes
- ½ onion
- 2 tablespoons of parsley
- 6 oz of feta
- ½ teaspoon of pepper
- ½ teaspoon of salt
- 2 teaspoons of lemon juice
- 3 tablespoon of oil
- 1/3 cup of olive oil

Directions:
1. Wash, clean and chop cucumber, pepper, tomatoes and onion in the pieces.
2. Place everything in the bowl.
3. Add fresh parsley, feta, pepper, salt, lemon juice, olive oil and mix everything well.
4. Sprinkle the Air Fryer with oil.
5. Then preheat it to 300F for 2-3 minutes.
6. Cook salad for 5 minutes.
7. Serve hot meal with few fresh basil leaves.

Nutrition:
- Calories: 136
- Fat: 2,3g
- Carbohydrates: 3,8g
- Protein: 1,2g

Salad with Chicken Curry

The great salad with meat. It is uncomplicated, wonderful and appetizing. Cook and check.

Prep time: 20 minutes | **Cooking time:** 20 minutes | **Servings:**4

Ingredients:
- 1 lb of chicken fillet
- 2 hard-boiled eggs
- ½ cup of mayonnaise
- ½ cup of celery
- ½ cup of apple
- ¼ cup of onion
- 1 teaspoon of curry
- ½ teaspoon of paprika
- ½ teaspoon of salt
- ½ teaspoon of pepper
- 2 tablespoons of oil

Directions:
1. Rinse and clean chicken.
2. Cut it in the pieces.
3. Chop eggs, apple, onion and celery.
4. Blend everything well.
5. Then add curry, paprika, pepper, salt and blend the components.
6. Sprinkle the Air Fryer with oil.
7. Preheat the Air Fryer at 350F for 5 minutes.
8. Cook the food for 20 minutes.
9. Serve hot with sauce or pasta.
10. Eat and you will see that it is tasty.

Nutrition:
- Calories: 156
- Fat: 3,5g
- Carbohydrates: 4,7g
- Protein: 3,1g

Cabbage with Bacon

You cannot imagine how appetizing and easy it is. Just cook and you will see that this meal is fantastic.

Prep time: 20 minutes | **Cooking time:** 20 minutes | **Servings:**4

Ingredients:

- 6 pieces of bacon
- ½ teaspoon of salt
- ½ teaspoon of pepper
- ½ teaspoon of paprika
- 1 tablespoon of oil
- ½ onion
- ½ cabbage
- 1 oz of butter
- ½ cup of red wine

Directions:

1. Sprinkle the Air Fryer with oil.
2. Preheat the Air Fryer to 300F for 2 minutes.
3. Chop bacon in the pieces.
4. Then cut onion, cabbage and blend everything with bacon.
5. After that add salt, pepper, paprika, butter and red wine.
6. Blend all ingredients.
7. Cook for 10 minutes.
8. Then blend everything well and cook for 10 minutes more.
9. Serve hot with parsley.
10. Cook and enjoy.

Nutrition:

- Calories: 147
- Fat: 3,8g
- Carbohydrates: 4,9g
- Protein: 4,2g

Appetizing and Piquant Rice

Prepare the greatest meal for you. It is unassuming in preparing.

Prep time: 10 minutes | **Cooking time:** 20 minutes | **Servings:**4

Ingredients:

- ½ teaspoon of pepper
- ½ teaspoon of salt
- 2 tablespoons of oil
- 1 tablespoon of ghee
- 1 cinnamon stick
- 2 cardamoms
- 3 cloves of garlic
- 1 cup of milk
- 1 cup of tomato pasta
- 2 cups of rice
- 1 onion
- ½ teaspoon of paprika
- ½ teaspoon of dry herbs

Directions:

1. Sprinkle the Air Fryer with oil.
2. Cook the Air Fryer to 300F.
3. Put rice with pepper, salt, ghee, cinnamon and cardamoms and blend them.
4. Then add chopped garlic, milk, tomato pasta, paprika and dry herbs.
5. Blend everything.
6. Chop onion. Then add onion rings to rice.
7. Pour rice with water.
8. Cook the meal for 10 minutes.
9. Then blend all products. Cook for 10 minutes.

Nutrition:

- Calories: 67
- Fat: 1,1g
- Carbohydrates: 2,8g
- Protein: 1g

Fried Artichokes

It is extremely delicious meal, which you can prepare. Cook and you will like it forever.

| **Prep time:** 10 minutes | **Cooking time:** 15 minutes | **Servings:** 4 |

Ingredients:
- 2 tablespoons of oil
- ½ teaspoon of pepper
- ½ teaspoon of salt
- 1 lb of artichokes
- 2 teaspoons of rosemary
- 1/3 cup of red wine
- ½ teaspoon of dry herbs
- 1/3 teaspoon of paprika

Directions:
1. Chop the artichokes in the pieces.
2. Then blend them with pepper, salt, rosemary, dry herbs and paprika.
3. Sprinkle the Air Fryer with oil.
4. Preheat the Air Fryer to 350F for 2-3 minutes.
5. Cook artichokes for 10 minutes.
6. Then blend the components, add red wine and cook for 5 minutes more.
7. Serve hot with salad, basil leaves or with different sauces
8. Enjoy with the meal!

Nutrition:
- Calories: 138
- Fat: 1,4g
- Carbohydrates: 4,7g
- Protein: 1g

Appetizing and Piquant Tofu

The components create the great meal. It is actually scrumptious.

| **Prep time:** 10 minutes | **Cooking time:** 10 minutes | **Servings:** 4 |

Ingredients:
- 5 oz of tofu
- 1 tablespoon of fish sauce
- 1 tablespoon of light soy sauce
- 1 tablespoon of dark soy sauce
- 1 tablespoon of oyster sauce
- 1 tablespoons of whiskey
- 2 tablespoons of oil
- 5 oz of cashews
- 1 onion
- 5 cloves of garlic
- 2 big red peppers
- 4 spring onions
- 3 tablespoons of water

Directions:
1. Firstly, chop tofu cheese in the pieces.
2. Then cut onion in the rings, garlic, spring onions and also peppers.
3. Blend them.
4. Then add fish sauces, light, dark soy sauces and also oyster sauce with the whiskey
5. Sprinkle the Air Fryer with oil.
6. Preheat the Air Fryer for 5 minutes to 350F.
7. Then cook the food it for 5 minutes.
8. After that add water and cashews. Then cook for 5 minutes.
9. To get it very scrumptious, serve meat hot with vegetables or cheese.

Nutrition:
- Calories: 121
- Fat: 1,5g
- Carbohydrates: 4,6g
- Protein: 1,1g

Backed Tomatoes with Cheese

These tomatoes are wonderful and appetizing. You can cook them any time you wish.

Prep time: 10 minutes | **Cooking time:** 15 minutes | **Servings:**4

Ingredients:
- 4 large tomatoes
- 4 tablespoons of mayonnaise
- 2 oz of cheese
- 1 tablespoon of mustard
- ½ teaspoon of pepper
- ½ teaspoon of salt
- 2 tablespoons of oil
- ½ teaspoon of oregano
- ½ teaspoon of paprika
- 1 teaspoon of parsley

Directions:
1. Chop tomatoes in the pieces.
2. Then add mustard, pepper, salt, oregano, paprika and parsley.
3. Blend everything well.
4. Then add mayonnaise.
5. Sprinkle the Air Fryer with oil.
6. Then preheat the Air Fryer to 350F for 3 minutes.
7. Place tomatoes in the Air Fryer and cook for 10 minutes.
8. Then cover tomatoes with cheese and cook for 5 minutes more.
9. Serve hot with vegetables.

Nutrition:
- Calories: 145
- Fat: 3,2g
- Carbohydrates: 5,2g
- Protein: 2,6g

Flavorsome Potatoes with Parsley and Cheese

This meal is appetizing and mouthwatering. Cook and you will be satisfied with the result.

Prep time: 10 minutes | **Cooking time:** 15 minutes | **Servings:**4

Ingredients:
- 4 potatoes
- 1 tablespoon of fresh parsley
- 2 tablespoon of grated cheese
- ½ teaspoon of salt
- ½ teaspoon of pepper
- ½ teaspoon of cumin
- 1/3 teaspoon of oregano
- 1/3 teaspoon of paprika
- 2 tablespoons of oil

Directions:
1. Wash and clean potatoes.
2. Then chop potatoes in the pieces.
3. Rub potatoes with parsley, salt, pepper, cumin, paprika and oregano.
4. Then sprinkle the Air Fryer with oil.
5. Preheat the Air Fryer to 340F for 3 minutes.
6. Cook potatoes for 10 minutes.
7. Then cover the meal with cheese and cook for 5 minutes.
8. Serve hot with sauce.

Nutrition:
- Calories: 121
- Fat: 1,6g
- Carbohydrates: 2,5g
- Protein: 1,2g

Appetizing Cheese with Fiery Chili

It is piquant and wonderful meal. Cook scrumptious meal.

Prep time: 10 minutes	**Cooking time:** 15 minutes	**Servings:** 4

Ingredients:
- 1 lb of frozen seasoned chips
- 2 tablespoons of water
- 2 tablespoons of flour
- 2 cups of milk
- 1 tablespoon of margarine
- 8 pieces of cheese
- 1 lb of chili pepper
- ½ teaspoon of salt
- ½ teaspoon of pepper
- ½ teaspoon of paprika
- 2 tablespoons of oil

Directions:
1. Blend flour, chips, margarine, pepper, salt, chopped chili pepper and paprika in the bowl.
2. Then add milk.
3. Sprinkle the Air Fryer with oil.
4. Then preheat the Air Fryer to 300F for 2-3 minutes.
5. Cook meal for 10 minutes.
6. After that add the cheese. Cook the meal for 5 minutes.
7. Serve it hot with pasta and parsley.

Nutrition:
- Calories: 135
- Fat: 1,9g
- Carbohydrates: 2,6g
- Protein: 1,1g

Wonderful and Appetizing Zucchini

You cannot even think that zucchini can be so appetizing. Cook and taste.

Prep time: 10 minutes	**Cooking time:** 20 minutes	**Servings:** 4

Ingredients:
- ½ teaspoon of pepper
- ½ teaspoon of salt
- 2 tablespoon of oil
- 2 zucchinis
- 2 tablespoons of butter
- 2 tablespoons of lemon juice
- ½ teaspoon of paprika
- ½ teaspoon of oregano

Directions:
1. Chop zucchinis in the pieces.
2. Then place pepper, salt, butter, lemon juice, paprika and oregano in the bowl.
3. Rub zucchinis with spices.
4. Sprinkle the Air Fryer with oil.
5. Preheat the Air Fryer to 290F for 3 minutes.
6. Cook the meal for 10 minutes.
7. Then blend all products.
8. Cook the meal for 10 minutes more.
9. Serve hot with salad or with peppery sauce.

Nutrition:
- Calories: 112
- Fat: 1,5g
- Carbohydrates: 2,3g
- Protein: 1,2g

Backed Vegetables with Spices

This meal is healthy. Cook it and enjoy with flavorsome food.

| **Prep time:** 20 minutes | **Cooking time:** 45 minutes | **Servings:** 4 |

Ingredients:
- ½ teaspoon of pepper
- ½ teaspoon of salt
- 2 tablespoons of oil
- 2 large zucchinis
- 6 tomatoes
- 1 big pepper
- 1 onion
- 1 cup of mushrooms
- ½ cup of white wine

Directions:
1. Cut tomatoes, pepper and zucchinis in the pieces.
2. Then chop onion and blend everything well.
3. Rub vegetables with pepper, salt.
4. Then chop mushrooms and blend the ingredients.
5. Sprinkle the Air Fryer with oil.
6. Preheat the Air Fryer for 5 minutes to 350F.
7. Cook the meal for 20 minutes.
8. Then add white wine and cook for 25 minutes.
9. Serve hot with parsley.
10. Enjoy with wonderful meal.
11. It is really tasty and you will like it forever.

Nutrition:
- Calories: 123
- Fat: 1,7g
- Carbohydrates: 2,8g
- Protein: 1,2g

Pasta with Corn

This pasta is scrumptious and appetizing. It is not complicated for preparing.

| **Prep time:** 10 minutes | **Cooking time:** 50 minutes | **Servings:** 4 |

Ingredients:
- 1 lb of kernel corn
- 1 lb of creamed corn
- ½ teaspoon of pepper
- ½ teaspoon of salt
- 1 tablespoon of oil
- 1 cup of pasta
- 4 oz of butter
- 1 cup of cheese
- ½ teaspoon of oregano
- ½ teaspoon of paprika

Directions:
1. Blend kernel corn and creamed corn.
2. Then add pepper, salt, pasta, butter, oregano and paprika.
3. Blend the ingredients well.
4. Sprinkle the Air Fryer with oil.
5. Preheat the Air Fryer for 3 minutes to 350F.
6. Then cook for 20 minutes.
7. After that add butter and blend everything well.
8. Cook for 20 minutes more.
9. Then cover with cheese and cook for 10 minutes.

Nutrition:
- Calories: 125
- Fat: 1,9g
- Carbohydrates: 2,9g
- Protein: 1,3g

Delectable Mushrooms with Vegetables

It is appetizing combination of the ingredients. Tempting, simple and delicious.

| **Prep time**: 10 minutes | **Cooking time:** 45 minutes | **Servings:**4 |

Ingredients:
- 1 lb of mushrooms
- ½ teaspoon of pepper
- ½ teaspoon of salt
- 2 tablespoons of oil
- 1 onion
- 2 cloves of garlic
- 1 green capsicum
- ½ teaspoon of dry herbs
- 1 teaspoon of parsley
- 1 teaspoon of butter

Directions:
1. Wash and clean mushrooms.
2. Then chop them in the pieces.
3. Chop onion in the rings.
4. Chop capsicum and add to the rest of ingredients.
5. Then blend vegetables with pepper, salt, chopped garlic, dry herbs, parsley and butter.
6. Sprinkle the Air Fryer with oil.
7. Preheat the Air Fryer for 3 minutes to 350F.
8. Cook the meal for 25 minutes.
9. Then blend everything and cook for 20 minutes more.
10. Serve hot with sauce and vegetables.

Nutrition:
- Calories: 137
- Fat: 1,7g
- Carbohydrates: 2,6g
- Protein: 1,1g

Fried Tofu and Celery

If you cook this meal for the first time, you will like it forever. Cook the easy, appetizing and delicious meal.

| **Prep time:** 15 minutes | **Cooking time:** 10 minutes | **Servings:**4 |

Ingredients:
- ½ teaspoon of pepper
- ½ teaspoon of salt
- 2 tablespoons of oil
- 2 tablespoons of wine
- 8 oz of tofu
- 2 spring onions
- 1 chili pepper
- 5 oz of celery
- ½ teaspoon of dry herbs
- ½ teaspoon of red chili pepper

Directions:
1. Chop tofu in the pieces.
2. Then cut spring onions and chili pepper and blend with tofu.
3. Sprinkle the Air Fryer with oil.
4. Preheat the Air Fryer for 3 minutes to 300F.
5. Add pepper, salt, celery, dry herbs and red chili pepper to the ingredients.
6. Blend everything well and cook for 5 minutes.
7. Then add the wine and cook for 5 minutes more.
8. Serve hot with basil leaves.

Nutrition:
- Calories: 146
- Fat: 1,9g
- Carbohydrates: 2,8g
- Protein: 1,3g

Mashed Carrots

Carrot has a lot of vitamins. This meal is vigorous and delicious.

Prep time: 10 minutes | **Cooking time:** 25 minutes | **Servings:**4

Ingredients:
- 2 oz of butter
- 1 onion
- 1 lb of carrot
- 1 lb of chicken stick
- ½ teaspoon of salt
- ½ teaspoon of pepper
- ½ teaspoon of dry herbs
- ½ teaspoon of cumin
- ½ teaspoon of garlic powder
- 2 tablespoons of oil

Directions:
1. Wash and clean carrot and onion.
2. Chop them in the pieces and place in the bowl.
3. Then add salt, pepper, dry herbs, cumin and garlic.
4. Blend everything well.
5. Sprinkle the Air Fryer with oil.
6. Preheat the Air Fryer for 2 minutes to 350F.
7. Cook vegetables for 10 minutes.
8. Then add butter and chicken stock.
9. Cook this meal for 15 minutes.
10. Serve hot with parsley.

Nutrition:
- Calories: 156
- Fat: 3,2g
- Carbohydrates: 5,2g
- Protein: 4,5g

Backed Mixed Vegetables

These vegetables are delicious. Easy, flavorsome and soft.

Prep time: 10 minutes | **Cooking time:** 5 minutes | **Servings:**4

Ingredients:
- 1 red capsicum
- ½ teaspoon of salt
- ½ teaspoon of pepper
- 2 tablespoons of olive oil
- 6 oz of frozen peas
- 1 teaspoon of coriander
- ½ teaspoon of dry herbs
- ½ teaspoon of paprika

Directions:
1. Chop red capsicum in the pieces.
2. Add salt, pepper, coriander, paprika and dry herbs.
3. Blend everything well.
4. Then add the peas.
5. Blend the ingredients again.
6. Sprinkle the Air Fryer with olive oil.
7. Preheat the Air Fryer for 2 or 5 minutes to 360F.
8. Cook fresh vegetables for 5 minutes.
9. Then serve hot with pasta or basil leaves.

Nutrition:
- Calories: 112
- Fat: 1,3g
- Carbohydrates: 3,2g
- Protein: 1,1g

Cabbage with Noodles and Egg

This meal is not hard and it is appetizing. You will not spend a lot of your efforts.

| **Prep time:** 10 minutes | **Cooking time:** 35 minutes | **Servings:**4 |

Ingredients:

- 1 lb of noodles
- ½ teaspoon of salt
- ½ teaspoon of pepper
- 2 tablespoons of oil

- 3 tablespoons of butter
- 1 lb of bacon
- 1 onion
- 1 cabbage

- ½ teaspoon of garlic
- ½ teaspoon of mustard
- 1 teaspoon of paprika

Directions:

1. Boil noodles in water.
2. Blend bacon with salt, pepper, garlic, mustard and paprika.
3. Then add noodles.
4. Blend the components.
5. Chop onion in the rings.
6. Cut cabbage in the pieces.
7. Then blend everything and add butter.
8. Sprinkle the Air Fryer with oil.
9. Preheat the Air Fryer for 3 minutes to 350F.
10. Cook the meal for 20 minutes.
11. Blend everything well and cook for 15 minutes.

Nutrition:

- Calories: 165
- Fat: 4,3g

- Carbohydrates: 6,7g
- Protein: 4,2g

Piquant Chips with Garlic and Cheese

These chips are peppery and tempting. Do not miss your chance to prepare them.

| **Prep time:** 20 minutes | **Cooking time:** 20 minutes | **Servings:**4 |

Ingredients:

- 3 large potatoes
- ½ leaspoon of pepper
- ½ teaspoon of salt

- ½ teaspoon of red chili pepper
- ½ teaspoon of cumin
- 2 tablespoons of oil

- 2 oz of cheese
- 1 teaspoon of dry herbs

Directions:

1. Rinse and clean potatoes.
2. Then cut them in the slices.
3. Rup potatoes with pepper, salt, cumin, red chili pepper and dry herbs.
4. Sprinkle the Air Fryer with oil.
5. Preheat the Air Fryer to 350F for 3 minutes.
6. Cook chips for 10 minutes.
7. Then shake them well and cook for 10 minutes more.
8. Serve the meal hot with sauces.

Nutrition:

- Calories: 115
- Fat: 1,2g

- Carbohydrates: 1,7g
- Protein: 1,1g

Appetizing Green Bean Casserole

It is tremendously scrumptious meal. Cook and try flavorsome beans.

Prep time: 10 minutes | **Cooking time:** 30 minutes | **Servings:**4

Ingredients:
- 1 cup of mushrooms
- ½ teaspoon of pepper
- ½ teaspoon of salt
- 2 tablespoons of oil
- 8 oz of green beans
- 1 lb of mushrooms soup
- 1 cup of milk
- ½ teaspoon of paprika
- ½ teaspoon of garlic powder
- ½ teaspoon of dry herbs

Directions:
1. Firstly, chop mushrooms, beans in the pieces.
2. Add pepper, salt, paprika, garlic powder, dry herbs.
3. Blend them.
4. Add mushrooms soup and milk.
5. Blend the components.
6. Sprinkle the Air Fryer with oil.
7. Preheat the Air Fryer for 3 minutes to 350F.
8. Cook the meal for 15 minutes.
9. Then blend everything.
10. Cook for 15 minutes.

Nutrition:
- Calories: 113
- Fat: 1,5g
- Carbohydrates: 4,2g
- Protein: 1,1g

Delicious Cucumber with Piquant Sauce

This meal is unassuming and easy. Also, it is appetizing. Just cook.

Prep time: 10 minutes | **Cooking time:** 5 minutes | **Servings:**4

Ingredients:
- 2 big cucumbers
- 5 dried red chili peppers
- 1 clove of garlic
- 1 spring onion
- 1 teaspoon of sugar
- 5 tablespoons of soy sauce
- 2 teaspoons of hot chili sauce
- 1 teaspoon of sesame oil
- ½ teaspoon of vinegar
- 2 tablespoons of oil

Directions:
1. Rinse and clean cucumbers.
2. Then slice them in the strings.
3. Rub cucumbers with garlic, sugar, soy sauce, hot chili sauce, sesame oil and vinegar.
4. Chop peppers and add them also.
5. Blend everything well.
6. Cut spring onion and add there.
7. Sprinkle the Air Fryer with oil.
8. Preheat the Air Fryer to 300F for 3 minutes.
9. Cook meal for 5 minutes in the Air Fryer.

Nutrition:
- Calories: 103
- Fat: 2,6g
- Carbohydrates: 6,2g
- Protein: 1,2g

Appetizing Zucchini with Fresh Basil

The meal is easy for preparing. Also, it is scrumptious and flavorsome.

Prep time: 10 minutes | **Cooking time:** 20 minutes | **Servings:** 4

Ingredients:
- 1 large zucchini
- ½ teaspoon of pepper
- ½ teaspoon of salt
- 3 teaspoons of oil
- 2 tablespoons of basil leaves
- ½ teaspoon of paprika
- ½ teaspoon of oregano
- 3 cloves of garlic

Directions:
1. At the beginning, cut zucchini in the pieces.
2. Then rub with pepper, salt, paprika, oregano and garlic.
3. Sprinkle the Air Fryer with oil.
4. Preheat the Air Fryer to 350F for 3 minutes.
5. Cook meal in the Air Fryer for 10 minutes.
6. Then blend everything well.
7. Cook for 10 minutes more at the same temperature.
8. Serve the meal hot with basil leaves.

Nutrition:
- Calories: 112
- Fat: 2,3g
- Carbohydrates: 6,3g
- Protein: 1,1g

Appetizing Fried Lettuce

It is delectable and quickly meal. Just cook and eat.

Prep time: 10 minutes | **Cooking time:** 10 minutes | **Servings:** 4

Ingredients:
- 1 tablespoon of oil
- ½ teaspoon of salt
- ½ teaspoon of pepper
- 4 cloves of garlic
- 2 spring onions
- 1 lb of lettuce
- 2 tablespoons of vinegar
- 1 tablespoon of oyster sauce
- ½ teaspoon of red chili pepper
- ½ teaspoon of paprika
- ½ teaspoon of cumin

Directions:
1. Chop lettuce in the pieces.
2. Slice spring onions in the pieces.
3. Then combine onions with the lettuce.
4. Blend with salt, pepper, chopped garlic, red chili pepper, paprika and cumin.
5. Sprinkle the Air Fryer with oil.
6. Preheat to 300F for 5 minutes.
7. Cook salad for 10 minutes.
8. Sprinkle with oyster sauce and vinegar.
9. Blend everything well.

Nutrition:
- Calories: 78
- Fat: 1,2g
- Carbohydrates: 5,2g
- Protein: 1g

Potato with Olives and Feta

It is actually delicious and appetizing meal. You will have the food for your whole family.

Prep time: 10 minutes	Cooking time: 25 minutes	Servings:4

Ingredients:
- 1 lb of potatoes
- ½ teaspoon of pepper
- ½ teaspoon of salt
- 2 tablespoons of oil
- 1 spring rosemary
- ½ teaspoon of paprika
- ½ teaspoon of red chili pepper
- 3 oz of olives
- 4 oz of feta
- 3 cloves of garlic
- ½ teaspoon of onion powder

Directions:
1. Wash and clean potatoes.
2. Then chop potatoes in the pieces.
3. Blend with salt, pepper, rosemary, paprika, red chili pepper, chopped garlic and onion powder.
4. Sprinkle the Air Fryer with oil.
5. Preheat it for 3 minutes to 340F.
6. Cook potatoes for 15 minutes.
7. Then blend everything, add olives and chopped feta and cook for 10 minutes more.

Nutrition:
- Calories: 145
- Fat: 1,7g
- Carbohydrates: 5,9g
- Protein: 1g

Flavorsome and Piquant Rice with Cheese

It is not very complicated in the preparing. Just cook it.

Prep time: 15 minutes	Cooking time: 25 minutes	Servings:4

Ingredients:
- 1 lb of leek
- ½ teaspoon of salt
- ½ teaspoon of pepper
- 3 tablespoons of oil
- 1 lb of beef stock
- 2 oz of butter
- 1 lb of rice
- 3 oz of cheese
- ½ teaspoon of garlic powder
- ½ teaspoon of red chili pepper
- ½ teaspoon of paprika

Directions:
1. Wash and chop leek.
2. Then blend rice with salt, pepper, butter, garlic powder, paprika and red chili pepper.
3. Sprinkle the Air Fryer with oil.
4. Preheat to 350F for 2-3 minutes.
5. Then blend rice with the leek.
6. Add the beef stock.
7. Cook for 20 minutes in the Air Fryer.
8. Then blend everything.
9. Cover with cheese and cook for 5 minutes.
10. Serve the meal hot with vegetables and pasta.

Nutrition:
- Calories: 121
- Fat: 1,3g
- Carbohydrates: 5,4g
- Protein: 1g

Luscious Peppery Rice with Browned Vegetables

It is the appetizing rice and roasted vegetables. Easy, delicious and scrumptious.

Prep time: 15 minutes | **Cooking time:** 25 minutes | **Servings:** 4

Ingredients:
- 1 packet of frozen vegetables
- ½ teaspoon of pepper
- ½ teaspoon of salt
- 2 tablespoons of oil
- 5 pieces of bacon
- 1 onion
- 4 cups of rice (cooked)
- 1 tablespoon of soy sauce
- 2 eggs
- ½ teaspoon of garlic powder
- ½ teaspoon of paprika
- ½ teaspoon of red chili pepper
- ½ teaspoon of cumin

Directions:
1. Slice bacon in the pieces.
2. Blend the pieces of bacon with pepper, salt, soy sauce, garlic powder, paprika, cumin, red chili pepper. Then cut onion in the rings
3. Blend with rice.
4. Add bacon. Sprinkle the Air Fryer with oil.
5. Preheat it to 360F for 2 minutes.
6. Then add vegetables to the other ingredients.
7. Cook everything in the Air Fryer for 15 minutes.
8. Blend the meal.
9. Then cook for 10 minutes. Serve hot meal with parsley.

Nutrition:
- Calories: 147
- Fat: 3,2g
- Carbohydrates: 5,8g
- Protein: 3,1g

Appetizing Carrot and Fennel with Cream

It is delectable and flavorsome meal. Also, it is not difficult for the preparing.

Prep time: 15 minutes | **Cooking time:** 15 minutes | **Servings:** 4

Ingredients:
- ½ teaspoon of salt
- 2 tablespoons of oil
- ½ teaspoon of pepper
- 3 carrots
- 1 fennel bulb
- 1/3 cup of cream
- ½ teaspoon of red chili pepper
- ½ teaspoon of onion powder
- ½ teaspoon of paprika

Directions:
1. Sprinkle the Air Fryer with oil.
2. Preheat it to 350F. Then grill carrots.
3. Add salt, pepper, onion powder, red chili pepper and paprika to carrot.
4. Blend everything. Then cut fennel bulb in the pieces.
5. Blend the components and cook for 10 minutes.
6. Then shake the ingredients and cook the meal for 5 minutes.

Nutrition:
- Calories: 123
- Fat: 2,1g
- Carbohydrates: 4,6g
- Protein: 1,2g

Piquant and Flavorsome Broccoli with Cheese

It is wonderful meal. Broccoli is truly flavorsome. Just cook this appetizing meal and check it.

Prep time: 5 minutes | **Cooking time:** 25 minutes | **Servings:** 4

Ingredients:
- 2 heads of broccoli
- 3 cups of sauce
- 1 tablespoon of parsley
- 1 cup of cheese
- ½ teaspoon of paprika
- ½ teaspoon of salt
- ½ teaspoon of pepper
- 2 tablespoons of oil
- ½ teaspoon of cumin
- 1/3 teaspoon of red chili pepper
- 1/3 teaspoon of rosemary

Directions:
1. Firstly, chop fresh broccoli in the pieces.
2. Then blend broccoli with parsley, paprika, salt, cumin, red chili pepper, rosemary.
3. Sprinkle the Air Fryer with oil.
4. Preheat it to 320F for 3 minutes.
5. Cover broccoli with sauce and blend.
6. Cook for 20 minutes in the Air Fryer.
7. Add cheese.
8. Cook for 5 minutes more.
9. Serve hot with vegetables.

Nutrition:
- Calories: 113
- Fat: 1,9g
- Carbohydrates: 4,8g
- Protein: 1,2g

Scrumptious Capsicum, Mushroom Salad with Pasta

This salad is enjoyable and soft. Cook and eat.

Prep time: 10 minutes | **Cooking time:** 15 minutes | **Servings:** 4

Ingredients:
- 8 oz of spaghetti
- ½ teaspoon of salt
- ½ teaspoon of pepper
- 2 tablespoons of oil
- 5 oz of mushrooms
- 1 red capsicum
- ¼ cup of rice vinegar
- 3 tablespoons of soy sauce
- 2 cloves of garlic
- ½ teaspoon of paprika
- ½ teaspoon of onion powder
- ½ teaspoon of ginger
- 1 teaspoon of parsley

Directions:
1. Boil spaghetti with water.
2. Leave in the bowl.
3. Blend with salt, pepper, soy sauce, chopped garlic, paprika, onion powder, parsley and ginger.
4. Then cut capsicum and mushrooms in the pieces.
5. Blend all ingredients well.
6. Sprinkle the Air Fryer with oil.
7. Preheat to 350F for 3 minutes.
8. Cook the meal for 10 minutes.
9. Then blend everything well and cook for 5 minutes more.

Nutrition:
- Calories: 134
- Fat: 1,7g
- Carbohydrates: 4,9g
- Protein: 1,2g

Scrumptious Browned Capsicum

This meal is vigorous and appetizing. Cook this flavorsome meal.

| **Prep time:** 15 minutes | **Cooking time:** 40 minutes | **Servings:**4 |

Ingredients:

- 3 green capsicums
- ½ teaspoon of salt
- ½ teaspoon of pepper
- 2 tablespoons of oil

- 1 onion
- 1 teaspoon of parsley
- ½ teaspoon of paprika

- ½ teaspoon of red chili pepper
- ½ teaspoon of cumin
- 3 cloves of garlic

Directions:

1. Rinse and slice capsicums in the pieces.
2. Then blend capsicums with salt, pepper, parsley, paprika, red chili pepper, cumin and chopped garlic.
3. Cut onion in the rings.
4. Add to the capsicum.
5. Sprinkle the Air Fryer with oil.
6. Preheat the Air Fryer to 350F for 3 minutes,
7. Cook capsicum for 20 minutes.
8. Then blend the components and cook for 20 minutes.
9. Serve hot with sauce.

Nutrition:

- Calories: 102
- Fat: 1,2g

- Carbohydrates: 4,5g
- Protein: 1,2g

Appetizing Backed Potato with Piquant Rosemary

It is peppery and appetizing meal. Make and enjoy.

| **Prep time:** 15 minutes | **Cooking time:** 40 minutes | **Servings:**4 |

Ingredients:

- 1 lb of potatoes
- ½ teaspoon of pepper
- ½ teaspoon of salt
- 1 teaspoon of rosemary

- 2 tablespoons of oil
- 1 onion
- ½ teaspoon of red chili pepper

- ½ teaspoon of paprika
- ½ teaspoon of cumin
- ½ teaspoon of oregano

Directions:

1. Rinse and clean potatoes
2. Chop in the pieces.
3. Place pepper, salt, rosemary, red chili pepper, cumin, paprika and oregano in the bowl.
4. Then cover potatoes with these spices.
5. Chop onion in the rings.
6. Add to potatoes.
7. Sprinkle the Air Fryer with oil.
8. Preheat it to 360F.
9. Cook potatoes for 20 minutes.
10. Then shake and cook for 20 minutes more.

Nutrition:

- Calories: 113
- Fat: 1,2g

- Carbohydrates: 2,6g
- Protein: 1,2g

MAIN DISHES

Chicken Curry

You even cannot imagine how flavorsome it is. Your guests will be surprised when they try this meal.

Prep time: 15 minutes | **Cooking time**: 20 minutes | **Servings**: 4

Ingredients:
- ½ teaspoon of salt
- ½ teaspoon of pepper
- 2 tablespoons of oil
- 5 tablespoons of garlic
- 2 tomatoes
- 3 tablespoons of cream
- 4 cloves of garlic
- 1 ginger
- 1 green chili
- 1 tablespoon of garam masala
- 3 onions
- ½ teaspoon of turmeric
- ½ teaspoon of red chili pepper
- 2 black cardamom
- 4 green cardamom
- 2 bay leaves
- 2 lbs of chicken fillets

Directions:
1. Wash and cut chicken fillet in the pieces.
2. After that blend salt, pepper, garlic, ginger, garam masala, turmeric, red chili pepper, cardamom and bay leaves together in the bowl.
3. Rub the pieces of chicken with these spices. Sprinkle the Air Fryer with oil.
4. Preheat it to 350F for 5 minutes. Place chicken in the Air Fryer and cook for 5 minutes.
5. Chop tomatoes and green chili with onions. Add them to the rest of the products.
6. Then add cream and blend. Cook for 15 minutes more.

Nutrition:
- Calories: 287
- Fat: 8,9g
- Carbohydrates: 10,3g
- Protein: 5,6g

Tasty and Spicy Chicken Stew

When you taste this meal for the first time, you will like it. Delicious and spicy, it is very tasty.

Prep time: 15 minutes | **Cooking time**: 30 minutes | **Servings**: 4

Ingredients:
- ½ teaspoon of salt
- ½ teaspoon of pepper
- 2 tablespoons of oil
- 1 tablespoon of flour
- 4-5 corns
- 3 oz of mushrooms
- 4 cloves of garlic
- 1 onion
- ½ red capsicum
- ½ green capsicum
- 1 broccoli
- 1 carrot
- 5-7 beans
- ¼ teaspoon of rosemary
- 2 tablespoons of oil
- 7 oz of chicken fillet

Directions:
1. Wash and clean chicken fillet.
2. Then chop it in the pieces. Mix salt, pepper, flour, garlic, rosemary in the bowl.
3. Mix chicken with these spices. Then chop mushrooms, onion, carrot, broccoli and mix with chicken. After that, add the corns and beans.
4. Preheat it to 350F. Cook the mixture in the Air Fryer for 15 minutes.
5. Then mix everything and cook for 15 minutes more.

Nutrition:
- Calories: 156
- Fat: 7,3g
- Carbohydrates: 9,8g
- Protein: 4,6g

Piquant Curry with Mutton

This curry meal is perfect. All components are appetizing.

Prep time: 20 minutes | **Cooking time**: 40 minutes | **Servings**: 4

Ingredients:
- 2 tablespoons of oil
- ½ teaspoon of salt
- ½ teaspoon of pepper
- 4 tablespoon of mustard oil
- 1 tablespoon of garam masala
- 1 teaspoon of red chili pepper
- 1 teaspoon of cumin
- 1 teaspoon of turmeric
- 6 oz of onions
- 1 tablespoon of ginger
- 1 lb of tomatoes
- 2 lbs of mutton

Directions:
1. Grease the Air Fryer with oil.
2. Preheat it for 5 minutes to 350F.
3. Rinse and clean meat. Cut it in the pieces.
4. Then rub meat with salt, pepper, mustard oil, garam masala, red chili pepper, cumin and turmeric. Cut tomatoes, onions and ginger in the pieces and blend everything.
5. Cook the food for 20 minutes.
6. Then blend everything and cook for 20 minutes.

Nutrition:
- Calories: 245
- Fat: 10,3g
- Carbohydrates: 9,7g
- Protein: 7,9g

Sharp and Yummy Chicken in Appetizing Yogurt Sauce

It is flavorsome meal. This chicken is tempting.

Prep time: 20 minutes | **Cooking time**: 30 minutes | **Servings**: 4

Ingredients:
- ½ tablespoon of coriander
- 2 tablespoons of oil
- ½ teaspoon of pepper
- ½ teaspoon of salt
- ¼ teaspoon of turmeric
- 2 tablespoons of mustard oil
- ½ tablespoon of cumin
- 1 cup of yogurt
- 2 tomatoes
- 5 cloves of garlic
- 1 teaspoon of red chili pepper
- 3 onions
- 2 lbs of chicken fillets

Directions:
1. Sprinkle the Air Fryer with oil.
2. Preheat it to 350F for 3 minutes.
3. Rinse and clean chicken.
4. Chop meat in the pieces.
5. Blend the coriander, pepper, salt, turmeric, mustard oil, cumin, garlic and red chili pepper in the bowl. Then rub chicken pieces with spices.
6. Cook the poultry in the Air Fryer for 10 minutes. Then chop tomatoes, onions in the pieces.
7. Blend everything, cover with yogurt. Cook for 20 minutes.

Nutrition:
- Calories: 245
- Fat: 10,3g
- Carbohydrates: 9,7g
- Protein: 7,9g

Wonderful Jackfruit with Vegetables

It you like vegetables, this meal will be perfect for you. Cook and enjoy with it.

Prep time: 30 minutes	**Cooking time**: 45 minutes	**Servings**: 4

Ingredients:

- 1 teaspoon of coriander
- ½ teaspoon of salt
- 2 tablespoons of oil
- ½ teaspoon of pepper
- 1 cup of yogurt

- 5 tablespoons of butter
- 7 oz of onion
- 1 garlic
- ½ teaspoon of red chili pepper

- ½ teaspoon of coriander
- 2 potatoes
- 8 oz of jackfruit

Directions:

1. Cut potatoes and jackfruit in the pieces and mix them.
2. Then rub these products with salt, pepper, butter, red chili pepper, coriander.
3. Sprinkle the Air Fryer with oil.
4. Preheat the Air Fryer to 300F for 2-3 minutes.
5. Cook the products for 20 minutes.
6. Then chop onion and add to potatoes.
7. Cover everything with yogurt and cook for 25 minutes more.

Nutrition:

- Calories: 178
- Fat: 7,9g

- Carbohydrates: 9,3g
- Protein: 5,7g

Appetizing Chana Masala

It is unusual meal but you will like it. The unique ingredients are very simple in preparing.

Prep time: 10 minutes	**Cooking time**: 30 minutes	**Servings**: 4

Ingredients:

- 8 tablespoons of mustard pasta
- ½ teaspoon of salt
- ½ teaspoon of pepper
- 1 tablespoon of garam masala

- ½ teaspoon of turmeric
- ½ teaspoon of coriander
- 8 tomatoes
- 3 tablespoon of garlic pasta

- 3 tablespoons of ginger pasta
- 5 onions
- 1 lb of kabuli chana
- 2 tablespoons of oil

Directions:

1. Sprinkle the Air Fryer with oil.
2. Then preheat it for 5 minutes to 300F.
3. Blend mustard pasta, salt, pepper, garam masala, turmeric, coriander, garlic pasta and ginger pasta in the bowl.
4. The chop tomatoes in the pieces.
5. Cut onions in the rings and add to tomatoes.
6. After that cook the kabuli chana for 15 minutes in the Air Fryer.
7. Then add all spices, tomatoes and onions and blend them together.
8. Cook for 15 minutes more.

Nutrition:

- Calories: 189
- Fat: 2,3g

- Carbohydrates: 8,5g
- Protein: 3,1g

Appetizing and Smoked Mince

It is uncomplicated and simple meal. Enjoy with this main dish.

Prep time: 30 minutes | **Cooking time**: 45 minutes | **Servings**: 4

Ingredients:

- 2 tablespoons of oil
- ½ teaspoon of salt
- ½ teaspoon of pepper
- ½ teaspoon of red chili pepper
- 1 teaspoon of cumin
- 1 tablespoon of fresh coriander
- 1 ginger
- 1 garlic
- 4 onions
- 1 cup of yogurt
- 10 tablespoons of ghee
- 2 lbs of minced meat

Directions:

1. Place meat in the bowl.
2. Sprinkle the Air Fryer with oil.
3. Then preheat it to 350F for 5 minutes.
4. Place salt, pepper, cumin, red chili pepper, coriander, chopped ginger, garlic and ghee to the bowl with meat.
5. After that blend the ingredients. Cook meat in the Air Fryer for 20 minutes.
6. Then chop onions in the pieces and add to meat. Blend everything well and cook for 15 minutes.
7. Then cover the combination with yogurt and cook for 10 minutes.

Nutrition:

- Calories: 146
- Fat: 3,5g
- Carbohydrates: 8,4g
- Protein: 2,1g

Tasty Potatoes with Soft Yogurt

This meal is very delicious and tasty. The unique combination of potatoes and yogurt is very delicious.

Prep time: 30 minutes | **Cooking time**: 45 minutes | **Servings**: 4

Ingredients:

- ½ teaspoon of pepper
- ½ teaspoon of salt
- 2 tablespoons of oil
- 2 tablespoons of mustard oil
- 1 tablespoon of besan
- 1 coriander
- 2 curry leaves
- 1 tablespoon of turmeric
- ½ teaspoon of red chili pepper
- 2 green chili peppers
- 1 red pepper
- 1 tablespoon of cumin
- 1 lb of potatoes
- 1 garlic
- 1 cup of yogurt

Directions:

1. Mix pepper, salt, mustard oil, besan, coriander, turmeric, red chili peppers, cumin and garlic in the bowl. Wash and clean potatoes.
2. Chop them in the pieces. Mix potatoes with spices.
3. Sprinkle the Air Fryer with oil. Preheat it to 350F.
4. Then cook potatoes for 20 minutes. Chop red pepper, chili peppers in the pieces.
5. Add them to potatoes and cook for 20 minutes,
6. Cover everything with yogurt and cook for 5 minutes more.

Nutrition:

- Calories: 123
- Fat: 3,2g
- Carbohydrates: 8,5g
- Protein: 1,2g

Piquant Mutton

If you like to eat spicy food, then this meal is exactly for you. Cook and enjoy.

Prep time: 10 minutes | **Cooking time**: 30 minutes | **Servings**: 4

Ingredients:

- 2 lbs of mutton
- ½ teaspoon of salt
- ½ teaspoon of pepper
- 2 teaspoons of oil
- 2 tablespoons of lemon juice
- 1 tablespoon of almonds
- 3 tablespoons of poppy seeds
- 1 tablespoon of garam masala
- 1/3 tablespoon of turmeric
- 2 red chili peppers
- 2 green chili peppers
- 2 cloves of garlic
- 1 cup of yogurt
- 4 onions

Directions:

1. Sprinkle the Air Fryer with oil.
2. Then preheat the Air Fryer for 5 minutes to 350F.
3. Wash and clean mutton.
4. Then chop it in the small pieces.
5. Take the bowl and blend salt, pepper, lemon juice, almonds, garam masala, turmeric, red chili peppers, green chili peppers and garlic.
6. Rub meat with spices. Then cook mutton in the Air Fryer for 10 minutes.
7. Chop onions, chili peppers and add them to meat.
8. After that, cover meat with yogurt. Cook for 15 minutes more.
9. Then blend everything well and cook for 5 minutes.

Nutrition:

- Calories: 145
- Fat: 3,3g
- Carbohydrates: 9,3g
- Protein: 6,2g

Delicious Chicken with Spices

It is very easy and simple meal. When you try it, you will be very glad to prepare it again.

Prep time: 15 minutes | **Cooking time**: 45 minutes | **Servings**: 4

Ingredients:

- 1 fresh coriander
- ½ teaspoon of salt
- ½ teaspoon of pepper
- 2 tablespoons of oil
- 6 tablespoons of ghee
- ½ tablespoon of turmeric
- 10-12 peppercorns
- 4 cardamoms
- 1 tablespoon of cumin seeds
- 2 teaspoons of red chili pepper
- 2 onions
- 1 teaspoon of garlic
- 1 teaspoon of ginger
- 2 lbs of chicken

Directions:

1. Sprinkle the Air Fryer with oil. Then preheat it for 5 minutes to 350F.
2. Wash and clean chicken. Chop it in the pieces.
3. After that rub meat with coriander, salt, pepper, ghee, turmeric, chopped peppercorns, cumin seeds, garlic, ginger. Chop onions in the pieces and add red chili pepper.
4. Mix everything well. Cook for 20 minutes.
5. Then mix everything again and cook for 25 minutes more.

Nutrition:

- Calories: 146
- Fat: 2,1g
- Carbohydrates: 6,3g
- Protein: 5,6g

Tasty Curry with Coconut Milk

It is unusual and very delicious meal. Just cook it and you will see, how unique and tasty it is.

Prep time: 25 minutes | **Cooking time**: 35 minutes | **Servings**: 4

Ingredients:
- ½ teaspoon of pepper
- ½ teaspoon of salt
- 2 teaspoons of oil
- 1 tablespoon of coriander
- 1 teaspoon of turmeric
- 1 tablespoon of pasta
- 1 tablespoon of mustard seeds
- 2 cups of chicken stock
- 1 teaspoon of red chili pepper
- 1 ginger
- 3 green chili peppers
- 1 tablespoon of curry
- 2 cups of coconut milk
- 9 oz of tomatoes
- 1 tablespoon of garlic
- 2 lbs of shrimps
- 3 onions

Directions:
1. Sprinkle the Air Fryer with oil. Preheat it for 5 minutes to 350F.
2. Put pepper, salt, coriander, turmeric, pasta, mustard seeds, red chili pepper, ginger and garlic in the Air Fryer. Cook for 5 minutes.
3. Then chop green chili peppers and cook for 5 minutes more.
4. Chop tomatoes and add them to the products. Cook for 10 minutes more.
5. Then add chopped onion, shrimps, coconut milk and chicken stock.
6. Cook everything for 15 minutes.

Nutrition:
- Calories: 156
- Fat: 2,6g
- Carbohydrates: 8,9g
- Protein: 4,5g

Flavorsome Meat with Spices

This meat is really wonderful and if you like spices, it will be great. Cook and enjoy with it.

Prep time: 30 minutes | **Cooking time**: 40 minutes | **Servings**: 4

Ingredients:
- ½ teaspoon of pepper
- ½ teaspoon of salt
- 2 tablespoons of oil
- 2-3 dry red chili peppers
- 2 black cardamoms
- 1 cup of garlic oil
- ½ cup of curd
- 2 tablespoons of ginger
- 2 tablespoons of cumin
- 3 teaspoons of garlic
- 3 tablespoons of coriander seeds
- 4 onions
- 2 lbs of mutton

Directions:
1. Sprinkle the Air Fryer with oil. Preheat it for 3 minutes to 350F.
2. Wash and clean meat. Then chop it in the pieces.
3. Place meat in the Air Fryer and cook for 10 minutes.
4. After that add pepper, salt, cardamom, garlic oil, ginger, cumin, chopped garlic, coriander seeds and mix everything.
5. Then chop tomatoes in the pieces, add the curd and mix everything well.
6. Cook the products for 10 minutes.
7. Chop onions in the rings and decorate the food.
8. Add also the red chili peppers. Then cook everything for 20 minutes.

Nutrition:
- Calories: 189
- Fat: 5,2g
- Carbohydrates: 8,7g
- Protein: 4,9g

Sharp Chicken with Vegetables

This piquant chicken meal is appetizing. Make and eat it.

Prep time: 30 minutes | **Cooking time**: 30 minutes | **Servings**: 4

Ingredients:

- 1 lemon
- ½ teaspoon of pepper
- ½ teaspoon of salt
- 2 tablespoons of oil
- 2 green chili peppers
- 3 tablespoons of flour

- 5 oz of butter
- ½ tablespoon of garam masala
- ½ teaspoon of turmeric
- 1 teaspoon of red chili pepper

- ½ cup of yogurt
- 3 onions
- 1 tablespoon of garlic
- 2 lbs of chicken fillet

Directions:

1. Sprinkle the Air Fryer with oil.
2. Preheat the Air Fryer for 5 minutes to 350F.
3. Then slice meat in the pieces.
4. Then chop onion in the rings and blend with meat.
5. Cook in the Air Fryer for 10 minutes.
6. Then add lemon juice, pepper, salt, flour, butter, garam masala, turmeric, red chili pepper and garlic.
7. Blend everything well.
8. Cook appetizing meal for 10 minutes more.
9. Then cover cooked chicken with yogurt.
10. Cook for 5 minutes more.
11. Serve it hot with basil leaves or sprigs of mint.

Nutrition:

- Calories: 178
- Fat: 5,3g

- Carbohydrates: 8,6g
- Protein: 4,7g

Appetizing and Piquant Chicken Meat

The different combination of spices will be incredible scrumptious and delicious. Check it on your end, prepare this meat.

| **Prep time**: 20 minutes | **Cooking time**: 40 minutes | **Servings:** 4 |

Ingredients:

- ½ cup of flour
- ½ teaspoon of pepper
- 2 tablespoons of oil
- ½ teaspoon of salt
- 1 pinch of saffron
- ½ teaspoon of red chili pepper

- ½ teaspoon of turmeric
- 2 tablespoons of coriander
- 10-12 peppercorns
- 12-15 cashews
- 18-20 almonds
- 4 tomatoes
- 1 cup of yogurt

- 2 onions
- 2 tablespoons of ginger
- 2 teaspoons of garlic
- 1 lb of chicken

Directions:

1. Wash and clean chicken.
2. Cut it in the pieces.
3. Then rub with salt, pepper, saffron, red chili pepper, turmeric, coriander and garlic.
4. Cook meat for 13 minutes at 350F.
5. Then chop onions and tomatoes.
6. Blend with meat and cook for 17 minutes at 330F.
7. Then add peppercorns, yogurt and blend everything well.
8. Cook for 10 minutes more.

Nutrition:

- Calories: 169
- Fat: 5,3g

- Carbohydrates: 8,4g
- Protein: 4,8g

Chicken with Tomatoes and Spices

The great meal for the family. Flavorsome and appetizing meal.

Prep time: 20 minutes | **Cooking time**: 40 minutes | **Servings**: 4

Ingredients:
- 1 lb of chicken
- 1 curry leaf
- ½ teaspoon of pepper
- ½ teaspoon of salt
- 2 tablespoons of oil
- 3 onions
- 4 tomatoes
- ½ teaspoon of turmeric
- 1 teaspoon of red chili pepper
- 6-8 red peppers
- 1,5 cup of coconut
- 1 teaspoon of garlic
- 1 teaspoon of ginger
- 2 teaspoons of lemon juice

Directions:
1. Rinse and clean chicken.
2. Cut meat in the pieces.
3. Rub it with pepper, salt, turmeric, red chili pepper, coconut, garlic, ginger and lemon juice.
4. Chop tomatoes and onions in the pieces.
5. Add them to chicken.
6. Then cut peppers and blend everything well.
7. Cook the meal in the Air Fryer at 350F for 20 minutes.
8. Then shake everything and cook for 20 minutes more.

Nutrition:
- Calories: 157
- Fat: 5,7g
- Carbohydrates: 8,3g
- Protein: 4,9g

Appetizing Egg Curry

This meal is scrumptious. Also, it does not need a lot of efforts and it is not expensive.

Prep time: 20 minutes | **Cooking time:** 25 minutes | **Servings:** 4

Ingredients:
- 8 boiled eggs
- ½ teaspoon of salt
- ½ teaspoon of pepper
- 2 tablespoons of oil
- 1 tablespoon of garlic
- 1 tablespoon of ginger
- 6-7 peppercorns
- 2 onions
- 3 tomatoes
- 1 tablespoon of poppy seeds
- 1 tablespoon of coconut
- ½ teaspoon of paprika
- ½ teaspoon of red chili pepper

Directions:
1. Clean and chop eggs in the pieces.
2. Blend them with salt, pepper, garlic, ginger, poppy seeds, coconut, paprika and red chili pepper.
3. After that chop onions in the rings.
4. Cut tomatoes and peppercorns in the pieces.
5. Blend everything well.
6. Cook the meal in the Air Fryer for 15 minutes.
7. Then blend everything and cook for 10 minutes.

Nutrition:
- Calories: 123
- Fat: 3,5g
- Carbohydrates: 6,9g
- Protein: 2,8g

Flavorsome Chicken Ghee

It is unusual meal but it is delicious. Meat is soft and appetizing.

Prep time: 20 minutes | **Cooking time:** 30 minutes | **Servings:** 4

Ingredients:

- 1,5 lb of chicken
- 1 cup of yogurt
- 1 teaspoon of red chili pepper
- ¼ teaspoon of turmeric
- 1/2 teaspoon of ginger
- ½ teaspoon of garlic
- 2 tablespoons of lime juice
- 7 tablespoons of ghee
- 10 curry leaves
- 2 tablespoons of coriander seeds
- ½ tablespoon of cumin seeds
- 2 tablespoons of oil

Directions:

1. Wash and clean chicken.
2. Chop it in the pieces.
3. Take the bowl and blend the red chili pepper, turmeric, ginger, chopped garlic, lime juice, ghee, coriander seeds, curry leaves and cumin seeds there.
4. Place chicken there and blend everything well.
5. After that sprinkle the Air Fryer with oil.
6. Preheat the Air Fryer to 350F for 2-3 minutes.
7. Cook meal for 20 minutes.
8. Then blend everything and cook for 10 minutes.

Nutrition:

- Calories: 178
- Fat: 5,2g
- Carbohydrates: 7,3g
- Protein: 4,2g

Tasty Curry with Meatballs

It is great meal if you are waiting for the guests. Simple, delicious, tasty and not expensive.

Prep time: 25 minutes | **Cooking time:** 25 minutes | **Servings:** 4

Ingredients:

- 1 lb of minced meat
- 2 onions
- 2 green chili peppers
- 2 tablespoon of ginger
- 3 tomatoes
- 3 cloves of garlic
- ½ teaspoon of dry herbs
- ½ teaspoon of oregano
- 1/3 teaspoon of turmeric
- 1 tablespoon of dill
- 1 tablespoon of parsley
- 3 tablespoons of oil

Directions:

1. Put meat in the bowl.
2. Add ginger, garlic, dry herbs, oregano, turmeric, parsley and dill there.
3. Mix everything well.
4. Then cut tomatoes in the pieces.
5. Add them to meat.
6. Chop onion in the rings.
7. Then blend all components.
8. Cook the meal for 15 minutes.
9. Then mix everything.
10. Cook for 10 minutes more.

Nutrition:

- Calories: 165
- Fat: 5,3g
- Carbohydrates: 7,1g
- Protein: 4,5g

Spinach with Meat

This appetizing combination is very easy for preparing. Meat is soft and scrumptious.

Prep time: 25 minutes | **Cooking time:** 50 minutes | **Servings:** 4

Ingredients:

- 1 lb of beef
- ½ teaspoon of pepper
- ½ teaspoon of salt
- 3 tablespoons of oil
- 1 ginger

- 4 onions
- 8 oz of spinach
- 3 cloves of garlic
- ½ cup of yogurt
- 4 tomatoes

- 2 tablespoons of coriander
- ¼ cup of butter
- 1 teaspoon of cumin

Directions:

1. Wash and clean the beef.
2. Chop meat in the pieces.
3. Take the bowl and place salt, pepper, chopped ginger, garlic, coriander, cumin and butter.
4. Then blend everything well and add meat there.
5. Chop onions in the rings.
6. Add them to spices and meat.
7. Cut spinach in the pieces.
8. Chop tomatoes and blend everything well.
9. Sprinkle the Air Fryer with oil.
10. Cook the meal for 25 minutes at 300F.
11. Then blend everything well, cover with yogurt and cook for 25 minutes more.
12. Serve hot with basil leaves.

Nutrition:

- Calories: 177
- Fat: 5,2g

- Carbohydrates: 7,6g
- Protein: 4,9g

Mouthwatering Chicken

This meat is enticing. Prepare this delectable meal.

Prep time: 25 minutes	**Cooking time:** 20 minutes	**Servings:** 4

Ingredients:

- 1 lb of chicken fillet
- ½ teaspoon of salt
- ½ teaspoon of pepper
- 3 tablespoons of oil
- 1 cup of flour
- 1 cup of bread crumbs
- 2 eggs
- 2 tablespoons of sesame seeds
- 1 teaspoon of parsley
- ½ teaspoon of red pepper
- ½ teaspoon of paprika
- 1 teaspoon of lemon juice

Directions:

1. Cut meat in the parts. Beat eggs.
2. Then rub meat with salt, pepper, sesame seeds, parsley, red pepper, paprika, lemon juice.
3. Place the piece of meat in flour, then in eggs.
4. After that blend the yummy components with bread crumbs.
5. Sprinkle the Air Fryer with oil.
6. Preheat it to 350F for 3 minutes. Cook meat for 10 minutes.
7. Then shake and cook for 10 minutes.
8. Serve the hot meal with pasta. Decorate with lemon and parsley.

Nutrition:

- Calories: 168
- Fat: 4,3g
- Carbohydrates: 7,8g
- Protein: 4,8g

Flavorsome Bitter Gourd

This meal is appetizing and delicious. The components are usual, but their combination created the yummy recipe.

Prep time: 25 minutes	**Cooking time:** 20 minutes	**Servings:** 4

Ingredients:

- 4 tablespoons of oil
- ½ teaspoon of pepper
- ½ teaspoon of salt
- ½ teaspoon of turmeric
- 8 oz of bitter gourd
- 4 onions
- ½ teaspoon of red chili pepper
- ½ teaspoon of onion powder
- ½ teaspoon of paprika
- 1/3 teaspoon of cumin
- 3 cloves of garlic

Directions:

1. Wash and clean the bitter gourd. Cut it in the pieces.
2. Then rub them with pepper, salt, turmeric, red chili pepper, onion powder, paprika, cumin and chopped garlic.
3. Cut onions in the rings. Blend everything well.
4. Sprinkle the Air Fryer with oil.
5. Preheat it to 350F. Cook the meal for 10 minutes.
6. Then shake everything and cook for 10 minutes more.

Nutrition:

- Calories: 95
- Fat: 2,1g
- Carbohydrates: 6,2g
- Protein: 1,1g

The Piquant Curry with Flavorsome Eggs

Appetizing and sharp meal. It is uncomplicated for preparing and flavorsome.

Prep time: 25 minutes | **Cooking time:** 20 minutes | **Servings:** 4

Ingredients:
- 4 eggs
- ½ teaspoon of salt
- ½ teaspoon of pepper
- 3 tablespoons of oil
- 2 tablespoons of poppy seeds
- 2 tablespoons of mustard
- 1 teaspoon of red chili pepper
- ½ teaspoon of paprika
- ½ teaspoon of onion powder
- 4 cloves of garlic

Directions:
1. Beat eggs in the container.
2. Then add salt, pepper, poppy seeds, mustard, chili pepper, paprika, onion powder.
3. Blend the components of the meal.
4. Chop garlic in the pieces. Then add to eggs.
5. After that grease the Air Fryer with oil.
6. Preheat it to 350F.
7. Cook eggs for 10 minutes. Then shake them and cook for 10 minutes.

Nutrition:
- Calories: 87
- Fat: 2,2g
- Carbohydrates: 3,4g
- Protein: 1,6g

Appetizing Spinach with Groundnuts

This meal is uncommon and delicious. Cook and you will be delighted with flavorsome meal.

Prep time: 10 minutes | **Cooking time:** 15 minutes | **Servings:** 4

Ingredients:
- 1 tablespoon of ghee
- ½ tablespoon of red chili pepper
- ¼ tablespoon of cumin
- ½ teaspoon of salt
- ½ teaspoon of pepper
- 2 tomatoes
- 3 oz of groundnuts
- 6 oz of spinach
- 3 cloves of garlic
- ½ teaspoon of paprika
- ½ teaspoon of onion powder

Directions:
1. Wash and chop spinach in the pieces.
2. Then add red chili pepper, ghee, cumin, salt, pepper, groundnuts, garlic, paprika and onion powder.
3. Blend everything well.
4. After that chop tomatoes in the pieces. Blend everything well.
5. Sprinkle the Air Fryer with oil.
6. Preheat it to 350F for 3 minutes. Cook the meal in the Air Fryer for 10 minutes.
7. Then shake well and cook for 5 minutes more.

Nutrition:
- Calories: 103
- Fat: 2,1g
- Carbohydrates: 3,8g
- Protein: 1,1g

Appetizing Piquant Cheese in Gravy

This meal is fantastic. Flavorsome meat with cheese is for the family dinner.

Prep time: 15 minutes | **Cooking time:** 20 minutes | **Servings:** 4

Ingredients:
- 1 cup of bread crumbs
- ½ teaspoon of pepper
- ½ teaspoon of salt
- 3 tablespoons of oil
- 2 tablespoons of yogurt
- ½ tablespoon of red chili pepper
- 1 tablespoon of ginger pasta
- 1 tablespoon of garlic pasta
- 1 tablespoon of honey
- 6 tomatoes
- 1 cup of cheese
- 4 tablespoons of cream
- 3 tablespoons of ketchup

Directions:
1. Slice tomatoes in the pieces.
2. Then add pepper, salt, red chili pepper, ginger pasta, honey, garlic pasta and ketchup.
3. Blend everything. Sprinkle the Air Fryer with oil.
4. Preheat it to 360F. Then add bread crumbs to tomatoes.
5. Blend the ingredients and cook them for 10 minutes.
6. Then add yogurt, cream and cheese. Cook for 10 minutes more.

Nutrition:
- Calories: 137
- Fat: 2,5g
- Carbohydrates: 5,2g
- Protein: 1,4g

Flavorsome Mutton in Herbs and Spices

The delicious meat. Simple and wonderful. Just try to cook.

Prep time: 15 minutes | **Cooking time:** 45 minutes | **Servings:** 4

Ingredients:
- 1 lb of mutton
- 3 onions
- ½ teaspoon of pepper
- ½ teaspoon of salt
- 3 tablespoons of oil
- 2 tablespoons of ginger
- 2 tablespoons of garlic
- 6-7 tablespoons of ghee
- 4 oz of yogurt
- 1/3 teaspoon of red chili pepper
- ½ teaspoon of onion powder
- ½ teaspoon of rosemary
- 2 eggs

Directions:
1. Wash and clean meat. Cut mutton in the tiny pieces.
2. Blend with pepper, salt, ginger, garlic, ghee, red chili pepper, onion powder and rosemary.
3. Beat eggs and add to meat.
4. Chop onions in the pieces and blend everything well.
5. Create cutlets.
6. Sprinkle the Air Fryer with oil. Preheat to 350F.
7. Cook cutlets for 25 minutes.
8. Then cover them with yogurt. Cook for 20 minutes.

Nutrition:
- Calories: 156
- Fat: 5,8g
- Carbohydrates: 5,6g
- Protein: 4,6g

Flavorsome and Fiery Aubergine

This meal has unusual note. Cook and check it.

| **Prep time:** 15 minutes | **Cooking time:** 20 minutes | **Servings:** 4 |

Ingredients:
- 9 oz of aubergines
- 2 onions
- 5 cloves of garlic
- ½ teaspoon of salt
- ½ teaspoon of pepper
- 2 tablespoons of oil
- 1 tablespoon of sesame seeds
- 1 tablespoon of coriander seeds
- 1 tablespoon of cumin
- 4 tablespoons of butter
- ½ teaspoon of onion powder
- ½ teaspoon of dry herbs
- ½ teaspoon of parsley

Directions:
1. Wash and clean aubergines.
2. Then cut them in the pieces.
3. Rub vegetables with salt, pepper, garlic, sesame seeds, cumin, coriander seeds, butter, parsley, onion powder and dry herbs.
4. Chop onions in the rings. Blend everything.
5. Sprinkle the Air Fryer with oil. Preheat it for 5 minutes to 300F.
6. Then cook the meal for 10 minutes. Blend everything well and cook for 5 minutes.

Nutrition:
- Calories: 112
- Fat: 3,2g
- Carbohydrates: 7,3g
- Protein: 1,2g

Appetizing Mutton with Ginger

This meat is scrumptious. It has flavorsome aroma.

| **Prep time:** 30 minutes | **Cooking time:** 45 minutes | **Servings:** 4 |

Ingredients:
- ½ teaspoon of salt
- ½ teaspoon of pepper
- 3 tablespoons of oil
- 1 lb of mutton
- 2 onions
- 2 big red peppers
- ½ teaspoon of dry herbs
- ½ teaspoon of garlic powder
- ½ teaspoon of cumin
- 1 tablespoon of lemon juice
- 1 tablespoon of ketchup
- 1 tablespoon of cream

Directions:
1. Rinse and clean mutton. Then chop it in the pieces.
2. Cut onions and peppers and mix everything well.
3. Then add salt, pepper, dry herbs, garlic powder, cumin and blend everything well.
4. Preheat the Air Fryer to 300F for 3 minutes.
5. Then place meat in the Air Fryer. Cook for 20 minutes.
6. Then sprinkle with lemon juice, add ketchup and cream, blend everything well and cook for 25 minutes.

Nutrition:
- Calories: 136
- Fat: 6,7g
- Carbohydrates: 7,1g
- Protein: 5,5g

Piquant and Appetizing Meat

It is not complicated to prepare this meat. It is tempting and peppery.

Prep time: 30 minutes | **Cooking time:** 45 minutes | **Servings:** 4

Ingredients:

- 1 lb of mutton
- ½ teaspoon of salt
- ½ teaspoon of pepper
- 5 onions
- 5 tomatoes
- 2 tablespoons of ginger
- 2 tablespoons of cumin
- ½ teaspoon of oregano
- ½ teaspoon of red chili pepper
- 1 teaspoon of paprika
- 2 tablespoons of mustard
- 2 tablespoons of lemon juice
- 1 teaspoon of garlic powder
- 2 tablespoons of oil

Directions:

1. Slice meat in the pieces.
2. Rub with salt, pepper, ginger, garlic, cumin, oregano, red chili pepper, paprika, mustard, lemon juice.
3. Grease the Air Fryer with oil. Preheat the Air Fryer to 320F for 2-3 minutes.
4. Cook meat for 25 minutes.
5. Then blend everything. Cut onions and tomatoes in the pieces.
6. Add them later to mutton.
7. Blend the components. Cook for 20 minutes.

Nutrition:

- Calories: 145
- Fat: 6,8g
- Carbohydrates: 7,2g
- Protein: 5,9g

Tempting Chicken with Piquant Gravy

It is very peppery meal but also, it is appetizing. Cook and you will like it. Easy and not complicated.

Prep time: 20 minutes | **Cooking time:** 30 minutes | **Servings:** 4

Ingredients:

- 1 lb of chicken breasts
- ½ teaspoon of pepper
- ½ teaspoon of salt
- 3 tablespoons of oil
- 3 tablespoons of lemon juice
- 1 tablespoon of garlic pasta
- 1 tablespoon of cream
- 1 cup of ketchup
- 1 tablespoon of garam masala
- ½ teaspoon of oregano
- ½ teaspoon of cumin
- 4 tomatoes
- 3 peppers
- 2 onions

Directions:

1. Sprinkle the Air Fryer with oil. Preheat it to 300F for 1-2 minutes.
2. Chop peppers, tomatoes and onions in the pieces.
3. Wash and clean meat. Cut it in the pieces.
4. Then rub meat with cumin, oregano, garam masala, garlic pasta, lemon juice, salt and pepper. Cook meat for 20 minutes.
5. Then add lemon juice, cream and ketchup and cook for 10 minutes more.

Nutrition:

- Calories: 136
- Fat: 6,9g
- Carbohydrates: 7,5g
- Protein: 5,3g

Fiery Meat with Appetizing Fried Rice

The great combination of rice and meat will be the favorite one. This meal is easy for cooking.

Prep time: 20 minutes	**Cooking time:** 40 minutes	**Servings:** 4

Ingredients:

- 1 lb of meat
- ½ teaspoon of pepper
- ½ teaspoon of salt
- 2 tablespoons of oil
- 1 lb of yogurt
- 3 green chili peppers
- 3 cloves of garlic
- ½ teaspoon of oregano
- 1 teaspoon of paprika
- ½ teaspoon of cumin
- 1 onion
- 1 cup of cooked rice.

Directions:

1. Sprinkle the Air Fryer with oil.
2. Preheat it to 350F.
3. Cut meat in the pieces.
4. Then rub it with salt, pepper, garlic, oregano, paprika, cumin.
5. Cook meat for 20 minutes in the Air Fryer.
6. Then chop onion and pepper in the pieces.
7. Add them to meat.
8. Then add prepared rice and cover everything with yogurt.
9. Cook for 20 minutes more in the Air Fryer.

Nutrition:

- Calories: 147
- Fat: 6,7g
- Carbohydrates: 7,8g
- Protein: 5,6g

Appetizing Curry with Fiery Spring Onions

It is not usual meal. Cook this appetizing meat.

Prep time: 15 minutes	**Cooking time:** 50 minutes	**Servings:** 4

Ingredients

- 6 oz of lentil
- ½ teaspoon of pepper
- ½ teaspoon of salt
- 3 tablespoons of oil
- 2 green chili peppers
- 3 spring onions
- ½ teaspoon of oregano
- ½ teaspoon of rosemary
- 1 teaspoon of cumin
- 1 teaspoon of garlic powder
- 1 teaspoon of onion powder
- 1 carrot
- 2 tablespoons of mustard
- 1 cup of ketchup
- 1 teaspoon of curry

Directions:

1. Rinse and clean carrot, chili peppers, spring onions.
2. Cut them in the pieces.
3. Then blend them with lentil.
4. Add pepper, salt, oregano, rosemary, cumin, garlic powder and curry.
5. Sprinkle the Air Fryer with oil.
6. Preheat it to 300F.
7. Cook this meal for 30 minutes.
8. Then add ketchup and blend the components.
9. Cook the whole combination of the products for 20 minutes.

Nutrition:

- Calories: 138
- Fat: 6,3g
- Carbohydrates: 7,2g
- Protein: 5,5g

Piquant Mutton with Almonds and Saffron

Meat has pleasant and appetizing aroma. It is appetizing and great.

Prep time: 25 minutes | **Cooking time:** 50 minutes | **Servings:** 4

Ingredients:
- 1 lb of mutton
- ½ teaspoon of salt
- ½ teaspoon of pepper
- 2 tablespoons of oil
- 1 tablespoon of coconut
- 1 cup of cheese
- 15 almonds
- ½ teaspoon of dry herbs
- 1/3 tablespoon of turmeric
- 3 cloves of garlic
- 2 tablespoons of mustard pasta
- 1 onion
- 3 green chili peppers
- 1/8 tablespoon of saffron

Directions:
1. Chop mutton in the pieces.
2. Take the bowl and put salt, pepper, coconut, dry herbs, turmeric, garlic, mustard pasta and saffron there. Then rub meat with spices.
3. Chop onion, green chili peppers and blend with the components.
4. Sprinkle the Air Fryer with oil.
5. Preheat it to 300F. Cook meat for 25 minutes.
6. Then add almonds and cover everything with cheese. Cook for 25 minutes more.

Nutrition:
- Calories: 128
- Fat: 5,9g
- Carbohydrates: 7,1g
- Protein: 5,3g

Appetizing Rezala with Spicy Mutton

It is the easiest and very delicious meal with mutton. Cook and check.

Prep time: 20 minutes | **Cooking time:** 40 minutes | **Servings:** 4

Ingredients:
- 1 lb of mutton
- ½ teaspoon of pepper
- ½ teaspoon of salt
- ½ teaspoon of oregano
- 2 tablespoons of oil
- 6 oz of ghee
- 3 oz of green chili peppers
- 1 onion
- 8 oz of cheese
- 1 tablespoon of garlic pasta
- 1 tablespoon of ginger pasta
- 1 teaspoon of paprika
- 1 teaspoon of red chili pepper

Directions:
1. Cut meat in the pieces.
2. Rub them with salt, pepper, oregano, ghee, garlic pasta, paprika, red chili pepper and ginger pasta. Sprinkle the Air Fryer with oil.
3. Preheat it to 280F. Cook meat in the Air Fryer for 20 minutes.
4. Then chop onion, green chili peppers in the pieces.
5. Blend everything well and add cheese.
6. Cook for 20 minutes more.

Nutrition:
- Calories: 142
- Fat: 5,6g
- Carbohydrates: 7,5g
- Protein: 5,6g

Appetizing Meat in Aromatic Spices

This meal is scrumptious and appetizing. Flavors add the unusual note to the aroma.

Prep time: 25 minutes | **Cooking time:** 30 minutes | **Servings:** 4

Ingredients:
- 1 lb of lamb
- ½ teaspoon of salt
- 1 teaspoon of pepper
- 2 tablespoons of oil
- 8 tablespoons of butter
- 2 tablespoons of lemon juice
- 1 cauliflower
- 2 onions
- ½ teaspoon of paprika
- ½ teaspoon of red chili pepper
- 1/3 tablespoon of dry herbs
- ½ teaspoon of cumin

Directions:
1. Sprinkle the Air Fryer with oil. Preheat to 360F.
2. Then cut lamb in the pieces.
3. Rub meat with salt, pepper, butter, lemon juice, paprika, red chili pepper, dry herbs with cumin.
4. Cook in the Air Fryer for 10 minutes.
5. Then chop onion in the rings.
6. Add to meat. Cut cauliflower and blend everything.
7. Cook for 10 minutes. Then blend everything well and cook for 10 minutes more.
8. Serve hot with vegetables or with basil leaves and parsley.

Nutrition:
- Calories: 156
- Fat: 5,7g
- Carbohydrates: 7,2g
- Protein: 5,9g

Flavorsome Fried Risotto with Mint

This meal is unique, appetizing and wonderful. Roast and you will prepare it very often.

Prep time: 25 minutes | **Cooking time:** 35 minutes | **Servings:** 4

Ingredients:
- ½ teaspoon of salt
- ½ teaspoon of pepper
- 2 tablespoons of oil
- 6 big shrimps
- 1 tablespoon of red chili flakes
- 3 tablespoons of butter
- 1 onion
- 5 cloves of garlic
- 1 cup of rice
- 1 cup of parsley
- 1 cup of cheese
- ½ teaspoon of oregano
- ½ teaspoon of paprika
- 1/3 teaspoon of cumin

Directions:
1. Cook rice in the boiled water. Then wash and clean mint.
2. Rub them with salt, pepper, red chili flakes, butter, parsley, oregano, paprika and cumin.
3. Sprinkle the Air Fryer with oil. Then preheat it to 350F.
4. Cook mint for 10 minutes in the Air Fryer.
5. Then add rice, chopped onion and garlic.
6. Blend everything well. Cook for 25 minutes more.

Nutrition:
- Calories: 189
- Fat: 3,2g
- Carbohydrates: 10,4g
- Protein: 5,8g

Appetizing Chicken with Flavors

This chicken is peppery, but also it is yummy. The meal is tempting.

Prep time: 5 minutes | **Cooking time:** 40 minutes | **Servings:** 4

Ingredients:
- 2 lbs of chicken
- 3 onions
- ½ teaspoon of pepper
- ½ teaspoon of salt
- 2 teaspoons of oil
- ½ teaspoon of garam masala
- 2 tablespoons of garlic pasta
- 2 tablespoons of ginger pasta
- 3 tablespoons of lemon juice
- 1/3 teaspoon of oregano
- 1/3 tablespoons of dry herbs
- ½ teaspoon of red chili pepper
- ½ tablespoon of cumin seeds

Directions:
1. Cut chicken in the pieces.
2. Blend pepper, salt, garam masala, ginger and garlic pasta, lemon juice, oregano, herbs, chili pepper and cumin seeds in the bowl. Rub meat with flavors.
3. Then sprinkle the Air Fryer with oil.
4. Preheat it to 340F. Cook meat for 20 minutes.
5. Then place meat on the other side.
6. Slice onion in the rings, cover meat and cook for 20 minutes.

Nutrition:
- Calories: 184
- Fat: 5,3g
- Carbohydrates: 9,5g
- Protein: 5,8g

Juicy and Peppery Mutton Mince

This meal is incredibly delicious and succulent. Cook and you will like this special taste and aroma.

Prep time: 5 minutes | **Cooking time:** 40 minutes | **Servings:** 4

Ingredients:
- 4 green cardamoms
- 4 cloves
- 4-6 red chili peppers
- 1 tablespoon of sesame seeds
- 1 tablespoon of white poppy seeds
- 1 lb of meat
- 5 tablespoons of ghee
- 1 onion
- 3 cloves of garlic
- 1 ginger
- ½ teaspoon of turmeric
- 2 tablespoons of almonds
- 2 tablespoons of cashew
- 1 cup of milk

Directions:
1. Preheat it to 300F for 5 minutes. Then chop meat in the pieces.
2. Take the bowl and place chopped red chili peppers, sesame seeds, poppy seeds, ghee, turmeric, almonds, cashew there.
3. Blend meat with spices. After that cook meat for 10 minutes.
4. Then chop onion in the pieces and add to meat. Cook for 20 minutes.
5. Then cover everything with milk and cook for 10 minutes.

Nutrition:
- Calories: 178
- Fat: 6,7g
- Carbohydrates: 10,1g
- Protein: 7,2g

Piquant Potato Curry with Scrumptious Cauliflower and Coconut Milk

This meal is delicious and appetizing. You can easily cook it and enjoy with this main dish.

Prep time: 20 minutes | **Cooking time:** 20 minutes | **Servings:** 3

Ingredients:

- 1 cup of coconut
- ½ teaspoon of pepper
- ½ teaspoon of salt
- 1 lb of cauliflower
- 10-12 curry leaves
- 3 potatoes
- 1 tablespoon of ginger

- 6 cloves of garlic
- 4 peppercorns
- ½ teaspoon of turmeric
- ¼ teaspoon of cumin seeds
- ¼ teaspoon of mustard seeds

- 5 red chili peppers
- 9 oz of onions
- 7-8 tablespoons of oil
- 1 cup of coconut milk

Directions:

1. Chop potatoes in the pieces.
2. Then chop cauliflower in the pieces and blend with potatoes.
3. Add pepper, salt, curry leaves, chopped ginger, garlic, turmeric, cumin seeds and mustard seeds to potatoes with cauliflower.
4. Blend everything well.
5. Then chop peppercorns and onions.
6. Blend everything again.
7. Sprinkle the Air Fryer with oil
8. Then preheat it to 360F.
9. Cook the meal for 10 minutes.
10. Then shake the products well and add the coconut milk.
11. Cook it for 10 minutes.
12. Serve hot with parsley and sauce.
13. Enjoy with the tasty meal.

Nutrition:

- Calories: 134
- Fat: 3,8g

- Carbohydrates: 9,6g
- Protein: 1,4g

Flavorsome Balls with Potatoes

The recipe of this meal is piquant and modest. Prepare and enjoy.

Prep time: 10 minutes | **Cooking time**: 10 minutes | **Servings**: 2

Ingredients:
- ½ teaspoon of salt
- ½ teaspoon of pepper
- 3 tablespoons of oil
- 1 teaspoon of coriander
- 2 green chilies
- ½ tablespoon of chili powder
- 1 tablespoon of mango powder
- 1 tablespoon of cumin seeds
- 1 black cardamom
- 7 oz of potatoes

Directions:
1. Preheat it to 340F for 3 minutes.
2. Wash and clean potatoes in the small pieces.
3. Add salt, pepper, coriander, chili powder, mango powder, cumin seeds and black cardamom.
4. Rub potatoes with these spices.
5. Then chop the green chilies.
6. Blend everything together. Create small balls.
7. Place these balls in the Air Fryer.
8. Then cook for 5 minutes.
9. Then shake the food and cook for 5 minutes.

Nutrition:
- Calories: 145
- Fat: 2,9g
- Carbohydrates: 8,5g
- Protein: 1,2g

Spicy Chicken Curry with Fresh Tomatoes and Onion Rings

It is hot and appetizing. Cook and you will be glad with the result.

Prep time: 20 minutes | **Cooking time**: 25 minutes | **Servings**: 4

Ingredients:
- ½ teaspoon of salt
- ½ teaspoon of pepper
- 2 tablespoons of oil
- 5 tomatoes
- ½ teaspoon of garam masala
- 1 teaspoon of coriander
- ¼ tablespoon of ginger
- 4 cloves of garlic
- 5 onions
- 2 green chili peppers
- 1 chicken

Directions:
1. Wash and clean chicken.
2. Then cut it in the pieces.
3. Add salt, pepper, garam masala, ginger, coriander, garlic.
4. Blend everything well. Chop onions in the rings.
5. Blend with chicken. Then preheat it to 300F.
6. Cook chicken for 10 minutes. Then chop tomatoes in the pieces.
7. Cut onions in the rings and blend everything with chicken. Cook for 15 minutes.

Nutrition:
- Calories: 189
- Fat: 6,5g
- Carbohydrates: 8,7g
- Protein: 6,4g

Flavorsome Curry with Onion

It is peppery and appetizing meal. Cook this meal and taste it.

Prep time: 30 minutes | **Cooking time:** 30 minutes | **Servings:** 4

Ingredients:

- ½ teaspoon of salt
- ½ teaspoon of pepper
- 3 tablespoons of oil
- 1 chicken
- 12 onions
- 15-17 peppercorns
- 2 large potatoes
- ½ teaspoon of red chili pepper
- ½ teaspoon of cumin
- 1 teaspoon of parsley
- 1 teaspoon of dill
- 1 teaspoon of curry
- 3 basil leaves
- 3 tablespoons of oil

Directions:

1. Sprinkle the Air Fryer with oil. Preheat it to 350F for 3 minutes.
2. Then rinse and clean chicken. Chop it in the pieces.
3. Then add salt, pepper, red chili pepper, cumin, parsley, dill, curry and rub meat with these spices. Cook it in the Air Fryer for 10 minutes.
4. Slice onions, peppercorns and blend them with chicken.
5. Cook for 20 minutes.
6. Serve hot with sauce and basil leaves.

Nutrition:

- Calories: 178
- Fat: 6,3g
- Carbohydrates: 8,9g
- Protein: 6,8g

Flavorsome Cutlets

These cutlets are delicious and appetizing. They are easy for cooking.

Prep time: 15 minutes | **Cooking time:** 40 minutes | **Servings:** 4

Ingredients:

- 6 oz of chickpeas
- 2-3 tablespoons of oil
- ½ teaspoon of pepper
- ½ teaspoon of salt
- 1 tablespoon of ginger pasta
- 1 tablespoon of parsley
- 3 cloves of garlic
- ½ teaspoon of red chili pepper
- ½ teaspoon of paprika
- 3 tomatoes
- 4 onions
- 2 tablespoons of tomato puree
- ½ teaspoon of cumin

Directions:

1. Take the bowl and place the chickpeas there.
2. Add pepper, salt, ginger pasta, parsley, garlic, red chili pepper, paprika, cumin and the puree with tomatoes. Blend the components.
3. Grease the Air Fryer with oil. Preheat it to 340F for 5 minutes.
4. Cook the meal for 10 minutes. Cut tomatoes and onions in the pieces.
5. Add to meat and blend.
6. Create cutlets and cook them for 30 minutes.

Nutrition:

- Calories: 189
- Fat: 6,8g
- Carbohydrates: 8,6g
- Protein: 6,3g

Appetizing Meat with Flavors

This meal is peppery and scrumptious. Cook and you will see it.

Prep time: 20 minutes	**Cooking time:** 50 minutes	**Servings:** 4

Ingredients:

- 1 lb of mutton
- 2 onions
- 10-12 tablespoons of ghee
- 2 tablespoons of garlic pasta

- 2 tablespoons of ginger pasta
- 2 tablespoons of coriander seeds
- 3-4 red chili peppers
- ¼ tablespoons of turmeric

- 1 cup of yogurt
- 4-5 tablespoons of cream
- ½ teaspoon of pepper
- ½ teaspoon of salt

Directions:
1. Cut mutton in the pieces.
2. Then rub meat with garlic pasta, ginger pasta, coriander seeds, turmeric, pepper and salt.
3. Chop onions in the pieces.
4. Then cut the red chili peppers. Blend everything well.
5. Cook for 20 minutes at 300F. Then add cream and yogurt.
6. Blend everything well. Cook for 20 minutes.

Nutrition:
- Calories: 178
- Fat: 6,3g
- Carbohydrates: 8,5g
- Protein: 6,2g

Appetizing Rice with Meat and Spices

This meal is appetizing and peppery. Cook and enjoy with it.

Prep time: 20 minutes	**Cooking time:** 50 minutes	**Servings:** 4

Ingredients:

- 1 lb of rice
- ½ teaspoon of pepper
- ½ teaspoon of salt
- 3 tablespoons of oil
- 2 cups of water

- 2 tablespoons of lemon juice
- 1 lb of mutton
- ½ teaspoon of red chili pepper

- 2 onions
- ½ teaspoon of paprika
- ½ teaspoon of cumin

Directions:
1. Wash and clean meat. Then cut it in the pieces.
2. Place meat in the bowl and add pepper, salt, lemon juice, red chili pepper, paprika and cumin. Then blend everything.
3. Sprinkle the Air Fryer with oil. Preheat it to 360F.
4. Then cook meat for 20 minutes.
5. Then add rice and water and cook for 20 minutes.
6. Chop onions and red chili pepper in the pieces.
7. Cook for 10 minutes.

Nutrition:
- Calories: 186
- Fat: 6,7g
- Carbohydrates: 8,4g
- Protein: 6,7g

Peppery Chicken with Appetizing Tomatoes

It is really great meal. It is flavorsome and delicious.

Prep time: 30 minutes | **Cooking time:** 20 minutes | **Servings:** 4

Ingredients:
- 1 lb of chicken
- 5 big tomatoes
- 2 tablespoons of lemon juice
- ½ teaspoon of pepper
- ½ teaspoon of salt
- 2 tablespoons of oil
- ½ teaspoon of red chili pepper
- 1 onion
- ½ tablespoon of garlic powder
- ½ tablespoon of ginger
- 1 teaspoon of oregano

Directions:
1. Wash and cut chicken in the pieces.
2. Rub meat with lemon juice, pepper, salt, red chili pepper, garlic powder, ginger and oregano.
3. Blend them well.
4. Then chop onion in the rings. Add to chicken.
5. Sprinkle the Air Fryer with oil. Then preheat it to 320F.
6. Cook chicken for 10 minutes.
7. Then add onions and chopped tomatoes.
8. Blend everything well. Cook for 10 minutes more.

Nutrition:
- Calories: 173
- Fat: 6,9g
- Carbohydrates: 8,3g
- Protein: 6,2g

Appetizing Chicken with Scrumptious Cheese

This meal is mouthwatering and piquant. It is scrumptious.

Prep time: 10 minutes | **Cooking time:** 15 minutes | **Servings:** 4

Ingredients:
- 1 cup of chicken
- ½ teaspoon of salt
- ½ teaspoon of pepper
- 2 tablespoons of oil
- 2 cloves of garlic
- 1 lb of chicken
- ½ teaspoon of dry herbs
- ½ teaspoon of oregano
- ½ teaspoon of paprika
- ½ teaspoon of red chili pepper
- 1 ginger
- 2 teaspoons of lemon juice

Directions:
1. Rinse and clean chicken. Cut it in the pieces.
2. Then take the bowl and add salt, pepper, garlic, dry herbs, oregano, paprika, red chili pepper, chopped ginger and lemon juice there.
3. Blend chicken with flavors.
4. Then sprinkle the Air Fryer with oil. Preheat it to 380F.
5. Place the meal in the Air Fryer. Cook it for 10 minutes.
6. Then blend everything and cook 5 minutes.

Nutrition:
- Calories: 173
- Fat: 6,5g
- Carbohydrates: 8,7g
- Protein: 6,9g

Piquant Curry with Mutton and Tomatoes

This meal is too peppery but it is flavorsome. You can eat the curry for dinner.

Prep time: 25 minutes | **Cooking time:** 35 minutes | **Servings:** 4

Ingredients:
- ½ teaspoon of salt
- ½ teaspoon of pepper
- 3 tablespoon of oil
- 1 lb of mutton
- 6 tomatoes
- 2 onions
- 3 green peppers
- ½ teaspoon of oregano
- ½ teaspoon of dry herbs
- ½ teaspoon of paprika
- 1/3 teaspoon of cumin

Directions:
1. Sprinkle the Air Fryer with oil.
2. Then preheat it to 370F.
3. Chop tomatoes and out them in the bowl.
4. Then cut onions. Blend them together.
5. Wash and clean mutton. Chop it in the pieces.
6. Then add pepper, salt, oregano, dry herbs, paprika and cumin.
7. Blend everything well.
8. Cook in the Air Fryer for 20 minutes.
9. Then cut peppers in the pieces and cook 15 minutes.

Nutrition:
- Calories: 169
- Fat: 6,4g
- Carbohydrates: 8,9g
- Protein: 6,2g

Appetizing Chicken in White Gravy

This meal is tempting and delicious. Flavors add unique aroma to the meal.

Prep time: 25 minutes | **Cooking time:** 35 minutes | **Servings:** 4

Ingredients:
- ¾ cup of yogurt
- 1 tablespoon of poppy seeds
- ½ teaspoon of pepper
- ½ teaspoon of salt
- 2 tablespoons of oil
- 1 lb of chicken
- 1 teaspoon of paprika
- ½ teaspoon of cumin
- 1/3 teaspoon of oregano
- ½ teaspoon of dry herbs
- 2 onions
- 5 peppers

Directions:
1. Sprinkle the Air Fryer with oil.
2. Preheat it to 350F. Then cut chicken in the pieces.
3. Rub meat with the poppy seeds, pepper, salt, paprika, cumin, oregano and dry herbs.
4. Then slice onions in the pieces.
5. Add to meat. Cut pepper in the strings.
6. Blend everything well.
7. Cook for 20 minutes.
8. After that cover the meal with yogurt. Cook for 15 minutes,

Nutrition:
- Calories: 187
- Fat: 6,9g
- Carbohydrates: 8,8g
- Protein: 6,2g

Spaghetti with Appetizing Sauce

This meal is great for dinner. It is flavorsome and delicious.

Prep time: 20 minutes	**Cooking time:** 20 minutes	**Servings:** 4

Ingredients:

- 3/4 cup of cheese
- ½ teaspoon of pepper
- ½ teaspoon of salt
- 2 tablespoons of oil
- 3 tomatoes
- 3 tablespoons of red wine
- 2 cups of spaghetti
- ½ teaspoon of paprika
- 2 tablespoons of red chili flakes
- 1 onion
- ½ teaspoon of dry herbs
- ½ teaspoon of cumin

Directions:

1. Boil spaghetti in water.
2. Place on the plate.
3. Then add salt, pepper, red wine, paprika, red chili flakes, dry herbs and cumin.
4. Blend everything well.
5. Chop onion and tomatoes in the pieces.
6. Add to spaghetti and blend everything.
7. Then sprinkle the Air Fryer with oil.
8. Preheat it to 360F.
9. Cook for 10 minutes.
10. Then shake everything and cook for 10 minutes.
11. Decorate with cheese and parsley.

Nutrition:

- Calories: 121
- Fat: 2,5g
- Carbohydrates: 4,7g
- Protein: 1,2g

Spicy and Appetizing Chicken

This chicken is scrumptious and piquant. It is needed to prepare it.

Prep time: 20 minutes	**Cooking time:** 20 minutes	**Servings:** 4

Ingredients:

- ½ teaspoon of pepper
- 2 tablespoons of oil
- ½ teaspoon of salt
- ½ teaspoon of dry herbs
- 1 lb of chicken
- 1 teaspoon of rosemary
- 1 onion
- 1 tomato
- ½ teaspoon of oregano
- ½ teaspoon of red chili pepper
- 1 teaspoon of paprika

Directions:

1. Sprinkle the Air Fryer with oil. Cook up it to 380F.
2. Then cut chicken in the pieces.
3. Take the container and place pepper, salt, dry herbs, rosemary, oregano, red chili pepper and paprika. Blend meat with spices.
4. Then cook it for 10 minutes.
5. Cut onion and tomato. Add them to meat.
6. Blend everything well. Cook for 10 minutes.

Nutrition:

- Calories: 178
- Fat: 7,5g
- Carbohydrates: 5,9g
- Protein: 6,2g

Delightful Mutton with Spices

The meal is appetizing and fiery.

| **Prep time:** 20 minutes | **Cooking time:** 20 minutes | **Servings:** 4 |

Ingredients:

- 1 teaspoon of pepper
- 1 teaspoon of salt
- 3 tablespoons of oil
- 1 lb of mutton
- 1 teaspoon of paprika
- 1 teaspoon of dry herbs
- ½ teaspoon of red chili pepper
- 2 oz of mushrooms
- 2 teaspoon of lemon juice
- ½ teaspoon of garlic powder
- ½ teaspoon of onion powder

Directions:

1. Sprinkle the Air Fryer with oil.
2. Preheat it to 380F for 2 minutes. Chop meat in the pieces.
3. Then blend it with pepper, salt, paprika, dry herbs, red chili pepper, lemon juice, garlic powder and onion powder. Chop mushrooms in the pieces.
4. Then blend them with meat.
5. Cook the meal for 10 minutes. Then blend everything.
6. Cook the meal for 10 minutes.

Nutrition:

- Calories: 189
- Fat: 7,4g
- Carbohydrates: 5,6g
- Protein: 6,9g

Flavorsome Lamb with Chicken and Spices

This meal is really great. It is appetizing and piquant. Just cook it.

| **Prep time:** 20 minutes | **Cooking time:** 25 minutes | **Servings:** 4 |

Ingredients:

- ½ lb of lamb
- ½ lb of chicken
- ½ teaspoon of pepper
- ½ teaspoon of salt
- 3 tablespoons of oil
- 2 onions
- 2 tomatoes
- 2 peppers
- 1 cup of cheese
- ½ teaspoon of dry herbs
- 1 teaspoon of paprika
- ½ teaspoon of oregano
- ½ teaspoon of garlic powder
- 1/3 teaspoon of red chili pepper

Directions:

1. Sprinkle the Air Fryer with oil.
2. Preheat it to 380F for 5 minutes. Wash and cut meat.
3. Then cut chicken and lamb in the pieces.
4. Place meat in the bowl.
5. Add pepper, salt, dry herbs, paprika, oregano, garlic powder and red chili pepper to meat.
6. Rub meat well. Then cook meat for 10 minutes.
7. Cut onions, peppers and tomatoes in the pieces.
8. Add to meat and cook 10 minutes.
9. Decorate everything with cheese and cook 5 minutes.

Nutrition:

- Calories: 168
- Fat: 4,9g
- Carbohydrates: 5,9g
- Protein: 6,8g

Tempting Spaghetti with Piquant Chicken

It is really appetizing combination of the product. The meal is peppery and delicious.

Prep time: 20 minutes | **Cooking time:** 35 minutes | **Servings:** 4

Ingredients:

- 2 cups of cooked spaghetti
- ½ teaspoon of salt
- ½ teaspoon of pepper
- 3 tablespoons of oil
- 1 lb of chicken
- 1 cup of cheese
- ½ teaspoon of oregano
- ½ teaspoon of red chili pepper
- 2 cloves of garlic
- ½ teaspoon of onion powder
- ½ teaspoon of rosemary

Directions:

1. Sprinkle the Air Fryer with oil.
2. Preheat it to 380F.
3. Then was and clean chicken.
4. Cut it in the pieces.
5. Rub with pepper, salt, oregano, red chili pepper, garlic, rosemary and onion powder.
6. Then cook the meal for 10 minutes.
7. Shake everything well and cook for 15 minutes more.
8. Then cover spaghetti with cheese and cook for 10 minute.

Nutrition:

- Calories: 189
- Fat: 6,2g
- Carbohydrates: 5,3g
- Protein: 6,7g

Appetizing and Piquant Chicken Stew

This meal is fantastic. It is flavorsome and peppery.

Prep time: 15 minutes | **Cooking time:** 30 minutes | **Servings:** 4

Ingredients:

- ½ teaspoon of pepper
- ½ teaspoon of salt
- 3 tablespoons of oil
- ½ cup of white wine
- 2 chicken breasts
- 1 teaspoon of parsley
- ½ teaspoon of paprika
- 2 teaspoons of lemon juice
- ¼ teaspoon of garlic powder
- ½ teaspoon of rosemary
- ½ teaspoon of cumin

Directions:

1. Sprinkle the Air Fryer with oil. Preheat it to 360F.
2. Then slice chicken breasts in the pieces.
3. Place salt, pepper, wine, parsley, lemon juice, garlic powder, rosemary and cumin in the bowl. Add meat and blend. Then cook for 15 minutes.
4. Shake meat and cook for 15 minutes more.
5. Serve hot with sauces.

Nutrition:

- Calories: 178
- Fat: 6,5g
- Carbohydrates: 5,8g
- Protein: 6,5g

Appetizing Peppery Chicken Legs with Pickle Juice

It is unusual and scrumptious meal. Cook and taste it.

Prep time: 15 minutes | **Cooking time:** 30 minutes | **Servings:** 4

Ingredients:
- ½ teaspoon of salt
- ½ teaspoon of pepper
- 3 tablespoons of oil
- 1 lb of chicken legs
- ½ teaspoon of paprika
- ½ teaspoon of cumin
- 1 teaspoon of dry herbs
- ½ teaspoon of garlic powder
- ½ teaspoon of onion powder
- 2 eggs
- ½ cup of bread crumbs
- ½ cup of flour
- 1 cup of pickle juice.

Directions:
1. Rub chicken legs with salt, pepper, paprika, cumin, dry herbs, garlic powder, onion powder.
2. Then beat eggs in the bowl.
3. Place chicken legs in the pickle juice, then in the cup of flour.
4. After that cover them with egg and bread crumbs.
5. Sprinkle the Air Fryer with oil.
6. Preheat it to 380F for 5 minutes.
7. Cook chicken legs for 15b minutes. Then shake them. Cook for 15 minutes.

Nutrition:
- Calories: 169
- Fat: 6,9g
- Carbohydrates: 5,9g
- Protein: 6,8g

Appetizing Salmon with Piquant Tomatoes

It is incredibly delicious meal. Tomatoes are too peppery.

Prep time: 20 minutes | **Cooking time:** 35 minutes | **Servings:** 4

Ingredients:
- 1 lb of salmon
- ½ teaspoon of pepper
- 2 tablespoons of oil
- ½ teaspoon of salt
- 3 tablespoons of lemon juice
- 5 tomatoes
- 1 onion
- ½ teaspoon of red chili pepper
- ½ teaspoon of garlic powder
- 1 ginger
- 1/ teaspoon of onion powder
- ½ teaspoon of dry herbs

Directions:
1. Sprinkle the Air Fryer with oil. Preheat it to 350F.
2. Wash and clean salmon. Chop it in the pieces.
3. Add lemon juice, pepper, salt, garlic powder, red chili pepper, chopped ginger, onion powder and dry herbs to salmon.
4. Then cut tomatoes and onion in the pieces. Add them to fish.
5. Cook everything for 20 minutes.
6. Then blend the meal well and cook for 15 minutes more.

Nutrition:
- Calories: 178
- Fat: 7,9g
- Carbohydrates: 5,8g
- Protein: 6,9g

Mouthwatering Salmon with Vegetables

This meal is flavorsome. Vegetables are peppery and delicious.

Prep time: 20 minutes | **Cooking time:** 40 minutes | **Servings:** 4

Ingredients:
- 1 lb of salmon
- ½ teaspoon of pepper
- ½ teaspoon of salt
- 2 teaspoon of oil
- 1 pepper
- 1 tomato
- 1 carrot
- 2 onions
- ½ teaspoon of paprika
- 2 teaspoon of lemon juice
- ½ teaspoon of oregano
- ½ teaspoon of dry herbs
- ½ teaspoon of red chili pepper

Directions:
1. Cut salmon in the pieces.
2. Chop pepper, tomato, carrot, onions in the pieces.
3. Then add them to salmon.
4. Blend them with salt, pepper, paprika, lemon juice, oregano, dry herbs and red chili pepper.
5. Sprinkle the Air Fryer with oil.
6. Preheat it to 350F for 5 minutes.
7. Cook the meal in the Air Fryer for 20 minutes. Then blend it and cook for 20 minutes more.

Nutrition:
- Calories: 167
- Fat: 7,8g
- Carbohydrates: 5,2g
- Protein: 6,8g

Cooked and Flavorsome Salad

This meal is appetizing. Just cook and try.

Prep time: 20 minutes | **Cooking time:** 20 minutes | **Servings:** 4

Ingredients:
- 2 cups of cooked spaghetti
- 1 cup of cheese
- 1 pepper
- 2 tomatoes
- 1 onion
- ½ teaspoon of salt
- ½ teaspoon of pepper
- 2 teaspoons of oil
- ½ teaspoon of dry herbs
- ½ teaspoon of red chili pepper
- ½ teaspoon of cumin

Directions:
1. Place pasta on the plate.
2. Then add salt, pepper, dry herbs, red chili pepper and cumin.
3. Blend everything well. After that slice tomatoes.
4. Add them to spaghetti.
5. Then slice onion in the rings.
6. Cut pepper in the strings. Blend them with spaghetti.
7. Sprinkle the Air Fryer with oil. Then preheat it to 350F.
8. Cook the meal for 10 minutes. Then cover it with cheese.
9. Cook for 10 minutes.

Nutrition:
- Calories: 179
- Fat: 7,9g
- Carbohydrates: 5,5g
- Protein: 1,3g

Fiery Vegetables with Cheese

This meal is healthy and scrumptious. Cook it and enjoy.

Prep time: 20 minutes	Cooking time: 30 minutes	Servings: 4

Ingredients:

- ½ teaspoon of pepper
- ½ teaspoon of salt
- ½ teaspoon of dry herbs
- 2 tablespoons of oil
- 2 tomatoes

- 3 peppers
- 2 onions
- 1 cup of mushrooms
- 1 cup of cheese

- ½ teaspoon of red chili pepper
- 1 teaspoon of parsley
- 1 teaspoon of dill
- 1/3 teaspoon of coriander

Directions:

1. Wash and clean vegetables.
2. Then chop tomatoes, peppers and onions. Please them in the bowl.
3. Then add salt, pepper, dry herbs, red chili pepper, coriander, parsley and dill.
4. Cut mushrooms in the pieces. Blend everything well.
5. Sprinkle the Air Fryer with oil.
6. Preheat it to 380F. Cook the meal for 20 minutes.
7. Then shake it well and cover with cheese.
8. Cook for 10 minutes more.

Nutrition:

- Calories: 145
- Fat: 3,9g

- Carbohydrates: 5,9g
- Protein: 1,2g

Peppery Potatoes with Fried Mushrooms and Vegetables

Here are a lot of components in this meal. It is really flavorsome.

Prep time: 20 minutes	Cooking time: 35 minutes	Servings: 4

Ingredients:

- 1 lb of potato
- 1 cup of mushrooms
- ½ teaspoon of salt
- ½ teaspoon of pepper

- ½ teaspoon of dry herbs
- 1/3 teaspoon of cumin
- 2 onions
- 2 peppers

- 2 tomatoes
- 2 tablespoons of oil
- ½ teaspoon of paprika
- 1/3 teaspoon of rosemary

Directions:

1. Wash and clean potatoes
2. Then chop potatoes in the pieces.
3. Add chopped pepper, onions and tomatoes.
4. Blend everything well.
5. Then add salt, pepper, cumin, paprika, rosemary and dry herbs.
6. Blend the products.
7. Sprinkle the Air Fryer with oil.
8. Then preheat it to 380F.
9. Cook the meal for 20 minutes.
10. Then shake it well and cook for 15 minutes again.

Nutrition:

- Calories: 138
- Fat: 3,3g

- Carbohydrates: 5,4g
- Protein: 1,2g

SNACKS AND APPETIZERS

Bread Rolls with Potatoes

If you have unexpected guests, then these snacks will be a good idea. They are easy and delicious and you will be delighted with the result.

Prep time: 10 minutes | **Cooking time**: 12 minutes | **Servings**:4

Ingredients:
- ½ teaspoon of salt
- ½ teaspoon of pepper
- 5 potatoes
- 2 sprigs of curry
- ½ tablespoon of mustard seeds
- ½ tablespoon of turmeric
- 1 teaspoon of coriander
- 2 onions
- 2 green chili peppers
- 8 pieces of bread
- 2 tablespoons of oil

Directions:
1. Cook potatoes and after that mix them with the spoon.
2. Then add salt, pepper, mustard seeds, coriander, turmeric and mix everything well.
3. Chop onion, add to the bowl with potatoes.
4. Then cut the green chili pepper in small pieces. Mix everything again.
5. After that put bread in water and them divide the potato mixture in 8 parts.
6. Put the mixture in bread and make the rolls. Sprinkle the Air Fryer with oil.
7. Then put the rolls in the Air Fryer and cook for 12 minutes at 300F.
8. Put in on the plate and decorate with the curry leaves.

Nutrition:
- Calories: 145
- Fat: 2,1g
- Carbohydrates: 6,8g
- Protein: 1,1g

Mutton Chops

These snacks are tasty, not complicated and flavorsome. They do not take a lot of your efforts.

Prep time: 15 minutes | **Cooking time**: 10-11 minutes | **Servings**:4

Ingredients:
- 3 tablespoons of oil
- 1 tablespoon of garam masala
- ½ teaspoon of salt
- ½ teaspoon of pepper
- 1 tablespoon of ginger
- 1 tablespoon of garlic
- 3 tablespoon of red chili pepper
- 2 eggs
- 2 cups of bread crumbs
- 2 lbs of mutton chops

Directions:
1. Mix red chili pepper, garlic, ginger, pepper, salt and garam masala in the bowl.
2. After that rub meat with these flavors. Beat eggs.
3. Take meat, place it in egg and after that in the cup of bread crumbs.
4. Cook in the Air Fryer for 5-6 minutes at 300F. Then put meat on the other side. Cook for 5 minutes more.

Nutrition:
- Calories: 359
- Fat: 10,8g
- Carbohydrates: 9,3g
- Protein: 17,3g

Chicken Bites with Ginger and Curry

It is very juicy and appetizing snack. Your guests will like them a lot because these chicken bites are very delicious.

Prep time: 15 minutes | **Cooking time**: 20 minutes | **Servings**:4

Ingredients:
- 4 tablespoons of oil
- Coriander for decoration
- ½ teaspoon of salt
- ½ teaspoon of pepper
- ½ tablespoon of garam masala
- ¼ tablespoon of turmeric
- 1 tablespoon of rec chili pepper
- 4 sprigs of curry
- ¼ cinnamon stick
- 2 tablespoon of ginger
- 3 green cardamom
- 1 bay leaf
- 1 lb of chicken

Directions:
1. Cut chicken in the pieces.
2. Then take the bowl and mix salt, pepper, garam masala, turmeric, red chili pepper, cinnamon, bay leaf, ginger and cardamom.
3. Rub the pieces of chicken with the mixture of seasonings.
4. Sprinkle the Air Fryer with oil.
5. After that preheat it to 300F. Then cook it for 10 minutes.
6. After that shake the pieces of chicken well and cook for 10 minutes more at the same temperature.

Nutrition:
- Calories: 340
- Fat: 11,2g
- Carbohydrates: 9,7g
- Protein: 17,9g

Banana Chips

This snack is very easy in preparing and your guests will be surprised to see the banana chips. They are delicious and fantastic. Just try!

Prep time: 15 minutes | **Cooking time**: 10 minutes | **Servings**:4

Ingredients:
- 4 bananas
- 1 teaspoon of salt
- 1 teaspoon of pepper
- ½ teaspoon of turmeric
- ½ teaspoon of paprika
- ½ teaspoon of chat masala
- 3 tablespoons of oil
- 2 cups of water

Directions:
1. Mix salt, turmeric with water. Put bananas in this water.
2. If you put them there, they will have yellow color for the long time.
3. Leave them there for 10 minutes.
4. Then put bananas and mix with 1 tablespoon of oil, chat masala, pepper and paprika.
5. Sprinkle the Air Fryer with the rest of oil.
6. Preheat it to 260F. Cook them for 5 minutes.
7. Then shake well and cook for 5 minutes more.

Nutrition:
- Calories: 78
- Fat: 2,1g
- Carbohydrates: 6,7g
- Protein: 1,5g

Vegetable Rolls

It is an excellent snack - pleasant, gentle, but at the same time very hearty! Just cook and you will like it.

Prep time: 15 minutes | **Cooking time**: 20 minutes | **Servings**:4

Ingredients:
- 1 spring onion
- 2 tablespoons of oil
- 1 teaspoon of soy sauce
- ½ teaspoon of salt
- ½ teaspoon of pepper
- 1 teaspoon of sugar
- 1 teaspoon of paprika
- 1 teaspoon of garlic powder
- ½ tablespoon of capsicum
- ½ teaspoon of ginger
- 2 cups of cabbage
- 1 carrot
- 2 tablespoons of flour
- 10 spring rolls sheets

Directions:
1. Chop cabbage in the small pieces and put them in the bowl.
2. Then cut carrot and mix everything.
3. Add soy sauce, salt, pepper, sugar, paprika, garlic powder, capsicum ginger and flour.
4. Mix everything well.
5. Sprinkle the Air Fryer with oil. Preheat it to 300F.
6. Put the mixture on spring roll sheets and make the rolls.
7. Put them in the Air Fryer and cook for 10 minutes at 250F.
8. Then put them on another side and cook for 10 minutes more.

Nutrition:
- Calories: 137
- Fat: 2,6g
- Carbohydrates: 6,2g
- Protein: 1,1g

Tortilla Chips

If you wish to prepare easy, but at the same time delicious snack, then you found the needed recipe. The result will be fantastic.

Prep time: 15 minutes | **Cooking time**: 8 minutes | **Servings**:4

Ingredients:
- 8 corn tortillas
- ½ teaspoon of salt
- ½ teaspoon of paprika
- ½ teaspoon of red chili pepper
- 3 tablespoons of oil

Directions:
1. Sprinkle the frying basket with oil.
2. Preheat the Air Fryer to 280F. Take tortillas and cut then in the slices.
3. After that take the plate and mix salt, paprika and chili pepper there.
4. Rub the pieces of tortillas with spices.
5. Then put them in the Air Fryer. Cook for 5 minutes.
6. Then shake them well and cook for 3 minutes more. The temperature should be 260F.
7. Serve hot with ketchup.

Nutrition:
- Calories: 98
- Fat: 2,3g
- Carbohydrates: 5,4g
- Protein: 1

Appetizing Tacos

It is the recipe of unusual snakes. Your family will appreciate your efforts.

Prep time: 15 minutes | **Cooking time**: 10 minutes | **Servings**:4

Ingredients:
- 1 cup of feta
- ½ teaspoon of salt
- ½ teaspoon of pepper
- 2 limes
- ½ teaspoon of onion powder
- ½ teaspoon of paprika
- ½ teaspoon of red chili pepper
- 1 tablespoon of coconut oil
- 1 onion
- 3 tablespoons of olive oil
- 8 corn tortillas

Directions:
1. Take the bowl and mix salt, pepper, onion powder, paprika, red chili pepper, coconut oil there.
2. Then cut the feta in the pieces.
3. Chop onion in the rings.
4. Add onion and feta to spices.
5. Mix everything well.
6. Divide the mixture in the parts and place on tortillas.
7. Sprinkle the air frying basket with oil. Then preheat it to 300F.
8. Put the tacos in the Air Fryer and cook for 5 minutes.
9. Then, put them on the other side and cook for 5 minutes more.

Nutrition:
- Calories: 156
- Fat: 3,1g
- Carbohydrates: 8,6g
- Protein: 1,5g

Shrimp with Lime and Tequila

These shrimps are very delicious and easy in preparing. You can be sure that you will like them a lot.

Prep time: 15 minutes | **Cooking time**: 15 minutes | **Servings**:4

Ingredients:
- 1 lime
- 12 big shrimps
- 2 oz of tequila
- 2 tablespoons of oil
- ½ teaspoon of salt
- ½ teaspoon of pepper
- ½ teaspoon of onion powder
- ½ teaspoon of garlic powder
- 1 onion

Directions:
1. Mix 1 tablespoon of oil, salt, pepper, onion powder, tequila, garlic powder and blend all well.
2. Then chop onion in the pieces and mix again. Wash and clean mint.
3. Rub them with spices. Leave in marinade for 10 minutes.
4. Sprinkle the frying basket with oil.
5. Preheat the Air Fryer to 350F.
6. Then put mint in the Air Fryer. Cook mint for 10 minutes.
7. After that put them on the other side, and cook for 5 minutes more.

Nutrition:
- Calories: 136
- Fat: 2,7g
- Carbohydrates: 9,4g
- Protein: 10,2g

Garlic Shrimps with Spinach

This combination of shrimps and spinach will surprise your guests a lot. It is very delicious and amazing. You should cook it.

Prep time: 15 minutes	**Cooking time**: 15 minutes	**Servings**:4

Ingredients:
- 1 cup of cooked shrimps
- 3 cups of spinach
- ½ teaspoon of salt
- ½ teaspoon of pepper
- 1 teaspoon of paprika
- 2 tablespoons of oil
- 1 onion
- ½ teaspoon of garlic powder

Directions:
1. Cook spinach and when it is ready just chop it in the small pieces.
2. After that mix salt, pepper, garlic powder, paprika and 1 tablespoon of oil.
3. Then chop onion and mix everything together.
4. Sprinkle the Air Fryer with oil.
5. Preheat it to 350F.
6. Then add the cooked shrimps and put in the Air Fryer.
7. Cook for 10 minutes at 350F.
8. Then mix everything and cook for 5 minutes more.
9. Enjoy with this snack.

Nutrition:
- Calories: 161
- Fat: 2,3g
- Carbohydrates: 9,7g
- Protein: 10,9g

Mexican Chicken

This snack is very easy and will not take a lot of your time. Also, they are very delicious. Just cook and check it on your end.

Prep time: 15 minutes	**Cooking time**: 25 minutes	**Servings**:4

Ingredients:
- ½ teaspoon of salt
- ½ teaspoon of pepper
- 3 tablespoons of lime juice
- ¼ cup of cilantro
- ¼ cup of salsa
- ½ teaspoon of ground coriander
- ½ tablespoon of cumin
- 1 cup of cooked chicken

Directions:
1. Take the bowl and mix salt, pepper, cilantro, salsa, ground coriander, cumin and lime juice together.
2. Then chop chicken in the pieces.
3. Rub them with spices.
4. After that sprinkle the Air Fryer basket with oil.
5. Then cook chicken for 20 minutes at 200F.
6. After that, when you see the crispy skin, put chicken on the other side.
7. Cook for 5 minutes more.

Nutrition:
- Calories: 239
- Fat: 7,2g
- Carbohydrates: 8,4g
- Protein: 10,8g

Crab Sticks

It is very interesting and flavorsome snack. If you wish to prepare something unusual for your guests, you should prepare exactly this meal.

Prep time: 15 minutes | **Cooking time**: 23 minutes | **Servings**:4

Ingredients:

- 1 packet of ready frozen crab sticks
- ½ teaspoon of pepper
- ½ teaspoon of salt
- ½ teaspoon of garlic powder
- ½ teaspoon of onion powder
- ½ teaspoon of paprika
- 2 tablespoons of oil

Directions:

1. Mix pepper, salt, garlic powder, onion powder, paprika and 1 tablespoon of oil in the container.
2. If you wish, it is possible to cut the crab sticks in the small parts.
3. Then rub them with spices.
4. After that sprinkle the basket with the rest of oil.
5. Cook the crab sticks for 20 minutes at 260F.
6. When they have golden color, put then on the other side. Cook for 3 minutes.
7. Serve warm and enjoy with your great crab snacks.

Nutrition:

- Calories: 135
- Fat: 2,1g
- Carbohydrates: 7,8g
- Protein: 10,9g

Potato Chips

These potato chips will be the best recipe for you. They are crispy and delicious.

Prep time: 5 minutes | **Cooking time:** 22 minutes | **Servings:** 3

Ingredients:

- ½ teaspoon of salt
- ½ teaspoon of pepper
- ½ teaspoon of paprika
- ½ teaspoon of red chili pepper
- 2 tablespoons of oil
- 5 big potatoes

Directions:

1. Wash and clean potatoes.
2. Then cut them in the slices.
3. After that mix salt, pepper, paprika, 1 tablespoon of oil and red chili pepper in the bowl.
4. Rub potatoes with the different spices.
5. Sprinkle the frying basket with two tablespoons of oil.
6. Place chips in the Air Fryer and cook for 12 minutes at 260F.
7. Then shake chips well and cook for 10 minutes more at 230F.
8. Serve hot meal with the different sauces or fresh vegetables.

Nutrition:

- Calories: 136
- Fat: 3,4g
- Carbohydrates: 2,2g
- Protein: 1,2g

Cauliflower Bites

It is healthy and delicious snack. You will spend only 20 minutes for the preparing this meal

| **Prep time:** 5 minutes | **Cooking time:** 25 minutes | **Servings:** 4 |

Ingredients:
- 2/3 cup of hot sauce
- ½ teaspoon of salt
- ½ teaspoon of pepper
- ½ teaspoon of garlic powder
- ½ teaspoon of onion powder
- 1 tablespoon of coconut oil
- 2 tablespoons of oil
- 1 big head of cauliflower

Directions:
1. Wash and clean cauliflower.
2. Then chop it in the pieces.
3. Put in the container and mix with salt, pepper, garlic powder and onion powder.
4. Blend these ingredients well.
5. Then sprinkle the Air Fryer basket with 2 tablespoons of oil.
6. Preheat it to 350F.
7. Cook cauliflower for 15 minutes.
8. Then add coconut oil, blend the components and cook for 5 minutes.
9. After that cover all products with sauce. Cook for 5 minutes more at the same temperature.

Nutrition:
- Calories: 120
- Fat: 3,1g
- Carbohydrates: 8,9g
- Protein: 1,1g

Grilled Broccoli

This snack is fantastic. Broccoli with spices is very delicious. Your guests will be surprised with this meal a lot.

| **Prep time:** 5 minutes | **Cooking time:** 10 minutes | **Servings:** 4 |

Ingredients:
- 4 cups of broccoli
- 2 teaspoons of garlic powder
- 1 teaspoon of pepper
- ½ teaspoon of salt
- 1/8 teaspoon of paprika
- 1/6 teaspoon of oregano
- 1 tablespoon of olive oil
- 1 tablespoon of coconut oil
- 1 big red pepper
- ½ teaspoon of onion powder
- ½ cup of sauce

Directions:
1. Wash and cup broccoli in the pieces.
2. Wash and chop the red pepper in the strings. Mix the red pepper with broccoli.
3. Then add pepper, salt, paprika, oregano, coconut oil and onion powder to the bowl with vegetables.
4. Mix everything well. Sprinkle the crying basket with oil.
5. Preheat the Air Fryer to 350F. Cook broccoli for 5 minutes at 350F.
6. Then shake well, cover with sauce and cook for 5 minutes again.

Nutrition:
- Calories: 89
- Fat: 2,1g
- Carbohydrates: 10,1g
- Protein: 1,2g

Cauliflower with Turmeric and Garlic

You will like this cauliflower because of the different spices. This snack is very delicious and tasty. Do not miss your chance to cook it.

| **Prep time:** 5 minutes | **Cooking time:** 30 minutes | **Servings:** 4 |

Ingredients:

- 3 tablespoons of chopped cilantro
- 3 scallions
- 1 cauliflower
- ½ teaspoon of salt
- ½ teaspoon of pepper
- ½ teaspoon of ground cumin
- 1 teaspoon of ground turmeric
- 4 garlic cloves
- 2 tablespoons of lemon juice
- 3 tablespoons of oil

Directions:

1. Preheat the Air Fryer to 350F.
2. Sprinkle it with oil.
3. Then wash and chop cauliflower in the small pieces.
4. Add salt, pepper, scallions, ground cumin, ground turmeric, chopped garlic cloves and mix the components.
5. Then place in the Air Fryer and cook at 350F for 20 minutes.
6. Then mix cauliflower and add 2 tablespoons of lemon juice.
7. After that cook for 10 minutes at 300F.

Nutrition:

- Calories: 110
- Fat: 1,6g
- Carbohydrates: 8,2g
- Protein: 1,2g

Broccoli Pesto with Quinoa

The combination of these ingredients is fantastic. You will prepare uncomplicated and delicious snack in a few minutes.

| **Prep time:** 15 minutes | **Cooking time:** 15 minutes | **Servings:** 4 |

Ingredients:

- 1 cup of quinoa
- 2 cups of water
- 5 cups of broccoli
- 1 tablespoon of basil
- ½ teaspoon of salt
- ½ teaspoon of pepper
- ¼ cup of cream
- 2 tablespoons of lemon juice
- ¼ cup of oil
- 2/3 cup of almonds
- 4 garlic cloves
- 1 cup of cheese

Directions:

1. Cook the quinoa with 2 cups of water.
2. When it is ready, place it in the bowl.
3. Then add broccoli and blend the products well.
4. After that, put salt, pepper, chopped basil, almonds, cloves of garlic and blend the components well. Sprinkle the Air Fryer with oil.
5. Then preheat it to 350F. Cook for 10 minutes.
6. Then shake everything, add cream, lemon juice and cheese.
7. Cook for 5 minutes more.

Nutrition:

- Calories: 115
- Fat: 4,2g
- Carbohydrates: 8,2g
- Protein: 1,3g

Black Beans and Quinoa

Delicious and fragrant snack, which can be easily prepared at home.

Prep time: 15 minutes | **Cooking time:** 35 minutes | **Servings:** 4

Ingredients:

- 1/3 cup of hot sauce
- 1 cup of cooked quinoa
- 1 tablespoon of oil
- 1 onion
- 1 teaspoon of garlic powder
- 1 teaspoon of pepper
- 1 potato
- ½ teaspoon of cumin
- ½ teaspoon of oregano
- ½ cup of potatoes
- 1 green pepper
- 1 red pepper
- 6 oz of cooked black beans

Directions:

1. Preheat the Air Fryer to 390F. Cut potatoes in the pieces.
2. Mix with oil and cook in the Air Fryer for 20 minutes.
3. Then chop pepper and onion and put in the bowl.
4. Add beans and mix together.
5. After that add cooked quinoa, pepper, salt, cumin, oregano, chopped potatoes and mix everything well. Cook for 10 minutes more at the same temperature.
6. Then cover with sauce and cook for 5 minutes.

Nutrition:

- Calories: 178
- Fat: 5,3g
- Carbohydrates: 9,6g
- Protein: 2,5g

Black Bean Burgers

Cutlets for these burgers are prepared in the Air Fryer and it makes them juicy and gives the burgers a special flavor.

Prep time: 15 minutes | **Cooking time:** 20 minutes | **Servings:** 4

Ingredients:

- 1 egg
- 1 teaspoon of hot chili pepper
- ½ teaspoon of salt
- 1 onion
- ½ teaspoon of pepper
- ½ teaspoon of cumin
- 1 big garlic
- ¼ cup of the green or red pepper
- ½ cup of water
- ½ cup of bread crumbs
- ¼ cup of quinoa
- 6 oz of black beans
- 2 teaspoons of oil

Directions:

1. Sprinkle the Air Fryer basket with oil. Then preheat it to 300F.
2. Boil the quinoa with water. When it is ready, put it in the bowl.
3. Chop onion, green and red peppers and add to quinoa.
4. Then add black beans and bread crumbs.
5. After that mix everything well.
6. Then add all spices and 1 egg. Chop garlic and mix everything.
7. After that create cutlets and put them in the Air Fryer.
8. Cook for 10 minutes and then out them on the other side.

Nutrition:

- Calories: 190
- Fat: 4,6g
- Carbohydrates: 9,3g
- Protein: 2,1g

Kale Chips

If you did not hear about this snack, you should cook it. It is really simple in preparing and you will have the appetizing and wonderful meal.

Prep time: 3 minutes | **Cooking time:** 10 minutes | **Servings:** 4

Ingredients:
- 1 head of kale
- 1 teaspoon of salt
- 1 teaspoon of pepper
- ½ teaspoon of red chili pepper
- ½ teaspoon of onion powder
- ½ teaspoon of garlic powder
- 2 tablespoons of olive oil
- 2 tablespoons of coconut oil

Directions:
1. Sprinkle the frying basket with olive oil. Preheat it to 350F.
2. Cut the kale in the pieces. Sprinkle the kale with the coconut oil.
3. Then add salt, garlic powder, onion powder, red chili pepper, salt and pepper.
4. Rub the pieces of kale with spices and mix them.
5. After that place them in the Air Fryer and cook 5 minutes.
6. Then shake them well and cook for 5 minutes more.

Nutrition:
- Calories: 56
- Fat: 1,5g
- Carbohydrates: 9,8g
- Protein: 1,2g

Cauliflower Gratin

This snack is very unusual. Healthy, simple and delicious!

Prep time: 10 minutes | **Cooking time:** 20 minutes | **Servings:** 4

Ingredients:
- ¼ cup of cheese
- ½ cup of cheese
- 1/8 teaspoon of ground nutmeg
- 1 cup of milk
- ½ teaspoon of salt
- ½ teaspoon of pepper
- 4 tablespoons of oil
- 2 tablespoons of flour
- 1 cauliflower

Directions:
1. Sprinkle the Air Fryer with oil. Preheat the Air Fryer to 350F.
2. Wash and clean cauliflower. Cut cauliflower in the pieces.
3. Then place in the Air Fryer.
4. Then pour the cup of milk in the bowl.
5. Add salt, pepper, flour, ground nutmeg there.
6. Blend the components well.
7. Cook it for 15 minutes in the Air Fryer.
8. Then cover with cheese. Cook for 5 minutes.
9. After that serve hot with sauce.

Nutrition:
- Calories: 138
- Fat: 2,5g
- Carbohydrates: 7,5g
- Protein: 1,5g

Tempting Chicken Wings

This chicken meal is scrumptious and peppery. Just make these mouthwatering snacks.

Prep time: 10 minutes | **Cooking time:** 20 minutes | **Servings:** 4

Ingredients:
- ½ teaspoon of red chili flakes
- ½ teaspoon of salt
- ½ teaspoon of pepper
- ½ teaspoon of oregano
- ½ teaspoon of coriander
- ½ teaspoon of paprika
- ½ teaspoon of onion powder
- ½ teaspoon of garlic powder
- ½ cup of butter
- 1 tablespoon of lemon juice
- 3 lbs of chicken wings
- 2 tablespoons of oil

Directions:
1. Sprinkle the Air Fryer with oil. Preheat it to 390F.
2. Cook lemon with butter.
3. Wash and clean chicken wings.
4. Place salt, pepper, red chili flakes, oregano, coriander, paprika and garlic in the bowl with butter. Then cover chicken wings with the fiery sauce.
5. Place meat in the Air Fryer. Cook for 20 minutes. Serve warm with parsley.
6. Decorate it with basil leaves and ketchup.

Nutrition:
- Calories: 290
- Fat: 7,9g
- Carbohydrates: 9,3g
- Protein: 12,5g

Roasted Piquant Chicken Wings

Make these snacks for the picnic. They are uncomplicated and flavorsome.

Prep time: 10 minutes	**Cooking time:** 25 minutes	**Servings:** 4

Ingredients:

- 1 teaspoon of pepper
- 1 teaspoon of salt
- 1 teaspoon of cayenne pepper
- 2 teaspoons of chili powder
- 1 teaspoon of garlic powder
- 1 teaspoon of onion powder
- 3 teaspoons of sugar
- 1 tablespoons of oil
- ¼ cup of maple syrup
- 1 lb of chicken wings
- ½ cup of sauce

Directions:

1. Sprinkle the Air Fryer basket with oil.
2. After that preheat it to 300F.
3. Wash and clean chicken wings.
4. Then mix pepper, salt, cayenne pepper, chili powder, garlic powder, onion powder, sugar in the container.
5. After that rub chicken wings with this spices.
6. Then place them in the Air Fryer. Cook meat for 15 minutes.
7. After that blend sauce with maple syrup.
8. Pour meat with sauce. Cook for 10 minutes more.

Nutrition:

- Calories: 279
- Fat: 7,7g
- Carbohydrates: 9,2g
- Protein: 12,7g

Tomato with Cucumber and Feta

These snacks are very easy and will be perfect for the picnic in hot summer days. The spicy note can create the great impression and you will like this meal.

Prep time: 10 minutes	**Cooking time:** 10 minutes	**Servings:** 4

Ingredients:

- 2 tablespoons of basil leaves
- 1 teaspoon of pepper
- ½ teaspoon of salt
- ½ teaspoon of garlic powder
- ½ teaspoon of onion powder
- ½ cup of sauce
- ¼ cup of feta cheese
- 1 big cucumber
- 2 tablespoons of oil

Directions:

1. Cut cucumber in the pieces.
2. Then cut the feta cheese in the pieces and mix with cucumber.
3. Sprinkle the frying basket with oil. Preheat it to 300F.
4. Mix cucumber and feta with pepper, salt, garlic powder, onion powder.
5. Cook in the Air Fryer at 5 minutes.
6. Then add sauce and cook for 5 minutes.

Nutrition:

- Calories: 110
- Fat: 5,3g
- Carbohydrates: 8,3g
- Protein: 7,4g

Cheesy Garlic Bread

Slices of crispy bread with baked cheese and garlic – this lunch can be both perfect appetizer and great variant for the quick dinner in the office!

Prep time: 5 minutes
Cooking time: 20 minutes
Servings: 4

Ingredients:

- Pizza dough
- Salt
- Pepper
- 4.4oz butter
- 1 teaspoon parsley
- 1 teaspoon garlic puree
- 0.53oz cheese
- Flour

Directions:

1. Put some flour on the table and roll pizza dough.
2. Cover it with the cheese.
3. Turn on air Fryer and preheat up to 340°F.
4. Warm butter on the frying pan and add garlic with parsley, salt and pepper.
5. Pout this mixture on the cheese.
6. Place dough into the Air Fryer and cook for 20 minutes.
7. Serve with fresh herbs.

Nutrition:

- Calories: 120
- Fat: 7g
- Carbohydrates: 13g
- Protein:3g

Cooked Mushrooms

The meal is very tasty and delicious, it can be also cooked for the holiday. This snack is very delicious.

| **Prep time:** 10 minutes | **Cooking time:** 30 minutes | **Servings:** 4 |

Ingredients:

- 1 lb of fresh mushrooms
- ½ teaspoon of pepper
- ½ teaspoon of salt
- ½ teaspoon of dry herbs
- ½ teaspoon of cumin
- 2 tablespoons of parsley
- 2 teaspoons of garlic sauce
- 2 teaspoons of oil

Directions:

1. Sprinkle the Air Fryer with oil.
2. Then preheat it to 350F.
3. Wash and clean mushrooms.
4. Then mix salt, pepper, dry herbs, cumin and garlic sauce in the bowl.
5. Cover mushrooms with the mixture. Cook in the Air Fryer to 30 minutes.
6. Decorate with parsley and serve hot.
7. Also, it is possible to serve with different mushroom sauces.

Nutrition:

- Calories: 102
- Fat: 3,6g
- Carbohydrates: 10,5g
- Protein: 2,3g

Roasted Mushrooms with Quinoa

It is elegant, fast, tasty and satisfying snack. Your guests will appreciate your efforts and will ask you about recipe of this meal.

| **Prep time:** 20 minutes | **Cooking time:** 23 minutes | **Servings:** 4 |

Ingredients:

- 1/3 cup of cheese
- 1 teaspoon of red chili flakes
- ½ teaspoon of pepper
- ½ teaspoon of salt
- 3 tablespoons of parsley
- ½ teaspoon of oregano
- ¼ cup of cleaned pistachios
- ¼ cup of batter
- ¼ cup of onion
- 20 white mushrooms
- 6 tablespoons of water
- 3 tablespoons of quinoa

Directions:

1. Sprinkle the frying basket with oil.
2. Then preheat the Air Fryer to 350F.
3. Wash and clean mushrooms.
4. Put the red chili flakes, pepper, salt, parsley, oregano in the bowl.
5. Mix them well. Then chop onion, add pistachios and mix them.
6. Cook the quinoa with water.
7. Then add to the rest of products.
8. Divide the mixture in 20 parts and put in mushrooms.
9. Cook for 20 minutes.
10. Then cover with cheese and cook for 3 minutes more.

Nutrition:

- Calories: 168
- Fat: 3,5g
- Carbohydrates: 9,5g
- Protein: 1,2g

Fried Pickles

These snacks are very appetizing. Also, they are uncomplicated for the preparing.

Prep time: 20 minutes | **Cooking time:** 13 minutes | **Servings:** 4

Ingredients:
- 2 tablespoons of oil
- ½ teaspoon of salt
- ½ teaspoon of paprika
- ½ teaspoon of pepper
- ¼ cup of milk
- ½ cup of flour
- 1 egg
- 16 oz of pickle wedges

Directions:
1. Take pickles and cut them in the pieces.
2. Mix butter and milk in the same bowl.
3. Then mix flour, pepper, paprika, salt in the separate bowl.
4. Put pickle wedges in flour with spices and after that in beaten egg.
5. Sprinkle the Air Fryer with oil.
6. Then preheat it to 350F.
7. Put pickles in the Air Fryer and cook them for 10 minutes.
8. After that shake them well and cook for 3 minutes more.
9. Serve hot with parsley.

Nutrition:
- Calories: 139
- Fat: 2.9g
- Carbohydrates: 8.8g
- Protein: 1,5g

Flavorsome Mac and Cheese Wheel

Delicious and scrumptious snack. Make it in 15 minutes.

Prep time: 20 minutes | **Cooking time:** 15 minutes | **Servings:** 4

Ingredients:
- 1 tablespoon of butter
- ¼ cup of cheese
- ¼ cup of bread crumbs
- ½ cup of cream
- ½ teaspoon of salt
- ½ teaspoon of pepper
- ½ teaspoon of onion powder
- ½ teaspoon of garlic powder
- ½ lb of your favorite pasta
- 2 teaspoons of oil

Directions:
1. Cook pasta in water and then place in the bowl.
2. Then add salt, pepper, onion powder, garlic powder and blend the components.
3. Sprinkle the frying basket with oil.
4. Then preheat the Air Fryer to 300F.
5. Put the tablespoon of butter, then add bread crumbs and put mix it well.
6. Create the wheel from the mixture.
7. Then cook in the Air Fryer at 300F for 10 minutes.
8. Then cover with cheese and cook for 5 minutes more.
9. Serve hot with ketchup or sauces.

Nutrition:
- Calories: 168
- Fat: 2.8g
- Carbohydrates: 8.5g
- Protein: 1,3g

Mushroom, Onion and Ham Quiche

This meal is very tasty. Simple, satisfying and appetizing food. And the most important fact - the cooking does not take too much time.

Prep time: 20 minutes	**Cooking time:** 15 minutes	**Servings:** 4

Ingredients:
- 1/3 cup of cheese
- ½ teaspoon of pepper
- ½ teaspoon of salt
- 3 eggs
- ½ cup of cream
- ½ teaspoon of cumin
- ½ teaspoon of garlic powder
- 1/3 cup of ham
- 1/3 cup of mushrooms
- 2 tablespoons of oil
- 1 prepared pie dough

Directions:
1. Cook mushrooms in the boiled water.
2. When they are ready, chop and put them in the bowl.
3. After that put salt, pepper, cumin and garlic powder in the bowl with mushrooms.
4. Mix them well.
5. Then chop ham and add it with eggs to the mixture.
6. Sprinkle the Air Fryer with oil.
7. Then preheat it to 350F.
8. Put the pie dough in the Air Fryer.
9. Then put the mixture on it. Cook for 5 minutes at 350F.
10. Then cover with cream and cheese and cook for 10 minutes more.

Nutrition:
- Calories: 176
- Fat: 3,1g
- Carbohydrates: 8.9g
- Protein: 1,1g

Flavorsome Salmon Croquets

These snacks with fish are appetizing. They are easy for cooking.

Prep time: 20 minutes	**Cooking time:** 12 minutes	**Servings:** 4

Ingredients:
- 1/3 cup of oil
- 3 oz of bread crumbs
- ½ teaspoon of pepper
- ½ teaspoon of salt
- ½ teaspoon of paprika
- ½ teaspoon of garlic powder
- ½ teaspoon of cumin
- ½ teaspoon of onion powder
- 1 lb of salmon
- 2 eggs

Directions:
1. Sprinkle the frying basket with oil.
2. Then preheat it to 350F. Chop salmon and blend with eggs.
3. Then add such spices as: pepper, salt, paprika, garlic powder, cumin and onion powder.
4. After that all components should be mixed well.
5. Place the pieces of fish in bread crumbs.
6. Then cook in the Air Fryer at 350F for 7 minutes.
7. Then shake then well and cook for 5 minutes.

Nutrition:
- Calories: 147
- Fat: 2,9g
- Carbohydrates: 6.4g
- Protein: 3,3g

Chips with Plantain

Cook chips not with potatoes, but also with the plantain. Try and you will like them.

Prep time: 5 minutes | **Cooking time:** 10 minutes | **Servings:** 4

Ingredients:
- 2 tablespoons of coconut oil
- 4 plantains
- 1/3 teaspoon of salt
- ¼ teaspoon of pepper
- ¼ teaspoon of paprika
- ¼ teaspoon of garlic powder
- 1/3 teaspoon of rosemary

Directions:
1. Sprinkle the frying basket with oil.
2. After that preheat the Air Fryer to 300F.
3. Wash and clean bananas.
4. Chop them in the small pieces.
5. After that place them in salt, pepper, paprika, rosemary and garlic powder.
6. Rup the plantains with spices.
7. Then place in the Air Fryer and cook for 5 minutes.
8. After that shake the and cook for 5 minutes more. Serve hot with the different sauces.

Nutrition:
- Calories: 130
- Fat: 2,3g
- Carbohydrates: 8.7g
- Protein: 1,1g

Scrumptious Cooked Calamari

Make the great snacks from the seafood. Uncomplicated, flavorsome and fantastic meal.

Prep time: 10 minutes | **Cooking time:** 15 minutes | **Servings:** 3

Ingredients:
- ½ teaspoon of pepper
- ½ teaspoon of salt
- ½ teaspoon of dry herbs
- ½ teaspoon of rosemary
- ½ teaspoon of cumin
- ½ teaspoon of garlic powder
- ½ teaspoon of onion powder
- ½ cup of flour
- 1 lb of calamari
- 2 teaspoons of oil
- 2 eggs
- 1/3 cup of bread crumbs

Directions:
1. Wash and clean the calamari.
2. Then slice the seafood in the pieces.
3. After that blend salt, pepper, cumin, rosemary, onion powder, garlic powder and dry herbs.
4. Beat eggs in the big bowl or in the container.
5. Place the seafood in eggs and after that in bread crumbs.
6. Sprinkle the frying basket with oil. Preheat it to 300F.
7. Cook the calamari for 10 minutes at 350F.
8. Shake them well. Cook for 5 minutes.
9. Serve the calamari hot, decorate with the fresh sprigs of parsley and sauces.

Nutrition:
- Calories: 192
- Fat: 4,5g
- Carbohydrates: 10,2g
- Protein: 7,8g

Fried Prawns with Garlic Sauce

Delicious and delicate snack. This meal is tasty and uncomplicated for the preparing at all.

Prep time: 10 minutes | **Cooking time:** 15 minutes | **Servings:** 3

Ingredients:
- 1 lb of cooked prawns
- ½ teaspoon of salt
- ½ teaspoon of pepper
- ½ teaspoon of seasoning for prawns
- ½ teaspoon of garlic powder
- ½ cup of sauce
- 1/3 cup of cheese
- 2 tablespoons of oil

Directions:
1. Wash and clean the prawns.
2. Chop them in 2 pieces but not till the end.
3. Rub the prawns with salt, pepper, seasonings, garlic powder.
4. Then sprinkle the Air Fryer basket with oil.
5. Preheat the Air Fryer to 390F.
6. Cook the prawns for 10 minutes.
7. Then cover them with sauce and cheese and cook for 5 minutes at 350F.
8. Serve it hot with the different sauces.

Nutrition:
- Calories: 187
- Fat: 3,4g
- Carbohydrates: 9,7g
- Protein: 10,2g

Cheese Chicken Pieces

Do you want to prepare some snacks with meat? Try juicy and delicate little chicken chopped chives!

Prep time: 10 minutes | **Cooking time:** 20 minutes | **Servings:** 3

Ingredients:
- 1 egg
- 1 teaspoon of Italian herbs
- ½ teaspoon of salt
- ½ teaspoon of pepper
- ½ cup of cheese
- 1 oz of butter
- 1 cup of bread crumbs
- 8 pieces of chicken pieces
- 2 teaspoons of oil

Directions:
1. Wash and clean chicken.
2. Cut it in the pieces.
3. Rub with butter, Italian herbs, salt, pepper.
4. Then put chicken in bread crumbs.
5. Leave for 5 minutes there.
6. Sprinkle the frying basket with oil.
7. Preheat the Air Fryer to 350F.
8. Then beat egg in the bowl and put the pieces of chicken there.
9. After that put them again in bread crumbs and then cook for 10 minutes at 350F.
10. Put them on the other side and cook for 10 minutes more.
11. Serve hot with ketchup.

Nutrition:
- Calories: 198
- Fat: 3,9g
- Carbohydrates: 9,9g
- Protein: 10,8g

Cheese with Cookies

The process of preparation of these snacks is very simple. Cook this meal once, and it will be your favorite one in the future.

Prep time: 10 minutes | **Cooking time:** 16 minutes | **Servings:** 3

Ingredients:
- 2 cups of macaroni
- 1 tablespoon of cheese
- 15 pieces of cookies
- 1 teaspoon of cloves powder
- ½ teaspoon of salt
- ½ teaspoon of pepper
- 2 tablespoons of oil
- 1 lb of milk
- 2 oz of cheese
- 2 oz of butter

Directions:
1. Crush cookies and blend them with the tablespoons of cheese.
2. Then leave it aside.
3. Cook butter, salt, pepper, 1 tablespoon of oil, milk and cloves powder will butter will melt.
4. Then add the combination to macaroni and blend well.
5. Sprinkle the frying basket with oil.
6. Preheat for 10 minutes to 350F.
7. Then cover with cheese and cook for 6 minutes more.
8. It should have golden color.

Nutrition:
- Calories: 189
- Fat: 3,7g
- Carbohydrates: 9,6g
- Protein: 6,2g

Codfish with Fried Mushrooms

It is special kind of snake which you can easily prepare at home. They are very delicious and tasty and your relatives will like them.

Prep time: 10 minutes | **Cooking time:** 20 minutes | **Servings:** 3

Ingredients:
- 1 lb of codfish
- 1/8 teaspoon of salt
- ½ teaspoon of pepper
- 6 mushrooms
- ½ teaspoon of garlic powder
- 2 teaspoons of oil
- For sauce:
- 2 tablespoons of soy sauce
- 1 teaspoon of sugar
- 1 teaspoon of water
- 2 teaspoons of mirin

Directions:
1. Sprinkle the Air Fryer with oil.
2. Then preheat to 390F for 3 minutes.
3. Wash and clean the codfish.
4. Cut it in the pieces.
5. Then rub with salt, pepper and garlic powder.
6. Mix sugar, soy sauce, water and mirin. Wash and slice mushrooms.
7. Cut them in the pieces and put on the codfish. Then cover with sauce.
8. Cook in the Air Fryer at 350F for 20 minutes.

Nutrition:
- Calories: 210
- Fat: 10,9g
- Carbohydrates: 12,5g
- Protein: 15,3g

Cheese and Mushroom Balls

Preparation of chicken cutlets with cheese and greens takes a little time and minimum of products. You can prepare it very easily.

Prep time:10 minutes	Cooking time: 20 minutes	Servings: 3

Ingredients:
- 8 fresh mushrooms
- ½ teaspoon of salt
- ½ teaspoon of pepper
- 2 tablespoons of oil
- ½ teaspoon of dry herbs
- 1 teaspoon of butter
- 2 oz of cheese
- 3 pieces of crackers
- 1 egg

Directions:
1. Crush the crackers into tiny pieces.
2. Then wash and clean mushrooms.
3. Mix egg with salt, pepper, dry herbs and butter.
4. Then cover mushrooms with this mixture.
5. Then put mushrooms in the pieces of cracker.
6. Sprinkle the frying basket with oil.
7. Then preheat the Air Fryer to 350F.
8. Cook mushrooms at 350F for 10 minutes.
9. Then add cheese and cook for 5 minutes more.

Nutrition:
- Calories: 140
- Fat: 5,6g
- Carbohydrates: 10,2g
- Protein: 2,3g

Cooked Balls with Onion

These balls can be the great snack. Delicious and easy for cooking. The great choice for the picnic.

Prep time: 3 minutes	Cooking time: 15 minutes	Servings: 8

Ingredients:
- 1 tablespoon of sage
- 1/3 teaspoon of salt
- ¼ teaspoon of pepper
- 1/3 teaspoon of oregano
- ¼ teaspoon of paprika
- ½ teaspoon of garlic powder
- 3 tablespoons of bread crumbs
- 1 tablespoons of oil

Directions:
1. Take the plate and mix sage, salt, garlic powder, oregano, paprika and pepper.
2. Sprinkle the Air Fryer with oil.
3. Preheat it to 350F.
4. Make the balls from the mixture.
5. Put them in the Air Fryer and cook for 10 minutes.
6. Then put on another side and cook for 5 minutes.
7. They should have golden color.
8. Serve hot and decorate with fresh vegetables.

Nutrition:
- Calories: 157
- Fat: 5,2g
- Carbohydrates: 7,3g
- Protein: 2,2g

Chicken Tikkas

You will have the success if you prepare these chicken snacks. Everyone will ask you about the recipe of delicious tikkas.

Prep time: 10 minutes | **Cooking time:** 15 minutes | **Servings:** 3

Ingredients:
- 1 teaspoon of garam masala
- 2 tablespoons of oil
- 2 tablespoons of cumin powder
- 2 tablespoons of coriander
- 1 tablespoon of turmeric
- 2 tablespoons of red chili pepper
- 3 oz of tomatoes
- 1 tablespoon of garlic pasta
- 6 oz of yogurt
- 3 green pepper
- 1 onion
- 1 lemon
- 1 lb of chicken

Directions:
1. Put garlic pasta, red chili pepper, turmeric, coriander, cumin and garam masala and mix.
2. Then cut chicken in the pieces and put them in the bowl with spices.
3. Chop onion in the pieces.
4. Then cut pepper and add it to onion.
5. Chop tomatoes.
6. Take the skewers and put chicken, pepper, onion and tomatoes on it.
7. Then sprinkle the Air Fryer basket with oil.
8. Cook for 10 minutes at 350F.
9. Then cook on the other side for 5 minutes.

Nutrition:
- Calories: 137
- Fat: 3,8g
- Carbohydrates: 7,1g
- Protein: 2,1g

Fried Toast

Unusual and tasty snack for the picnic or for the holiday. It is easy in preparing and also it is not expensive.

Prep time: 5 minutes | **Cooking time:** 12 minutes | **Servings:** 4

Ingredients:
- 2 teaspoons of icing sugar
- 1/3 teaspoon of salt
- 1/3 teaspoon of pepper
- 1/5 teaspoon of nutmeg
- 2 tablespoons of butter
- ¼ teaspoon of cinnamon
- 8 pieces of bread
- 2 eggs

Directions:
1. Beat eggs in the bowl. Sprinkle the frying basket with oil.
2. Then preheat it to 340F for 2 minutes.
3. Rub bread with the nutmeg, salt, pepper and cinnamon.
4. Then melt butter in eggs and cover bread with this mixture. Cook in the Air Fryer at 6 minutes.
5. Then shake the components well and cook for 6 minutes more.
6. Serve hot with different vegetables.

Nutrition:
- Calories: 121
- Fat: 3,6g
- Carbohydrates: 9,7g
- Protein: 1,3g

Nuggets with Chicken

Crispy, soft and delicious. This meal has a lot of advantages like: it is cheap and easy.

Prep time: 20 minutes	**Cooking time:** 25 minutes	**Servings:** 4

Ingredients:

- 4 cups of flour
- 2 teaspoons of oil
- ¼ tablespoon of salt
- 1/5 tablespoon of pepper
- 4 eggs
- 3 teaspoons of garlic powder
- 8 pieces of chicken fillet

Directions:

1. Sprinkle the basket for frying with oil.
2. After that preheat the Air Fryer to 350F.
3. Mix garlic powder, pepper and salt in the bowl.
4. Wash chicken and cut meat in the pieces.
5. Then rub the pieces with pepper, salt and garlic powder.
6. Beat all eggs one by one in the bowl.
7. After that put all pieces of chicken in flour.
8. Put the pieces of meat in eggs and cover them with the mixture.
9. Then cook them in the Air Fryer for 15 minutes at 350F.
10. Shake them well and cook for 5 minutes more.

Nutrition:

- Calories: 190
- Fat: 7,3g
- Carbohydrates: 9,7g
- Protein: 9,3g

Cutlets with Salmon

This snack is really healthy. Fish has a lot of vitamins for your health.

Prep time: 25 minutes	**Cooking time:** 12 minutes	**Servings:** 4

Ingredients:

- 1 egg
- 1 cup of bread crumbs
- 2 teaspoons of oil
- 1 teaspoons of parsley
- 1 teaspoons of black pepper powder
- ½ cup of frozen vegetables
- 4 big potatoes
- ½ teaspoon of salt
- ½ lb of salmon

Directions:

1. Clean potatoes.
2. Then cook potatoes in water.
3. When it is ready – cut in the small pieces.
4. Leave for 10 minutes. Sprinkle the basket for Air Fryer.
5. Preheat it to 350F and cook salmon for 5 minutes.
6. Then add parsley, frozen vegetables, potatoes and salt and blend the products together.
7. Add egg and create cutlets.
8. Put the foil on the Air Fryer basket and then place cutlets on it.
9. Cook for 12 minutes at 350F.

Nutrition:

- Calories: 214
- Fat: 7,9g
- Carbohydrates: 9,6g
- Protein: 9,8g

Cooked Eggs

It is the great snack for different time of day. Easy in cooking and very delicious. Simple and tasty.

Prep time: 15 minutes	**Cooking time:** 15 minutes	**Servings:** 4

Ingredients:

- ½ teaspoon of pepper
- 4 tablespoons of cream
- ½ teaspoon of salt
- 1 oz of butter
- 1 tablespoon of oil
- 1 lb of cooked spinach
- 4 big eggs
- 6 oz of ham

Directions:

1. Take four ramekins and put butter there.
2. Cut spinach in the pieces.
3. Then mix the whole spinach with salt, oil, pepper and cream.
4. Put in the ramekins.
5. After that chop ham and add to the forms.
6. Add eggs there and after that preheat the Air Fryer to 350F.
7. Cook for 15-20 minutes and then put aside.
8. Serve hot and decorate with parsley.
9. Enjoy with simple and fast snack.
10. It is great meal for your guests. They will be delighted.

Nutrition:

- Calories: 140
- Fat: 4,8g
- Carbohydrates: 8,3g
- Protein: 7,1g

Cooked Burgers with Meat

They are tasty and soft. The combination of meat and flavors is truly great. The burgers are soft and crispy.

Prep time: 14 minutes	**Cooking time:** 30 minutes	**Servings:** 4

Ingredients:

- 1 salad for burgers
- 4 bread buns
- 1/3 teaspoon of pepper
- 1 oz of cheese
- ½ teaspoon of salt
- 1 tablespoon of basil
- 1 tablespoon of dry herbs
- 1 tablespoon of tomato puree
- 1 tablespoon of mustard
- 1 lb of mixed mince
- 1 tablespoon of garlic puree
- 1 onion

Directions:

1. Put mince in the bowl.
2. Then add pepper, salt, chopped basil, dry herbs, mustard, garlic puree.
3. Blend these ingredients together. Cut onion in the pieces.
4. Sprinkle the frying basket with oil. Preheat the Air Fryer to 360F.
5. Make cutlets from mince and cook in the Air Fryer at 360F for 20 minutes.
6. Then put them on the other side and cook for 10 minutes more at 360F also.
7. Put the cutlet on the bun, add cheese and salad.

Nutrition:

- Calories: 180
- Fat: 8,9g
- Carbohydrates: 8,2g
- Protein: 9,1g

Appetizing Tofu

The spicy tofu is a flavorsome snack. Delicious and with piquant note. It is needed to try this snack. Prepare and enjoy.

| **Prep time:** 15 minutes | **Cooking time:** 15 minutes | **Servings:** 4 |

Ingredients:

- 1/3 teaspoon of pepper
- 3 tablespoons of oil
- ½ teaspoon of salt
- ½ teaspoon of garlic powder
- ¼ teaspoon of oregano
- ½ lb of tofu
- ¼ cup of cheese
- ¼ cup of flour
- 2 tablespoons of corn starch

Directions:

1. Sprinkle the Air Fryer basket with oil.
2. Then preheat it to 300F.
3. Chop tofu in the pieces.
4. Rub with the oregano, garlic powder, pepper, salt and corn starch
5. After that place it in flour.
6. Mix the products well.
7. Then put in the Air Fryer and cook for 10 minutes.
8. After that shake it well and cook for 5 minutes.

Nutrition:

- Calories: 168
- Fat: 5,2g
- Carbohydrates: 8,3g
- Protein: 3,4g

Tasty Polenta

Usual, simple, but delicious snack. Prepare and enjoy with your friends.

| **Prep time:** 15 minutes | **Cooking time:** 15 minutes | **Servings:** 4 |

Ingredients:

- 1/7 teaspoon of salt
- 1/5 teaspoon of paprika
- 1/3 teaspoon of pepper
- 2 teaspoons of oil
- 2 teaspoons of nutritional yeast
- ¼ tube of polenta

Directions:

1. Sprinkle the Air Fryer basket with oil.
2. Then preheat it to 390F for 3 minutes.
3. Wash and clean the polenta.
4. Then chop it in the pieces and put in the bowl.
5. Add salt, paprika, yeast and pepper to the bowl.
6. Rub the pieces of appetizing polenta with spices.
7. Put the polenta in the Air Fryer and cook for 10 minutes.
8. Then put the pieces of polenta on the other side and cook for 2 minutes more.

Nutrition:

- Calories: 102
- Fat: 2,3g
- Carbohydrates: 4,5g
- Protein: 2,2g

Salt Potatoes

These potatoes can be served as the snack or as the main dish. Spicy, delicious and simple.

Prep time: 20 minutes | **Cooking time:** 10 minutes | **Servings:** 4

Ingredients:
- ½ cup of batter
- ½ teaspoon of salt
- ½ teaspoon of pepper
- 1/3 teaspoon of paprika
- ¼ teaspoon of cumin powder
- 1/3 teaspoon of onion powder
- ½ teaspoon of garlic pasta
- 6 cups of water
- 1 cup of salt
- 2 lbss of potatoes

Directions:
1. Wash and scrub potatoes.
2. Then put 1 cup of salt in water and leave potatoes for 20 minutes there.
3. Sprinkle the Air Fryer with oil.
4. Preheat to 350F.
5. Rub potatoes with pepper, cumin powder, salt, paprika, garlic past, cumin powder and onion powder.
6. Then put potatoes in the Air Fryer.
7. Cook for 5 minutes.
8. Then put on the other side and cook for 5 minutes more.
9. Cover with butter.
10. Serve hot with salad, sauces or vegetables.

Nutrition:
- Calories: 121
- Fat: 2,3g
- Carbohydrates: 4,5g
- Protein: 2,2g

Doughnuts with Sugar and Cinnamon

It is simple and quick recipe. Easy in cooking and tasty. Everyone will like these doughnuts. The cinnamon adds special flavor to the sweets.

Prep time: 10 minutes | **Cooking time:** 5 minutes | **Servings:** 4

Ingredients:
- ½ cup of sugar
- 2 teaspoons of cinnamon
- ½ cup of water
- 1 teaspoon of vanilla
- 1/8 teaspoon of salt
- 1 egg
- 2 teaspoons of oil

Directions:
1. Beat egg in the bowl. Add flour and mix it well.
2. Then add sugar and water. After that add vanilla and cinnamon.
3. Make the dough and create the doughnuts.
4. Sprinkle the Air Fryer basket with oil. After that preheat it for 3 minutes to 350F.
5. Place the doughnuts in the Air Fryer and cook for 3 minutes.
6. Then out then on the other side and cook for 2 minutes.

Nutrition:
- Calories: 215
- Fat: 2,3g
- Carbohydrates: 4,5g
- Protein: 2,2g

Sandwich with Chicken

The flavor of these burgers is more delicious then the usual ones. Here is one secret component in the recipe and because of it meat is very soft.

Prep time: 10 minutes | **Cooking time:** 16 minutes | **Servings:** 4

Ingredients:
- 4 toasted buns
- 1 teaspoon of pepper
- ½ teaspoon of salt
- ½ teaspoon of paprika
- ½ teaspoon of red chili pepper
- ½ cup of milk
- 2 tablespoons of sauce
- ½ cup of bread crumbs
- 2 lbs of chicken fillet
- ¼ teaspoon of celery
- 2 teaspoons of oil

Directions:
1. Sprinkle the Air Fryer with oil.
2. Wash and clean chicken fillet.
3. Cut it in the small pieces.
4. Put the paprika, pepper, salt, clery, red chili pepper in the bowl.
5. Rub the pieces of chicken with them. Then add milk and egg.
6. After that mix everything well. Add sauce and make cutlets.
7. Cook cutlets in the Air Fryer at 350F for 8 minutes.
8. Then put them on the other side and cook for 8 minutes more.

Nutrition:
- Calories: 168
- Fat: 2,9g
- Carbohydrates: 7,2g
- Protein: 10,5g

Flavorsome and Piquant Cauliflower

This meal is uncomplicated and delicious. It is the ideal option for the guests.

Prep time: 10 minutes | **Cooking time:** 15 minutes | **Servings:** 4

Ingredients:
- 1 cup of soy milk
- ½ teaspoon of pepper
- ½ teaspoon of salt
- 1 cauliflower
- 1 cup of flour
- ½ teaspoon of garlic powder
- ½ teaspoon of mustard pasta
- 1/3 teaspoon of onion powder

Directions:
1. Wash and clean cauliflower.
2. Cut it in the pieces.
3. Place pepper, salt, garlic powder, mustard pasta and onion powder in the bowl.
4. Then mix everything well.
5. Rub the pieces of cauliflower with these spices.
6. Then place them in the soy milk and cover completely with it.
7. After that place them in flour. Preheat it to 340F.
8. Place cauliflower in the Air Fryer and cook for 10 minutes.
9. Than shake them well and cook for 5 minutes more.

Nutrition:
- Calories: 97
- Fat: 2,3g
- Carbohydrates: 7,8g
- Protein: 1,2g

Fried Cajun Salmon

It is the unusual method of salmon's preparing. Salmon is flavorsome and peppery.

Prep time: 20 minutes | **Cooking time:** 10 minutes | **Servings:** 4

Ingredients:

- 2 teaspoons of lemon juice
- 1/3 teaspoon of sugar
- 1 lb of salmon
- ½ teaspoon of pepper
- ½ teaspoon of salt
- 1/3 teaspoon of cumin
- ¼ teaspoon of chili pepper
- 1/3 teaspoon of onion powder
- ½ teaspoon of Cajun

Directions:

1. Sprinkle the Air Fryer with oil.
2. Then preheat it to 350F.
3. Cut salmon in the pieces.
4. Blend sugar, salt, chili pepper, cumin, onion powder and pepper with Cajun in the bowl.
5. After that rub salmon with the species.
6. After that place fish in the Air Fryer and cook for 7 minutes.
7. Then place on another side. Cook for 3 minutes more.
8. Sprinkle with lemon juice.
9. Serve hot with the white wine.

Nutrition:

- Calories: 212
- Fat: 5,3g
- Carbohydrates: 7,3g
- Protein: 2,7g

Peppery Grilled Brussels Sprouts

It is vigorous and appetizing snack. Easy in cooking and delicious. Cook and check!

Prep time: 20 minutes | **Cooking time:** 15 minutes | **Servings:** 4

Ingredients:

- 1 lb of Brussels sprouts
- ½ teaspoon of pepper
- ½ teaspoon of salt
- ½ teaspoon of oregano
- ½ teaspoon of chili pepper
- 1/3 teaspoon of cumin powder
- 1/3 teaspoon of parsley
- 1 onion
- 2 teaspoons of oil

Directions:

1. Wash brussels sprouts.
2. Take the bowl and blend salt, oregano, pepper, cumin powder, chili pepper, parsley there.
3. Then rub brussels sprouts with all these spices.
4. After that chop onion.
5. Sprinkle the frying basket with oil.
6. Preheat it to 360F.
7. Then cook brussels sprouts in the Air Fryer for 6 minutes.
8. Then shake them well and cook for 5 minutes more.

Nutrition:

- Calories: 89
- Fat: 2,1g
- Carbohydrates: 8,3g
- Protein: 1,5g

Piquant Rolls with Vegetables and Spices

This snack is unique and delicious. It is meatless and tasty food. Cook and eat!

Prep time: 15 minutes | **Cooking time:** 10 minutes | **Servings:** 4

Ingredients:

- 10 rolls
- ½ teaspoon of pepper
- 2 cups of broccoli
- 1/3 teaspoon of salt
- 1 teaspoon of vinegar
- ½ teaspoon of onion powder
- ½ teaspoon of garlic
- 1/3 tablespoon of mustard pasta
- 1 green pepper
- 1 onion
- 1 carrot
- 2 tablespoons of flour

Directions:

1. Wash and cut broccolis in the pieces.
2. Then chop onion with carrot.
3. Mix everything together in the bowl.
4. Then add salt, vinegar, garlic, onion powder, mustard pasta and pepper and mix again.
5. Cut the green pepper in the strings and add to the mixture.
6. Then cover with flour and mix everything.
7. Sprinkle the Air Fryer with oil.
8. Preheat it to 350F. Take the rolls and put the mixture on them.
9. After that put them in the Air Fryer and cook for 5 minutes.
10. Put on the other side and cook for 5 minutes more.

Nutrition:

- Calories: 104
- Fat: 2,2g
- Carbohydrates: 8,8g
- Protein: 1,1g

Fiery Beans with Lemon

The vigorous and scrumptious snack. It is wonderful and uncomplicated.

Prep time: 15 minutes | **Cooking time:** 10 minutes | **Servings:** 4

Ingredients:

- 1/4 teaspoon of salt
- 1/3 teaspoon of pepper
- 1 lb of green beans
- 1 lemon
- 1/3 teaspoon of red chili pepper
- ½ teaspoon of garlic powder
- /5 tablespoon of oregano
- 1 teaspoon of ketchup
- 1 teaspoon of mustard
- 2 tablespoons of oil

Directions:

1. Cook beans in water. Then place them in the bowl.
2. Blend beans with garlic powder, salt, pepper, oregano, red chili pepper.
3. Then add ketchup and mustard.
4. Blend all ingredients well. Sprinkle with lemon juice.
5. Then mix everything again. Sprinkle the frying basket with oil.
6. Preheat the Air Fryer to 300F.
7. Place beans in the Air Fryer and cook for 10 minutes.

Nutrition:

- Calories: 94
- Fat: 1,5g
- Carbohydrates: 7,3g
- Protein: 1,2g

Appetizing Zucchini with Spices

The incredibly wonderful and flavorsome snack. Flavors give special note.

Prep time: 15 minutes | **Cooking time:** 10 minutes | **Servings:** 4

Ingredients:
- ¼ tablespoon of pepper
- ½ teaspoon of salt
- 2 tablespoon of oil
- 2 eggs
- 3 medium zucchinis
- 1/3 cup of cheese
- ½ cup of bread crumbs
- ½ teaspoon of paprika
- ½ tablespoon of ketchup
- ½ teaspoon of garlic powder
- ½ teaspoon of onion powder

Directions:
1. Cook zucchinis in water.
2. Then cut in the pieces and place on the plate.
3. Beat 2 eggs in the bowl.
4. Add salt, pepper, paprika, ketchup, onion powder and garlic powder to them.
5. Blend everything well.
6. After that place zucchinis in egg and then in bread crumbs.
7. Sprinkle the frying basket of the Air Fryer with oil. Preheat it to 330F.
8. Cook it for 10 minutes. Then shake well and cook for 3 minutes more.

Nutrition:
- Calories: 113
- Fat: 1,8g
- Carbohydrates: 6,7g
- Protein: 1,3g

Pickle Chips with Parmesan Cheese

These chips are incredible and delicious. They are very easy in preparing. Also, they are spicy and crispy.

Prep time: 14 minutes | **Cooking time:** 16 minutes | **Servings:** 4

Ingredients:
- 32 oz of large pickles
- ½ teaspoon of salt
- ½ teaspoon of pepper
- 1/3 teaspoon of chili pepper
- 1/3 teaspoon of cumin
- ¼ teaspoon of garlic pasta
- 1/3 teaspoon of mustard
- 1/3 teaspoon of onion powder
- 2 tablespoons of oil
- 2 eggs
- 1 cup of bread crumbs

Directions:
1. Then preheat the Air Fryer to 350F for 5 minutes. Put the pickles in the bowl.
2. After that mix them with pepper, salt, cumin, red chili pepper, mustard, onion powder and garlic in this bowl. Beat eggs and put the pickles in them.
3. Cover the pickles well. Then put them in bread crumbs.
4. Cook in the Air Fryer at 350F for 10 minutes.
5. After that put in the other side and cook for 6 minutes more.

Nutrition:
- Calories: 115
- Fat: 1,7g
- Carbohydrates: 6,9g
- Protein: 1,1g

Polenta Bites with Cheese

Such tasty and delicious. This snack is very easy in preparing. It is fantastic.

Prep time: 14 minutes	**Cooking time:** 16 minutes	**Servings:** 4

Ingredients:
- 2 tablespoons of oil
- ½ teaspoon of pepper
- ½ teaspoon of salt
- 1 lb of Palenta
- ¼ cup of potato starch
- 1 tablespoon of olive oil
- ½ cup of cheese
- ½ teaspoon of chili pepper
- 1/3 teaspoon of onion powder

Directions:
1. Wash and clean the Polenta.
2. Then cut it in the pieces.
3. Rub with pepper, salt, olive oil, chili pepper and onion powder.
4. Then sprinkle the frying basket with oil.
5. Preheat the Air Fryer to 350F.
6. Put the Polenta in the Air Fryer and cook for 10 minutes.
7. Then put it on the other side, cover with cheese and cook for 5 minutes.

Nutrition:
- Calories: 121
- Fat: 1,8g
- Carbohydrates: 6,4g
- Protein: 1,2g

Cutlets with Tomatoes and Cheese

If you are too busy, prepare this snack from tomatoes and cheese. It is very easy for cooking. Also, this snack is special and delicious.

Prep time: 14 minutes	**Cooking time:** 16 minutes	**Servings:** 4

Ingredients:
- 1 tablespoon of sauce
- ½ teaspoon of pepper
- 1 cup of rice
- ¼ cup of dry wine
- 1 cup of water
- 1 cup of chicken stock
- 2 eggs
- ½ cup of cheese
- 1 onion
- ½ teaspoon of parsley
- ½ teaspoon of onion powder
- ½ teaspoon of garlic powder
- ½ cup of bread crumbs
- ½ cup of tomatoes

Directions:
1. Cook rice with the cup of water.
2. Put it in the deep bowl. Then cut tomatoes and onion in the pieces.
3. After that mix them with tomatoes and onion.
4. Beat eggs in the bowl. Make cutlets from the mixture.
5. Put them in eggs and after that in bread crumbs.
6. Sprinkle the frying basket with oil. Preheat it to 350F.
7. Cook cutlets for 10 minutes.
8. Then cover them with sauce and cheese and cook for 5 minutes more.

Nutrition:
- Calories: 146
- Fat: 2,5g
- Carbohydrates: 6,8g
- Protein: 1,3g

Peppery Rings with Onion

Delicious and very easy rings with onion for your guests. The best snack for the picnic. Simple and tasty.

Prep time: 15 minutes | **Cooking time:** 13 minutes | **Servings:** 4

Ingredients:

- 2/3 cup of flour
- ¾ cup of beer
- 1 teaspoon of salt
- 1 teaspoon of pepper
- ½ teaspoon of soda

- 1 beaten egg
- 1 cup of bread crumbs
- 1/3 teaspoon of onion powder

- 1/3 teaspoon of garlic powder
- 3 onions
- 2 tablespoons of oil

Directions:

1. Chop onion in the rings.
2. Mix flour, eggs, soda and beer in the bowl.
3. Then put salt, pepper, onion powder and garlic powder on the plate.
4. Mix these spices well.
5. Rub onion rings with them.
6. Then put onion rings in the mixture with eggs and beer.
7. After that cover the rings with bread crumbs.
8. Sprinkle the frying basket with oil.
9. Then preheat the Air Fryer to 350F.
10. Cook them for 10 minutes.
11. Then shake well and cook for 3 minutes more.
12. Serve hot with sauces.

Nutrition:

- Calories: 129
- Fat: 2,3g

- Carbohydrates: 3,4g
- Protein: 1,2g

Sandwich with Ham

Incredibly delicious and simple meal. It is very easy for preparing and you will enjoy with the flavor of ham and bread.

Prep time: 10 minutes | **Cooking time:** 3 minutes | **Servings:** 1

Ingredients:
- 2 pieces of bread
- 2 pieces of cheese
- 1 tablespoon of ketchup
- 1 tablespoon of mustard
- 1 piece of tomato
- 1 tablespoon of cheese
- 4 pieces of ham.

Directions:
1. Take the pieces of bread and put them on the plate.
2. Then mix ketchup and mustard together.
3. Cover bread with the mixture of mustard and ketchup.
4. Then put ham and 2 pieces of cheese.
5. After that put the tomato and cover with cheese.
6. Sprinkle the frying basket with oil.
7. After that preheat the Air Fryer to 350F for 5 minutes.
8. Then put the sandwich in the Air Fryer.
9. Cook it for 3 minutes.
10. Serve warm with salad.

Nutrition:
- Calories: 145
- Fat: 4,6g
- Carbohydrates: 5,9g
- Protein: 2,7g

Avocado with Tomatoes and Basil

The combination of the products is strange, but the meal is incredibly delicious. You can cook it quickly and easy.

Prep time: 10 minutes | **Cooking time:** 4 minutes | **Servings:** 1

Ingredients:
- 1 bagel
- ½ avocado
- ½ tomato
- ½ teaspoon of balsamic vinegar
- ¼ teaspoon of pepper
- 1/5 teaspoon of salt
- 6 basil leaves
- 1 teaspoon of butter
- 2 teaspoons of oil
- ½ teaspoon of sauce

Directions:
1. Sprinkle the frying basket of the Air Fryer with butter.
2. Then preheat it for 5 minutes to 330F.
3. Cook the bagel in the Air Fryer for 2 minutes. Then cover it with sauce.
4. Cut avocado and tomato in the pieces. Mix them together.
5. Then add salt and pepper and mix well.
6. Put the mixture on the bagel and then add basil leaves.
7. Sprinkle with balsamic vinegar.
8. Cook in the Air Fryer for 2 minutes.

Nutrition:
- Calories: 49
- Fat: 1,1g
- Carbohydrates: 2,7g
- Protein: 1,1g

FISH AND SEAFOOD

Air Fryer Fish Chips

Delicious chips for the big company. Just try and enjoy.

Prep time:10 minutes	**Cooking time**:15 minutes	**Servings**:4

Ingredients:
- 1 tablespoon of parsley
- Salt
- Pepper
- 1 egg
- 2 fish fillets
- 1 oz of chips
- 1 big lemon
- 3 tablespoons of bread crumbs

Directions:
1. Cut every fillet into two pieces. You should have 4 parts of fish fillet.
2. Mix lemon juice with seasonings and put aside.
3. Put in the food processor salt, pepper, parsley, rest of lemon, chips and bread crumbs. Then just grind them. Put the mixture in the backing basket for the Air Fryer.
4. Fish should be placed in beaten egg firstly and covered with it.
5. Then put fish in the mixture of bread crumbs and seasonings.
6. The process of cooking takes 15 minutes and the temperature should be 370F.

Nutrition:
- Calories: 830
- Fat: 13,1g
- Carbohydrates: 125,1g
- Protein: 43,2g

Lemon Fish

If you like fish, then this recipe is the best choice. Fish will be the main dish on your table after reading it.

Prep time:0-5 minutes	**Cooking time**: 31minutes	**Servings**:4

Ingredients:
- Lettuce 2-3 leaves
- 1 teaspoon of red chili sauce
- 4 teaspoons of corn flour slurry
- 1 egg (white)
- Juice of lemon
- 2 teaspoons of oil
- 2 teaspoons of green chili sauce
- Salt
- ¼ cup sugar
- 1 big lemon

Directions:
1. Chop lemon. Put it in the bowl. Boil half of cup of water and add sugar.
2. Stir it till sugar dissolves completely. Take the deep bowl.
3. Put egg white, 2 tablespoons of oil, salt, 1 cup of flour, green chili sauce in the bowl.
4. Mix the ingredients well. Then add 3 tablespoons of water and whisk it.
5. Put fillets in butter and after that cover with the refined flour.
6. Brush the basket with oil and also cook the Air Fryer.
7. Put fillets in the basket for Air Fryer and cook for 15-20 minutes. The temperature should be 365F.
8. Add salt to sugar. Mix it well in the pan. Then add red chili sauce, corn flour slurry, lemon and lemon juice and mix everything.

Nutrition:
- Calories: 972
- Fat: 15,6g
- Carbohydrates: 155,1g
- Protein: 49,5g

Fish and Chips with Tartar Sauce

Do you want to find the easy and at the same time simple fish meal? You have just found it.

| **Prep time**: 30 minutes | **Cooking time**: 40 minutes | **Servings**:3 |

Ingredients:

Tartar sauce:
- Salt and black pepper
- 1 lemon (juice)
- 1 little shallot
- 2 tablespoons of jalapenos
- 3 tablespoons of capers
- 1 cup of mayonnaise

Chips:
- 2 pieces of garlic
- 1 tablespoon of oil
- 1 teaspoon of rosemary
- 2 big potatoes

Fish:
- 1 teaspoon of salt
- 1 teaspoon of pepper
- 1 tablespoon of oil
- 1 tablespoon of parsley
- ½ cup bread crumbs
- ½ cup flour
- 2 eggs
- 15 oz of white fish fillet

Directions:

1. The Air Fryer should be preheated to 392F for 5 minutes.
2. Take the bowl and mix salt, pepper, oil, parsley and bread crumbs.
3. Fish should be chopped into 8 pieces.
4. Put one piece of fish in flour.
5. After that, put fish into beaten egg and after that in bread crumbs.
6. Put fish in the Air Fryer. Cook up to 15 minutes.
7. Cut potatoes for chips, chop them into slices and put in the bowl with salted water for 20 minutes.
8. Preheat the Air Fryer up to 360F for 5 minutes.
9. Mix the ingredients and put them in Air Fryer for 20 minutes.
10. For sauce just mix the ingredients and leave them for 20 minutes.

Nutrition:

- Calories: 856
- Fat: 16g
- Carbohydrates: 159,7g
- Protein: 44,9g

Broiled Tilapia

This recipe will surprise you a lot. You will not spend too much time on preparing it and it is very delicious.

Prep time: 10 minutes | **Cooking time**: 7 minutes | **Servings**:2

Ingredients:

- Tilapia fillets 1 lb
- Lemon pepper
- Salt
- 1 tablespoon of oil

Directions:

1. If the pieces of fillet are frozen, thaw them.
2. Spray the basket for your Air Fryer with oil. Also, it is possible to use the cooking spray.
3. Preheat the Air Fryer for 5 minutes to the temperature 392F.
4. Put fish in the basket.
5. Set the temperature 360F and cook it for 7 minutes.
6. Fish should have golden color. If you have too big pieces of fish, cook it a bit longer, for example 2-3 minutes more.
7. It is possible to add your favorite vegetables like tomato, cucumber or something like this to fish.

Nutrition:

- Calories: 900
- Fat: 17g
- Carbohydrates: 160g
- Protein: 43g

Cod Fish with Crispy Skin

This is very healthy food and it is really worth to taste. It will be great meal for dinner.

Prep time: 2 minutes | **Cooking time**: 7 minutes | **Servings**:4

Ingredients:

- Coriander
- Green onion
- White onion
- 5 pieces of ginger
- 3 tablespoons of oil
- 5 teaspoons of sugar
- 5 teaspoons of soy sauce
- 1 cup of water
- Sesame oil
- Salt and sugar
- 15 oz of cod fish

Directions:

1. Wash fish and after that dry it.
2. Add salt, 3 teaspoons of sugar and oil to fish and leave for 15 minutes.
3. Preheat the Air Fryer to 350F for 3 minutes.
4. Cook fish during 12 minutes.
5. Then prepare sauce.
6. Pour 1 cup of water in the pan and boil.
7. Add sugar, soy sauce and wait up to 5 minutes.
8. Cook oil in the small pen, add onion and ginger. It will take 10 minutes.
9. Take fish from Air Fryer and out on the dish. Pour with sauce and oil.

Nutrition:

- Calories: 890
- Fat: 16g
- Carbohydrates: 170g
- Protein: 45g

Tasty Fish

Prepare it quickly and delicious. It will not take too much of your time and money.

| **Prep time**: 10 minutes | **Cooking time**: 12 minutes | **Servings**:4 |

Ingredients:
- 1 lemon
- 1 egg
- 4 tablespoons of oil
- 4 fish fillets
- 15 oz of bread crumbs

Directions:
1. Put fish and wash it.
2. Preheat the Air Fryer up to 370F for 4-5 minutes.
3. Mix oil and bread crumbs together.
4. Put the piece of fish fillet into beaten egg. Then put it in the bowl with bread crumbs.
5. Check if fish is covered with bread crumbs completely.
6. Put fish in the Air Fryer and cook it for 12 minutes. The temperature of the Air Fryer should be no more than 360F.
7. Take fish out of Air Fryer and sprinkle it with lemon.
8. Serve it hot, because it is the most delicious when it has been just prepared.

Nutrition:
- Calories: 883
- Fat: 17,5g
- Carbohydrates: 169g
- Protein: 49g

Herb and Garlic Fish Fingers

This recipe can be used by everyone. Try to prepare fish and you will get the perfect dish in the result.

| **Prep time**: 10 minutes | **Cooking time**: 30 minutes | **Servings**:4 |

Ingredients:
- Oil
- 1 cup of bread crumbs
- ¼ teaspoon of backing soda
- 2 eggs
- 2 tablespoons of lemon juice
- 2 tablespoons of cornflour
- 2 tablespoons of maida
- 1 teaspoon of garlic
- ½ teaspoon of pepper
- 2 teaspoons of mixed herbs
- ½ teaspoon of red chili pepper
- ½ teaspoon of turmeric
- ½ teaspoon of salt
- 10 oz of seer fish

Directions:
1. Wash fish and put in the bowl.
2. Add salt, pepper, red chili pepper, lemon juice, herbs, garlic and mix everything.
3. Put aside for 10 minutes.
4. Mix the corn flour, maida, egg and soda in another bowl.
5. Add fish from the first bowl in this one and leave for another 10 minutes.
6. Mix herbs and garlic and cover fish fingers with them.
7. Preheat the Air Fryer to 370F for 2-3 minutes.
8. Put the foil on the backing basket.
9. Then sprinkle the foil with oil and put fish fingers. Cook up to 10 minutes.

Nutrition:
- Calories: 869
- Fat: 19,1g
- Carbohydrates: 130g
- Protein: 46,8g

Grilled Fish Fillet with Pesto Sauce

You can use this recipe of fish every day. It will be great as for the usual meal as for your guests.

| Prep time: 10 minutes | Cooking time: 8 minutes | Servings:3 |

Ingredients:

- 1 cup of olive oil
- 1 tablespoon of parmesan cheese
- 2 pieces of garlic
- 2 tablespoons of pinenuts
- 1 bunch of basil
- Pepper and salt
- 3 big pieces of white fish fillets

Directions:

1. Firstly, preheat the Air Fryer tO 365F.
2. Then wash fish.
3. Cover it with oil and add salt and pepper.
4. Put it in the cooking basket and then put in the Air Fryer.
5. Cook it for 8 minutes.
6. Take basil and grind with cheese, garlic, pinenuts in the food processor.
7. Add salt.
8. Put fish on the dish and cover with sauce.
9. There is no need to serve it hot, so it is possible to wait 10-15 minutes.

Nutrition:

- Calories: 785
- Fat: 8g
- Carbohydrates: 120g
- Protein: 47g

Fish and Chips

You can prepare this meal even if you are too busy. It is very easy and delicious.

| Prep time: 40 minutes | Cooking time: 12 minutes | Servings:4 |

Ingredients:

- ½ tablespoon of lemon juice
- 1 tablespoon of oil
- 10 oz of red potatoes
- 1 big egg
- 1 oz of chips
- 6 oz of white fish fillet

Directions:

1. The Air Fryer should be preheated to 370F for 2-3 minutes.
2. Fish should be divided into 4 pieces.
3. Then rub it with salt, pepper and lemon juice.
4. Leave it for 5 minutes.
5. Grind chips with the help of food processor.
6. Beat egg into the bowl.
7. Put the piece of fish in egg firstly and then into the pieces of chips.
8. Clean potatoes and divide into long pieces. Leave them in water for 25-30 minutes.
9. After that dry the potato and put in oil. Boil potatoes for 5 minutes.
10. After that, the separator should be inserted in the Air Fryer.
11. Put potatoes on one side and fish on another one.
12. Cook for 12 minutes at 360F.

Nutrition:

- Calories: 691
- Fat: 12g
- Carbohydrates: g
- Protein: 41g

Fish Sticks

The easiest and very cheap snack from fish. You can enjoy it any time you wish, because it will not take a lot of efforts to be prepared.

Prep time: 10-15 minutes	**Cooking time**: 12 minutes	**Servings**:4

Ingredients:
- 3 tablespoons of milk
- 1 cup of flour

- ½ teaspoon of black pepper
- ¼ of teaspoon of sea salt

- 1 cup Panko
- 1 big egg
- 1 pound of cod

Directions:
1. Mix milk and egg in the bowl.
2. Put bread crumbs on the bottom of the pan.
3. Add seasonings to milk and egg.
4. Then mix everything well.
5. Put fish and cover it with bread crumbs.
6. After that put the dish in the fry basket.
7. Pour fish with the mixture of egg, milk and seasonings.
8. Cook it for 12 minutes at 390F.
9. Then take it out of Air Fryer and leave for 5-10 minutes, because it will be very hot.

Nutrition:
- Calories: 737
- Fat: 15,9g

- Carbohydrates: 121g
- Protein: 46,8g

Fish Chili Basil

The interesting combinations of ingredients are hidden in this recipe. When you try it, you will not be able to refuse from this fish anymore.

Prep time: 0-5 minutes	**Cooking time**: 16-20 minutes	**Servings**: 4

Ingredients:
- 2 teaspoons of red chili pepper
- 2 tablespoons of soy sauce
- 1 tablespoon of garlic

- 1 tablespoon of oil
- Salt
- Pepper
- ¼ cup and 1 tablespoon of cornstarch

- 6-7 red chilies
- 15 oz of fish fillet

Directions:
1. Mix fish with salt, pepper and 1 cup of cornstarch
2. Preheat the Air Fryer for 3 minutes to 370F
3. Put fish into the basket and cook for 8 minutes. Fish should have golden color.
4. Cook oil (1 tablespoon) and mix it with garlic and red chili, which should be chopped.
5. After that add water to the mixture.
6. Then add chili flakes and soy sauce.
7. Put 1 tablespoon of cornstarch and wait. Sauce should be thickened.

Nutrition:
- Calories: 1157
- Fat: 89,3g

- Carbohydrates: 127g
- Protein: 60,4g

Cajun Fish

Do you have some unexpected guests? Do not worry, this recipe can help in these situations, because it needs only a few minutes of your time.

Prep time: 0-5 minutes | **Cooking time**: 6-10 min | **Servings**: 4

Ingredients:
- 1 tablespoon of lemon juice
- 2 pieces of fish fillets
- 2 tablespoons of refined flour
- 1 tablespoon of red chili flakes
- ½ tablespoon of garlic
- Salt
- 1 teaspoon of stock cubes
- 1 teaspoon of herbs
- 1 teaspoon of red chili powder
- 2 tablespoons of oil

Directions:
1. Grind salt, garlic, herbs, chili powder, stock cubes and chili flakes in the food processor.
2. After that add the refined flour and mix.
3. Divide fillet into the pieces.
4. Rub these pieces with lemon juice.
5. Preheat the Air Fryer. It is required 2 minutes to392F.
6. Then put fish into sauce and after that cook it in the Air Fryer for 7 minutes. The temperature should be 370F.

Nutrition:
- Calories: 1011
- Fat: 73,9g
- Carbohydrates: 26g
- Protein: 60,3g

Steamed Basa Fish

According to this recipe you will get incredibly juicy, delicate and delicious fish. Just try and you will see it.

Prep time: 11-15 minutes | **Cooking time**: 11-15 min | **Servings**: 4

Ingredients:
- Salt
- 1 tablespoon of lemon juice
- 8-10 sprigs of coriander
- 1 teaspoon of cumin
- 1 green chili pepper
- ½ tablespoon of garlic
- ¼ cup coconut
- 2-3 leaves of basil
- 1 tablespoon of black pepper
- 1 tablespoon of oil
- 1 tablespoon of herbs
- 15 oz of Basa fish fillets

Directions:
1. Wash and cut fish into the pieces.
2. Rub it with salt and black pepper.
3. Preheat the Air Fryer for 2 minutes under 350F.
4. Put fish into the backing basket, but firstly put the foil and sprinkle it with 1 tablespoon of oil.
5. Mix the seasoning in the bowl.
6. After that put everything from the bowl into the backing basket on fish and mix it.
7. Cook for 11-15 minutes under 390F. Fish should have brown color.

Nutrition:
- Calories: 1025
- Fat: 78g
- Carbohydrates: 29g
- Protein: 63,5g

Spinach Fish Rolls

You should not visit restaurant to try this meal. It is easy to prepare these rolls at home.

Prep time: 0-5 minutes | **Cooking time**: 8-10 min | **Servings**: 4

Ingredients:

For sauce:
- 1 teaspoon of lemon juice
- 3-4 chopped chives
- 1 tablespoon of oil

For fish:

- 1 teaspoon of red chili flakes
- 1 cup of cheese (paneer)
- 2 teaspoons of lemon juice
- 2 teaspoons of garlic pasta

- 1 teaspoon of mustard pasta
- 1 teaspoon of black pepper
- Salt
- 8-10 Spinach leaves

Directions:

1. Preheat the Air Fryer to 392F for 5 minutes.
2. Chop fish into pieces and put in the bowl.
3. Add lemon juice, pepper, garlic pasta, mustard pasta and mix them together.
4. Put aside for 15 minutes.
5. After that put cheese in another bowl.
6. Add red chili flakes and salt.
7. Put fish on the plate. Then put spinach on it and after that put the mixture of cheese.
8. Roll everything tightly.
9. Put them in the Air Fryer and cook for 8-10 minutes at 370F.

Nutrition:
- Calories: 1080
- Fat: 72g
- Carbohydrates: 49g
- Protein: 69,9g

Lemon Chili Fish with Kurmura

It is very easy in preparing, but you even cannot imagine how delicious this fish is. Prepare and enjoy.

Prep time: 6-10 minutes | **Cooking time**: 16-25 min | **Servings**: 4

Ingredients:

- 2-3 teaspoons of castor sugar
- 1 teaspoon of coriander
- 1 red capsicum
- 15-18 curry leaves

- 1 teaspoon of red chili pepper
- Salt
- ¼ teaspoon of turmeric
- 1 onion

- 3-4 green chilies
- 1 lemon juice
- 2 cups of puffed rice
- 2 pieces of fish fillets

Directions:

1. Wash fish and chop it.
2. Chop onion in the smallest pieces. Add there chopped green chili.
3. Put rice in the Air Fryer and cook it with the cup of water for 10 minutes at 350F.
4. Take rice out of Air Fryer into the bowl.
5. Add the turmeric and red chili pepper. Add the green chili, curry and onion.
6. After that chop red capsicum and add coriander with lemon juice.
7. Put everything in the backing basket and add fish,
8. Cook for 10 minutes at 360F.

Nutrition:
- Calories: 966
- Fat: 72g
- Carbohydrates: 64,3g
- Protein: 36,9g

Grilled Fish Coriander Butter

What can be better than inviting your friends at your place? Only fish, which you can prepare for them and they will enjoy with this delicious meal.

Prep time: 0-5 minutes | **Cooking time:** 1-1.3 hour | **Servings:** 4

Ingredients:
- 6-8 leaves of arugula lettuce
- 4-5 leaves of iceberg lettuce
- 1 tablespoon of olive oil
- 1 teaspoon of red chili flakes
- Salt
- 3 lemons
- 3 tablespoons of butter.
- 18-20 sprigs of coriander
- 2 big pieces of Basa fish fillets

Directions:
1. For preparing the coriander butter, chop the coriander into the small pieces, put it in the bowl.
2. Add salt and pepper and mix them together.
3. Grate the whole lemon and add it to the bowl. After that add butter and mix everything.
4. Take the foil and put one sheet of foil on another one.
5. Put the mixture in the center and create the cylinder with the foil.
6. Leave it for 30 minutes. Put fish in another bowl and add oil, red chili pepper and salt.
7. Put fish in the Air Fryer and cook at 370F up to 10 minutes.
8. Take the leaves of the lettuce and put on the plate.
9. The coriander butter should be chopped into roundels.

Nutrition:
- Calories: 883
- Fat: 77,5g
- Carbohydrates: 34,1g
- Protein: 12,2g

Fish Coconut Chili Fry

Fish turns out to be spicy, tender and very tasty. Also, it has a lot of vitamins and minerals for you.

Prep time: 31-40 minutes | **Cooking time:** 11-15 minutes | **Servings:** 4

Ingredients:
- 2 tablespoons of coriander
- 2 tablespoons of oil
- 2-3 curry leaves
- Salt
- 3 teaspoons of red chili
- 1 teaspoon of turmeric
- 2 small onions
- 1 teaspoon of fennel seeds
- ¼ cup coconut
- 2 pieces of fish fillets

Directions:
1. Wash and clean fish. Leave them aside in the bowl.
2. After that crush the seeds and also leave them, Then crush onions and coconut into pasta.
3. Take the bowl with fish and add curry leaves, salt, red chili pepper, turmeric and coconut.
4. Mix everything very well.
5. Then leave it for 30 minutes in the fridge. After that put fish in the Air Fryer.
6. It should be cooked with oil up to 3-5 minutes at 390F.
7. After that put fish on another side and cook for 3-5 minutes again.

Nutrition:
- Calories: 850
- Fat: 73,9g
- Carbohydrates: 28,1g
- Protein: 15g

Fish Cutlet

Delicious, fragrant and the main advantage - a very simple dish of fish in cooking. It will be great dinner for the whole family.

Prep time: 11-15 minutes	**Cooking time:** 11-15 minutes	**Servings:** 4

Ingredients:

- 1 cup of bread crumbs
- Oil
- ½ tablespoon of turmeric
- 1 egg
- ½ bunch of coriander
- Salt
- 1 tablespoon of corn starch
- 2 green chilies
- ½ teaspoon of garam masala
- 2 bread slices
- 2 teaspoons of bread crumbs
- 17 oz of fish mince

Directions:

1. Take fish mince and put it in the bowl.
2. Put bread in the bowl with water for 15 minutes.
3. After that add bread to fish and mix them.
4. Add one by one turmeric, egg, salt, corn starch, coriander and garam masala.
5. Mix everything in the bowl.
6. Chop the chilies and add them to the mixture.
7. Create cutlets. Put bread crumbs in the bowl and dip every cutlet into it.
8. Cook in the Air Fryer for 10-15 minutes at 392F.

Nutrition:

- Calories: 886
- Fat: 70g
- Carbohydrates: 26g
- Protein: 14g

Fish with Coconut

This simple recipe will be appreciated by your relatives and friends. Everyone will ask for the second portion of this fish.

Prep time: 11-15 minutes	**Cooking time:** 16-20 minutes	**Servings:** 4

Ingredients:

- 2 tablespoons of coconut
- 2 lb of fish fillet
- 3 kokum petals
- 2 curry leaves
- 5-6 green chilies
- 2 tablespoons of garlic
- ¼ teaspoon of turmeric
- 1 lb of shallot
- 2 big cups of coconut
- 1 tablespoon of lemon juice

Directions:

1. Put fish in the bowl and add lemon juice. Mix it well.
2. Put the curry leaves in the second bowl. Chop chilies and add there.
3. Then add turmeric, coconut, shallot to the second bowl and mix everything.
4. Take the backing basket of the Air Fryer and sprinkle it with oil if there is the need.
5. Put fish on it and add to it salt, kokum petals and coconut mixture.
6. Cook 20 minutes at 350F Before serving, sprinkle fish with the coconut oil.

Nutrition:

- Calories: 960
- Fat: 95g
- Carbohydrates: 34,2g
- Protein: 17g

Tuna Thoran

If you say that it is delicious – it means, that you said nothing. The incredibly delicious fish, which can be on your dinner table in a few minutes.

Prep time: 26-30 minutes	Cooking time: 11-15 minutes	Servings: 4

Ingredients:
- Salt
- 2-3 green chilies
- 1 onion
- 3-4 curry leaves
- 2 dry red chilies
- ½ teaspoon of mustard seeds
- 1 cup of coconut
- 3 tablespoons of oil
- ½ teaspoon of turmeric
- 3 teaspoon of coriander
- 3 teaspoons of coconut
- 1 lb of tuna fish

Directions:
1. Mix together oil, red chilies, coriander and turmeric. Grate the coconut and add it to the mixture.
2. After that add the curry leaves and mix everything.
3. Then add dry red chilies and mustard seeds. Chop onion and add there also.
4. Finally put fish, green chopped chilies, salt and half of cup of water.
5. Cook it in Air Fryer during 10-15 minutes. There should not be water when fish is ready.

Nutrition:
- Calories: 925
- Fat: 87g
- Carbohydrates: 41g
- Protein: 19g

Rohu Fish in White Gravy

It is very easy and quick recipe of fish. The result will be great, just try and get the tasty food.

Prep time: 10-15 minutes	Cooking time: 10-13 minutes	Servings: 4

Ingredients:
- 4 pieces of Rohu fish
- 6 teaspoons of sesame pasta
- 4 teaspoons of poppy seed pasta
- ½ teaspoon of cumin seeds
- 1 teaspoon of turmeric
- 2 tablespoons of oil
- Salt
- ½ teaspoon of onion seeds
- 3 teaspoons of mustard pasta

Directions:
1. Rub it with the turmeric and salt. Leave it for 15 minutes.
2. Add oil into basket, put fish there and cook for 4-5 minutes at 392F.
3. Then put fish on another side and do the same for 5 minutes.
4. Fish should have golden or easy brown color. After that put fish on the plate.
5. After that put oil into the backing basket, add onion seeds and cumin seeds. After that add mustard pasta, poppy pasta and sesame pasta. Mix everything well.
6. Add salt and ½ cup of water. After that cook everything for 5-6 minutes in the Air Fryer at 385F.

Nutrition:
- Calories: 916
- Fat: 82g
- Carbohydrates: 43g
- Protein: 17g

Muri Ghonto

It is very tasty dish of backed fish with potatoes. This dish is the dream of every gourmet.

Prep time: 6-10 minutes | **Cooking time:** 11-15 minutes | **Servings:** 4

Ingredients:
- 2-3 Rohu fish
- 2 tablespoons of potatoes
- 2 teaspoons of soaked rice
- 2 teaspoons of rice
- 1 teaspoon of coriander
- 1 teaspoon of garam masala
- 1 teaspoon of turmeric
- 1 teaspoon of red chili pepper
- 2 chopped potatoes
- 2 onions
- ½ teaspoon of cumin seeds
- Salt

Directions:
1. Sprinkle the backing basket with oil and add cumin seeds.
2. Onion should be chopped into small pieces.
3. Add turmeric, red chili pepper, rice and garam masala.
4. Cook it in the Air Fryer for 3-5 minutes at 380F.
5. Then put fish, ½ cup of water and cook at the same temperature for 6-7 minutes. Fish should be soft.
6. Serve with the hot rice.

Nutrition:
- Calories: 934
- Fat: 71g
- Carbohydrates: 47g
- Protein: 13g

Fish and Chips

People that do not have enough time to prepare something will like this recipe. No much time, efforts and money.

Prep time: 6-10 minutes | **Cooking time:** 12 minutes | **Servings:** 4

Ingredients:
- ½ tablespoon of lemon juice
- 1 tablespoon of oil
- 1 middle egg
- 1 oz of tortilla chips
- 7 oz of white fish fillet
- 9 oz of potatoes
- Salt
- Pepper

Directions:
1. Preheat the Air Fryer to 356F.
2. Chop fish into several pieces.
3. Then rub them with some lemon juice, salt and pepper. After that leave them for 5 minutes.
4. Grind chips in the food processor and put them in the bowl.
5. Beat egg in the deep bowl.
6. Put the pieces of fish in egg and later in chips. Potatoes should be sliced.
7. Take one piece of potato, put fish on it and put on it another piece of potatoes.
8. When you have them a lot, put them in the basket and put the basket in the Air Fryer for 12 minutes.

Nutrition:
- Calories: 903
- Fat: 85g
- Carbohydrates: 39g
- Protein: 15g

Fried Cocktail Hot Prawns

If you have the picnic, these prawns will be the great choice. They are very delicious and can will become your favorite meal.

| **Prep time:** 5-10 minutes | **Cooking time:** 8 minutes | **Servings:** 4 |

Ingredients:

- ½ teaspoon of salt
- ½ teaspoon of black pepper
- 1 teaspoon of chili flakes
- 1 tablespoon of ketchup
- 1 table spoon of cider or wine vinegar
- 3 tablespoons of mayonnaise
- 9-11 king prawns

Directions:

1. Preheat the Air Fryer to 353F.
2. Then mix all seasonings together.
3. Add the prawns to spices and mix them together.
4. Check if the prawns are completely covered with spices.
5. After that put the prawns in the Air Fryer basket for 8 minutes.
6. Mix ketchup, cider and mayonnaise together.
7. Serve the prawns with sauce, but wait up to 5-10 minutes, because they are too hot.
8. You will be delighted with the result.

Nutrition:

- Calories: 420
- Fat: 3g
- Carbohydrates: 22g
- Protein: 18,9g

Salmon Quiche

Fish can be not only tasty but also very delicious. If you try this salmon, you will like it forever.

| **Prep time:** 15 minutes | **Cooking time:** 20 minutes | **Servings:** 4 |

Ingredients:

- Black pepper
- ½ tablespoon of lemon juice
- 1 green onion
- 1 teaspoon of mustard
- 2 eggs and 1 egg yolk
- 3 tablespoons of whipping cream
- 2 oz of cold butter
- 4 oz flour
- 6 oz salmon

Directions:

1. Preheat the Air Fryer to 353F.
2. Cop salmon and mix it with lemon juice, salt and pepper.
3. Leave it for some time.
4. Mix butter with egg yolk in the bowl. Add the tablespoon of cold water and place into the ball.
5. Then roll the dough.
6. Put the round dough in the pan.
7. Beat egg into the bowl with salt, pepper, mustard and cream.
8. Place the mixture in the pan and add salmon with onion.
9. Put your pan in the fryer basket in your Air Fryer.
10. Cook for 20 minutes.

Nutrition:

- Calories: 553
- Fat: 10g
- Carbohydrates: 26.6g
- Protein: 20,5g

Bhapa Chingry

Only 30 minutes of your time and you will get the best prawns on the world. Your family will like them and you will need to prepare them almost every day.

Prep time: 11-15 minutes	**Cooking time:** 26-30 minutes	**Servings:** 4

Ingredients:

- 2 tablespoons of cream
- 2 tablespoons of mustard oil
- ¼ teaspoon of sugar
- Salt
- 2-3 green chilies
- ½ teaspoon of turmeric
- 2 teaspoons of mustard pasta
- ¼ cup of coconut
- 1 lb of Jumbo prawns

Directions:

1. Grind the coconut in food processor and add water to get pasta. Clean the prawns.
2. Mix cream, mustard oil, sugar, salt, chopped chilies, turmeric, mustard pasta in the bowl.
3. Add the prawns and mix everything again.
4. Put everything in the basket for Air Fryer and cook for 25-30 minutes at 340F.
5. Turn off the Air Fryer and leave the prawns for 10 minutes.

Nutrition:

- Calories: 458
- Fat: 18,6g
- Carbohydrates: 24,4g
- Protein: 19,8g

Tiger Prawns with Herbs

The incredibly delicious prawns, which do not need a lot of efforts to be cooked. Prepare them for your friends or relatives.

Prep time: 16-20 minutes	**Cooking time:** 26-30 minutes	**Servings:** 4

Ingredients:

- ½ cup of coconut milk
- Salt
- 2 teaspoons of coriander
- ½ teaspoon of turmeric
- 2 teaspoons of red chili pepper
- ½ cup of mint leaves
- 3 green chilies
- 1 big tomato
- 1 teaspoon of ginger-garlic pasta
- 2 medium onions
- 4 cloves
- ½ inch stick of cinnamon
- 2 green cardamoms
- 2 tablespoons of oil
- 20 tiger prawns

Directions:

1. Then add there cinnamon, cloves and cardamoms. Fry in the Air Fryer for 1 minutes at 370F.
2. Then add chopped onion and cook it for 3-4 minutes.
3. Add water and pasta after you cooked onion.
4. Chop the tomato, green chilies, mint and coriander and cook for a few minutes.
5. Then add red chili pepper, turmeric and prawns.
6. Also, it is needed to add ½ cup of water in the basket.
7. Then cook it at the same temperature for 4-5 minutes. Add coconut oil and cook till the prawns are ready.

Nutrition:

- Calories: 439
- Fat: 17,2g
- Carbohydrates: 27g
- Protein: 18,8g

Stir Fried Prawns

Delicious, fragrant and very simple dish with prawns. It is possible to have a great meal if you have any visitors.

Prep time: 11-15 minutes	**Cooking time:** 11-15 minutes	**Servings:** 4

Ingredients:

- 2 tablespoon of coriander leaves
- 1 green capsicum
- 2 onions
- Black pepper
- 2 green chilies
- 1 teaspoon of ginger pasta
- 2 tablespoons of oil
- 1 tablespoon of rice flour
- 1 tablespoon of lemon juice
- Salt
- ¼ tablespoon of turmeric
- 10-13 tiger prawns

Directions:

1. Rub the prawns with salt, lemon juice, turmeric and rice flour and leave it aside for up to 30 minutes.
2. Add one tablespoon of oil to the basket in Air Fryer and cook the prawns for 3-4 minutes at 350F. The prawns should be pink.
3. Then add green chilies and pasta and cook for 1 minute.
4. Then add onion and green capsicum and cook for 3 minutes.
5. Add the prawns and pepper. Mix everything together and cook for 3 minutes.

Nutrition:

- Calories: 445
- Fat: 16,7g
- Carbohydrates: 30g
- Protein: 18,2g

Prawn Green Masala

Do you want to cook something in the summer? You have found it. These prawns will be good snack for you and your family.

Prep time: 6-10 minutes	**Cooking time:** 20 minutes	**Servings:** 4

Ingredients:

- Salt
- 2 tomatoes
- ½ teaspoon of turmeric
- Black pepper
- 4-5 cloves
- ½ inch stick of cinnamon
- 2 onions
- 2 tablespoons of oil
- 3 green chilies
- 6 cloves of garlic
- 3-5 leaves of fresh mint
- 1 bunch of coriander
- 1 lb of prawns

Directions:

1. Rub the prawns with lemon juice and leave for 20 minutes.
2. Grind in the food processor mint, garlic, coriander and water. It should be like pasta.
3. Preheat the oil in an Air Fryer up to 1 minute to 380F.
4. Add in the basket onion, pepper and cinnamon and cook for a few minutes. Onion should be golden. Add the turmeric and chopped tomatoes and cook for 3 minutes.
5. Then add prawns and salt. Mix everything.
6. Cook in the Air Fryer for another 3-5 minutes at the same temperature.

Nutrition:

- Calories: 356
- Fat: 17,2g
- Carbohydrates:291g
- Protein: 18,5g

Hot Garlic Prawns

This meal will be good as for some holiday as for the usual breakfast. You can share the recipe with your friends and enjoy together with the delicious prawns.

Prep time: 6-10 minutes	Cooking time: 16-20 min	Servings: 4

Ingredients:

- Salt
- 2 tablespoons of coriander leaves
- 2 tablespoons of soya sauce
- 1 tablespoon of vinegar
- 2 tablespoons of green chilies
- 1 tablespoon of ginger
- 3 tablespoons of garlic
- 2 tablespoons of oil
- 10-13 prawns

Directions:

1. Take the basket of Air Fryer, add oil and cook garlic with the ginger up to 2 minutes at 370F.
2. Then add prawns, salt and soya sauce. Cook it in the same conditions for 1-2 minutes.
3. Add vinegar and cook for another 2 minutes.
4. Serve with the coriander leaves. Put them on the plate and put the prawns on them.

Nutrition:

- Calories: 366
- Fat: 16,7g
- Carbohydrates: 25,2g
- Protein: 18,3g

Prawn Malai Curry

Do not want to waste your time on something boring? Prepare this curry and get a lot of satisfaction because of it delicious meal.

Prep time: 6-10 minutes	Cooking time: 16-20 min	Servings: 4

Ingredients:

- ½ teaspoon of sugar
- ½ cup of milk
- Salt
- 4 cloves of garlic
- 1 teaspoon of garam masala
- 2 bay leaves
- 3 tablespoons of mustard oil
- 1 tablespoon of lemon juice
- 1 cup of coconut pasta
- 8 peeled and deveined prawns

Directions:

1. The prawns should be rubbed with salt and lemon juice.
2. Leave them for 15 minutes.
3. Preheat the Air Fryer to 350F for 2 minutes.
4. Add oil and bay leaves, garam masala. Cook for 30 seconds.
5. Then add garlic pasta and cook for 1-2 minutes.
6. Put the prawns in the basket and cook for 4-5 minutes. The temperature of the Air Fryer should be the same.
7. Then add milk, coconut pasta and simmer. It will take 3-5 minutes.
8. Add salt, sugar and ½ cup of water. Cook for 5 minutes.

Nutrition:

- Calories: 458
- Fat: 16,3g
- Carbohydrates: 21,1g
- Protein: 17,3g

Prawn Thoran

The prawns, which are cooked in the Air Fryer are not dry, but delicate and tasty. It is recommended to check and to try.

Prep time: 5-11 minutes | **Cooking time:** 5-11 min | **Servings:** 4

Ingredients:

- 1 teaspoon of garam masala
- Salt
- 8-10 curry leaves
- 4 green chili peppers
- 1 piece of ginger
- ½ teaspoon of turmeric
- 1 teaspoon of mustard seeds
- 2 tablespoons of coconut oil
- 2 cups of coconut
- 1 teaspoon of black pepper
- 1 teaspoon of coriander
- 1 teaspoon of red chili pepper
- 1 lb of sliced coconut
- 2 lb of prawns

Directions:

1. Preheat the Air Fryer up to 1 minutes to 390F.
2. Mix in the bowl turmeric, red chili pepper and coriander.
3. Add mustard seeds and coconut.
4. Put oil into fry basket and add the mixture from the bowl in the basket.
5. Cook for 1-2 minutes.
6. Then add green chilies and curry.
7. Add the prawns and change the temperature at 392F for 4-5 minutes.
8. Add salt and ¼ cup of water. Cook for 3 minutes more.
9. Add coconut mixture and garam masala.
10. You will not spend too much of your time and will get the great result.

Nutrition:

- Calories: 356
- Fat: 16,5g
- Carbohydrates: 21,3g
- Protein: 17,8g

Hot Prawns

If you want something delicious, fragrant and useful at the same time, choose hot prawns. This recipe will diversify your menu a lot.

Prep time: 5 minutes | **Cooking time:** 16 minutes | **Servings:** 4

Ingredients:

- 8-10 king prawns
- ½ teaspoon of black pepper
- ½ teaspoon of salt
- 1 teaspoon of chili powder
- 1 teaspoon of chili flakes

Directions:

1. Preheat your Air Fryer to 353F. Take the deep bowl.
2. Put chili flakes, salt, chili powder and black pepper in the bowl and mix them there.
3. Then add the prawns in spices and also mix.
4. After that put prawns with seasonings into the basket for Air Fryer.
5. Cook for 6-8 minutes at the same temperature. The time of cooking depends on the size of the prawns.

Nutrition:

- Calories: 457
- Fat: 16,2g
- Carbohydrates: 33,2g
- Protein: 17,9g

Appetizing Shrimps

New and delicious meal, which will take the first place on your table. Try, enjoy and surprise your relatives or friends.

Prep time: 10 minutes	**Cooking time:** 10 minutes	**Servings:** 2

Ingredients:

- 1 cup of white flour
- 1 cup of Panko

- 1 tablespoon of corn starch
- 1 cup of coconut

- 1 cup of egg white
- 1 lb of large shrimps

Directions:
1. Put mint in the bowl.
2. Mix coconut and panko together in the bowl and leave aside.
3. Then mix the corn starch and flour together.
4. Put egg white in the bowl.
5. Dip mint firstly in flour, then in egg white and after that in coconut mixture.
6. Then put mint in the basket for Air Fryer.
7. After that press the button "M" and scroll down to the "fish" icon.
8. Cook 10 minutes at 662F.
9. After that put them on the plate and wait for 10 minutes. It is possible to decorate them with some vegetables.
10. This meal will be great for the picnic.

Nutrition:

- Calories: 349
- Fat: 16,9g

- Carbohydrates: 24,4g
- Protein: 18,2g

Crumped Prawns

The simple and delicious recipe of air fried crumped prawns will surprise you a lot with it's delicious flavor. This simple and fragrant dish will be appreciated by all your family.

Prep time: 6-10 minutes	**Cooking time:** 21-25 minutes	**Servings:** 4

Ingredients:

- 1 tablespoon of oil
- 7-8 potato chips
- 10-12 fresh coriander sprigs

- 1 lemon juice
- 1 teaspoon of red chili powder
- Salt

- 1 cup of bread crumbs
- 12-16 prawns

Directions:
1. Take the deep bowl.
2. Put the red chili powder, lemon juice and prawns in the bowl and mix everything together.
3. Chol the leaves of coriander and add them into the bowl.
4. Crush chips and add them to the mixture.
5. Then add oil and bread crumbs. Mix everything well.
6. Leave it for 10-15 minutes.
7. Put the prawns and marinade in your Air Fryer and cook for 6-7 minutes at 392F.

Nutrition:

- Calories: 585
- Fat: 20,3g

- Carbohydrates: 37,5g
- Protein: 62,8g

Honey Garlic Prawns

Gently, juicy, fragrant! Everything is very simple and fast, but the result is excellent!

Prep time: 6-10 minutes

Cooking time: 6-10 minutes

Servings: 4

Ingredients:
- Salt
- 1 tablespoon of soy sauce
- 1 red chilies
- 2 tablespoons of sesame oil
- 6-8 cloves of garlic
- ½ tablespoon of honey
- 16-20 middle prawns
- Onion greens

Directions:
1. Put oil in the basket. If you have oil spray, use it.
2. Add garlic and red chili pepper in the basket for Air Fryer.
3. Then add prawns and cook them at 350F for 3-4 minutes.
4. Then add salt, honey and sauce and cook another 2-3 minutes.
5. Add onion greens and mix everything well. Onion should be chopped in the small pieces.
6. Wait up to 10 minutes and then serve.
7. It is possible to decorate them with the leaves of basil or mint.
8. It is easy and delicious.

Nutrition:
- Calories: 600
- Fat: 19,3g
- Carbohydrates: 35,5g
- Protein: 63,8g

Backed Butter Garlic Prawns

Very simple, very fast and very delicious recipe. Indispensable for a quick snack or for a picnic.

Prep time: 6-10 minutes

Cooking time: 10 minutes

Servings: 2-3

Ingredients:
- Black pepper
- 1 lemon juice
- 1 teaspoon of coriander
- 1/3 teaspoon of salt
- 2 tablespoon of garlic
- 1 tablespoon of oil
- 1 oz of melted butter
- 1 lb of prawns

Directions:
1. Wash the prawns
2. Then clean them.
3. Preheat the Air Fryer to 374F for 3-5 minutes.
4. Put the prawns in the bowl.
5. Add all spices one by one and mix everything well.
6. It is important to mix everything, because the prawns should be completely in spices.
7. Put everything in the basket for Air Fryer.
8. Bake for 10 minutes at 374F.
9. The prawns are pink when they are ready.
10. Put them on the plate and wait up to 5-10 minutes. They should not be too hot.
11. Your family will ask for another portion.

Nutrition:
- Calories: 590
- Fat: 18g
- Carbohydrates: 32,4g
- Protein: 53,8g

Seafood Kebab

The delicious and interesting recipe, which you will like. Easy in preparing and it will not take much of your time.

Prep time: 16-20 minutes	Cooking time: 10 minutes	Servings: 4

Ingredients:

- Onion rings
- 2 teaspoons of chaat masala
- Butter
- 2-3 tablespoons of oil
- 1 teaspoon of garam masala

- 1 teaspoon of green cardamom
- Salt
- 1 tablespoon of lemon juice
- 1 inch of ginger
- 2-3 cloves of garlic
- 2 green chilies

- Leaves of coriander
- 1 large onion
- 1 cup of prawns
- 1 cup of melted white fish fillet

Directions:

1. Put minced fish, onion, prawns, coriander leaves, green chilies, ginger, garlic, lemon juice, salt and cardamom powder in a bowl. Then add garam masala and mix everything well.
2. Make some cutlets from this mixture.
3. Preheat your Air Fryer to 354F for 2 minutes.
4. Cook them at the same temperature for 5 minutes on one side.
5. Then turn them on another side and cook for 5 minutes.
6. Add chaat masala on the top.

Nutrition:

- Calories: 595
- Fat: 23g

- Carbohydrates: 36,4g
- Protein: 60,8g

Prawns with Honey

If you wish to prepare something delicious and a bit sweet, try these prawns. The most delicious meal you have never tasted.

Prep time: 6-10 minutes	Cooking time: 10 minutes	Servings: 4

Ingredients:

- Spring onion greens
- Salt
- 1 tablespoon of soy sauce

- 1 red chili pepper
- 15 prawns

- 2 tablespoons of sesame oil
- 1 ½ tablespoon of honey

Directions:

1. Clean the prawns.
2. Put them in the bowl and add red chili pepper.
3. Mix everything well.
4. Add oil to the fryer basket and put the prawns with pepper in the basket.
5. Cook for 3-4 minutes at 390F.
6. Add salt, honey and soy sauce. Cook for 3-4 minutes more.
7. Add the green onions. Leave for 2-3 minutes.
8. Then serve the prawns, but wait 2-5 minutes, because it is impossible to eat the prawns when they are too hot.

Nutrition:

- Calories: 530
- Fat: 23g

- Carbohydrates: 35g
- Protein: 61,7g

Crispy Indian Prawns

Fast, tasty, but at the same time not quite usual due to its serving and the way of cooking a dish.

Prep time: 6-10 minutes | **Cooking time:** 10 minutes | **Servings:** 4

Ingredients:

- 1 tablespoon of chaat masala
- ½ cup of bread crumbs
- 2 tablespoons of oil
- 2-3 tablespoons of gram flour
- ½ cup of yogurt
- 2 teaspoons of red chili pepper
- 1 teaspoon of cumin
- 1 tablespoon of ginger-garlic pasta
- Salt
- 1 tablespoon of lemon juice
- 20-25 prawns

Directions:

1. Put the prawns in the bowl.
2. Add yogurt, red chili pepper, lemon juice, cumin and garlic-ginger pasta.
3. Mix everything well.
4. Beat egg in another bowl. Then add ½ of the bowl with egg to the prawns.
5. Add gram flour and mix it again.
6. Put bread crumbs on the plate and covered the prawns with them.
7. Put oil in the fryer basket and put the prawns there.
8. Cook 5-10 minutes in the Air Fryer.
9. After that sprinkle the prawns with chaat masala.

Nutrition:

- Calories: 570
- Fat: 25g
- Carbohydrates: 31g
- Protein: 58,7g

Chicken and Prawn Rice with Peppers

Do you want to have meat and seafood in the same dish? There is nothing easier, because when you try it, you will not be able to refuse from this meal.

Prep time: 26-30 minutes | **Cooking time:** 16-18 minutes | **Servings:** 4

Ingredients:

- 3-4 cups of chicken stock
- 6-8 florets of broccoli
- 1 teaspoon of paprika
- Salt
- 1 tomato
- 1 onion
- 1 tablespoon of garlic
- ½ tablespoon of oil
- 1 green capsicum
- 1 green paprika
- 1 yellow capsicum
- 1 ½ cup of rice
- 8-10 prawns
- 1lb of boneless chicken

Directions:

1. Add garlic, chopped tomato and onion. Add salt and paprika and mix well.
2. Cook it in the Air Fryer up to 3 minutes at 390F.
3. Add chicken and cook for 1 minute. Then add rice and mix everything well.
4. Add capsicums, broccoli, chicken stock and paprika and cook for 5 minutes.
5. Add the prawns and cook everything for another 3-4 minutes at the same temperature.

Nutrition:

- Calories: 579
- Fat: 29g
- Carbohydrates: 35g
- Protein: 58,2g

Thai Red Prawn Curry

It is not usual dish because of the ingredients. Enjoy with this tasty meal and prepare it for your friends.

Prep time: 11-15 minutes	Cooking time: 16-20 minutes	Servings: 4

Ingredients:

- 5-6 basil leaves
- 4 kaffir lime leaves
- 1 cup of coconut milk
- 4-5 mushrooms
- 1 teaspoon of sugar
- 1 tablespoon of lemon juice
- Salt

- 1 onion
- 2 tablespoons of oil
- 1 tablespoon of rice flour pasta
- ½ teaspoon of powered black pepper
- 4-5 bird's eye chili
- 1 tablespoon of galangal

- 1 tablespoon of lemon grass
- 2 tablespoons of coconut
- 1 tablespoon of red curry pasta
- 1 cup of prawns

Directions:

1. Chop and mix together rice flour, pepper, turmeric, bird's eye chili, galangal, lemon grass and coconut.
2. Add oil in the Air Fryer and put curry pasta.
3. Chop onion and add prawns.
4. Cook it for 5 minutes in the Air Fryer at 370F.
5. Add sugar, lemon juice and salt.
6. Mix everything well.
7. Add some water and cook everything for another 5 minutes.
8. Then add mushrooms and milk.
9. Change the temperature to 350F and cook for 3-4 minutes.
10. Add the leaves of basil and kaffir lime and serve hot.
11. Do not miss your chance.

Nutrition:

- Calories: 638
- Fat: 31g
- Carbohydrates: 37g
- Protein: 54,2g

Sweet and Sour Prawns

If the guests are on the doorstep, then this salad is for you! Fast, tasty, without hassle!

Prep time: 21-25 minutes | **Cooking time:** 11-15 minutes | **Servings:** 4

Ingredients:

- Spring onion greens
- 2 ½ tablespoon of vinegar
- 1 green capsicum
- ½ teaspoon of celery
- 1 tablespoon of ginger
- 1 tablespoon of garlic
- 1 tablespoon of corn starch
- 1 tablespoon of oil
- 1 ½ tablespoon of red chili pasta
- Salt
- Pepper
- ¾ cup of ketchup
- 8-10 prawns

Directions:

1. Put the prawns in the bowl and add salt, ½ spoon of pasta and pepper. Leave for 10-15 minutes.
2. Preheat the Air Fryer to 390F for 2 minutes.
3. Put oil in the basket.
4. Mix the prawns with flour and add them in the basket.
5. Cook for 3 minutes at 350F.
6. The add garlic, ginger, celery and vinegar.
7. Mix everything together and cook for 3-4 minutes.
8. Add the rest of pasta and cook for 5 minutes.
9. Serve with onion rings.
10. This meal will be your favorite one.

Nutrition:

- Calories: 613
- Fat: 30g
- Carbohydrates: 29,7g
- Protein: 53g

Spicy Garlic Prawns

It will be some new and exotic recipe in your collection. Everyone will like the incredibly delicious prawns.

Prep time: 12 minutes	**Cooking time:** 8 minutes	**Servings:** 4

Ingredients:

- Salt
- 1 garlic
- 1 tablespoon on sweet chili sauce
- 1 teaspoon of black pepper
- 1 teaspoon of chili powder
- 1 ½ tablespoon of oil
- 15 prawns
- 1 onion

Directions:

1. Preheat the Air Fryer to 356F.
2. Clean and wash the prawns.
3. After that put them in the bowl.
4. Then add chopped onion, garlic, oil, pepper, chili in the bowl.
5. Mix everything well.
6. After that add salt to the mixture
7. Put everything in the Air Fryer.
8. Cook for 8 minutes at 356F. You will see that the prawns will have the delicious flavor.
9. Then take out if Air Fryer and put in the bowl. The prawns should be warm, but not too hot.

Nutrition:

- Calories: 602
- Fat: 28g
- Carbohydrates: 25,7g
- Protein: 49g

Crispy and Spicy Prawns

Tasty and beautiful. As it was checked, it is instantly eaten!

Prep time: 2 minutes	**Cooking time:** 18 minutes	**Servings:** 2

Ingredients:

- Salt
- Pepper
- 1 tablespoon of Chinese five spices
- 1 tablespoon of mixed spices
- 1 tablespoon of coriander
- 1 lime
- 1 tablespoons of coconut milk
- 3 tablespoons of coconut (dry)
- 1 egg
- 1 lb of prawns
- 3 oz Granola

Directions:

1. Wash and clean the prawns.
2. Grind the granola in food processor.
3. Add all spices in blender and also coconut. Beat egg in the bowl.
4. Put the prawns in egg and later in flour, which you got from food processor.
5. After that put the prawns in the Air Fryer.
6. Cook for 18 minutes at 356F.
7. You will see that they are ready, because all prawns will have golden or even brown color. It means that they are ready.

Nutrition:

- Calories: 591
- Fat: 29,3g
- Carbohydrates: 26,7g
- Protein: 45,7g

Prawns with Wasabi

Do you like spicy food? Enjoy with these prawns, because they are really hot and spicy.

Prep time: 20 minutes | **Cooking time:** 5 minutes | **Servings:** 2

Ingredients:

Wasabi:
- 3 tablespoons of Mayo
- Wasabi pasta

Prawns:
- 2 tablespoons of oil
- 1 egg white
- 2 teaspoons of backing powder
- 4 teaspoons of corn flour
- 10 prawns

Directions:
1. Preheat the Air Fryer to 392F.
2. Mix flour and baking powder together.
3. Put the prawns into flour.
4. Then put them in beaten egg.
5. After that our them in flour again.
6. Cover the prawns with oil and put in the Air Fryer.
7. Cook up to 5 minutes.
8. Mix all ingredients for wasabi.
9. Pour the prawns with sauce.
10. They should be warm and also, it is possible to put every prawn in sauce or just mix them together in the separate bowl.
11. Eat this meal with your family or friends.

Nutrition:
- Calories: 587
- Fat: 22,6g
- Carbohydrates: 27,1g
- Protein: 46,9g

Prawn with Buffalo

Prepare a quick, healthy breakfast for your family. It will not take too much of your time.

Prep time: 70 minutes | **Cooking time:** 10-13 minutes | **Servings:** 2

Ingredients:
- 6-10 prawns
- 2-3 tablespoons of oil
- 2 tablespoon of garlic
- A pinch of salt
- A pinch of pepper
- A pinch of basil
- A pinch of oregano leaves (they should be only dry)

Directions:
1. Mix the prawns in the bowl with all ingredients.
2. Leave them in the fridge for 1 hour.
3. Then put them in the Air Fryer.
4. Bake for 10 minutes at 350F.
5. If you use the huge prawns, increase the time to 12 minutes to cook them completely.
6. In 8 minutes put the prawns on the second side and cook for 3-5 minutes.
7. Then take them and put on the plate. You can serve them with vegetables of leaves of mint or basil. It is up to you what to choose.

Nutrition:
- Calories: 561
- Fat: 19,9g
- Carbohydrates: 26,5g
- Protein: 45,7g

Shrimp with Spicy Apricot Sauce and Coconut

Are you looking for something new and not usual? Taste these shrimps and you will not be able to refuse from them later because of their spacy and delicious flavor.

Prep time: 5-10 minutes | **Cooking time:** 5 minutes | **Servings:** 2

Ingredients:

- 1 tablespoon of vinegar
- ½ teaspoon of soy sauce
- 2 tablespoons of apricots
- Spicy apricot sauce
- 1 beaten egg
- ¼ cup of bread crumbs
- ¼ cup of coconut
- 2 tablespoon of flour
- 3 oz of shrimps

Directions:
1. Preheat your Air Fryer to 352F
2. Take 3 bowls: 1 with beaten egg, 1 with flour and 1 with crumbs and coconut.
3. Put the prawns in flour and then in egg.
4. Then put it in the mixture of coconut and crumbs.
5. Cook for 5-10 minutes. It depends on the size of mint.
6. At this moment, mix all ingredients for sauce. Cook sauce till it is melted well.
7. Serve hot and enjoy.

Nutrition:
- Calories: 581
- Fat: 20,3g
- Carbohydrates: 24,5g
- Protein: 48,3g

Scrumptious Shrimps

Very tasty and easy-it's all about shrimps. Like the main dish or snack – it is up to you.

Prep time: 5-10 minutes | **Cooking time:** 5-8 minutes | **Servings:** 2

Ingredients:

- 2 tablespoons of sweet chili sauce
- 2 tablespoons of oil
- ¼ teaspoon of cayenne pepper
- ½ cup of coconut zest
- ½ cup of bread crumbs
- 2 egg whites
- ½ cup of flour
- 16-20 shrimps

Directions:
1. Prepare 3 bowls.
2. Put flour with salt and pepper in the first bowl and mix them.
3. Beat eggs in the second bowl.
4. In the third bowl mix the coconut, bread crumbs and cayenne pepper.
5. Preheat the Air Fryer up to 400F.
6. Put every shrimp in flour, egg and coconut.
7. Cook for 5-6 minutes at 400F.
8. It is important to divide the cooking in two parts.
9. When mint is ready, put them in the Air Fryer again and cook for 2 minutes.
10. Then add sweet sauce and serve.

Nutrition:
- Calories: 546
- Fat: 25,3g
- Carbohydrates: 23,5g
- Protein: 47,1g

Fried Hot Prawns with Cocktail Sauce

It is very tasty and fragrant homemade dish. The cocktail sauce adds some spicy note to the prawns and you will like it.

Prep time: 10 minutes | **Cooking time:** 6 minutes | **Servings:** 4

Ingredients:
- 1 tablespoon of cider
- 1 tablespoon of ketchup
- 3 tablespoons of mayonnaise
- 10-12 king prawns
- ½ teaspoon of pepper
- ½ teaspoon of salt
- 1 teaspoon of chili powder
- 1 teaspoon of chili flakes

Directions:
1. Preheat the Air Fryer to 350F.
2. Mix all spices in the bowl.
3. Add there the prawns and mix everything well.
4. After that put all prawns with spices in the basket for Air Fryer.
5. Cook for 5-6 minutes.
6. It depends on the size of the prawns. If they are large, cook them for 6-8 minutes.
7. When they are pink, it means that they are ready.
8. Mix the ingredients for sauce in the bowl.
9. Put the prawns on the plate and pour with sauce.

Nutrition:
- Calories: 715
- Fat: 18g
- Carbohydrates: 20,5g
- Protein: 12g

Garlic Prawn Pasta

There is no any need to eat pasta in the restaurant. You can prepare it at home and spend less money.

Prep time: 10 minutes | **Cooking time:** 15 minutes | **Servings:** 2

Ingredients:
- 5 oz of spaghetti pasta
- 10-15 prawns
- 1 tablespoon of butter
- 2 tablespoons of olive oil
- ¼ teaspoon of black pepper
- 1 teaspoon of chili flakes
- ½ teaspoon of chicken powder
- 5 cloves of garlic

Directions:
1. Put spaghetti in the pan with boiled water.
2. Add salt and oil.
3. Cook for 8 minutes. Take the air fry basket.
4. Add 1 spoon of oil, butter and prawns in the basket.
5. Cook for 10 minutes at 356F.
6. Then add spaghetti, chicken granula, pepper, oil, chili flakes and garlic.
7. Mix everything and cook for 5 minutes.
8. When everything is ready, put it in the bowl and decorate with vegetables.

Nutrition:
- Calories: 340
- Fat: 25g
- Carbohydrates: 15g
- Protein: 16g

Backed Drunken Prawns

It is very fast and delicious. Also, this meal is not very expensive and everyone can cook it.

Prep time: 10 minutes | **Cooking time:** 7-9 minutes | **Servings:** 2

Ingredients:
- 1 tablespoon of oil
- ½ teaspoon of sugar
- ¼ teaspoon of salt
- 2 ginger
- 1 clove of garlic
- 1 teaspoon of wolfberries
- 2,5 tablespoon of red wine
- 8 big prawns

Directions:
1. Clean and wash the prawns. Leave them aside.
2. Dry the wolfberries.
3. Leave them in the wine for 10 minutes.
4. Put the prawns in the large bowl and add the wolfberries with the wine.
5. Mix everything well.
6. Place the foil in the basket for Air Fryer.
7. Put the prawns on the foil and pour with the rest of wine.
8. Cook at 356F for 8-9 minutes. It depends on the size of prawns.
9. When they are ready, take them out of Air Fryer and wait till they will be warm, because they will be very hot and it will be impossible to eat them.

Nutrition:
- Calories: 480
- Fat: 18,8g
- Carbohydrates: 13,9g
- Protein: 14,7g

Shrimps with Coconut Sauce

It is difficult to believe that these two things can be combined. But you will enjoy with the incredibly delicious flavor of these shrimps.

Prep time: 30 minutes | **Cooking time:** 8 minutes | **Servings:** 4

Ingredients:
- ¼ teaspoon of pepper
- ½ teaspoon of salt
- ½ cup of coconut
- 1 cup of milk
- ½ cup of bread crumbs
- 2 eggs
- ½ cup of flour
- 16 large shrimps

Directions:
1. Put mint in the bowl.
2. Rub them with salt and pepper.
3. Put flour in the second bowl.
4. Beat eggs.
5. Cover mint with flour and them with beaten eggs.
6. Preheat the Air Fryer to 340F.
7. Put mint in the Air Fryer and cook for 8 minutes.
8. Mix milk and coconut.
9. Put mint on the plate and pour with sauce of coconut and milk.
10. Also, it is possible to pour sauce in the separate cup and just put mint one by one there.
11. You will everything with the satisfaction.

Nutrition:
- Calories: 437
- Fat: 14,9g
- Carbohydrates: 9,3g
- Protein: 19,3g

Cajun Shrimp

This meal can be prepared in a few minutes. Just prepare and enjoy, because it is easy and very delicious.

Prep time: 30 minutes	**Cooking time:** 8 minutes	**Servings:** 4

Ingredients:

- ¼ teaspoon of salt
- ¼ teaspoon of smoked paprika
- ½ teaspoon of seasonings
- ¼ teaspoon of cayenne pepper
- ½ pound of shrimps

Directions:

1. Preheat the Air Fryer to 385-390F for 3 minutes.
2. Add salt, smoked paprika, seasonings, cayenne pepper in the bowl.
3. Mix everything well.
4. Then add mint to the bowl.
5. Mix everything. All shrimps should be in spices.
6. Put mint in the fry basket and cook for 6 minutes.
7. The mix them again and cook for 2 minutes more.
8. After that serve them with some leaves of basil or mint, for example. If you like vegetables, feel free to take them.

Nutrition:

- Calories: 439
- Fat: 14,7
- Carbohydrates: 13,3g
- Protein: 17,9g

Goan Dry Prawns

Pay attention to this meal, because it is easy for preparing and you can cook it if you do not have time. Also, it is tasty and delicious.

Prep time: 30 minutes	**Cooking time:** 8 minutes	**Servings:** 4

Ingredients:

- 3-4 tablespoons of rice flour
- 1 tablespoon of oil
- Salt
- ½ tablespoon of lemon juice
- 1 teaspoon of coriander
- ½ teaspoon of turmeric
- 1 teaspoon of red chili pepper
- ½ tablespoon of ginger-garlic pasta
- 2 lb of prawns

Directions:

1. Wash and clean the prawns.
2. Put salt, oil, coriander, turmeric and chili pepper in the bowl.
3. Add ½ tablespoon of lemon juice and water. You will get pasta.
4. Mix the prawns with this pasta.
5. Put in the fridge for 30 minutes.
6. The preheat the Air Fryer for 5 minutes to 350F.
7. Put oil on the Air Fryer tray.
8. Put flour on this tray. Then put the prawns on flour.
9. Mix them together and cook for 7-8 minutes at 350F.

Nutrition:

- Calories: 455
- Fat: 19,7
- Carbohydrates: 12,3g
- Protein: 16,2g

Mint with Spicy Marmalade Sauce

If you have a party, mint can be the great snack on it. You can be sure, that the delicious marmalade sauce will add the incredible flavor to mint.

Prep time: 10 minutes | **Cooking time:** 20 minutes | **Servings:** 2

Ingredients:
- ¼ teaspoon of hot sauce
- 1 teaspoon of mustard
- 1 tablespoon of honey
- ½ cup of orange marmalade
- ¼ teaspoon of black pepper
- ¼ teaspoon of salt
- ½ teaspoon of cayenne pepper
- ½ cup of panko bread
- ½ cup of coconut
- 8 oz of coconut milk
- 8 big shrimps

Directions:
1. Wash and clean all shrimps.
2. Put milk, salt and pepper into the small bowl and mix everything.
3. In the second bowl add the coconut, salt, pepper and panko.
4. Dip the shrimp in the coconut milk, then in panko.
5. Put mint in the fry basket. Cook in the Air Fryer for 20 minutes at 662F.
6. Put the marmalade, honey, sauce and mustard in the bowl and mix them.
7. Mint should be poured with sauce.

Nutrition:
- Calories: 537
- Fat: 18,2
- Carbohydrates: 13,3g
- Protein: 14,1g

Prawns with Cheese

If you like cheese, then you will prepare these prawns a few times a week. They are healthy and very tasty.

Prep time: 10 minutes | **Cooking time:** 13-15 minutes | **Servings:** 2

Ingredients:
- ¼ teaspoon of pepper
- 4 oz cheese
- Salt
- Pepper
- ½ cup of flour
- 10 tiger prawns
- 2 eggs
- ¼ teaspoon of garlic
- 2 tablespoons of oil

Directions:
1. Wash the prawns in the warm water.
2. Put them in the bowl and leave for some time.
3. Then put eggs in the bowl and beat them.
4. Chop cheese in the small pieces. Rub the prawns with salt, pepper and garlic.
5. Preheat the Air Fryer to 350F for 2 minutes.
6. Then take the prawns and put them in flour and then in egg.
7. Cook in the Air Fryer for 5-7 minutes and then put the prawns on another side and cook for 5 minutes more. Add cheese and cook for 3 minutes.

Nutrition:
- Calories: 680
- Fat: 25,5
- Carbohydrates: 15g
- Protein: 16,1g

Crispy Nachos Prawns

It will be the best choice for the picnic. You will have a lot of energy and also, they are very tasty and delicious.

Prep time: 30 minutes | **Cooking time:** 8 minutes | **Servings:** 2

Ingredients:

- 2 eggs
- 8 oz of nacho flavored chips
- 18 prawns

Directions:

1. Wash and clean the prawns.
2. They dry them. After that leave them aside.
3. Beat eggs in the bowl.
4. Crush nachos in another bowl. They should be tiny.
5. Put every prawn in egg. You should do it step by step with all prawns.
6. Then put it in the nachos.
7. Preheat the Air Fryer to 350F.
8. Put the prawns in the backing basket and cook for 8 minutes.
9. It is possible to serve with sauce cream.
10. If you like, you can decorate them with onion rings or with basil or mint leaves.
11. Just put them on the dish and put the prawns on them.

Nutrition:

- Calories: 648
- Fat: 23,2
- Carbohydrates: 14,5g
- Protein: 17,2g

Honey Tossed Calamari

Enjoy with the tasty seafood and get a lot of vitamins. Try to prepare it and you will get the incredibly delicious snacks.

Prep time: 20 minutes | **Cooking time:** 13 minutes | **Servings:** 3

Ingredients:

- 1 teaspoon of red chili flakes
- ½ cup of honey
- Salt
- Pepper
- 1 cup of flour
- 1 cub of soda
- 1/2lb calamari tubes
- 1 tablespoon of oil

Directions:

1. Wash and clean calamari. Then dry them.
2. Chop them into the rounds. They should not be too thick or too thin.
3. Put them in the bowl with water and add soda.
4. Leave the calamari for 10 minutes.
5. Mic flour with pepper and salt. Put the calamari one by one in flour.
6. Sprinkle the basket for Air Fryer with oil.
7. Put the calamari in the basket.
8. Cook for 10 minutes at 350F.
9. Then add honey and cook for 3 minutes more.

Nutrition:

- Calories: 748
- Fat: 17,2
- Carbohydrates: 13,6g
- Protein: 14,2g

Frito Misto With Chips

The mixture of potatoes and shrimps will be liked by everyone. This delicious seafood will get together the whole family.

Prep time: 20 minutes	**Cooking time:** 35-36 minutes	**Servings:** 3

Ingredients:

Salad:
- ½ cup of parsley
- ½ lemon
- 1 fennel

Sauce:
- ½ cup of lime juice
- 1 teaspoon of sweet chili

- 1 teaspoon of soy sauce
- 1 teaspoon of fish sauce
- ¾ cup of oil

Main dish:
- 6 oz of shrimps
- 4 oz of squid heads
- 7 oz of maya fillet

- 1 cup of bread crumbs
- 1 cup of flour
- 2 eggs
- 1 oz chips
- 1 potato (chips)

Directions:

1. Cut potatoes and chips into the pieces and put in the Air Fryer.
2. Cook for 15 minutes at 392F.
3. Take 3 separate bowls for flour, eggs and bread crumbs.
4. Put fish fillet in flour, eggs and bread crumbs.
5. Then cook for 9 minutes in the Air Fryer.
6. The same for the squid and shrimps, but cook them for 7 minutes.
7. Mix the ingredients for sauce and also for salad.
8. Add salt.
9. Eat with the satisfaction.

Nutrition:

- Calories: 734
- Fat: 35,2
- Carbohydrates: 16,9g
- Protein: 15,4g

POULTRY

Chicken Nuggets

This meal will decorate every dish. It is very tasty and does not take too much time for preparing.

Prep time:10 minutes | **Cooking time**: 10-15 minutes | **Servings**:4

Ingredients:
- Salt
- Pepper
- 1 tablespoon of parsley
- 1 tablespoon of paprika
- 1 tablespoon of oil
- 2 beaten eggs
- 1 tablespoon of ketchup
- 1 tablespoon of garlic puree
- 1 lb of chicken breast
- 2 pieces of wholemeal bread (bread crumbs)

Directions:
1. Mix bread crumbs with paprika, pepper and salt.
2. After that add oil and mix everything well.
3. You should get the batter.
4. Grid chicken in the food processor and then add ketchup, one beaten egg, garlic and parsley.
5. Put the second beaten egg into the bowl.
6. Create cutlets and put them in chicken nuggets and after cover completely with egg.
7. Cook for 10-15 minutes at 392F.

Nutrition:
- Calories: 332
- Fat: 13,7g
- Carbohydrates: 7g
- Protein: 38g

Chicken Kievs

Incredibly delicious pieces of chicken. You even cannot imagine, that it can be so tasty.

Prep time:10 minutes | **Cooking time**: 25 minutes | **Servings**:2

Ingredients:
- Salt
- Pepper
- 1 big egg
- 1 tablespoon of parsley
- ¼ tablespoon if garlic puree
- 4 oz of soft cheese (the flavor of herb and garlic)
- 1 large chicken breast
- Bread crumbs

Directions:
1. Put in the bowl cheese, half of parsley and garlic.
2. Mix everything well.Divide chicken into two pieces.
3. Put the mixture of garlic, parsley and cheese between two pieces of chicken.
4. Then take the bowl and put salt, pepper, parsley and bread crumbs there
5. Beat eggs and cover chicken with it.
6. Then put chicken in bread crumbs.
7. Cook in the Air Fryer for 25 minutes at 356F.

Nutrition:
- Calories: 356
- Fat: 14,7g
- Carbohydrates: 6,5g
- Protein: 38,5g

Chicken Wings

If you are looking for something that can be great for the picnic – then these wings will be the great choice. Spicy and tasty, you will want more them to eat.

Prep time:5 minutes | **Cooking time**: 30 minutes | **Servings**:2

Ingredients:
- Salt
- Pepper
- 1 tablespoon of Chinese spices
- 1 tablespoon of mixed spices
- 1 tablespoon of soy sauce
- 4 chicken wings

Directions:
1. Mix salt, pepper, soy sauce and spices in the deep bowl.
2. After that put chicken wigs in spices and cover the wigs with these spices.
3. Then put the silver foil in the basket for Air Fryer.
4. Put chicken wings on the foil.
5. Add the rest or spices in the bowl.
6. Cook at 356F for 15 minutes.
7. Then put the wings on another side and cook for another 15 minutes at 392F
8. Serve hot and get the delicious chicken wings for your family.

Nutrition:
- Calories: 372
- Fat: 15,2g
- Carbohydrates: 7,1g
- Protein: 37,5g

Popcorn Chicken

Do you want to get the tasty, juicy and fragrant chicken? You will not spend too much of your time to prepare delicious chicken.

Prep time:10 minutes | **Cooking time**: 12 minutes | **Servings**:12

Ingredients:
- Pepper
- Salt
- 2 oz of flour
- 1 egg
- 3 oz of bread crumbs
- 2 teaspoon of chicken spices
- 1 chicken breast

Directions:
1. Put chicken in the food processor and blend it.
2. You should get minced chicken in the result.
3. Take the bowl and put flour there.
4. After that beat egg in another bowl.
5. Mix chicken spices, bread crumbs, salt and pepper in the third bowl.
6. Create the balls from chicken and put them in flour.
7. After that put these balls in egg and cover completely.
8. Then put them in bread crumbs with spices.
9. Put in the Air Fryer and cook for 10-12 minutes at 356F.
10. At a result, you will get the golden chicken balls with the crispy skin.

Nutrition:
- Calories: 362
- Fat: 14,8g
- Carbohydrates: 6,7g
- Protein: 36,8g

Chicken Burger

If you wish to have some simple, but at the same time delicious snack with chicken – then you should prepare this chicken burger. You will be really surprised with this recipe.

Prep time:10 minutes | **Cooking time**: 15 minutes | **Servings**:4

Ingredients:

- 1 tablespoon of paprika
- 1 tablespoon of mustard powder
- 1 tablespoon of Worcester sauce
- ½ cup of bread crumbs
- 1 tablespoons of chicken spices
- 2 oz of flour
- 6 chicken breasts
- 1 egg
- Salt
- Pepper

Directions:

1. Blend chicken with the help of the food processor.
2. After that put chicken in the bowl.
3. Add mustard, salt, pepper, paprika and Worcester sauce.
4. Create the little burgers from chicken and leave them.
5. Beat egg in one bowl.
6. Put flour in the second one.
7. Mix bread crumbs and chicken spices in the separate bowl.
8. Then put your burgers in flour and after that in the bowl with egg.
9. When they are completely covered with egg, put them in the bowl with bread crumbs and spices.
10. After that put chicken in the Air Fryer.
11. It should be cooked for 15 minutes at 356F.
12. When chicken burgers are ready, enjoy them, because they can be the great snack.

Nutrition:

- Calories: 368
- Fat: 14,5g
- Carbohydrates: 6,2g
- Protein: 36,4g

Chicken Strips

A delicious meal from usual ingredients. Your guests will be delighted - all without exception.

Prep time:10 minutes | **Cooking time**: 12 minutes | **Servings**:8

Ingredients:
- Salt
- Pepper
- 2 tablespoons of dry coconut
- 2 tablespoons of plain oats
- 1 teaspoon of chicken spices
- 1 egg
- 2 oz of flour
- 3 oz of bread crumbs
- 1 chicken breast

Directions:
1. Take the bowl and chop chicken into small pieces.
2. Put pepper, salt, bread crumbs, coconut, oats and chicken spices in another bowl.
3. Mix everything well.
4. Then beat egg in another bowl.
5. Take the third bowl and put flour there
6. Take the piece of chicken and put it in flour, then in egg and after that in the mixture of different spices.
7. Cook in the Air Fryer at 360F for 8 minutes.
8. After that put chicken on another side and cook for 4 minutes at 320F.
9. Then enjoy with the tasty and delicious chicken at dinner table.

Nutrition:
- Calories: 364
- Fat: 14,7g
- Carbohydrates: 5,9g
- Protein: 36,9g

Tasty Backed Chicken

This meal is very easy. If you prepare it one time, you will often prepare it for different holidays.

Prep time:10 minutes | **Cooking time**: 18 minutes | **Servings**:4

Ingredients:
- 2 oz of flour
- 2 eggs
- 2 tablespoons of chicken spices
- 9 oz of bread crumbs
- 1 chicken
- 6 oz of cheese

Directions:
1. Chop chicken in the small pieces.
2. Take the bowl and mix spices with flour.
3. But bread crumbs in another bowl.
4. Beat eggs in the bowl well.
5. Take the piece of chicken and put in flour.
6. Then cover it with egg and put in bread crumbs.
7. Sprinkle the Air Fryer basket with oil.
8. Cook for 350F for 15 minutes.
9. Then add cheese and cook for 3 minutes more.
10. You will appreciate this recipe, because it is very tasty.

Nutrition:
- Calories: 371
- Fat: 15,9g
- Carbohydrates: 6,5g
- Protein: 36,8g

Buffalo Chicken

This dish is suitable for a holiday table and for a very ordinary dinner. It will be appreciated as by sportsmen as by gourmets.

Prep time: 20 minutes | **Cooking time:** 16 minutes | **Servings:** 4

Ingredients:
- A cup of bread crumbs
- 1 teaspoon of hot sauce
- 1 tablespoon of hot sauce
- ¼ cup of egg substitute
- ½ cup of plain fat-free Greek yogurt
- 1 tablespoon of cayenne pepper
- 1 tablespoon of garlic pepper seasoning
- 1 tablespoon of sweet paprika
- 1 pound of skinless chicken

Directions:
1. Put one tablespoon of hot sauce and egg substitute in the bowl.
2. Then whisk yogurt and add the teaspoon of hot sauce.
3. Mix everything in the bowl.
4. After that put garlic pepper, bread crumbs, paprika and cayenne pepper in another bowl.
5. Mix everything well.
6. Then put the pieces of chicken in yogurt. Leave them for 2-3 minutes there.
7. After that put every piece of chicken in the crumbs and cover completely.
8. Then put them in the Air Fryer. Cook for 8 minutes at 370F on one side.
9. After that put them on another side and cook for another 8 minutes.
10. Enjoy with the ready chicken pieces. They should have brown color.

Nutrition:
- Calories: 376
- Fat: 15,1g
- Carbohydrates: 6,3g
- Protein: 36,6g

Peppery Chicken

This meal will be the favorite one. It is easy in preparing and too tasty.

Prep time: 10 minutes | **Cooking time:** 20 minutes | **Servings:** 4

Ingredients:
- 1 big egg
- Backing spray
- 1 teaspoon of pepper
- 1 teaspoon of salt
- 2 cups of flour
- 1 cup of buttermilk
- 3/2 pounds of chicken parts

Directions:
1. Wash chicken and put it in the bowl with buttermilk.
2. Mix salt, pepper and flour together in the bowl and add to chicken.
3. Rub chicken with the mixture of spices and four.
4. After that beat egg in the bowl and cover chicken with it. It should be completely covered with egg.
5. Sprinkle the backing basket with the backing spray.
6. Cook at 390F for 20 minutes.
7. As the result, you will get the hot chicken parts with the crispy skin.
8. You will be delighted with this meal.

Nutrition:
- Calories: 376
- Fat: 16,3g
- Carbohydrates: 6,2g
- Protein: 36,1g

Roast Chicken

This ruddy chicken has the crispy crust? This tasty meal is fantastic, you will like it.

Prep time: 10 minutes | **Cooking time:** 50 minutes | **Servings:** 4

Ingredients:

- 2 tablespoons of garlic pepper
- 2 tablespoon of cayenne pepper
- 2 tablespoons of dry mustard
- 2 tablespoons of dried thyme
- ¼ cup of brown sugar
- ¼ cup of Italian seasoning
- ¼ cup of garlic powder
- ¼ cup of onion powder
- ¼ cup of paprika
- ¾ cup of kosher salt
- 4,25 pound of chicken

Directions:

1. Wash, clean and dry chicken.
2. Then rub it with all seasonings.
3. Spray the basket for Air Fryer with the cooking spray and put chicken there.
4. Cook it in the Air Fryer for 30 minutes at 330F.
5. After that put chicken on the other side.
6. Cook it for 20 minutes more.
7. Serve it hot and your family will be glad to eat this meal.

Nutrition:

- Calories: 369
- Fat: 14,9g
- Carbohydrates: 7,1g
- Protein: 34,9g

Fried Crispy Chicken

Roast chicken is a familiar meal. However, note that this recipe contains some interesting nuances.

Prep time: 15 minutes | **Cooking time:** 35 minutes | **Servings:** 4

Ingredients:

- 2 beaten eggs
- ¼ cup of milk
- Pepper
- Salt
- 1 teaspoon of barbecue chicken spice
- 1 teaspoon of basil
- 2 teaspoons of paprika
- 2 teaspoons of garlic
- 2 teaspoons of seasoning salt
- 3 cups of flour

Directions:

1. Put 1 cup of flour in the bowl and add salt and pepper there.
2. Mix everything.
3. Beat eggs in another bowl and add milk there.
4. Put 2 cups of flour in the third bowl and add spices.
5. Put your chicken in flour with salt and pepper, after that cover the whole chicken with eggs and after that with the rest of flour.
6. Then put oil in the basket for Air Fryer and put chicken.
7. Cook it for 35 minutes at 360F, but after 20 minutes you should put it on another side.
8. Just enjoy with crispy, juicy and amazing chicken.

Nutrition:

- Calories: 372
- Fat: 15,3g
- Carbohydrates: 6,3g
- Protein: 36,2g

Chicken Sandwich

Sometimes, you can face the fact that chicken meal is too fry. However, here you will get only delicious and soft chicken.

Prep time: 40 minutes | **Cooking time:** 16 minutes | **Servings:** 2

Ingredients:

- ¼ teaspoon of red pepper for spicy sandwiches
- 7 dill pickle chips
- 4 toasted hamburger buns
- 1 oil mister
- 1/3 tablespoon of oil
- 1/2 teaspoon of celery

- 1/3 teaspoon of garlic powder
- 1/3 teaspoon of black pepper
- 1 teaspoon of salt
- 1 teaspoon of paprika
- 1 teaspoon of powdered sugar

- 1 cup of flour
- 2 eggs
- ½ cup of milk
- ½ cup of dill pickle juice
- 2 chicken breasts (boneless and skinless)

Directions:

1. Cut chicken into the pieces.
2. Then put chicken in the bowl and rub with juice.
3. Leave if for 25-30 minutes.
4. Mix all eggs with milk in the bowl.
5. Put chicken in the bowl with milk.
6. Take another bowl and mix flour with all spices.
7. Then put chicken in this bowl.
8. Spray the backing basket for the Air Fryer with oil.
9. Put chicken in the Air Fryer and sprinkle with oil too.
10. Cook it for 6 minutes at 350F.
11. Then put chicken on another side, sprinkle with oil again and cook for 6 minutes more.
12. Increase the temperature at 360F and cook for 2 minutes for every side of chicken.
13. Serve hot and on buns. Also, it is possible to put 2 chips on every bun and if you like, you can add the ¼ teaspoon of mayonnaise on every bun. You will be surprised how delicious chicken can be.

Nutrition:

- Calories: 369
- Fat: 16,3g

- Carbohydrates: 7,3g
- Protein: 34,8g

Flavorsome Grilled Chicken

It has some unusual ingredients. Meat is juicy and crusty.

Prep time: 5 minutes | **Cooking time:** 1 hour | **Servings:** 4

Ingredients:
- 1 chicken (skinless)
- 1-2 tablespoons of oil or coconut oil
- 2 teaspoons of salt
- 3 teaspoons of celery
- 1 teaspoon of celery seeds
- 4 teaspoons of sugar
- ½ teaspoon of potato starch
- ½ teaspoon of garlic
- ½ teaspoon of onion powder
- 1 teaspoon of paprika
- ½ teaspoon of turmeric

Directions:
1. Wash and clean chicken.
2. Blend flavors with oil and rub chicken with this mixture.
3. Put chicken meat in the Air Fryer.
4. Cook chicken meat for 30 minutes at 360F.
5. Then place chicken on the other side.
6. Cook it for another 30 minutes.
7. After that, leave it for 10 minutes and serve hot.
8. Decorate with parsley and basil leaves.

Nutrition:
- Calories: 366
- Fat: 16,2g
- Carbohydrates: 6,4g
- Protein: 36,8g

Tasty Chicken Legs with Spices

Prepare this chicken. This meal is flavorsome and sharp.

Prep time: 2 hours | **Cooking time:** 20 minutes | **Servings:** 3

Ingredients:
- 1 cup of buttermilk
- 1 tablespoon of oil
- 1 tablespoon of paprika
- 1 teaspoon of cumin
- ½ teaspoon of poultry seasonings
- 1 teaspoon of onion powder
- 1 tablespoon of garlic powder
- 1 tablespoon of black pepper
- 2 cups of flour
- 3 chicken legs

Directions:
1. The legs of chicken should be placed in the container with buttermilk.
2. Then leave them for 2 hours. The poultry will have special note after that.
3. Blend the paprika, cumin, onion powder, black pepper and garlic powder.
4. Take the poultry out of fridge, place in flour.
5. Then cover chicken with buttermilk and two cups of flour.
6. After that set chicken legs in the fry basket in the Air Fryer.
7. Cook it for 20 minutes at 380F.
8. Turn the legs of chicken on the other side every 5-6 minutes.

Nutrition:
- Calories: 385
- Fat: 16,5g
- Carbohydrates: 6,8g
- Protein: 36,4g

Healthy Chicken Tenders

Chicken will be tasty and juice if you use this recipe. However, you even cannot imagine how simply and quickly it can be prepared.

Prep time: 10 minutes | **Cooking time:** 10 minutes | **Servings:** 3

Ingredients:
- Salt
- Pepper
- 1,5 oz of bread crumbs
- 1/8 cup of flour
- 1 big egg
- 12 oz of chicken breasts

Directions:
1. Cut all unneeded fat from chicken.
2. Wash it under the cold water.
3. Rub chicken with salt and pepper.
4. Put chicken in flour and cover it with flour.
5. Take another bowl and beat eggs there.
6. After that put it in beaten eggs.
7. Then cover chicken with bread crumbs.
8. Sprinkle the Air Fryer basket with oil and put chicken there.
9. Cook for 10 minutes at 352F.
10. When chicken is ready, server it hot. You will appreciate this recipe and will prepare it very often.

Nutrition:
- Calories: 388
- Fat: 15,6g
- Carbohydrates: 6,8g
- Protein: 36,7g

Mouthwatering and Peppery Chicken

It is unassuming, juicy, fragrant, tasty dish. Just try it!

Prep time: 15 minutes | **Cooking time:** 30 minutes | **Servings:** 4

Ingredients:
- ¼ teaspoon of garlic salt
- 1 big egg
- 1 egg white
- 3 tablespoons of dry ranch dressing mix
- ½ cup of buttermilk
- ½ cup of bread crumbs
- 4 pieces of chicken

Directions:
1. Blend the dry seasonings with buttermilk.
2. Cover chicken with the combination of spices and buttermilk.
3. Take the bowl and beat one egg and egg white.
4. Then place chicken into this bowl.
5. Take another bowl and put bread crumbs, garlic salt.
6. Mix everything well.
7. Place chicken in the bowl with bread crumbs.
8. Then place it in the Air Fryer and cook at 373F for 15 minutes.
9. After that turn chicken on another side and cook for 15 minutes again. If you like crisper chicken, increase the temperature to 380F and enjoy with crispy skin.

Nutrition:
- Calories: 379
- Fat: 15,5g
- Carbohydrates: 6,7g
- Protein: 35,2g

Crusty Chicken with Curry

Delicious. Fast. Cook this chicken!

Prep time: 10 minutes | **Cooking time:** 22 minutes | **Servings:** 4

Ingredients:

Marinate together:
- 1 egg
- 15 curry leaves
- ½ teaspoon of white pepper
- 1 teaspoon of cumin powder
- 1 teaspoon of sugar

- 1 teaspoon of salt
- 1 tablespoon of corn starch
- 1 tablespoon of curry powder
- 8 chicken thighs

Coating ingredients:

- 1 tablespoon of curry powder
- 4 tablespoons of potato starch
- 8 tablespoons of flour

Directions:
1. Remove all fat from chicken.
2. Place it in the bowl.
3. Then rub chicken with all marinating ingredients.
4. Mix 1 tablespoon of curry powder, flour and potato starch in the bowl.
5. Cover chicken with this mixture and leave for 3-5 minutes.
6. Preheat the Air Fryer to 392F for 10 minutes.
7. Place chicken in the Air Fryer and sprinkle with oil.
8. Cook for 10 minutes. After that place on another side and cook for 12 minutes.

Nutrition:
- Calories: 387
- Fat: 17,3g
- Carbohydrates: 6,5g
- Protein: 36,7g

Piquant and Tempting Wings

Flavorsome and interesting meat. It is aromatic and completely unusual.

Prep time: 10 minutes | **Cooking time:** 25 minutes | **Servings:** 4

Ingredients:
- ½ teaspoon of salt
- ½ cup of butter

- ½ cup of hot sauce
- ½ cup of flour

- 8 chicken wings

Directions:
1. Preheat the Air Fryer to 345F.
2. Take the bowl and blend flour and salt together.
3. Then place chicken wings in flour and cover with it.
4. Place chicken wings in this basket and put it in the Air Fryer.
5. You should cook chicken wings for 25 minutes, but it is needed to shake them for every 5 minutes.
6. Melt butter with sauce and blend them.
7. When chicken wings are ready, place them on the plate and pour with sauce.
8. Mix the wings with sauce.

Nutrition:
- Calories: 367
- Fat: 15,4g
- Carbohydrates: 6,4g
- Protein: 36,5g

Scrumptious Chicken with Sweat Honey

Do you want to surprise your friends and relatives? Prepare tender and flavorsome chicken right now.

Prep time: 10 minutes	**Cooking time:** 15-16 minutes	**Servings:** 4

Ingredients:
- ½ cup of honey
- ½ cup of barbecue sauce
- ½ cup of flour
- ½ teaspoon of pepper
- ½ teaspoon of salt
- 8 chicken wings

Directions:
1. Preheat your Air Fryer to 350F.
2. Wash the wings.
3. Put flour, salt and pepper in the deep bowl.
4. Then put chicken wings in the bowl and cover them with flour and spices.
5. Cook chicken wings in the Air Fryer for 7 minutes. After that shake them and cook for 5 minutes. The temperature should be 350F.
6. Mix the barbecue sauce and honey in the bowl.
7. Cover every piece of chicken with the honey and sauce.
8. After that cook for 3-4 minutes. The incredibly delicious chicken wings will melt in the mouth.

Nutrition:
- Calories: 373
- Fat: 15,4g
- Carbohydrates: 6,5g
- Protein: 35,3g

Marinated Chicken Wings

Delicate juicy chicken with a piquant taste. A meal that does not require a side dish.

Prep time: 10 minutes	**Cooking time:** 17-19 minutes	**Servings:** 3-4

Ingredients:
- 1 teaspoon of salt
- 1 teaspoon of pepper
- 1 tablespoon of paprika
- ½ cup of oil
- 7-8 chicken wings

Directions:
1. Preheat the Air Fryer to 390F.
2. Mix pepper, salt, paprika and oil in the deep bowl.
3. Put the wings in the bowl and mix everything well. Then leave them aside for some time.
4. Sprinkle the frying basket for the Air Fryer with oil.
5. Put chicken wings in the basket and fry for 10-12 minutes.
6. Then shake them a lot and cook for another 7 minutes.
7. Take out of Air Fryer and eat them with your family. You will see, that all members of your family will like them.
8. Cook and enjoy.

Nutrition:
- Calories: 365
- Fat: 15,7g
- Carbohydrates: 6,4g
- Protein: 36,3g

Appetizing Wings with Cheese and Garlic

You will like these wings. Just no words from admiration! This is the best meal that came up!

| **Prep time:** 15 minutes | **Cooking time:** 25minutes | **Servings:** 4 |

Ingredients:

- ¼ teaspoon of paprika
- ½ teaspoon of pepper
- ½ teaspoon of salt
- 1 teaspoon of oregano
- 1 teaspoon of rosemary
- 2 cloves of garlic
- ¼ cup of butter
- ¼ cup of parmesan
- 32 oz of chicken wings

Directions:

1. Preheat the Air Fryer to 390F.
2. Put chicken wings in the Air Fryer and cook them for 25 minutes.
3. Mix garlic and butter and melt these ingredients.
4. Add paprika, salt, pepper, oregano and rosemary to butter and garlic and mix everything well.
5. Take chicken wings out of Air Fryer.
6. Put them on the plate and pour with sauce.
7. Add chicken on the top of chicken wings.
8. Serve and eat, because they are really amazing.

Nutrition:

- Calories: 376
- Fat: 15,2g
- Carbohydrates: 5,9g
- Protein: 36,8g

Dry Rub Chicken Wings

Everyone dreams about a festive meal, which is prepared itself. Also, it should be appetizing, delicious, juicy and fragrant. That is it. Just try and prepare.

| **Prep time:** 13 minutes | **Cooking time:** 20 minutes | **Servings:** 4 |

Ingredients:

- ½ teaspoon of salt
- ½ teaspoon of black pepper
- ½ teaspoon of chili pepper
- 1 teaspoon of garlic powder
- 32 oz of wings

Directions:

1. Preheat the Air Fryer to 350F.
2. Then wash and clean chicken wings.
3. Put them in the bowl.
4. Take another bowl and put salt, pepper, chili pepper and garlic powder.
5. Mix everything well.
6. Put chicken wings in the bowl and cover them completely with the mixture.
7. Cook them in the Air Fryer for 20 minutes.
8. If you wish to have golden color, shake chicken wings every 5 minutes.
9. After that you will see, that it the easiest and the most delicious meal.

Nutrition:

- Calories: 381
- Fat: 16,4g
- Carbohydrates: 5,7g
- Protein: 35,9g

Yummy and Fiery Chicken Wings

Chicken wings, which are prepared according to this recipe will have a crispy crust. You should try it.

Prep time: 15 minutes | **Cooking time:** 18 minutes | **Servings:** 4

Ingredients:
- ½ teaspoon of salt
- 4 cloves of garlic
- ¼ cup of butter
- ¼ cup of honey
- ¾ cup of flour
- 30 ox of chicken wings

Directions:
1. Preheat the Air Fryer to 350F.
2. Mix salt and flour in one deep bowl.
3. Put chicken wings in this bowl and cover with this mixture.
4. After that sprinkle the Air Fryer basket with oil and put chicken wings in it.
5. Cook them up to 7 minutes.
6. Shake meat and cook for 5 minutes more.
7. Melt garlic, butter and honey in the small pan.
8. Take chicken wings on the plate.
9. You can decorate them with basil leaves.
10. After that, cover chicken wings with the honey sauce.

Nutrition:
- Calories: 359
- Fat: 15,9g
- Carbohydrates: 6g
- Protein: 36,9g

Fried and Hot Chicken

The delicious, tender chicken, baked in its own juice. This meal is for the whole family. It is prepared easily and quickly.

Prep time: 15 minutes | **Cooking time:** 18 minutes | **Servings:** 4

Ingredients:
- 1 teaspoon of cumin
- 1/2 tablespoon of paprika
- 1 teaspoon of onion powder
- 1/3 teaspoon of creole seasonings
- 1 tablespoon of garlic powder
- ½ teaspoon of salt
- ¼ teaspoon of black pepper
- 2 cups of flour
- 1 cup of buttermilk
- 8-10 chicken Drumettes

Directions:
1. Place chicken in buttermilk and leave it for some time.
2. Blend flour and all seasonings in the separate bowl.
3. Take chicken from buttermilk and cover with seasonings.
4. Then put again in the bowl with buttermilk and again cover with spices and flour.
5. Place every piece of chicken in the Air Fryer.
6. Cook up to 20 minutes at 360F.
7. It is important to turn chicken wings on another side every 5-6 minutes.

Nutrition:
- Calories: 369
- Fat: 15,6g
- Carbohydrates: 6,2g
- Protein: 36,6g

Backed Buffalo Wings

Home fast food is always better and tastier! Therefore, just cook a delicious chicken in bread crumbs!

Prep time: 15 minutes	**Cooking time:** 26 minutes	**Servings:** 4

Ingredients:
- 1 teaspoon of salt
- ½ cup of butter
- ½ cup of hot sauce
- ½ cup of flour
- 4 chicken wings

Directions:
1. Preheat the Air Fryer to 350F.
2. Wash and clean chicken wings.
3. After that take a big bowl.
4. Mix flour and salt.
5. Put chicken wings in this bowl. Rub them with flour and salt well.
6. Cook in the Air Fryer for 25 minutes.
7. Mix butter with sauce and cover chicken with this mixture.
8. Cook for 1 minutes more. Then take out of Air Fryer.
9. Serve it hot and also, it is possible with the leaves of mint or basil. You will see how delicious it is.
10. Cook this meal for your relatives and friends.

Nutrition:
- Calories: 380
- Fat: 17g
- Carbohydrates: 6,5g
- Protein: 36,7g

Sweat and Scrumptious Chicken Wings

These wings are unique. They are juicy, flavor and very tasty.

Prep time: 10 minutes	**Cooking time:** 16 minutes	**Servings:** 4

Ingredients:
- ½ cup of honey
- ½ cup of sauce
- ½ cup of flour
- ½ teaspoon of salt
- ½ teaspoon of pepper
- 4 chicken wings

Directions:
1. Preheat the Air Fryer to 376F.
2. Cut chicken wings into 2-3 pieces.
3. Wash and clean them.
4. Rub chicken wings with salt, pepper and flour.
5. Sprinkle the backing basket with oil and place chicken wings in the basket.
6. Cook then for 8 minutes.
7. After that place them on another side and cook for another 5 minutes.
8. Mix honey, butter and sauce in the bowl and cover chicken with this mixture.
9. Shake chicken wings well and cook them for 3 minutes.

Nutrition:
- Calories: 381
- Fat: 16,8g
- Carbohydrates: 6,4g
- Protein: 36,5g

Flavorsome and Piquant Wings with Marinade

Chicken in this marinade is incredibly delicious. You can make it spicy or soft – it depends only on you.

Prep time: 10 minutes | **Cooking time:** 20 minutes | **Servings:** 4

Ingredients:
- ¼ teaspoon of salt
- ¼ teaspoon of pepper
- ¼ teaspoon of sweet paprika
- ¼ teaspoon of hot paprika
- ½ cup of oil
- 4 chicken wings

Directions:
1. Preheat the Air Fryer to 392F.
2. Take the bowl and mix the paprika, pepper, salt and oil together.
3. Rub chicken wings with all these spices well.
4. Sprinkle the Air Fryer with oil.
5. Put chicken wings there.
6. Cook for 8 minutes at 392F.
7. Then put hem om another side and cook for 12 minutes more at the same temperature.
8. When chicken wings are ready, you will see, that they are golden.
9. Serve them hot and enjoy with the wine.

Nutrition:
- Calories: 379
- Fat: 16,4g
- Carbohydrates: 6,5g
- Protein: 36,3g

Chicken Wings with Garlic and Cheese

If you like garlic, this recipe will be your favorite one. It is very tasty and delicious.

Prep time: 10 minutes | **Cooking time:** 23-24 minutes | **Servings:** 4

Ingredients:
- 1 tablespoon of paprika
- ½ tablespoon of salt
- 2 tablespoons of oregano
- 1,5 tablespoon of rosemary
- 2 cloves of garlic
- ¼ cup of butter
- ¼ cup of cheese
- 2 pounds of chicken wings

Directions:
1. Preheat the Air Fryer to 390F.
2. Sprinkle the backing basket with oil.
3. Put chicken wings in the Air Fryer and cook for 12 minutes.
4. Then shake them well and cook for 12 minutes again.
5. Melt butter and add garlic to it.
6. After that add paprika, salt, oregano, rosemary to sauce.
7. When chicken wings are ready, cover then with sauce.
8. Decorate everything with cheese and enjoy.

Nutrition:
- Calories: 384
- Fat: 15,9g
- Carbohydrates: 6,7g
- Protein: 36,6g

Scrumptious and Dry Chicken Wings

Pepper and spices create the great combination together with chicken wings. It is flavorsome meat.

| **Prep time:** 10 minutes | **Cooking time:** 20 minutes | **Servings:** 4 |

Ingredients:

- ½ tablespoon of black pepper
- ½ tablespoon of chili powder
- ½ tablespoon of garlic powder
- ½ teaspoon of salt
- 12 chicken wings

Directions:

1. Mix salt, pepper, garlic and chili powder in the bowl.
2. Rub chicken wings with this mixture.
3. Preheat the Air Fryer to 350F.
4. Sprinkle the backing basket with olive oil spray and put chicken wings in it.
5. Place the basket in the Air Fryer and cook 10 minutes.
6. Then shake chicken wings. Cook them for 10 minutes again.
7. You will get the great snack, which you can eat any time you wish.

Nutrition:

- Calories: 382
- Fat: 15,7g
- Carbohydrates: 6,4g
- Protein: 36,4g

Spicy and Appetizing Chicken

Delicious and very hearty meal. You can make it for dinner and breakfast.

| **Prep time:** 10 minutes | **Cooking time:** 30 minutes | **Servings:** 4 |

Ingredients:

- 1 tablespoon of olive oil
- 1-2 cup of cheese
- 2 tablespoons of butter
- 1 cup of heavy cream
- 7-8 gloves of garlic
- Salt
- Pepper
- 3 cups of chicken stock
- 2 cups of spinach leaves
- 4 boneless chicken breasts
- 1 lb of pasta

Directions:

1. Rub chicken with salt and pepper.
2. Take the backing basket and sprinkle with oil.
3. Put chicken there.
4. Add garlic and chicken stock.
5. Then add pasta to the rest of ingredients.
6. Add butter and cream to chicken.
7. Cook everything for 30 minutes at 320F.
8. After that add cheese and blend everything well.
9. Then chop chicken into small pieces.

Nutrition:

- Calories: 390
- Fat: 17g
- Carbohydrates: 6,9g
- Protein: 36,9g

Scrumptious Chicken Meal with Noodles

It is very tasty and juicy chicken meal. You can prepare it for the picnic or when you are waiting for guests.

Prep time: 10 minutes

Cooking time: 9-10 minutes

Servings: 4

Ingredients:
- ¼ cup of corn starch
- ½ cup of chicken stock
- 10 oz of egg noodles
- 1 cup of marsala wine
- 2 cloves of garlic
- 1 tablespoon of oil
- Salt
- 4 boneless chicken breasts
- 1 cup of mushrooms

Directions:
1. Rub chicken with salt.
2. Then add oil to the Air Fryer basket.
3. Put chicken in the basket and add chopped garlic.
4. Then add mushrooms, egg noodles and wine.
5. Mix everything well.
6. Cook for 7 minutes at 350F.
7. Then mix chicken stock and corn starch.
8. Pour chicken with the stock.
9. Cook chicken for another 2 minutes.
10. Serve it hot and you will see, that mushrooms and wine can add some special note to the meal.

Nutrition:
- Calories: 388
- Fat: 16,5g
- Carbohydrates: 6,7g
- Protein: 36,2g

Yummy Grilled Chicken

Extremely delicious, chicken is very juicy and sauce deserves special attention. The dish is prepared simply and relatively quickly.

Prep time: 10 minutes

Cooking time: 18 minutes

Servings: 4

Ingredients:
- 2 lbs of skinless, boneless chicken breast
- 1 tablespoon of chopped chives
- 8 ox of cream cheese
- 12 pieces of bacon

Directions:
1. Cut chicken into small pieces.
2. Cook bacon in the Air Fryer at 350F for 5 minutes.
3. Put bacon in the bowl.
4. Mix 1 tablespoon of chopped chives with cream cheese well.
5. Then put the mixture on every piece of chicken, add bacon and roll them.
6. After that sprinkle the fry basket with oil.
7. Put the rolls into the basket and cook for 13 minutes at 350F.
8. Your children will like these rolls, because they are very tasty.

Nutrition:
- Calories: 379
- Fat: 15,5g
- Carbohydrates: 7,7g

Parmesan Chicken

The incredibly delicious and tasty chicken meal. One piece of this chicken and you will not want to eat anything else.

Prep time:31-40 minutes	Cooking time: 41-50 minutes	Servings: 4

Ingredients:

- 1 teaspoon of black pepper powder
- 1 egg
- 6 tablespoons of oil
- 2 teaspoons of red chili
- Salt
- 2 fresh sprigs of thyme
- 2 fresh sprigs of rosemary
- 4-5 sprigs of parsley
- 8-10 cloves of garlic
- 6-8 pieces of white bread
- 2 tablespoon of cheese
- 3 oz of chopped cheese
- 2 chicken breasts

Directions:

1. Mix the pieces of bread with the 2 tablespoons of cheese, garlic, parsley, rosemary, thyme, salt, black pepper and chili pepper. Grid them with the help of the food processor.
2. Mix 3 tablespoons of oil with egg.
3. Then cover chicken pieces with egg and after that rub them with the mixture of spices.
4. Then preheat the Air Fryer to 390F.
5. Sprinkle the fry basket with oil and put chicken in the Air Fryer.
6. Cook for 7-8 minutes.
7. After that decrease the temperature at 320F and cook at 10 minutes.
8. Then just serve hot and you will see how quickly chicken will be eaten.

Nutrition:

- Calories: 1880
- Fat: 124,2g
- Carbohydrates: 89,4g
- Protein: 108,2g

Piquant Chicken

Minimum of products! Tender and juicy chicken! Very tasty and satisfying!

Prep time: 35 minutes	Cooking time: 15 minutes	Servings: 2

Ingredients:

- 2 tablespoons of oil
- 2 chicken drumsticks
- ¼ teaspoon of cayenne pepper
- ¼ teaspoon of paprika
- ¼ teaspoon of oregano
- ¼ teaspoon of garlic powder
- 1/3 teaspoon of onion powder

Directions:

1. Place chicken in the bowl.
2. Then rub chicken with cayenne pepper, paprika, oregano, garlic powder, onion powder.
3. Leave chicken for 30 minutes in the bowl.
4. Preheat the Air Fryer to 400F.
5. Cook chicken for 15 minutes at this temperature.
6. Then enjoy with delicious drumsticks with your friends and relatives.
7. Serve hot with sauces.
8. Decorate with mint leaves, vegetables and basil leaves.

Nutrition:

- Calories: 680
- Fat: 103,2g
- Carbohydrates: 69,4g
- Protein: 98,2g

Cooked Chicken Wings

It is possible to prepare these wings and you will not be tired of them. It is not very difficult for preparing and also it is very delicious.

Prep time: 10 minutes	**Cooking time:** 28 minutes	**Servings:** 4

Ingredients:
- ¼ cup of wings sauce
- 2 lb of chicken wings
- ¼ teaspoon of salt
- ½ teaspoon of pepper
- ½ teaspoon of oregano
- ½ teaspoon of chili
- ½ teaspoon of cumin

Directions:
1. Preheat the Air Fryer to 362F.
2. Then sprinkle the frying basket with oil.
3. Rub chicken wings with salt, pepper, chili, oregano and cumin.
4. Cook chicken wings for 28 minutes.
5. You should shake every 5 minutes the wings in the basket.
6. After that put chicken wings in the bowl.
7. Cover chicken wings with sauce.
8. Serve hot and decorate with fresh leaves of mint.

Nutrition:
- Calories: 590
- Fat: 92,2g
- Carbohydrates: 63,4g
- Protein: 88,2g

Wonderful Chicken with Parmesan

Flavorsome, fast and great recipe. As children as adult will like them.

Prep time: 10 minutes	**Cooking time:** 17-18 minutes	**Servings:** 4

Ingredients:
- 1 teaspoon of black pepper
- 1 egg
- 6 tablespoons of oil
- ½ teaspoon of black pepper
- ½ teaspoon of chili pepper
- 4-5 sprigs of parsley
- 1-2 sprigs of rosemary
- 2 sprigs of thyme
- 8-10 cloves of garlic
- 6-8 pieces of bread
- 2 tablespoons of parmesan
- 2 pieces of chicken fillet

Directions:
1. Mix all seasonings with bread in the bowl.
2. Place them in the food processor and grind everything.
3. Add 3 tablespoons of oil and mix everything again.
4. Then chop chicken fillet into small pieces.
5. Rub them with the mixture of the different spices.
6. Preheat the Air Fryer to 380F.
7. Cook chicken in the Air Fryer for 7-8 minutes.
8. Then shake chicken and cook for 10 minutes at 10 minutes.

Nutrition:
- Calories: 580
- Fat: 62,2g
- Carbohydrates: 53,4g
- Protein: 78,2g

Flavorsome Salad with Chicken

If you wish to prepare delicious, spicy and aromatic salad, you have made the right choice. It does not take too much of your time.

| **Prep time:** 10-15 minutes | **Cooking time:** 15-17 minutes | **Servings:** 4 |

Ingredients:

- ½ teaspoon of salt
- 1 inch of lemon juice
- ½ teaspoon of pepper
- ½ tablespoon of thai green pasta
- 2 tablespoons of rice vinegar

- 2 tablespoon of oil
- 2 tablespoons of peanuts
- ¼ cup of coriander leaves
- Spring onion
- 1 medium of red capsicum
- 1 medium carrot
- 1 medium cucumber

- 1 lettuce iceberg
- 2 tablespoons of green curry pasta
- 2 teaspoons of lemon juice
- ¼ cup of quinoa
- 2 chicken breasts

Directions:

1. Cut chicken in the pieces. Add lemon juice, curry pasta, salt and pepper.
2. Leave for 10-15 minutes.
3. Preheat the Air Fryer to 380F.
4. Mix Thai green pasta, rice vinegar and oil.
5. Take the lettuce, cucumber, carrot, capsicum, green leaves, coriander and peanuts. Mix everything well.
6. Sprinkle the basket with oil.
7. Put chicken in the Air Fryer and cook for 2 minutes.
8. Then shake them and cook for another 2 minutes.
9. Put the foil in the Air Fryer, put chicken on it and cover with the mixture of vegetables.
10. Cook for 10-13 minutes.
11. When chicken is ready, put it on the plate and decorate with the lettuce.

Nutrition:

- Calories: 237
- Fat: 73,2g

- Carbohydrates: 50,4g
- Protein: 64,2g

Peppery Backed Chicken

Delicate chicken in crispy crust. Incredibly tender and juicy meat with a light piquant note and a crispy crust.

Prep time: 3-4 hours | **Cooking time:** 10-15 min | **Servings:** 4

Ingredients:

- ½ tablespoon of oil
- 1 cup of flour
- 2 eggs
- 1 teaspoon of chaat masala
- 1 lemon

- 1-2 tablespoons of garlic pasta
- Salt
- 1-2 teaspoons of chili pepper
- 25-30 curry leaves

- 1 cup of sago
- 2 boneless chicken breasts

Directions:

1. Preheat the air fry to 350F.
2. Chop curry leaves and put them in the bowl.
3. Then add chili, salt, garlic and lemon.
4. Cover chicken with these spices. Leave for 3-4 hours.
5. After that mix sago, chili powder and chaat masala.
6. Beat eggs in the bowl.
7. Put flour on the plate.
8. Then put chicken in flour and then in egg.
9. Put chicken in the Air Fryer and cook for 10-15 minutes at 350F.
10. You will get tasty and delicious meat in the result and your big company will like it.

Nutrition:

- Calories: 582
- Fat: 89,2g

- Carbohydrates: 61,4g
- Protein: 62,2g

Chicken with Herbs

Chicken, baked with aromatic herbs is suitable as for a family dinner as for a holiday meal.

Prep time: 16-20 minutes | **Cooking time:** 6-10 min | **Servings:** 4

Ingredients:

- 1 tablespoon of balsamic vinegar
- 2 teaspoons of red chili flakes
- 2 teaspoon of dry herbs

- ¼ teaspoon of black pepper
- ¼ teaspoon of salt
- 1 cup of capsicum
- ½ medium zucchini

- 2 tablespoon of oil
- 2 chicken breasts

Directions:

1. Preheat the Air Fryer to 340F.
2. Chop chicken in the pieces.
3. Spray the Air Fryer basket with oil.
4. Put chicken on the basket. Then put pieces of zucchini.
5. Then sprinkle meat with salt, pepper, herbs and balsamic vinegar.
6. Cook for 6-10 minutes at 350F.

Nutrition:

- Calories: 539
- Fat: 82,2g

- Carbohydrates: 65,4g
- Protein: 61,2g

Appetizing Chicken with Citrus Salad

This meal can be prepared by everyone. It takes not too much of your time and efforts.

Prep time: 16-20 minutes | **Cooking time:** 11-15 min | **Servings:** 4

Ingredients:

- Fresh coriander leaves
- 1-2 tablespoons of feta cheese
- 1 tablespoon of peanuts
- 16 fresh arugula leaves
- 1 tablespoon of lemon juice
- 1 tablespoon of maple juice
- 1 teaspoon of mustard pasta
- ¼ cup of oil
- 2 teaspoons of chili pepper
- Salt
- 2 tablespoons of garlic
- 3-4 pomelo segments
- 2 medium oranges
- 4 chicken breasts

Directions:

1. Chop chicken and put in the bowl.
2. Add garlic, oil, mustard pasta, chili pepper, salt, garlic and black pepper.
3. Then put everything in the Air Fryer.
4. Cook for 3-4 minutes.
5. Then take pepper, lemon juice and maple juice. Then add ¼ cup of oil.
6. Put chicken in the Air Fryer and cook for 5 minutes.
7. Decorate it with arugula leaves, pomelo slices, orange segments, feta cheese and pine nuts.

Nutrition:

- Calories: 541
- Fat: 63,2g
- Carbohydrates: 51,4g
- Protein: 60,2g

Delicious Pesto Chicken

This meal will be great for holiday. You will see that it is possible to prepare in the short time.

Prep time: 16-20 minutes | **Cooking time:** 11-15 min | **Servings:** 4

Ingredients:

- Herbs for sprinkle
- 6 oz of cheese
- ¼ tablespoon of black pepper
- ½ teaspoon of salt
- 2 medium tomatoes
- 9 oz of chicken fillet
- ½ cup of pesto sauce

Directions:

1. Preheat the Air Fryer to 390F.
2. Chop tomatoes in the pieces and mix with salt and pepper.
3. Cut chicken in the slices and after that mix everything well.
4. Put the pesto sauce on chicken.
5. Also, sprinkle salt and pepper.
6. Put everything in the Air Fryer and cook for 8-10 minutes.
7. Cover it with the herbs and cheese.
8. Cook for 5 minutes.
9. When the meal is ready, you will be able to rate the flavor of this chicken.

Nutrition:

- Calories: 613
- Fat: 53,2g
- Carbohydrates: 49,4g
- Protein: 59,2g

Yummy Chicken with Varied Herbs

This meal is very easy for breakfast or dinner. It can be one of most popular meal on your table.

Prep time: 16-20 minutes | **Cooking time:** 6-10 min | **Servings:** 4

Ingredients:

- 1 oz of cheese
- 3-4 pieces of bacon
- 15-20 spinach leaves
- 1 teaspoon of sauce
- 1 teaspoon of mixed herbs
- 1 teaspoon of black pepper
- ½ teaspoon of salt
- 2 boneless chicken breasts

Directions:

1. Preheat the Air Fryer to 380F.
2. Chop chicken in small pieces.
3. Then add salt, peppers, herbs, sauce and pepper. Mix everything together.
4. Put bacon, cheese and spinach leaves between chicken.
5. Sprinkle the frying basket with oil.
6. Then place chicken in the Air Fryer.
7. Cook for 8-1- minutes
8. Your guests will appreciate the flavor of tasty chicken.

Nutrition:

- Calories: 621
- Fat: 55,2g
- Carbohydrates: 42,4g
- Protein: 49,2g

Delicious Cooked Chicken

If you wish to get something unusual and tasty, you made the right choice. This recipe is exactly for you.

Prep time: 15 minutes | **Cooking time:** 30 minutes | **Servings:** 4

Ingredients:

- 2 teaspoons of coriander flour
- 1 teaspoon of black pepper
- 2 teaspoons of Kasuri methi.
- 4 tablespoons of hung curd
- 1 tablespoon of turmeric powder
- 2 teaspoons of red chili powder
- 1 tablespoon of garam masala
- 1 teaspoon of cumin
- 3 table spoons of lemon juice
- 3 teaspoons of garlic pasta
- 3 teaspoons of ginger pasta
- 4 chicken legs

Directions:

1. Wash chicken and put in the bowl.
2. Then add spices to chicken. Mix them well.
3. After that leave them aside.
4. Put the silver foil in the basket for Air Fryer.
5. Preheat the Air Fryer to 350F.
6. Put chicken in the Air Fryer and cook for 18-20 minutes.
7. Then put chicken on another side and cook for 10 minutes.
8. Serve it with onion and mint. You will appreciate this meal a lot.

Nutrition:

- Calories: 612
- Fat: 53,2g
- Carbohydrates: 41,4g
- Protein: 43,2g

Buttermilk Chicken

Chicken will be delicious and fragrant. You can prepare it is easily, but cooking will take some time.

Prep time: 6 hours

Cooking time: 18-20 minutes

Servings: 4

Ingredients:

- 2 lbs of chicken fillet

Flour:

- 1 teaspoon of salt
- 1 tablespoon of pepper
- 1 tablespoon of garlic

- 1 tablespoon of paprika
- 1 tablespoon of backing powder
- 2 cups of flour

Marinade

- 1 teaspoon of cayenne pepper
- 1 teaspoon of black pepper
- 1 teaspoon of salt
- 2 cups of buttermilk

Directions:

1. Wash chicken and cut all fat.
2. Place chicken, salt, pepper and paprika in the bowl and mix everything.
3. Pour everything with buttermilk.
4. You should leave it for 6 hours.
5. Preheat the Air Fryer to 370F.
6. Blend salt, pepper, baking powder and flour in the bowl.
7. Sprinkle the basket with oil and put chicken there.
8. Cook in the Air Fryer 8 minutes.
9. Then lay chicken on another side and cook for 10 minutes.
10. You will get the delicious mean and your efforts will be appreciated.

Nutrition:

- Calories: 598
- Fat: 49,2g

- Carbohydrates: 39,4g
- Protein: 41,2g

Chicken Kabobs

Chicken, baked in the Air Fryer can decorate not only your breakfast or dinner table. It is possible to prepare it for holiday.

Prep time: 15 minutes | **Cooking time:** 15 minutes | **Servings:** 2

Ingredients:
- 2 chicken breasts
- 2 tablespoons of oil
- 3 bells of pepper
- 6 mushrooms
- 1 teaspoon of sesame
- 1 teaspoon of pepper
- ¼ teaspoon of salt
- 1/3 cup of soy sauce
- 1/3 cup of honey

Directions:
1. Cut chicken into few small pieces.
2. Put them in the bowl.
3. Add salt and pepper to that bowl with chicken
4. Then add honey, sesame and soy sauce in the bowl
5. Take some wooden skewers and put chicken, pepper, mushrooms on them.
6. Preheat the Air Fryer to 390F.
7. Then spray it with oil.
8. Cook 15-20 minutes.

Nutrition:
- Calories: 548
- Fat: 43,2g
- Carbohydrates: 32,4g
- Protein: 40,2g

Chicken Quesadillas

There is nothing easier than prepare this meal. The result will exceed your expectation.

Prep time: 10 minutes | **Cooking time:** 11 minutes | **Servings:** 4

Ingredients:
- 2 tablespoons of sour cream
- 3 tablespoons of Mexican cheese
- ½ cup of onion
- ½ cup of green pepper
- Chicken fajita strips
- Taco shells

Directions:
1. Preheat the Air Fryer to 370F.
2. Place 1 soft taco on the basket.
3. Put cream on the taco.
4. Chop onion, cheese and green pepper.
5. Mix them well.
6. After that put on the taco.
7. Add chopped chicken fajita strips.
8. Put the basket in the Air Fryer.
9. Cook for 4 minutes at 370F.
10. Then put on another side and cook for 6-7 minutes.
11. When the meal is ready, chop it into small pieces.

Nutrition:
- Calories: 493
- Fat: 29,2g
- Carbohydrates: 28,4g
- Protein: 38,2g

Nuggets with Chicken

Do you want something, that can be prepared easily? The answer was found. It is simple and delicious meal.

Prep time: 10 minutes	**Cooking time:** 15-17 minutes	**Servings:** 4

Ingredients:
- 1 cup of plain yogurt
- 1 teaspoon of paprika
- ½ teaspoon of pepper
- ½ teaspoon of salt.
- 1 cup of cheese
- 1 lb of chicken fillet
- 1 egg
- 1 cup of flour

Description:
1. Preheat your Air Fryer to 390F.
2. Chop chicken in the small pieces.
3. Then beat egg in the bowl.
4. Mix chicken with egg in the bowl.
5. Mix salt, paprika, pepper, cheese with flour.
6. Then cover chicken with this mixture.
7. Sprinkle the baking basket with oil.
8. Put chicken in the basket and cook for 10 minutes at 390F.
9. Then put the nuggets on another side and cook for 5-7 minutes.
10. Enjoy with your friends when you are watching TV, for example.

Nutrition:
- Calories: 485
- Fat: 33,2g
- Carbohydrates: 30,4g
- Protein: 45,2g

Piquant Cooked Chicken

If you like hot meal, then this chicken is for you. You can prepare this meal for everyone.

Prep time: 10 minutes	**Cooking time:** 22 minutes	**Servings:** 4

Ingredients:
- ½ cup of oil
- 1 teaspoon of salt
- 1 teaspoon of pepper
- 1 teaspoon of paprika
- 1 teaspoon of dry herbs
- 12 chicken pieces

Directions:
1. Wash and clean chicken.
2. Then cut the big pieces in the small ones.
3. Rub chicken pieces with salt, pepper, paprika and dry herbs.
4. After that sprinkle the Air Fryer basket with oil and put chicken and the mixture of spices in the basket.
5. Then cook them for 10 minutes at 350F and put on another side.
6. After that cook for 12 minutes.
7. The nuggets should have golden and even brown color.
8. They are easy in preparing and you will enjoy with your friends just in 20 minutes.

Nutrition:
- Calories: 460
- Fat: 35,2g
- Carbohydrates: 33,4g
- Protein: 42,2g

Chili Chicken

Chicken is always a delicious and hearty supper! Your efforts will be appreciated by your family and friends.

Prep time: 10 minutes | **Cooking time:** 20 minutes | **Servings:** 4

Ingredients:
- 3 oz of flour
- 3 eggs
- ¼ teaspoon of salt
- 1/3 teaspoon of paprika
- ½ of chili pepper
- 1 chicken

Directions:
1. Chop chicken in the pieces.
2. Then mix salt, paprika and pepper in the bowl.
3. Rub chicken with spices.
4. The whole chicken should be covered with spices completely.
5. Then beat eggs in the bowl.
6. Put flour in another bowl.
7. Take piece of chicken and put it in flour, then in egg and after that again in flour.
8. Preheat the Air Fryer to 390F.
9. Cook in the Air Fryer for 10 minutes.
10. Then shake chicken pieces and cook for 10 minutes more.

Nutrition:
- Calories: 477
- Fat: 39,2g
- Carbohydrates: 36,4g
- Protein: 41,2g

Crispy Chicken

The easiest way to prepare appetizing chicken pieces. You do not need more time to prepare it.

Prep time: 10 minutes | **Cooking time:** 45 minutes | **Servings:** 4

Ingredients:
- ½ cup of chopped pecans
- ½ cup of honey
- ½ cup of butter
- ½ cup of hot sauce
- ½ cup of buttermilk
- 1 teaspoon of dry mustard
- 3 teaspoons of Cajun seasonings
- 3 teaspoons of thyme
- 3 teaspoons of oregano
- 3 tablespoons of black pepper
- 3 teaspoons of salt
- 3 teaspoons of celery
- 1 teaspoon of onion
- 3 teaspoons of garlic powder
- 2 tablespoons of paprika
- 4 cups of bread crumbs
- 12 chicken pieces

Directions:
1. Mix chicken pieces, buttermilk and hot sauce in the bowl.
2. Then mix all spices with bread crumbs in the bowl.
3. Take the piece of chicken and put the one by in bread crumbs.
4. Preheat the Air Fryer to 368F.
5. Sprinkle the basket with oil.
6. Cook for 20 minutes and after that put on another side.
7. Cook for 25 minutes.
8. Cook butter with the honey.

Nutrition:
- Calories: 497
- Fat: 39,5g
- Carbohydrates: 36,9g
- Protein: 41,7g

Tao Chicken Wings

Stuffed chicken without bones is an incredibly tasty dish. It does not require special skills and a culinary diploma.

Prep time: 10 minutes | **Cooking time:** 20 minutes | **Servings:** 4

Ingredients:

- 2 lbs of chicken

Marinade:
- 1 teaspoon of black pepper
- 3 tablespoons of corn starch
- 1 beaten egg

- 3 tablespoons of soy sauce

Sauce:
- 2 tablespoon of corn starch
- 2 tablespoon of garlic
- 1 teaspoon of ginger

- ¾ cup of water
- 1 tablespoon of red wine
- 4 tablespoons of sugar
- 1,5 tablespoon of vinegar
- 1,5 tablespoons of oil
- 1 teaspoon of chili flakes

Directions:

1. Beat egg in the bowl.
2. Add black pepper, 3 tablespoons of corn starch, soy sauce and mix everything.
3. Chop chicken in the pieces and nix with marinade.
4. Leave aside for some time.
5. Then preheat the Air Fryer to 360F.
6. Put chicken in the Air Fryer and cook for 10 minutes.
7. Then shake them and cook for 10 minutes more.
8. After that mix chili flakes, oil, vinegar, sugar, wine, water, ginger, garlic and corn starch.
9. Mix everything well and pour chicken.
10. Serve hot and enjoy with the spicy and delicious chicken.

Nutrition:

- Calories: 492
- Fat: 37,5g
- Carbohydrates: 37,9g
- Protein: 42,7g

Chicken Legs

Do you want to prepare something delicious? Prepare chicken legs.

Prep time: 10 minutes | **Cooking time:** 23 minutes | **Servings:** 4

Ingredients:

- 2 cups of brown sugar
- 2 cups of sauce

- 1 teaspoon of pepper
- 1 teaspoon of salt

- 2 cups of flour
- 12 chicken legs

Directions:

1. Mix flour, salt and pepper together.
2. Put chicken legs in the mixture. Cover them with the mixture.
3. Preheat the Air Fryer to 390F.
4. Cook for 10 minutes at 390F and after that put them on another side.
5. Then cook for 10 minutes more at the same temperature. They should have golden color.
6. After that mix sauce with sugar and cover chicken.
7. Then cook for 3 minutes.

Nutrition:

- Calories: 487
- Fat: 37,5g
- Carbohydrates: 38,9g
- Protein: 43,7g

Panko Chicken with Mustard

Baked chicken with a crispy crust - appetizing, hearty dish. It will be great for the everyday life.

Prep time: 10 minutes | **Cooking time:** 20 minutes | **Servings:** 4

Ingredients:
- Salt
- Pepper
- 1/3 cup of bread crumbs
- 2-3 tablespoons of mustard
- 1 lb of skinless chicken cutlets

Directions:
1. Chop chicken in the pieces.
2. Rub chicken with salt and pepper.
3. Blend chicken with mustard.
4. Then put chicken in bread crumbs.
5. Cover chicken completely with bread crumbs.
6. Preheat the Air Fryer to 370F.
7. Sprinkle the frying basket with oil.
8. Place chicken in the Air Fryer and cook for 10 minutes.
9. After that shake chicken and cook again for 10 minutes.
10. The ready chicken pieces have golden brown.
11. Enjoy with the tasty meal.

Nutrition:
- Calories: 483
- Fat: 37,6g
- Carbohydrates: 38,7g
- Protein: 43,6g

Chicken with Bacon

It can be the simple, quick and delicious family dinner. You will not spend too much time and it is very delicious.

Prep time: 10 minutes | **Cooking time:** 15 minutes | **Servings:** 4

Ingredients:
- 12 pieces of bacon
- ¼ teaspoon of pepper
- ¼ teaspoon of salt
- 10 leaves of spinach
- 3 oz of cheese
- 1 chicken breast

Directions:
1. Chop chicken breast in the small pieces.
2. Rub it with salt and pepper completely.
3. Then take spinach and cheese and put them on chicken.
4. After that roll chicken and wrap the piece of bacon around it.
5. Take the fry basket and sprinkle with oil.
6. Then place chicken in the Air Fryer and cook for 10 minutes at 380F.
7. Put chicken on another side and cook 5 minutes.
8. Take chicken and place on the table.
9. Decorate with cheese.
10. Serve hot and you will be delighted with the tasty chicken snacks.

Nutrition:
- Calories: 457
- Fat: 37,2g
- Carbohydrates: 36,7g
- Protein: 45,2g

Tasty Chicken with Mushrooms and Vegetables

Extraordinarily soft meat, with noble sourness, slightly sweet.

Prep time: 10 minutes | **Cooking time:** 15 minutes | **Servings:** 4

Ingredients:

- 1 tablespoon of oil
- 1 tablespoon of ginger
- 2 tablespoon of fish sauce
- ½ cup of chicken broth
- 2 cups of broccoli
- 1 cup of white mushrooms
- ½ cup of snow peas
- 1 red onion
- 2 cloves of garlic
- ¼ cup of flour
- 1 lb of chicken

Directions:

1. Cut chicken in small pieces.
2. Then put them in flour.
3. Blend together fish sauce, chicken broth, oil and honey in the bowl.
4. Mix everything well and add the rest of chicken broth.
5. After that put all vegetables, chicken, ginger and garlic in the frying basket.
6. Place the basket in the Air Fryer and cook for 15 minutes at 380F.
7. Chicken should have crispy skin.

Nutrition:

- Calories: 468
- Fat: 37,5g
- Carbohydrates: 34,7g
- Protein: 43,2g

Crispy Hot Chicken

A delicious and juicy chicken will appear on the table after very little labor and a short time.

Prep time: 10 minutes | **Cooking time:** 15 minutes | **Servings:** 4

Ingredients:

- ¼ teaspoon of pepper
- ¼ teaspoon of salt
- 1/3 teaspoon of paprika
- 2 oz of cheese
- 2 chicken breasts
- 2 oz of fresh spinach
- 1 tablespoon of oil

Descriptions:

1. Wash and clean chicken.
2. Then cut spinach and mix the leaves with oil.
3. Add the mixture to the bowl with chicken. Mix everything well.
4. Rub chicken with salt and pepper.
5. Grate cheese and cover chicken with it.
6. Add the paprika.
7. Preheat the Air Fryer to 370F.
8. Then put chicken in the Air Fryer.
9. Cook for 8 minutes.
10. Then shake the basket and cook chicken for 7 minutes.
11. Just eat it because this meal is perfect and delicious.

Nutrition:

- Calories: 471
- Fat: 36,9g
- Carbohydrates: 33,7g
- Protein: 43,6g

Sweat Chicken with Marinade

Chicken in this sauce with a light note is sure to please your guests!

Prep time: 10 minutes | **Cooking time:** 15 minutes | **Servings:** 4

Ingredients:

Marinade:
- 2 tablespoons of oil
- ½ cup of flour
- 1 teaspoon of sesame
- 1 teaspoon of soy sauce
- 2 lbs of chicken

Sauce:
- 1 teaspoon of sugar
- 2 oz of water
- 3-4 tablespoons of ketchup
- 3 cloves of garlic

- 1 red onion
- 1 capsicum
- 2 tomatoes
- 2 tablespoons of oil

Directions:

1. Mix all ingredients for marinade, except of flour and oil.
2. Leave for 5-10 minutes.
3. Then put every piece of chicken in flour.
4. Sprinkle the Air Fryer with butter.
5. Cook chicken for 10 minutes at 380F.
6. Then add garlic.
7. Chop tomatoes and onion.
8. Add ketchup, sugar and water.
9. Mix everything together.
10. Cook for 5 minutes.

Nutrition:
- Calories: 485
- Fat: 36,3g
- Carbohydrates: 33,2g
- Protein: 43,4g

Fried Turkey with Spices

Turkey will be delicious, ruddy and incredibly tasty. You can prepare it very easily.

Prep time: 10 minutes | **Cooking time:** 23-25 minutes | **Servings:** 4

Ingredients:

- 1 tablespoon of butter
- 2 tablespoons of mustard
- ¼ cup of maple juice

- ½ teaspoon of pepper
- ½ teaspoon of salt
- ½ teaspoon of paprika

- 1 teaspoon of dry thyme
- 5 pounds of turkey
- 2 tablespoons of oil

Directions:

1. Chop turkey in the pieces.
2. Then mix mustard, pepper, butter, salt, paprika, dry thyme in the bowl.
3. Rub turkey with spices.
4. Then sprinkle turkey with maple juice and oil.
5. Take the basket and sprinkle it with oil.
6. Put turkey in the basket.
7. Cook for 10 minutes at 380F.
8. Then put it on another side and cook for 13-15 minutes.

Nutrition:
- Calories: 485
- Fat: 34,9g
- Carbohydrates: 33,6g
- Protein: 43,7g

Turkey with Mustard

Do you like to cook something tasty from the poultry? You will not forget this recipe, because this turkey is fantastic.

Prep time: 10 minutes	**Cooking time:** 35 minutes	**Servings:** 4

Ingredients:

- 1 tablespoon of butter
- 2 tablespoons of mustard
- ½ teaspoon of pepper
- 1 teaspoon of salt
- ½ teaspoon of paprika
- ½ teaspoon of dried sage
- 1 teaspoon of dried thyme
- 5 pound of turkey
- 2 teaspoons of oil

Directions:

1. Preheat the Air Fryer to 350F.
2. Wash and clean turkey.
3. Cut turkey in the pieces.
4. Sprinkle to turkey with oil.
5. Mix dried thyme, butter, dried sage, paprika, salt, pepper together.
6. Rub turkey with this mixture.
7. Put turkey in the Air Fryer.
8. Add mustard there.
9. Cook for 25 minutes at 350F.
10. Then put the pieces of turkey on another side.
11. Cook for 10 minutes.
12. Serve hot and with different vegetables or variety of sauces.

Nutrition:

- Calories: 490
- Fat: 36,9g
- Carbohydrates: 31,6g
- Protein: 43,2g

Flavorsome Turkey Cutlets with Mushrooms

Try the incredibly tasty cutlets with mushrooms. You will be surprised how delicious it is.

Prep time: 10 minutes	**Cooking time:** 10 minutes	**Servings:** 4

Ingredients:

- 1 lb of turkey
- ½ teaspoon of pepper
- ½ teaspoon of salt
- 1 teaspoon of onion powder
- 1 teaspoon of garlic powder
- 1 tablespoon of ketchup or sauce
- 6 big mushrooms

Directions:

1. Wash mushrooms and put in the food processor.
2. Grind them in the food processor.
3. Then mix pepper, salt, onion powder, garlic powder in the bowl.
4. Chop turkey in small pieces.
5. Rub them with spices and mushrooms.
6. Prepare cutlets from meat.
7. Then sprinkle the frying basket with oil and put cutlets in the Air Fryer.
8. Cook cutlets for 10 minutes at 380F.

Nutrition:

- Calories: 485
- Fat: 35,9g
- Carbohydrates: 33,6g
- Protein: 44,2g

Mustard Turkey Breast

You will like this turkey after you try it for the first time. This meal will be great for some holiday.

Prep time: 10 minutes | **Cooking time:** 40 minutes | **Servings:** 4

Ingredients:
- 4 pounds of turkey
- 2 tablespoons of oil
- 3 tablespoons of mustard
- ½ teaspoon of salt
- ½ teaspoon of pepper
- ½ teaspoon of paprika
- ½ teaspoon of chili
- ¼ cup of butter

Directions:
1. Preheat the Air Fryer to 380F.
2. Rub turkey with oil.
3. Then rub turkey with salt and pepper.
4. After that, mix paprika and chili.
5. Then mix turkey with the chili and paprika.
6. Cook turkey for 25 minutes at 380F.
7. Then put turkey on another side and cook for 10 minutes.
8. After that cook butter and mustard and cover turkey with it.
9. Then cook for 5 minutes more.
10. Eat the tasty meat with your favorite sauce. Serve hot.

Nutrition:
- Calories: 439
- Fat: 37,9g
- Carbohydrates: 35,6g
- Protein: 43,2g

Turkey with Mayo and Cheese

If your friends are going to visit you, prepare this turkey and they will be delighted.

Prep time: 10 minutes | **Cooking time:** 20 minutes | **Servings:** 4

Ingredients:
- ½ teaspoon of pepper
- 3 lbs of turkey
- ½ teaspoon of salt
- 2/3 teaspoon of paprika
- ¼ teaspoon of oregano
- 1/3 teaspoon of garlic powder
- 4 oz of cheese
- ½ teaspoon of cumin
- ½ teaspoon of chili

Directions:
1. Wash and clean turkey.
2. Then cut turkey in small pieces.
3. Put the deep bowl.
4. Mix pepper, salt, paprika, oregano, garlic, cumin and chili there.
5. Rub the pieces of turkey with spices.
6. Sprinkle the basket for Air Fryer with oil.
7. Cook for 10 minutes at 380F.
8. Then shake them and cook for another 10 minutes at 380F.
9. Chop cheese and cover turkey with it.
10. Enjoy with the red wine.

Nutrition:
- Calories: 425
- Fat: 36,9g
- Carbohydrates: 34,6g
- Protein: 42,2g

MEAT

Meat Burgers

If you wish to make the great and fast meat snacks, cook these fantastic burgers.

Prep time: 10 minutes | **Cooking time**: 10 minutes | **Servings**: 4

Ingredients:
- 1 pound of beef
- 1 teaspoon of dry parsley
- ½ teaspoon of oregano
- ½ teaspoon of salt
- ½ teaspoon of pepper
- ½ teaspoon of onion powder
- 1 tablespoon of sauce

Directions:
1. Put meat in the food processor and cut it.
2. Then put the beef in the bowl.
3. After that mix dry parsley, oregano, salt, pepper, onion powder and sauce in another bowl.
4. Then add all these spices to meat.
5. Mix everything well.
6. Make the small burgers.
7. Sprinkle the Air Fryer basket with oil.
8. Put the burgers in the Air Fryer.
9. Cook 10 minutes at 300F.
10. When the burgers are ready, serve them with buns, vegetables and sauces.

Nutrition:
- Calories: 148
- Fat: 4,6g
- Carbohydrates: 1,6g
- Protein: 24,2g

Balls with Bacon and Cheese

Do you need to prepare something interesting? The great mixture of cheese with bacon is very wonderful. Try to make and you will like it.

Prep time: 10 minutes | **Cooking time**: 10 minutes | **Servings**: 4

Ingredients:
- 1 cup of bread crumbs
- ¾ cup of flour
- 2 cups of milk
- 3 eggs
- 1/3 cup of cheese
- ¼ cup of bacon

Directions:
1. Beat three eggs in the bowl and mix them.
2. Chop cheese and bacon in the small pieces.
3. Add flour and mix everything well.
4. Make the balls from cheese and bacon with flour.
5. Take the ball, put it in milk and after that in bread crumbs.
6. All balls should be in bread crumbs and in milk.
7. After that preheat the Air Fryer to 350F.
8. Sprinkle the basket with oil.
9. Put the balls in the Air Fryer and cook for 5 minutes at 350F.
10. Then put them on another side and cook for 5 minutes more.
11. When the balls are ready, enjoy with them and add different sauces.

Nutrition:
- Calories: 165
- Fat: 5,6g
- Carbohydrates: 1,5g
- Protein: 24,3g

Beef Roll

It is very important to eat meat and because of this fact you can prepare the delicious, tasty and great meat. It will be great dinner for your family.

Prep time: 10 minutes | **Cooking time**: 14 minutes | **Servings**: 4

Ingredients:
- 1 teaspoon of pepper
- 1 teaspoon of salt
- ¾ cup of spinach
- 3 oz of red chili pepper
- 6 pieces of cheese
- 3 tablespoons of sauce
- 2 lb of beef steak

Directions:
1. Divide the steak in the separate pieces.
2. Rub the pieces of beef with salt and pepper.
3. Chop cheese, pepper and spinach into the small pieces.
4. Mix them together.
5. Then put the mixture on every piece of meat and roll them.
6. Sprinkle the Air Fryer basket with oil
7. Put the rolls in the Air Fryer.
8. Cook for 14 minutes at 380F.
9. Serve hot with sauce.
10. Enjoy with tasty rolls.

Nutrition:
- Calories: 156
- Fat: 5,8g
- Carbohydrates: 1,6g
- Protein: 24,6g

Beef Tenders

They are very easy for preparing and at the same moment they are very delicious. You can prepare the complete dinner for your family if you prepare this meal.

Prep time: 10 minutes | **Cooking time**: 15 minutes | **Servings**: 4

Ingredients:
- ½ cup of milk
- 1 tablespoon of oil
- ½ teaspoon of salt
- ½ teaspoon of oil
- 1 cup of bread crumbs
- ½ cup of flour
- 3 eggs
- 1 lb of meat

Directions:
1. Mix bread crumbs with oil.
2. Then take another bowl and mix eggs with milk.
3. Put flour in the third bowl.
4. Chop meat into middle pieces.
5. Take the piece of meat, put it in flour, then in beaten eggs and after that in bread crumbs.
6. Sprinkle the Air Fryer basket with oil.
7. Put the pieces of meet in the Air Fryer.
8. Cook them for 15 minutes at 380F.
9. Enjoy with this delicious meat.

Nutrition:
- Calories: 144
- Fat: 5,3g
- Carbohydrates: 1,2g
- Protein: 24,7g

20 Minutes Beef

This type of meat will be the beloved one, since it can be popular as for trip as for the typical dinner in 20 minutes only. You will like it as the beef is simple and pleasant. Just cook meat!

Prep time: 10 minutes | **Cooking time**: 20 minutes | **Servings**: 4

Ingredients:

- 1 egg
- ½ teaspoon of pepper
- ½ teaspoon of salt
- ½ teaspoon of cumin

- 1 tablespoon of tomato pasta
- 1 small onion
- 2 cloves of garlic

- 1 green pepper
- 1 tablespoon of oil
- 1 cup of flour

Directions:

1. Blend salt, pepper then cumin and garlic in the bowl.
2. Slice onion with pepper in small pieces.
3. Then mix them together.
4. Place oil and tomato pasta to the rest of products.
5. Mix them well.
6. Make cutlets from this mixture.
7. Sprinkle the Air Fryer basket with oil.
8. Then put cutlets in the Air Fryer.
9. Cook them for 15 minute at 300F and then put on other side and cook for 5 minutes.

Nutrition:

- Calories: 147
- Fat: 5,5g

- Carbohydrates: 1,3g
- Protein: 24,1g

Rib Eye Steak

If you wish to know how to prepare meat well and have what to show your guests, then this recipe is exactly for you. The guests will like it.

Prep time: 10 minutes | **Cooking time**: 21 minutes | **Servings**: 4

Ingredients:

- 1 teaspoon of oil
- ½ teaspoon of pepper

- ½ teaspoon of salt
- 1/3 teaspoon of dry herbs

- 2 lbs of steak rub

Directions:

1. Preheat the Air Fryer to 390F for 4 minutes.
2. Then mix salt, pepper, dry herbs and oil together.
3. After that rub meat with these spices.
4. Sprinkle the Air Fryer basket with oil.
5. Put meat in the Air Fryer.
6. Cook for 14 minutes at 390F.
7. Then put the steak on another side and cook for 7 minutes.
8. Decorate with vegetables and do not forget about sauces. Your guests will be surprised, because it will be too tasty.

Nutrition:

- Calories: 138
- Fat: 4,9g

- Carbohydrates: 1,5g
- Protein: 23,8g

Garlic Meat

It is for fans of spicy food. This garlic meat is delicious and spicy. It is very rare and tasty. Do not miss your chance.

Prep time: 10 minutes | **Cooking time**: 12 minutes | **Servings**: 4

Ingredients:
- 1 lb of meat.
- ½ teaspoon of salt
- ½ teaspoon of pepper
- 1/3 teaspoon of red chili pepper
- ½ teaspoon of garlic
- ½ teaspoon of mustard
- 3 eggs
- 1 cup of flour

Directions:
1. Take the deeps bowl.
2. Mix salt, pepper then red chili pepper, garlic, mustard in this bowl.
3. Then cut meat in the pieces.
4. Rub every piece of meat with spices.
5. Beat three eggs in the bowl and put flour in another bowl.
6. Then put every piece of meat in flour and then in egg,
7. Sprinkle the frying basket with oil.
8. Put the steaks in the Air Fryer.
9. Cook then for 6 minutes at 380F and then 6 minutes on the other side.
10. Serve hot with vegetables.

Nutrition:
- Calories: 135
- Fat: 4,6g
- Carbohydrates: 1,7g
- Protein: 23,5g

Tater Tots with Bacon

This meal seems to be original, but you even cannot imagine how flavorsome it is. The result of the cooked bacon will exceed all your expectation.

Prep time: 10 minutes | **Cooking time**: 8 minutes | **Servings**: 4

Ingredients:
- ½ cup of cheese
- ½ teaspoon of salt
- ½ teaspoon of pepper
- 1/3 teaspoon of paprika
- 3 tablespoons of sour cream
- 4 onions
- Frozen tater tots

Directions:
1. Chop bacon in the pieces.
2. Mix salt, pepper then paprika in the bowl.
3. Chop onions and add to all ingredients.
4. Crush every tater tots and mix with cheese.
5. Add to the rest of products.
6. Mix everything well.
7. Preheat the Air Fryer to 380F.
8. Sprinkle the basket with oil.
9. Put the assortment in the Air Fryer and cook for 8 minutes at 380F.

Nutrition:
- Calories: 158
- Fat: 4,8g
- Carbohydrates: 1,4g
- Protein: 22,5g

Easy Steak

Prepare this scrumptious meat, the easy steak is your true choice. The family will be shocked once they try it.

Prep time: 10 minutes | **Cooking time**: 8 minutes | **Servings**: 4

Ingredients:
- 1 teaspoon of pepper
- ½ teaspoon of salt
- 2 cups of milk
- 2 tablespoons of flour
- 1 teaspoon of garlic powder
- 1 teaspoon of onion powder
- 1 cup of flour
- 1 cup of bread crumbs
- 3 beaten eggs
- 6 oz of steak

Directions:
1. Take the bowl and mix bread crumbs with salt, pepper, onion powder and garlic powder.
2. Rub the pieces of steal in this mixture.
3. Then beat eggs in the bowl.
4. Put the steak in flour, then in beaten eggs and after that in bread crumbs.
5. Sprinkle the Air Fryer with oil.
6. Put meat in Air Fryer.
7. Cook for 12 minutes at 350F.
8. When it is ready, serve with sauce and enjoy.

Nutrition:
- Calories: 138
- Fat: 4,3g
- Carbohydrates: 1,2g
- Protein: 22,7g

Wonderful Potatoes with Scrumptious Pork

This pork meal is for dinner. It is delightful, uncomplicated and the potato is flavorsome.

Prep time: 10 minutes | **Cooking time**: 14 minutes | **Servings**: 4

Ingredients:
- 1 tablespoon of balsamic glaze
- 1 teaspoon of salt
- 1 teaspoon of parsley
- 1 teaspoon of pepper
- ½ teaspoon of onion powder
- ½ teaspoon of garlic powder
- ½ teaspoon of red chili pepper
- 1 red potatoes
- 2 lb of meat

Directions:
1. Wash and clean potatoes.
2. Slice the products in the pieces.
3. Rub them with salt, pepper, parsley then onion powder, garlic powder and red chili pepper.
4. Lay meat in the Air Fryer and cook for 7 minutes at 380F.
5. Then put meat on the dish.
6. Cook vegetables in the Air Fryer for 3 minutes and then 4 minutes on the other side.
7. Place all components on saucer, decorate with the root vegetables and pasta or basil leaves with parsley.

Nutrition:
- Calories: 147
- Fat: 4,6g
- Carbohydrates: 1,4g
- Protein: 22,76g

Hot Dogs

These hot dogs are the special ones. Attempt to create these hot dogs and you can be satisfied with the result. Your effort will be valued by the children.

| **Prep time**: 10 minutes | **Cooking time**: 3 minutes | **Servings**: 4 |

Ingredients:
- 1 tablespoon of ketchup
- 8 candies eyes
- 4 hot dogs
- ½ teaspoon of pepper
- ½ teaspoon of salt
- 2 tablespoons of oil
- 1 puff pastry sheet

Directions:
1. Rub sausages with salt and pepper.
2. Place the puff pastry sheet on the table.
3. Divide it in 5 strings.
4. Cover sausages with these strings.
5. Sprinkle the Air Fryer with oil.
6. Set the hot dogs in the Air Fryer for 3 minutes at 300F.
7. Then add the candies eyes.
8. Prepare hot with sauces. You can choose different ones.
9. Your kids will like them.
10. Cook and you will be delighted with it.

Nutrition:
- Calories: 119
- Fat: 4,1g
- Carbohydrates: 1,2g
- Protein: 22,1g

Turkey with Spices

Do you need to cook soft and tasty meat? Cook this turkey and you will use too little time preparing meat.

| **Prep time**: 15 minutes | **Cooking time**: 40 minutes | **Servings**: 4 |

Ingredients:
- 2 tablespoons of olive oil
- 1 teaspoon of salt
- 1 teaspoon of pepper
- 8 pounds of turkey.

Directions:
1. Take the bowl and mix salt, pepper and oil in it.
2. Rub turkey with these seasonings and oil.
3. Chop turkey in the pieces. It will be easier for you to cook if they will not be too big.
4. Then sprinkle the frying basket with oil.
5. Put the pieces of turkey in the Air Fryer.
6. Cook them for 20 minutes at 280F.
7. Then put them on other side and cook for 20 minutes again.
8. Put turkey in the plate.
9. Decorate with basil leaves, mint and do not forget about sauces.
10. It will be your favorite and delicious meal.

Nutrition:
- Calories: 138
- Fat: 4,2g
- Carbohydrates: 1,4g
- Protein: 22,5g

Meat with Herbs

It is enjoyable and peppery meal. It can be roasted for breakfast, for dinner and for lunch. Just attempt and you will definitely like this meat.

Prep time: 10 minutes	**Cooking time**: 20 minutes	**Servings**: 4

Ingredients:

- ½ teaspoon of salt
- ½ teaspoon of pepper
- ½ teaspoon of onion powder
- ½ teaspoon of garlic
- 1/3 teaspoon of cumin
- 2 lb of meat
- 7 oz of cheese

Directions:

1. Take the bowl and mix salt, pepper, onion powder, garlic and cumin in it.
2. Cut meat into the pieces and rub them with spices.
3. After that preheat the Air Fryer to 380F.
4. Sprinkle the basket with oil.
5. Put the pieces of meat in the Air Fryer.
6. Cook for 10 minutes at 380F and then shake well and cook for 10 minutes more.
7. Put on the plate and serve with potatoes and sauces.
8. Meat should be hot, it is the most delicious at this moment.

Nutrition:

- Calories: 146
- Fat: 4,7g
- Carbohydrates: 1,3g
- Protein: 22,5g

Meet Cheese

This meat with cheese is uncomplicated in preparing: just 7 minutes. Unassuming, easy and scrumptious meal.

Prep time: 10 minutes	**Cooking time**: 7 minutes	**Servings**: 4

Ingredients:

- ½ teaspoon of salt
- ½ teaspoon of garlic powder
- ½ teaspoon of pepper
- ½ teaspoon of oregano
- 1/3 teaspoon of cumin
- ½ teaspoon of onion powder
- 8 pieces of cheese
- 2 tablespoons of oil
- 4 tablespoons of coleslaw
- 4 pieces of bread
- 1 lb of meat

Directions:

1. Blend oil with bread.
2. Place bread on the dish.
3. Mix all flavors together in the bowl.
4. Rub meat with them.
5. Put the piece of meat on bread.
6. Then put the coleslaw on it.
7. After that sprinkle the Air Fryer basket with oil.
8. Preheat it to 380F.
9. Put the snacks in the Air Fryer and cook for 5 minutes at 380F.
10. Then add pieces of cheese and cook 2 minutes at 300F.

Nutrition:

- Calories: 165
- Fat: 5,7g
- Carbohydrates: 1,2g
- Protein: 23,5g

Meatlof

If you wish to prepare something interesting and delicious at the same time, you should prepare this meal.

Prep time: 10 minutes | **Cooking time**: 20 minutes | **Servings**: 4

Ingredients:
- 2 mushrooms
- ½ teaspoon of salt
- ½ teaspoon of oil
- ½ teaspoon of pepper
- 3 oz of salami
- 1 onion
- 1 beaten egg
- 3 tablespoons of bread crumbs

Directions:
1. Cut the salami into pieces and put in the bowl.
2. Then add salt, oil, pepper there.
3. Chop onion and add to the ingredient.
4. Mix everything well.
5. Beat egg and add chopped mushrooms in the bowl.
6. Mix all ingredients.
7. After that, sprinkle the Air Fryer basket with oil.
8. Then make the cutlet from the mixture, put them in bread crumbs and after that in the Air Fryer.
9. Cook for 10 minutes at 380F and them 10 minutes more at 200F.
10. Serve hot with potatoes and sauces.

Nutrition:
- Calories: 136
- Fat: 5,4g
- Carbohydrates: 1,3g
- Protein: 23,4g

Piquant Beef and Scrumptious Broccoli

This broccoli and beef meal is actual healthy. Cook peppery beef with the appetizing broccoli!

Prep time: 10 minutes | **Cooking time:** 20 minutes | **Servings:** 4

Ingredients:
- ½ teaspoon of ginger
- ½ teaspoon of pepper
- 1 teaspoon of onion powder
- ½ teaspoon of salt
- 1 teaspoon of sugar
- 1 tablespoon of soy sauce
- 1 tablespoon of ketchup
- 1 lb of broccoli
- 1 lb of beef.

Directions:
1. Rinse the beef and broccoli.
2. Cut them in the pieces.
3. Mix ginger, pepper then salt, onion powder, sugar and sauce with ketchup in the bowl.
4. Place meat in the bowl and blend with all seasonings.
5. Then sprinkle the Air Fryer with oil
6. Set meat there and cook for 10 minutes at 380F.
7. Then add the pieces of broccoli, blend everything and cook for 10 minutes more.
8. Serve hot with potatoes.
9. Decorate with parsley or mint leaves.

Nutrition:
- Calories: 145,9
- Fat: 5,12g
- Carbohydrates: 1,2g
- Protein: 23,5g

Spice Beef

If you like spicy food, it means, that you are on the right way. Cook this beef and you will like it forever. Healthy, delicious and incredibly tasty.

| **Prep time:** 10 minutes | **Cooking time:** 15 minutes | **Servings:** 4 |

Ingredients:

- ½ cup of sugar
- ½ teaspoon of pepper
- ½ teaspoon of salt
- 1/2teaspon of chili
- ½ teaspoon of garlic
- ½ teaspoon of ginger
- ½ cup of soy sauce

Directions:

1. Take the bowl and put sugar, pepper, salt, onion powder, pepper, garlic and ginger there.
2. Mix everything well.
3. Then wash and clean the beef.
4. Cut it in the pieces.
5. Put them in the bowl with spices and cover completely with them.
6. Sprinkle the Air Fryer with oil.
7. Put the foil on the basket.
8. Then put the pieces of meat on the foil.
9. Sprinkle with soy sauce.
10. Cook for 15 minutes at 390F.

Nutrition:

- Calories: 135
- Fat: 5,6g
- Carbohydrates: 1,4g
- Protein: 23,6g

Appetizing Meat Balls

If you demand something easy and yummy – these meat balls can be the solution. They are fantastic and delicious. They will be great for the picnic.

| **Prep time:** 10 minutes | **Cooking time:** 20 minutes | **Servings:** 4 |

Ingredients:

- ½ teaspoon of salt
- 1/3 teaspoon of pepper
- 1/3 teaspoon of cumin
- ½ teaspoon of garlic
- 1 tablespoon of soy sauce
- 1 onion
- 1 carrot
- 9 oz of pork.

Directions:

1. Wash and chop pork in the smallest pieces.
2. Take the bowl and mix salt, pepper, then garlic, cumin and soy sauce.
3. Then rub pork with these spices.
4. Slice onion in the pieces and add in the bowl.
5. Cut carrot in small pieces, add to the mixture and blend all components well.
6. Create the balls.
7. Preheat the Air Fryer to 370F.
8. Sprinkle the basket with oil.
9. After that, place the mixture in the Air Fryer and cook for 10 minutes.
10. Mix everything well and cook for 10 minutes more.

Nutrition:

- Calories: 146
- Fat: 5,3g
- Carbohydrates: 1,1g
- Protein: 23,7g

Meat with Vegetables

It is great recipe of meat and vegetables. Tasty, easy, wonderful and unassuming.

Prep time: 10 minutes | **Cooking time:** 20 minutes | **Servings:** 4

Ingredients:

- 1 pepper
- 1 tomato
- 1 cucumber
- 1 lb of pork
- ½ teaspoon of salt
- ½ teaspoon of pepper
- 1/3 teaspoon of cumin
- 1/3 teaspoon of garlic
- ½ teaspoon of onion powder
- 1/3 teaspoon of dry herbs

Directions:

1. Wash and chop meat in the pieces.
2. Mix salt, then pepper, cumin and rest or spices in the bowl.
3. Then rub pork with them.
4. Chop tomatoes in the pieces and pit on separate bowl.
5. Then chop cucumber and pepper in the pieces and add the products to the tomato.
6. Mix everything well.
7. Sprinkle the Air Fryer basket with oil.
8. Cook meat at 380F for 10 minutes.
9. Then add vegetables and cook for 10 minutes more.
10. Serve hot and enjoy.

Nutrition:

- Calories: 148
- Fat: 5,6g
- Carbohydrates: 1,2g
- Protein: 23,5g

Potatoes with Pork

If you need to make supper for the family, this pork with potatoes will be the great one. It is delightful, modest and uncomplicated.

Prep time: 10 minutes | **Cooking time:** 20 minutes | **Servings:** 4

Ingredients:

- 5 potatoes
- 1 lb of meat
- ½ teaspoon fo salt
- ½ teaspoon of pepper
- 1/3 teaspoon of cumin
- 1/3 teaspoon of breadcrumbs
- 1/3 teaspoon of dry herbs
- 2 tablespoons of oil

Directions:

1. Wash and clean potatoes.
2. Cut in the pieces.
3. Wash and clean meat.
4. Cut in the pieces too.
5. Then combine meat with potatoes.
6. Rub them with salt, pepper, cumin, dry herbs and breadcrumbs.
7. Preheat the Air Fryer to 380F.
8. Cook potatoes with meat for 10 minute.
9. Then put on another side and cook for 10 minutes.

Nutrition:

- Calories: 139
- Fat: 5,1g
- Carbohydrates: 1,3g
- Protein: 23,4g

Easy Beef

The title of the recipe means that it is very easy. You will be able to prepare the delicious meal.

Prep time: 10 minutes	**Cooking time:** 15 minutes	**Servings:** 4

Ingredients:

- 1 teaspoon of black pepper
- ½ teaspoon of chili
- ½ teaspoon of dry herbs
- 1 teaspoon of onion powder
- ½ teaspoon of cumin
- 2 tablespoons of oil
- 1 lb of beef

Directions:

1. Preheat the Air Fryer to 380F.
2. Then sprinkle the Air Fryer basket with oil.
3. Take the deep bowl.
4. Mix pepper, chili, herbs, onion powder, cumin and oil there.
5. Wash and clean meat.
6. Chop it in the pieces and rub with spices.
7. Put in the Air Fryer and cook for 10 minutes.
8. Then shake well and cook for 5 minutes more.
9. Serve hot with sauces, vegetables or salad.
10. This meat is really tasty and incredibly delicious.

Nutrition:

- Calories: 143
- Fat: 5,2g
- Carbohydrates: 1,3g
- Protein: 23,3g

Beef with Spices and Vegetables

If you need to make the special meal for Sunday, then you were given with the right recipe. Simple, easy and wonderful!

Prep time: 10 minutes	**Cooking time:** 20 minutes	**Servings:** 4

Ingredients:

- 1 lb of beef
- 8 potatoes
- 1 carrot
- 1 pepper
- 1 onion
- ½ teaspoon of salt
- ½ teaspoon of pepper
- ½ teaspoon of oregano
- 3 tablespoons of oil
- ½ teaspoon of garlic
- 1 tablespoons of ketchup

Directions:

1. Wash and clean potatoes.
2. Chop it in the pieces.
3. Wash meat and chop in the pieces also.
4. Then mix salt, pepper, oregano, then oil, garlic and ketchup together.
5. Rub meat and potatoes with them.
6. Slice onion in small pieces.
7. Then chop carrot with pepper and blend with onion.
8. Put meat and potatoes in the Air Fryer.
9. Cook for 10 minutes at 380F.
10. Then add vegetables. Mix everything well and cook for 10 minutes more.

Nutrition:

- Calories: 157
- Fat: 5,6g
- Carbohydrates: 1,4g
- Protein: 23,8g

Beef for Sunday

If the guests are coming, prepare this beef and they will be delighted. It is very soft, delicious and have crispy skin.

Prep time: 10 minutes

Cooking time: 22-23 minutes

Servings: 4

Ingredients:
- 1 big piece of beef
- 2 cups of spinach
- ½ teaspoon of salt
- ½ teaspoon of pepper
- 2 cloves of garlic
- 1/3 teaspoon of oregano
- ½ teaspoon of cumin

Directions:
1. Take the bowl and mix salt, pepper, garlic and cumin with oregano there.
2. Wash and clean meat.
3. Chop it in the pieces.
4. Then put in the bowl with spices and mix everything.
5. Meat should be completely covered with spices.
6. Then preheat the Air Fryer to 370F.
7. Cook meat for 12-13 minutes.
8. Wash and chop spinach.
9. Add spinach to meat and cook for 10 minutes and 280F.

Nutrition:
- Calories: 135
- Fat: 5,2g
- Carbohydrates: 1,3g
- Protein: 22,1g

Grilled Beef

This meal is very simple in preparing. You can make the original and tasty meal for your friends and relatives.

Prep time: 10 minutes

Cooking time: 20 minutes

Servings: 4

Ingredients:
- ½ teaspoon of salt
- ½ teaspoon of pepper
- 1 onion
- 2 lb of beef
- ½ cup of soy sauce
- ½ teaspoon of garlic
- ½ teaspoon of fry herbs

Directions:
1. Wash and clean meat.
2. Chop in the pieces.
3. Take the bowl.
4. Mix salt, pepper, dry herbs, garlic.
5. Then chop onion in the pieces.
6. Mix it with spices.
7. Rub meat with spices and onion.
8. Preheat the Air Fryer to 380F.
9. After that put meat in the Air Fryer. Cook for 10 minutes.
10. Then sprinkle with soy sauce and cook for 10 minutes more.

Nutrition:
- Calories: 128
- Fat: 4,9g
- Carbohydrates: 1,2g
- Protein: 22,5g

Steak with Spices

This meal is piquant and not everyone can eat it. But if you attempt, you can understand, that the spicy meat is incredibly delightful.

| **Prep time:** 30 minutes | **Cooking time:** 20 minutes | **Servings:** 4 |

Ingredients:

- 9 oz of free
- ½ teaspoon of salt
- ½ teaspoon of pepper
- 4 steaks
- 1 pepper
- 1 teaspoon of mustard
- ½ teaspoon of coriander
- 1 teaspoon of mustard
- 2 teaspoons of paprika
- 1 teaspoon of chili pepper

Directions:

1. Take the bowl and blend all flavors.
2. Then chop meat in the pieces and rub with spices.
3. Leave them aside for 20 minutes.
4. Preheat the Air Fryer to 380F.
5. Place peppery meat in the Air Fryer, cook for 10 minutes.
6. Wash and chop pepper.
7. Add it to Air Fryer, cook for 10 minutes more.

Nutrition:

- Calories: 123
- Fat: 4,8g
- Carbohydrates: 1,4g
- Protein: 22,7g

Ginger Beef

If you prepare this meal, you can be sure, that you will not be hungry. You will not spend a lot of your time to prepare it. Just try!

| **Prep time:** 10 minutes | **Cooking time:** 25 minutes | **Servings:** 4 |

Ingredients:

- ½ teaspoon of salt
- ½ teaspoon of pepper
- 1 teaspoon of red chili flakes
- 1 tablespoon of oil
- 3 tablespoons of soy sauce
- ¼ cup of ginger
- 3 onions
- 2 eggs
- 2 carrot
- ¾ cup of corn flour
- 1 lb of beef

Directions:

1. Take the bowl and mix spices there.
2. Wash and cut meat in the pieces.
3. Rub meat with spices.
4. Chop onion in the pieces.
5. Then chop carrot and add them to meat.
6. Beat eggs and mix everything well.
7. Preheat the Air Fryer to 350F.
8. Sprinkle the frying basket with oil.
9. Put the mixture in the Air Fryer and cook for 15 minutes.
10. Then add soy sauce and corn flour and cook for 10 minutes more.

Nutrition:

- Calories: 127
- Fat: 4,8g
- Carbohydrates: 1,5g
- Protein: 22,7g

Roles with Beef

These rolls are very wonderful. You can make these roles with the beef for friends or for the picnic. They can be ready even for the regular breakfast.

Prep time: 15 minutes | **Cooking time:** 10 minutes | **Servings:** 4

Ingredients:
- 10 egg roll wrappers
- ½ teaspoon of salt
- ½ teaspoon of pepper

- 4 cups of beef with cabbage
- 5 pieces of cheese

- 2 tablespoons of oil
- ½ cup of marmalade

Directions
1. Wash and cut meat in the pieces.
2. Rub it with salt and pepper.
3. Then add marmalade and mix everything well.
4. Cut cheese and add to the mixture.
5. Do not forget to cut cabbage.
6. Divide this mixture and put on the rolls.
7. Preheat the Air Fryer to 370F.
8. Sprinkle the frying basket with oil.
9. Put the mixture in the Air Fryer and cook for 10 minutes.
10. Enjoy with the delicious and spicy meat.

Nutrition:
- Calories: 137
- Fat: 4,3g

- Carbohydrates: 1,6g
- Protein: 24,7g

Piquant Taquitos with Beef

Your kids can eat these taquitos with the hot beef. You get pleasing, easy and peppery taquitos.

Prep time: 15 minutes | **Cooking time:** 15 minutes | **Servings:** 4

Ingredients:
- 2 tablespoons of oil
- ½ teaspoon of pepper
- ½ teaspoon of salt
- 1 teaspoon of coriander

- 1 teaspoon of cumin
- ¾ cup of cheese
- ½ teaspoon of garlic powder

- ½ teaspoon of paprika
- 18 ready tortillas
- 1 lb of beef

Directions:
1. Rinse and slice the beef.
2. Blend it with pepper, salt, then cumin, coriander, paprika and garlic.
3. Preheat the Air Fryer to 380F.
4. Sprinkle the frying basket with oil.
5. Take tortillas, place meat combination on them and cook for 10 minutes.
6. Then add cheese and cook 5 minutes more.
7. Enjoy with pasta.
8. Do not forget about juice – they are piquant.

Nutrition:
- Calories: 142,5
- Fat: 4,6g

- Carbohydrates: 1,2g
- Protein: 24,3g

Homemade Hot Dogs

If you need to make the hot dogs at home for your kids, you can do it in this second. Be sure, that these cooked hot dogs will be very scrumptious.

Prep time: 15 minutes | **Cooking time:** 15 minutes | **Servings:** 4

Ingredients:

- 2-3 teaspoons of chopped onion
- ½ teaspoon of salt
- ½ teaspoons of pepper
- 2 teaspoons of ketchup
- 2 teaspoon of mustard
- 8 pieces of bacon
- 1 tablespoon of mayo
- 4 buns for hot dogs

Directions:

1. Chop bacon in the small pieces and blend them with salt and pepper.
2. Take buns and split them in 2 pieces.
3. Put ketchup and mustard with mayo in the central of buns.
4. Then place bacon.
5. Put chopped onion on the top.
6. Preheat the Air Fryer to 380F.
7. Sprinkle the Air Fryer basket with oil.
8. Place the hot dogs in the Air Fryer and cook for 10-15 minutes.
9. Serve warm and enjoy with them.

Nutrition:

- Calories: 131
- Fat: 4,2g
- Carbohydrates: 1,1g
- Protein: 24,5g

Cooked Lamb

If someone demands for preparing something innovative with lamb, he/she should check this method. Lamb will be brilliant and soft.

Prep time: 15 minutes | **Cooking time:** 20 minutes | **Servings:** 4

Ingredients:

- 1 pound of lamb
- ½ cup of bread crumbs
- ½ teaspoon of salt
- ½ teaspoon of pepper
- 1 teaspoon of mustard
- 1 teaspoon of rosemary
- ½ teaspoon of oregano
- 2 tablespoons of oil

Directions:

1. Wash and chop lamb.
2. Then mix salt, pepper, mustard, oil, rosemary, oregano in the bowl.
3. Cover meat with this spices.
4. Then preheat the Air Fryer to 350F.
5. Sprinkle the frying basket with oil.
6. Cover lamb with bread crumbs.
7. Put lamb in the Air Fryer.
8. Cook for 10 minutes at 350F.
9. Then put on the other side and cook for 10 minutes more.
10. Serve warm with sauce.

Nutrition:

- Calories: 146
- Fat: 5,3g
- Carbohydrates: 1,2g
- Protein: 22,7g

Asparagus with Bacon

Do you have the huge desire to blend meat with the fresh vegetables? This recipe can provide you with the needed help. The meal will be actually scrumptious.

Prep time: 15 minutes | **Cooking time:** 15 minutes | **Servings:** 4

Ingredients:
- ½ teaspoon of pepper
- ½ teaspoon of salt
- Asparagus spears
- 8 pieces of bacon
- ½ teaspoon of paprika

Directions:
1. Wash and dry asparagus.
2. Then cut bacon in the strings.
3. Rub these strings with salt, pepper and paprika.
4. Preheat the Air Fryer to 370F.
5. Sprinkle the frying basket with oil.
6. Then take asparagus and wrap bacon strings around them.
7. Cook for 10 minutes in the Air Fryer.
8. Then shake them well and cook for 2 minutes more.
9. You will like them and will not be hungry.

Nutrition:
- Calories: 124
- Fat: 3,3g
- Carbohydrates: 1,1g
- Protein: 15,7g

Steaks with Mushrooms

It is the great mixture of these products - the family will estimate your effort. Mushrooms create the pleasant note for the whole meal.

Prep time: 15 minutes | **Cooking time:** 15-17 minutes | **Servings:** 4

Ingredients:
- 1 lb of steak
- 1 cup of mushrooms
- 2 tablespoons of oil
- ½ teaspoon of pepper
- ½ teaspoon of salt
- ½ teaspoon of oregano
- ½ cup of bread crumbs

Directions:
1. Wash and cup meat in the pieces.
2. Take the deep bowl and put salt, pepper and then oregano in it.
3. Rub meat with these spices.
4. Wash and cup mushrooms in the small pieces.
5. Place them in the bowl with meat.
6. After that cover everything with bread crumbs and mix well.
7. Preheat the Air Fryer to 340F.
8. Sprinkle the frying basket with oil.
9. Put meat with mushrooms in the Air Fryer.
10. Cook for 15 minutes.
11. Then shake them well and cook for 2-3 minutes more.

Nutrition:
- Calories: 146
- Fat: 5,3g
- Carbohydrates: 1,2g
- Protein: 15,8g

Cooked and Piquant Bacon

Do you plan to cook something original from bacon? Try this recipe and you will be shocked about how pleasant bacon is.

Prep time: 15 minutes	**Cooking time:** 10 minutes	**Servings:** 4

Ingredients:

- ½ teaspoon of salt
- ½ teaspoon of pepper
- 1 tablespoon of ketchup
- 1 tablespoon of soy sauce
- 3 cloves of garlic
- ½ teaspoon of paprika
- ½ teaspoon of oregano
- 1 lb of bacon
- 1 cup of breadcrumbs

Directions:

1. Blend salt, pepper, ketchup, garlic, paprika and oregano in the bowl.
2. Chop bacon in the small pieces and rub them with spices.
3. Then add soy sauce and blend all products well.
4. Cover everything with bread crumbs and mix all ingredients.
5. Preheat the Air Fryer to 350F.
6. Sprinkle the Air Fryer basket with oil.
7. After that cook it for 5 minutes.
8. Shake bacon well and cook for 5 minutes more.
9. Eat with your friends.

Nutrition:

- Calories: 148
- Fat: 5,5g
- Carbohydrates: 1,4g
- Protein: 22,7g

Steaks with Beef

You can prepare the great steaks with pasta. They are delicious, soft and fantastic. The great option for the picnic.

Prep time: 15 minutes	**Cooking time:** 15-17 minutes	**Servings:** 4

Ingredients:

- ½ teaspoon of pepper
- ½ teaspoon of salt
- ½ teaspoon of garlic
- ½ teaspoon of cumin
- 2 tablespoons of sauce
- 1 lb of beef

Directions:

1. Take the dep bowl and mix salt, cumin, pepper and garlic.
2. Wash and clean the beef.
3. Chop it in the pieces.
4. Rub the beef with seasonings.
5. Then rub them with sauce.
6. Preheat the Air Fryer to 380F.
7. Sprinkle the basket with oil.
8. Then put the pieces of meat in the Air Fryer.
9. Cook for 5 minutes, then shake well and cook for 5 minutes more.
10. Serve warm with vegetables and pastas.

Nutrition:

- Calories: 138
- Fat: 5,4g
- Carbohydrates: 1,3g
- Protein: 22,8g

Beef

The beef will be brilliant and soft. It is the innovative meat. Dinner is essentially delightful. You will not spend a lot of your time to prepare it. Just try!

Prep time: 15 minutes | **Cooking time:** 10 minutes | **Servings:** 4

Ingredients:

Gravy:

- 2 cups of milk
- 1 teaspoon of pepper
- 2 teaspoons of flour
- 6 oz of ground sausages

For steaks:

- 1 teaspoon of pepper
- 1 teaspoon of salt
- 1 teaspoon of onion powder

- 1 teaspoon of garlic powder
- 1 cup of bread crumbs
- 1 cup of flour
- 3 eggs
- 1 lb of beef

Directions:
1. Blend flavors in the container. Slice the meet in the pieces.
2. Rub with these flavors. Beat three eggs in the bowl.
3. Preheat the Air Fryer to 380F.
4. Leave the beef in flour. Then place it in eggs. After that put it in the crumbs of bread.
5. Cook in the Air Fryer for 5 minutes.
6. After that blend sausages, milk, flour and pepper.
7. Cover meat with the mixed components and cook for 5 minutes.

Nutrition:
- Calories: 156,3
- Fat: 6,9g
- Carbohydrates: 1,4g
- Protein: 22,9g

Beef for Sunday

If you have free time and you wish to prepare something delicious for dinner for your family – choose this one. The beef has crispy skin and is fantastic.

Prep time: 15 minutes | **Cooking time:** 15 minutes | **Servings:** 4

Ingredients:
- 1 marinade for beef
- ½ teaspoon of salt
- ½ teaspoon of pepper

- ½ teaspoon of paprika
- 1 onion
- ½ cup of mushrooms

- 6 oz of beef

Directions:
1. Take the bowl and mix salt, pepper and paprika there.
2. Wash and clean the beef.
3. Chop it in the pieces.
4. Rub with the mixture of seasonings.
5. Then chop onion and add there.
6. Cut mushrooms in the slices and mix everything well.
7. Preheat the Air Fryer to 365F.
8. Sprinkle the basket with oil. Add marinade to the mixture and make cutlets.
9. Put them in the Air Fryer and cook for 15 minutes.

Nutrition:
- Calories: 165
- Fat: 7g
- Carbohydrates: 1,3g
- Protein: 22,8g

Fiery Schnitzel with Beef

Cook this delicious schnitzel with the beef. It is piquant and amazing. The unusual note is in this meal.

Prep time: 10 minutes | **Cooking time:** 12 minutes | **Servings:** 1

Ingredients:

- 1 piece of lemon
- 1 thin beef schnitzel
- 1 egg
- 2 oz of bread crumbs
- 2 tablespoons of oil
- ½ teaspoon of salt
- ½ teaspoon of pepper

Directions:

1. Preheat the Air Fryer to 350F.
2. Then sprinkle the frying basket with oil.
3. Rub meat with salt and pepper.
4. Then blend bread crumbs and oil together.
5. Beat egg in the bowl.
6. Put meat in breadcrumbs. Then place it in egg. After that put the beef in breadcrumbs again.
7. Put in the Air Fryer and cook for 12-13 minutes.
8. Serve hot or warm, with the decorated lemon.

Nutrition:

- Calories: 127
- Fat: 6,3g
- Carbohydrates: 1,2g
- Protein: 22,6g

Beef with Fiery Red Pepper

This beef with pepper meal is flavorsome and delicious. The great breakfast, dinner, just cook and check.

Prep time: 10 minutes | **Cooking time:** 13 minutes | **Servings:** 4

Ingredients:

- 2 tablespoons of oil
- ½ teaspoon of pepper
- ½ teaspoon of salt
- 1/2 teaspoon of red chili flakes
- 3 cloves of garlic
- 1 onion
- 1 tablespoon of sauce
- 1 tablespoon of ketchup
- 1 lb of beef
- 6 tablespoons of corn flour
- 2 eggs

Directions:

1. Take the bowl and mix pepper, salt, chili flakes, garlic in it.
2. Wash and cut meat.
3. After that rub the beef with spices.
4. Then slice onion and mix everything.
5. After that add sauce and ketchup and mix everything.
6. Create cutlets from this mixture.
7. Put every cutlet in flour,
8. Then beat eggs and put cutlets in eggs and then again in flour.
9. Preheat the Air Fryer to 350F.
10. Cook them for 13 minutes.

Nutrition:

- Calories: 136
- Fat: 6,2g
- Carbohydrates: 1,3g
- Protein: 22,7g

Beef with Onion and Pepper

The great combination and this meal can be even for the holiday. It is easy and simple. Also, it will be great if you have a big family.

Prep time: 10 minutes | **Cooking time:** 11 minutes | **Servings:** 4

Ingredients:
- ½ teaspoon of pepper
- ½ teaspoon of salt
- 1 green pepper
- 1 onion
- 1 teaspoon of paprika
- 1 teaspoon of onion powder
- ½ teaspoon of oregano
- 2 tablespoons of oil.

Directions:
1. Wash and cut meat in the pieces.
2. Then rub meat with pepper, salt, paprika, onion powder and oregano.
3. Preheat the Air Fryer to 380F.
4. Make cutlets from the mixture and cook for 6 minutes.
5. Then chop onion in the pieces.
6. Chop pepper and mix with onion.
7. Then put them on other side, add onion with pepper and cook for 5 minutes more.
8. Enjoy with meat and vegetables.

Nutrition:
- Calories: 133
- Fat: 6,3g
- Carbohydrates: 1,5g
- Protein: 22,6g

Hot Beef with Mushrooms

Try these mushrooms with the piquant beef. The delicious, wonderful and scrumptious beef meal with mushrooms.

Prep time: 10 minutes | **Cooking time:** 18 minutes | **Servings:** 4

Ingredients:
- 2 tablespoons of flour
- ½ teaspoon of pepper
- ½ teaspoon of salt
- 3 oz of beef broth
- 2 oz of butter
- 9 oz of mushrooms
- 9 oz of onion
- 4 oz of sour cream

Directions:
1. Cut onion and put in the bowl.
2. Then cut mushrooms in the pieces and add to the bowl.
3. Then wash and cut the beef in the small pieces.
4. Blend the ingredients well.
5. Sprinkle the Air Fryer with oil.
6. Place meat in the Air Fryer and cook for 10 minutes at 290F.
7. Then add flour and beef broth and cook for 5 minutes more.
8. Add sour cream and cook 3 minutes.
9. Serve hot and enjoy with perfect meal.

Nutrition:
- Calories: 367
- Fat: 10,7g
- Carbohydrates: 1,4g
- Protein: 22,8g

Hamburgers with Beef

It is possible to prepare your favorite hamburgers at home and they will be even more delicious than hamburgers in the shop.

| Prep time:10 minutes | Cooking time: 13 minutes | Servings: 4 |

Ingredients:
- 1 lb of beef
- Buns for hamburgers
- ½ teaspoon of salt
- ½ teaspoon of pepper
- Tomato
- Onion
- 3 tablespoons of ketchup
- 3 tablespoons of mustard

Directions:
1. Wash and rub meat with salt and pepper.
2. Then cut it in the pieces.
3. Put buns and divide them in 2 parts.
4. After that cover the bun with ketchup and mustard.
5. Preheat the Air Fryer to 380F.
6. Sprinkle the frying basket with oil.
7. Then cook meat for 10 minutes.
8. Put the ready meat on buns.
9. Chop onion and tomato.
10. Decorate the bun with them.
11. Then put the second part of the bun above.
12. Put them in the Air Fryer for 3 minutes.

Nutrition:
- Calories: 345
- Fat: 10,9g
- Carbohydrates: 1,1g
- Protein: 22,6g

Cheese Meatballs with Macaroni

This meal is very delicious. It will not take a lot of your time and your guests will be delighted with the original meal on your table.

| Prep time:10 minutes | Cooking time: 13 minutes | Servings: 4 |

Ingredients:
- 2 tablespoons of onion
- ½ teaspoon of pepper
- ½ teaspoon of salt
- 3 tablespoons of bread crumbs
- 1 tablespoon of oil
- 1 cup of cheese
- 2 cups of milk
- 1 tablespoon of sauce
- 3 cups of macaroni
- Frozen meatballs

Directions:
1. Boil macaroni and leave them.
2. Preheat the Air Fryer to 350F.
3. Sprinkle the Air Fryer basket with oil.
4. Then cook meatballs for 3 minutes.
5. Put them on the plate.
6. Mix macaroni with the sale, pepper, oil, cheese, milk and sauce.
7. Add meatballs and cook for 10 minutes at the same temperature.

Nutrition:
- Calories: 368
- Fat: 13,9g
- Carbohydrates: 1,5g
- Protein: 25,7g

Bacon Cheeseburger

Now you will have the opportunity to prepare cheeseburger at home. It is easy and delicious. Try and enjoy.

Prep time: 10 minutes | **Cooking time:** 39 minutes | **Servings:** 4

Ingredients:
- ¼ cup of onion
- 2 cups of cheese
- 7 pieces of bacon
- 32 oz of potatoes
- ½ cup of sour cream
- ½ teaspoon of salt
- ½ teaspoon of pepper
- 1 lb of beef

Directions:
1. Cook the Air Fryer to 350F.
2. Sprinkle the Air Fryer basket with oil.
3. Chop onion and the beef.
4. Rub with salt and pepper.
5. Put in the Air Fryer and cook for 9 minutes.
6. Then cover them with sour cream and leave aside.
7. Put potatoes in the Air Fryer, then put meat and cover with cheese.
8. Cook for 30 minutes at 270F.
9. You will get the tasty meal, which you can show your guests.

Nutrition:
- Calories: 345
- Fat: 13,6g
- Carbohydrates: 1,7g
- Protein: 25,8g

Hamburger Hash

This meal will be melt in your mouth if you prepare it. The incredibly delicious and soft meat when will be often on your table in the future.

Prep time: 10 minutes | **Cooking time:** 35 minutes | **Servings:** 4

Ingredients:
- 1 teaspoon of pepper
- ½ teaspoon of salt
- 1 carrot
- 28 oz of potatoes
- ¾ cup of water
- 1 cup of beef stock
- 1 tomato puree
- 3 lb of beef

Directions:
1. Wash and cut the beef in the bowl.
2. Then mix it with salt and pepper.
3. After that preheat the Air Fryer to 380F.
4. Cook meat for 10 minutes.
5. After that add tomato puree, 1 chopped carrot and mix everything well.
6. Put potatoes in the Air Fryer.
7. Then put meat and pour with the beef stock.
8. Cook for 25 minutes at 290F.
9. Serve hot with vegetables.
10. Decorate with basil leaves.

Nutrition:
- Calories: 332
- Fat: 12,7g
- Carbohydrates: 1,1g
- Protein: 25,6g

Scrumptious Noodles with Piquant Beef

Easy, tasty and really fantastic meal. It is uncomplicated in the process of the preparing.

Prep time: 10 minutes	Cooking time: 30 minutes	Servings: 4

Ingredients:

- 4 oz of mushrooms
- 3 tablespoon of ketchup
- ½ teaspoon of dry herbs
- ½ cup of water
- 5 oz of ready noodles
- 1 onion
- 1 green pepper
- 1 lb of beef
- ½ teaspoon of salt
- ½ teaspoon of pepper

Directions:

1. Wash and slice the beef in the pieces.
2. Then add salt, pepper to it and mix everything.
3. Preheat the Air Fryer to 350F.
4. Sprinkle the Air Fryer basket with oil.
5. Then put the beef in the Air Fryer and cook for 10 minutes.
6. Chop pepper and onion.
7. Cook meat in the Air Fryer for 9-10 minutes.
8. Then place noodles, onion and pepper, blend all products well.
9. Cook for 10 minutes more at 250F.

Nutrition:

- Calories: 365
- Fat: 12,3g
- Carbohydrates: 1,2g
- Protein: 25,4g

Mushrooms with Beef

If you wish to prepare pasta with meat, then you should check this recipe. Pasta will be delicious and not too spicy. You will like it very much.

Prep time: 10 minutes	Cooking time: 30 minutes	Servings: 4

Ingredients:

- 2 tablespoons of parsley
- ½ teaspoon of pepper
- ½ teaspoon of salt
- 3 eggs
- 1/3 cup of cream
- 1 onion
- 2 cloves of garlic
- 8 oz of mushrooms
- ½ lb of beef
- 12 oz of spaghetti

Directions:

1. Boil spaghetti and leave aside.
2. Mix the beef with salt, pepper and garlic and cut in the small pieces.
3. Preheat the Air Fryer to 380F.
4. Sprinkle the Air Fryer with oil.
5. Put meat and cook for 10 minutes at 350F.
6. Then mix spaghetti with eggs and cream.
7. Chop onion and mushrooms and add them also there.
8. Then mix everything well.
9. Add meat and cook for 20 minutes at 350F.

Nutrition:

- Calories: 325
- Fat: 11,9g
- Carbohydrates: 1,3g
- Protein: 25,5g

Peppery Burrito with Flavorsome Beef

This meal will be the needed choice. Tasty and uncomplicated.

Prep time: 10 minutes	**Cooking time:** 25 minutes	**Servings:** 4

Ingredients:
- ¼ cup of onion
- ½ cup of sour cream
- 1 cup of cheese
- 4 flour tortillas
- 15 oz of black beans
- 1 cup of water
- ½ teaspoon of salt
- ½ teaspoon of pepper
- 1 lb of beef

Directions:
1. Preheat the Air Fryer to 380F.
2. Sprinkle the frying basket with oil.
3. Then wash and chop meat.
4. Rub it with salt and pepper.
5. Then cook in the Air Fryer for 10 minutes.
6. Chop onion in small pieces.
7. Mix the beef with onion, sour cream, cheese, beans.
8. Then divide the combination in the parts and put on tortillas.
9. Cook the food for 15 minutes in the Air Fryer.
10. Serve hot and decorate with fresh basil leaves.

Nutrition:
- Calories: 289
- Fat: 10,6g
- Carbohydrates: 1,2g
- Protein: 25,3g

Yummy and Original Cheeseburger

It is something innovative and wonderful. The products are very simple and not exclusive. Cook and adore.

Prep time: 10 minutes	**Cooking time:** 25 minutes	**Servings:** 4

Ingredients:
- 4 pieces of cheese
- 1 cup of croutons
- 2 tomatoes
- 1 box of macaroni
- 1 onion
- 2 cup of milks
- 1 lb of beef
- ½ teaspoon of pepper
- ½ teaspoon of salt

Directions:
1. Wash and chop meat.
2. Run the pieces of meat with salt and pepper.
3. Then chop onion with meat and mix everything.
4. Preheat the Air Fryer to 380F.
5. Sprinkle the frying basket with oil.
6. Then put meat in the Air Fryer and cook for 10 minutes.
7. After that add croutons and 2 cups of milk.
8. Put the ready macaroni in the Air Fryer and add chopped tomatoes.
9. Mix everything well.
10. Cook everything for 15 minutes at the same temperature.

Nutrition:
- Calories: 325
- Fat: 11,9g
- Carbohydrates: 1,3g
- Protein: 25,5g

Bacon Avocado Salad

It seems to be crazy, but it is very delicious. The meal has some new note and you will like it a lot. You can surprise your family with it.

Prep time: 10 minutes | **Cooking time:** 20 minutes | **Servings:** 4

Ingredients:
- 1 avocado
- 8 pieces of bacon
- 1 cup of aragula leaves
- 1 cup of cheese
- 1 cup of tomatoes
- 2 tablespoons of basil leaves
- ½ teaspoon of salt
- ½ teaspoon of pepper
- 1 tablespoon of vinegar
- ½ teaspoon of dry herbs
- ¼ tablespoon of oil
- 1 box of pasta

Directions:
1. Cook pasta and leave aside.
2. Then cut bacon in the small pieces.
3. Mix it with salt, pepper, dry herbs and vinegar.
4. Then add basil leaves and aragula leaves.
5. Preheat the Air Fryer to 380F.
6. Sprinkle the Air Fryer with oil.
7. Put the mixture in the Air Fryer and cook for 10 minutes.
8. Then add pasta and chopped tomatoes.
9. Decorate with cheese and cook for 10minutes.

Nutrition:
- Calories: 315
- Fat: 11,7g
- Carbohydrates: 1,2g
- Protein: 25,3g

Bacon Cheeseburger Casserole

This meal will melt in your mouth, because it is very soft and incredibly tasty. Prepare and you will see, that it is truc. This meat is fantastic.

Prep time: 10 minutes | **Cooking time:** 30 minutes | **Servings:** 4

Ingredients:
- ¼ cup of onion
- 2 cups of cheese
- 4 big pieces of bacon
- 32 oz of frozen potatoes
- 1 cup of onion soup
- ½ teaspoon of salt
- ½ teaspoon of pepper
- ½ teaspoon of paprika
- ½ teaspoon of dry herbs
- 1 lb of beef

Directions:
1. Preheat the Air Fryer to 360F.
2. Sprinkle the Air Fryer basket with oil.
3. Wash and cut bacon.
4. Mix it with salt, pepper, dry herbs, paprika in the bowl.
5. Then cook it in the Air Fryer for 10 minutes.
6. After that add potatoes, chopped onion and mix everything.
7. Pour with the soup and cook for 20 minutes at the same temperature.
8. Serve hot with parsley.

Nutrition:
- Calories: 303
- Fat: 11,5g
- Carbohydrates: 1,3g
- Protein: 25,6g

Savory Meat

It is very delicious and appetizing meal. Cook and like this type of scrumptious meat.

Prep time: 50 minutes | **Cooking time:** 20 minutes | **Servings:** 4

Ingredients:
- ¼ teaspoon of cumin
- 1 tablespoon of sauce chili
- 1/3 cup of spicy sauce
- ½ teaspoon of salt
- ½ teaspoon of pepper
- 1 lb of beef

Directions:
1. Cook the Air Fryer to 390F.
2. Sprinkle the frying basket with oil.
3. Cut the beef in the pieces.
4. Rub it with salt and pepper.
5. Then cover meat with the chili sauce and spicy sauce.
6. Leave it for 30 minutes.
7. Cook meat in the Air Fryer for 10 minutes at 380F.
8. Then shake them well and cook for 10 minutes more.
9. Take out of Air Fryer and put on the plate.
10. Decorate with basil leaves.
11. Serve hot with fresh vegetable salad.

Nutrition:
- Calories: 310
- Fat: 11,4g
- Carbohydrates: 1,2g
- Protein: 25,6g

Grilled Yummy Steak

It is uncomplicated, wonderful and unassuming.

Prep time: 1 hour 15 minutes | **Cooking time:** 15 minutes

Servings: 4

Ingredients:
- ½ teaspoon of salt
- ½ teaspoon of pepper
- 2 tablespoons of lemon juice
- 1/3 cup of mustard
- 1 cup of cheese
- 1 lb of beef

Directions:
1. Wash and clean the beef.
2. Take the bowl and mix mustard and lemon juice there.
3. Place the beef in the bowl and blend everything.
4. Leave for 1 hour in the fridge.
5. Then cut the beef in the parts.
6. Add salt and pepper and blend all ingredients well.
7. Preheat the Air Fryer to 380F.
8. Sprinkle the frying basket with oil.
9. Then place the beef in the Air Fryer and cook for 10 minutes.
10. Put meat on other side and cover with cheese.
11. Cook for 5 minutes more at 350F.

Nutrition:
- Calories: 269
- Fat: 10,6g
- Carbohydrates: 1,5g
- Protein: 21,9g

Scrumptious Burgers with Beef

Make these easy snacks for the picnic. The burgers with the beef are delightful and yummy.

Prep time: 20 minutes | **Cooking time:** 15 minutes | **Servings:** 4

Ingredients:

- 4 bread buns
- 1 oz of cheese
- ½ teaspoon of salt
- ½ teaspoon of pepper
- 1 teaspoon of dry herbs
- 1 tablespoon of mustard
- 1 tablespoon of tomato puree
- 1 tablespoon of basil
- 1 tablespoon of garlic puree
- 1 onion
- 12 oz of mixed mince

Directions:

1. Place meat in the bowl.
2. Then add salt, then pepper and dry herbs there.
3. Mix everything well.
4. Then add mustard, tomato puree, basil and garlic puree.
5. Mix all ingredients.
6. Make cutlets from this mixture.
7. Preheat the Air Fryer to 380F.
8. Cook cutlets for 5 minutes.
9. Then place them on the other side and cook for 5 minutes more.
10. Place them on buns, add piece of cheese and chopped onion.
11. Then set in the Air Fryer and cook for 5 minutes more.

Nutrition:

- Calories: 257
- Fat: 10,3g
- Carbohydrates: 1,2g
- Protein: 21,8g

Grilled Broccoli with Piquant Meat

It is the delicious, wonderful and healthy. Your gusts will be delighted with it.

Prep time: 3 minutes | **Cooking time:** 15 minutes | **Servings:** 4

Ingredients:

- 1 teaspoon of oil
- 1 small onion
- 1 teaspoon of onion powder
- 1 teaspoon of garlic powder
- ½ teaspoon of salt
- ½ teaspoon of pepper
- 1 tablespoon of sauce
- 1 lb of beef
- 1 cup of cooked broccoli

Directions:

1. Preheat the Air Fryer to 360F.
2. Sprinkle the Air Fryer basket with oil.
3. Divide the meet in the small pieces.
4. Rub the beef with salt, pepper, then garlic powder, sauce and onion powder.
5. Cook the beef in the Air Fryer for 10 minutes.
6. Then add broccoli, chopped onion and blend all components well.
7. Cook for 5 minutes.

Nutrition:

- Calories: 269
- Fat: 10,7g
- Carbohydrates: 1,1g
- Protein: 23,8g

Lamb Chops

This meat is usual one, but it is very delicious and tasty. The soft meat with the rest of ingredients can be prepared for some celebration. You can be sure, that the guests will like it.

Prep time: 15 minutes | **Cooking time:** 20 minutes | **Servings:** 4

Ingredients:

- 8 lamb chops
- ½ teaspoon of salt
- 1 teaspoon of pepper
- 1 teaspoon of oregano
- 1 teaspoon of garlic powder
- 1 teaspoon of cumin
- 1 teaspoon of dry herbs
- 2 tablespoons of oil
- 1 cup of cheese

Directions:

1. Wash and clean meat.
2. Preheat the Air Fryer to 370F.
3. Sprinkle the frying basket with oil.
4. Cut meat in the big pieces.
5. Then mix salt, pepper, dry herbs, cumin, garlic powder and oregano in the bowl.
6. Put the pieces of meat in spices and mix everything well.
7. Then put meat in the Air Fryer.
8. Cook for 10 minutes, then shake well and cook for 5 minutes more.
9. Add cheese and mix everything again.
10. After that cook for 5 minutes at 300F.

Nutrition:

- Calories: 239
- Fat: 11,2g
- Carbohydrates: 1,3g
- Protein: 23,4g

Cooked Peppery Lamb

This meal is basic in preparing. Meat is flavorsome and scrumptious.

Prep time: 15 minutes | **Cooking time:** 35 minutes | **Servings:** 4

Ingredients:

- 2 tablespoons of sauce
- 4 teaspoons of onion flakes
- 2 tablespoons of oil
- 4 teaspoons of rosemary
- 4 teaspoons of garlic
- 1 sweet potato
- 2 carrots
- 3 brushed potatoes
- 1 lb of lamb
- ½ teaspoon of salt
- 1 teaspoon of pepper

Directions:

1. Preheat the Air Fryer to 300F.
2. Slice carrots and potatoes in the pieces.
3. Place vegetables in the Air Fryer and cook for 20 minutes.
4. Cut lamb in the pieces.
5. Then rub lamb with garlic, rosemary, then salt and pepper.
6. Place the foil in the Air Fryer.
7. Then place meat, add onion flakes and sauce.
8. Blend all products well.
9. Cook for 15 minutes.

Nutrition:

- Calories: 260
- Fat: 11,8g
- Carbohydrates: 1,2g
- Protein: 23,9g

Appetizing Beef with Garlic and Cheese Sauce

This meal is spicy and yummy. Spices create the special aroma for the beef.

Prep time: 30 minutes | **Cooking time:** 20 minutes | **Servings:** 4

Ingredients:
- 4 beef chops
- ½ teaspoon of salt
- 1 teaspoon of pepper
- 1 teaspoon of cumin
- ½ teaspoon of oregano
- 1 teaspoon of chili pepper
- 1 cup of cheese
- 2 tablespoons of oil

Directions:
1. Wash the beef.
2. Then chop it in the pieces.
3. Take the bowl and mix chili pepper, cumin, oregano, then salt and pepper together.
4. Rub meat with spices.
5. Leave meat aside for 20 minutes.
6. Preheat the Air Fryer to 300F.
7. Cook meat for 10 minutes.
8. Then mix the components, add cheese and cook for 10 minutes.
9. Serve warm with pasta and red wine. Decorate with basil leaves or with parsley.

Nutrition:
- Calories: 289,2
- Fat: 12,7g
- Carbohydrates: 1,5g
- Protein: 24,7g

Spicy Potatoes with Mushrooms and Flavorsome Meat

This meat with flavorsome potatoes is for the ordinary dinner. The appetizing beef with the fiery potatoes is scrumptious.

Prep time: 20 minutes | **Cooking time:** 50 minutes | **Servings:** 4

Ingredients:
- 1 lb of potatoes
- ½ teaspoon of salt
- 1 teaspoon of pepper
- 3 tablespoons of oil
- 1 cup of mushrooms
- 1 cup of cheese
- ½ teaspoon of oregano
- ½ teaspoon of garlic
- 1 lb of beef

Directions:
1. Preheat the Air Fryer to 300F.
2. Wash and clean potatoes.
3. Sprinkle the Air Fryer with oil.
4. Place potatoes in the Air Fryer and cook for 20 minutes.
5. Chop the beef in the pieces.
6. Mix them with salt, oil, pepper, garlic and oregano.
7. Cook in the Air Fryer at 10 minutes.
8. Then place in the Air Fryer meet, potatoes, mushrooms and cheese and cook for 20 minutes.
9. Enjoy with the tasty dinner.
10. Serve hot with salad.

Nutrition:
- Calories: 290
- Fat: 12,3g
- Carbohydrates: 1,2g
- Protein: 24,5g

Scrumptious Cutlets with Beef and Cooked Spinach

Spinach is healthy and cutlets are original.

Prep time: 20 minutes	**Cooking time:** 30 minutes	**Servings:** 4

Ingredients:
- 1 cup of spinach
- 1 lb of beef
- ½ teaspoon of pepper
- ½ teaspoon of salt
- 3 tablespoons of oil
- 1 cup of bread crumbs
- 3 eggs
- 1 cup of flour
- ½ teaspoon of paprika

Directions:
1. Wash and chop meat in the pieces.
2. Then rub meat with salt, pepper, then paprika and spinach.
3. Preheat the Air Fryer to 300F.
4. Sprinkle the Air Fryer basket with oil.
5. Beat three eggs in the bowl.
6. Make cutlets from meat.
7. Put cutlets in flour, after that put them in eggs. Then place in bread crumbs.
8. Cook them in the Air Fryer at 300F for 20 minutes.
9. Then shake the spicy cutlets well and cook for 10 minutes more.
10. Eat with pasta.

Nutrition:
- Calories: 320
- Fat: 12,5g
- Carbohydrates: 1,5g
- Protein: 24,8g

Piquant Meat with Hot Pepper and Tomatoes

This combination of hot meat and fresh vegetables is wonderful. Enjoy with the smell of vegetables and flavorsome meat.

Prep time: 15 minutes	**Cooking time:** 30 minutes	**Servings:** 4

Ingredients:
- 1 big green pepper
- 2 tomatoes
- ½ lb of meat (up to you)
- 2 tablespoons of oil
- ½ teaspoon of salt
- 1 teaspoon of pepper
- 1 teaspoon of dry herbs
- 1 tablespoon of sauce

Directions:
1. Wash and cut the beef in the pieces.
2. Take the bowl and mix dry herbs, sauce, pepper, salt and 1 tablespoon of oil together.
3. Rub meat with these spices.
4. Preheat the Air Fryer to 290F.
5. Sprinkle the Air Fryer basket with oil.
6. Cook meat in the Air Fryer at 290F for 15 minutes,
7. Then chop tomatoes with pepper and put in the Air Fryer.
8. Cook the components with pasta for 15 minutes.
9. Serve hot with salad.

Nutrition:
- Calories: 321
- Fat: 12,6g
- Carbohydrates: 1,4g
- Protein: 24,9g

VEGETABLE MEALS

Flavorsome Cooked Avocado

It is very simple, easy to prepare and most importantly - an incredibly delicious meal.

| **Prep time**:10 minutes | **Cooking time**:10 minutes | **Servings**:4 |

Ingredients:

- ½ teaspoon of salt
- ½ teaspoon of pepper
- 1 big avocado
- 2 oz of white beans
- ½ cup of bread crumbs

Directions:

1. First of all, take the deep bowl.
2. Mix pepper, salt and bread crumbs.
3. Then place white beans in another bowl.
4. Chop avocado in small pieces.
5. Take the piece of avocado and put it in beans and after that in bread crumbs.
6. Preheat the Air Fryer to 390F.
7. Sprinkle the frying basket with oil.
8. After that put avocado pieces in the Air Fryer.
9. Cook for 5 minutes.
10. After that, shake avocado pieces well and cook for 5 minutes.
11. Serve hot and also you can take your favorite sauce.
12. Enjoy!

Nutrition:

- Calories: 212
- Fat: 20g
- Carbohydrates: 6g
- Protein: 2g

Apple Chips

The snacks, which are very easy for preparing. Also, these chips are very delicious.

Prep time:10 minutes | **Cooking time**:15 minutes | **Servings**:2

Ingredients:
- ¼ teaspoon of salt
- 1 tablespoon of sugar
- ½ teaspoon of cinnamon
- 1 big apple

Directions:
1. Firstly, preheat the Air Fryer to 380F.
2. Wash and clean the apple.
3. Chop the apple into the pieces.
4. Take small bowl and mix salt, sugar and cinnamon well.
5. Sprinkle the fry basket with oil or special spray.
6. Put the pieces of apple in the Air Fryer.
7. Cover the apple with salt, sugar and cinnamon.
8. Cook 7-8 minutes at 380F in Air Fryer.
9. Then put the pieces of the apple on another side and cook for 7-8 minutes again.
10. Then put them on the plate and wait 3-4 minutes till they are warm.

Nutrition:
- Calories: 253
- Fat: 0,2g
- Carbohydrates: 59g
- Protein: 2,2g

Crispy Tofu

The incredibly delicious meal. All your friends will like it.

Prep time:35 minutes | **Cooking time**:20 minutes | **Servings**:2

Ingredients:
- 1 tablespoon of potato starch
- 2 teaspoons of sesame oil
- ¼ teaspoon of salt
- ¼ teaspoon of pepper
- 1 teaspoon of vinegar
- 2 tablespoons of soy sauce
- 1 block of tofu

Directions:
1. Take the bowl.
2. Chop tofu into small pieces.
3. Put them in the bowl.
4. After that, add sesame oil, teaspoon of vinegar and mix everything well.
5. Then add soy sauce and mix everything again.
6. Also, put pepper and salt to the mixture.
7. Leave everything for 15-30 minutes.
8. After that, put the potato starch to tofu and mix together.
9. Put the frying basket.
10. Add oil there.
11. Then put the pieces of tofu in the Air Fryer.
12. Cook for 10 minutes at 370F.
13. Then shake well and cook for 10 minutes more.

Nutrition:
- Calories: 76
- Fat: 4,78g
- Carbohydrates: 1,88g
- Protein: 8,8g

Small Breakfast Burritos

If you wish to prepare something special for breakfast, then you made the right choice. These burritos are tasty and delicious.

Prep time:15 minutes	Cooking time:25 minutes	Servings:2

Ingredients:
- Pinch of spinach
- 6-8 fresh asparagus
- 1 small broccoli
- 8 strips of red pepper
- 1/3 cup of sweet potato

- 2 tofu scrambles
- 4 pieces of rice paper
- 1-2 tablespoons of water
- 1-2 tablespoons of liquid smoke

- 2-3 tablespoons of tamari
- 2 tablespoons of cashew butter

Directions:
1. Preheat the Air Fryer to 355F.
2. Put rice paper in Air Fryer.
3. Take small bowl.
4. Mix together liquid smoke, water, tamari and cashew butter.
5. Then chop asparagus, spinach, red pepper, sweet potato, tofu in the bowl and mix with the rest ingredients, which are in the bowl.
6. Put everything on rice paper and cook in the Air Fryer.
7. The burritos should be cooked at 350F for 10 minutes.
8. Then put the burritos on another side and cook for 15 minutes.
9. Serve warm and enjoy with the delicious snacks.

Nutrition:
- Calories: 132
- Fat: 8,5g

- Carbohydrates: 1,4g
- Protein: 8,3g

Ranch Kale Chips

These chips are very easy for preparing. The result will be great.

Prep time:5 minutes	Cooking time:5 minutes	Servings:4

Ingredients:
- ¼ teaspoon of salt
- ¼ teaspoon of oregano
- 1/3 teaspoon of garlic
- ½ teaspoon of turmeric

- 1 tablespoon of yeast flakes
- 2 teaspoon of seasonings
- 4 cups of kale

- 2 tablespoons of oil

Directions:
1. Preheat the Air Fryer to 370F.
2. Cut the kale into the pieces.
3. Then mix the kale with salt, oregano, turmeric, garlic powder, oil and yeast flakes in the bowl.
4. Put the kale in the Air Fryer.
5. Then cook it for 4-5 minutes in the Air Fryer.
6. It should have dark green color.
7. After that enjoy with the healthy and delicious kale.
8. It is possible to prepare with potatoes or decorate with the different vegetables.

Nutrition:
- Calories: 27
- Fat: 1g

- Carbohydrates: 4,7g
- Protein: 1,8g

Taco Crisp Wraps

It is tasty meal, which can be prepared as snack for guests. Easy in cooking and delicious.

Prep time:10 minutes | **Cooking time**:18 minutes | **Servings**:4

Ingredients:

- 4 tablespoons of vegan cheese
- Mixed greens
- Tortilla chips
- 1/3 cup of mango salsa
- 4 pieces of fish fillet
- 2 cobs of grilled corn
- 1 red pepper
- 1 yellow onion
- 4 burrito tortillas

Directions:

1. Preheat the Air Fryer to 390F.
2. Cut cheese and fish fillet in the pieces.
3. Then add the corn to it and mix everything.
4. Then cut the red pepper and onion.
5. Mix everything well with chips.
6. Take the burrito tortillas and divide the mixture in the same parts.
7. Put this mixture on tortillas.
8. Then roll them and put in the Air Fryer.
9. Cook for 12 minutes at 390F.
10. Then shake everything and cook for 6 minutes more.

Nutrition:

- Calories: 238
- Fat: 13,7g
- Carbohydrates: 9,6g
- Protein: 3,7g

Chonut Holes

This meal is tasty and delicious. It is very easy and simple in preparing. Your friends will like it.

Prep time:1h 15 minutes | **Cooking time**:11 minutes | **Servings**:4

Ingredients:

- 2 tablespoons of sugar
- 2 teaspoons of cinnamon
- ¼ cup of almond milk
- 2 tablespoons of aquafaba
- ½ teaspoon of salt
- 1 teaspoon of backing powder
- 1 cup of flour
- ¼ cup of sugar
- 1 red pepper

Directions:

1. Take the deep bowl.
2. Mix salt, aquafaba, sugar and ¼ cup of sugar together in the bowl.
3. Put the mixture aside for 1 hour.
4. Cut the red pepper in small pieces.
5. Mix the cinnamon and 2 tablespoons of sugar in the separate bowl.
6. After that, mix everything together with pepper.
7. Divide the mixture in 12 pieces and create the rolls.
8. Put the rolls in the Air Fryer.
9. Cook for 6 minutes at 370F.
10. Then shake them and cook 5 minutes more.

Nutrition:

- Calories: 197
- Fat: 13,2g
- Carbohydrates: 6,6g
- Protein: 2,7g

Tofu Scramble

This recipe will be the new one in your collection. Tasty and delicious. Just try!

Prep time: 5 minutes | **Cooking time**:30 minutes | **Servings**:4

Ingredients:
- 2 cups of broccoli
- 1 tablespoon of oil
- 2 cups of red potatoes
- ½ cup of onion
- ½ teaspoon of onion powder
- ½ teaspoon of garlic powder
- 1 teaspoon of turmeric
- 1 tablespoon of olive oil
- 2 tablespoons of sauce
- 1 block of tofu

Directions:
1. Chop broccoli, potatoes, onion.
2. Put them in the bowl.
3. Then add tofu, oil, onion powder, garlic powder and mix together.
4. Leave the mixture aside.
5. After that, put the mixture in the Air Fryer.
6. Do not forget to sprinkle the basket with oil.
7. Cook for 7-8 minutes at 350F.
8. Then put the mixture on another side and cook for 15 minutes at 370F.
9. Serve it hot.
10. You can decorate with the different vegetables or basil leaves.

Nutrition:
- Calories: 225
- Fat: 16,2g
- Carbohydrates: 7,6g
- Protein: 4,7g

Flavorsome Cauliflower

A fine dietary dinner or a side dish to the main course! It will be the great choice.

Prep time: 5 minutes | **Cooking time**:20-22 minutes | **Servings**:4

Ingredients:
- 4 cups of cauliflower
- 2 carrots
- 1 cup of bread crumbs
- 1 teaspoon of salt
- ¼ cup of vegan sauce
- ¼ cup of buffalo sauce
- ¼ teaspoon of pepper

Directions:
1. Mix the vegan sauce with the buffalo sauce.
2. Put every cauliflower in the mixture.
3. Then add salt, pepper and mix everything.
4. After that, chop carrots.
5. Put every cauliflower in bread crumbs and after that put in the Air Fryer.
6. Add carrot and cook for 14-17 minutes at 370F.
7. After that, shake everything well and cook for another 5 minutes.
8. When everything is ready, enjoy with the healthy and tasty food.

Nutrition:
- Calories: 139
- Fat: 15,2g
- Carbohydrates: 4,3g
- Protein: 4,2g

Brussels sprouts

It is really healthy meal. Also, you will see, that it is very delicious and children will like it.

Prep time: 5 minutes | **Cooking time**:10 minutes | **Servings**:4

Ingredients:
- ¼ teaspoon of salt
- ¼ teaspoon of pepper
- 1 tablespoon of oil
- ¼ teaspoon of paprika
- 1/3 teaspoon of oregano
- ½ teaspoon of garlic
- 1/3 teaspoon of ginger
- 1/3 teaspoon of cumin
- 2 cups of brussels sprouts

Directions:
1. Preheat the Air Fryer to 380F.
2. Put salt, pepper, oil, oregano and paprika in the bowl.
3. Mix everything well.
4. After that add garlic, cumin and ginger.
5. Mix these ingredients with the rest in the bowl.
6. You can cut brussels sprouts in 2 pieces.
7. Then rub every piece with spices.
8. Sprinkle the frying basket with oil.
9. Put brussels sprouts in the basket.
10. Cook for 8 minutes and then shake them.
11. After that, cook for another 8 minutes.
12. Serve hot and enjoy with healthy and crispy brussels sprouts with your family.

Nutrition:
- Calories: 86
- Fat: 6,2g
- Carbohydrates: 4,1g
- Protein: 2,2g

Piquant Chickpeas with Juice of Lemon

It is appetizing and vigorous meal. This meal is delectable and brilliant.

Prep time: 5 minutes | **Cooking time**:20 minutes | **Servings**:4

Ingredients:
- 2,5 tablespoons of juice of the fresh lemon
- ½ teaspoon of salt
- ½ teaspoon of pepper
- ½ teaspoon of paprika
- ½ teaspoon of cumin
- ½ teaspoon of oregano
- 2 tablespoons of oil
- 15 oz of chickpeas

Directions:
1. Take the small bowl.
2. After that blend the chickpeas with the fat in the container. When you are purchasing the chickpeas, you should not choose very big size.
3. Cook up the Air Fryer to 390F.
4. Then cook the chickpeas up to 15 minutes.
5. Later add rest of oil, oregano, cumin, paprika, then pepper, juice of lemon and salt.
6. Blend the foods in the bowl.
7. Place the chickpeas in the Air Fryer and cook for 5 minutes.
8. Serve with salad or vegetables.

Nutrition:
- Calories: 92
- Fat: 3,3g
- Carbohydrates: 3,2g
- Protein: 2,1g

Tofu

You can have the totally original and unusual meal, which will become your favored. There are countless minerals and different vitamins in this tofu meal.

| **Prep time**: 40 minutes | **Cooking time**:30 minutes | **Servings**:4 |

Ingredients:

- 1 teaspoon of salt
- 1 cup of bread crumbs
- ½ cup of vegan mayo
- 1 teaspoon of ginger
- ½ teaspoon of garlic
- 1 teaspoon of vinegar
- ¼ cup of soy sauce
- 1 tablespoon of sesame oil
- 1 block of tofu

Directions:

1. Make 8 cutlets of tofu.
2. Make marinade.
3. Mix sesame oil, soy sauce, garlic with vinegar and ginger together in the container.
4. Set cutlets on the plate and cover with marinade.
5. Leave the products for 30 minutes.
6. Place the vegan mayo in the bowl.
7. Mix salt and bread crumbs in another salt.
8. Put cheese in the mayo and then in bread crumbs.
9. Cook then for 20 minutes at 350F, then shake and cook for 10 minutes more.
10. You will get tasty cutlets, which can be good as for dinner as for breakfast.

Nutrition:

- Calories: 103
- Fat: 8,4g
- Carbohydrates: 5,1g
- Protein: 3,1g

Appetizing Potato

It is yummy meal and it is uncomplicated for preparing. Try and see.

| **Prep time**: 10 minutes | **Cooking time**: 35-40 minutes | **Servings**: 4 |

Ingredients:

- 1 teaspoon of salt
- 1 teaspoon of pepper
- 1 tablespoon of chives
- 1 tablespoon of Kalamata olives
- 1 piece of bacon
- 1 cup of vegan cream cheese
- 1/8 teaspoon of salt
- ¼ teaspoon of onion powder
- 1 teaspoon of oil
- 1 medium Russet potato

Directions:

1. Clean and wash potatoes
2. Then rub it with oil, onion powder and 1/8 teaspoon of salt.
3. Preheat the Air Fryer to 390F.
4. Put potatoes in the Air Fryer basket.
5. Cook potatoes for 35 minutes.
6. The potato should have the wonderful coffee color. Then place it on the other side and cook further.
7. Then add the rest of foodstuffs and cook for 5 minutes more.

Nutrition:

- Calories: 272
- Fat: 20.1g
- Carbohydrates: 37.1g
- Protein: 33.2g

Crispy Fried Pickles

You will get the most delicious and tasty meal. Enjoy with crispy skin of meal.

Prep time: 10 minutes	**Cooking time**: 35-40 minutes	**Servings**: 4

Ingredients:
- ½ cup of vegan sauce
- 2 teaspoons of oil
- ¼ teaspoon of cayenne pepper
- ½ teaspoon of paprika
- 6 tablespoons of bread crumbs
- 2 tablespoons of corn starch
- 2-3 tablespoons of water
- ¼ teaspoon of salt
- 3 tablespoons of dark beer
- 1/8 teaspoon of baking powder
- ¼ cup of flour
- 14 pickle slices

Directions:
1. Wash and clean the pickle slices, dry and leave aside.
2. Mix the baking powder, beer, salt and water together.
3. Then take two plates. Put the corn starch on the first plate.
4. Mix the paprika, salt, cayenne pepper and bread crumbs on the second plate.
5. Put every piece in the corn starch and after that in beer batter.
6. After that, put everything in bread crumbs.
7. Preheat the Air Fryer to 380F. Cook in the Air Fryer at 8 minutes and then shake well.
8. Cook for another 8 minutes.

Nutrition:
- Calories: 225
- Fat: 16.1g
- Carbohydrates: 33.1g
- Protein: 31.2g

Vegetable Fries

This meal will be great if you wish to prepare something easy and healthy. Everyone will like it, even children.

Prep time: 5 minutes	**Cooking time**: 15-20 minutes	**Servings**: 4

Ingredients:
- ¼ teaspoon of salt
- ¼ teaspoon of pepper
- 1 teaspoon of basil
- 1 tablespoon of mix spices
- 1 tablespoon if thyme
- 2 tablespoons of olive oil
- 6 oz of carrot
- 8 oz of courgette
- 8 oz of sweet potatoes
- ¼ teaspoon of paprika
- ¼ teaspoon of oregano
- 1/3 teaspoon of chili

Directions:
1. Clean and wash carrot and sweet potatoes. Then clean the courgetti and chop them in the small pieces. After that, chop the sweet potatoes and carrot into the slices.
2. Mix everything together.
3. After that, add salt, pepper, basil, mix spices, thyme, chili, pepper and oregano.
4. Sprinkle the frying basket with oil and put carrot, sweet potatoes and courgetti in the Air Fryer. Cook them for 18 minutes. Shake them after 5 and 12 minutes of the cooking.

Nutrition:
- Calories: 89
- Fat: 9.1g
- Carbohydrates: 25.1g
- Protein: 23.2g

Mediterranean Vegetables

The incredibly delicious vegetables, which are healthy and easy in preparing. Try and enjoy with this flavor.

Prep time: 5 minutes | **Cooking time:** 20 minutes | **Servings:** 4

Ingredients:
- 1/3 teaspoon of pepper
- 1/5 teaspoon of salt
- 2 teaspoons of garlic puree
- 1 teaspoons of mustard
- 2 teaspoons of honey
- 1 teaspoon of mixed herbs
- 1 big carrot
- 1 big parsnip
- 1 green pepper
- 1 large courgetti
- 2 oz of cherry tomatoes
- 3 tablespoons of oil

Directions:
1. Take the bowl plate.
2. Wash and clean tomatoes, pepper, courgetti and carrot.
3. After that, chop all vegetables in the small pieces and put in the bowl.
4. Add 3 tablespoons of oil and mix everything well.
5. Preheat the Air Fryer to 380F for 2 minutes.
6. Put vegetables with spices in the Air Fryer.
7. Cook for 15-20 minutes at 380F.
8. Put the rest of ingredients in the separate bowl and mix them.

Nutrition:
- Calories: 103
- Fat: 9,6g
- Carbohydrates: 21.1g
- Protein: 18.2g

Piquant Cauliflower with Honey

The honey makes the original aroma. It is flavorsome and tasty.

Prep time: 5 minutes | **Cooking time:** 20 minutes | **Servings:** 4

Ingredients:
- ¼ teaspoon of salt
- ¼ teaspoon of pepper
- 1 tablespoon of mix herbs
- 1 tablespoon of mixed spices
- 2 tablespoons of soy sauce
- 2 tablespoons of honey
- 1 big egg
- 1/3 teaspoon of coconut
- 1/3 cup of flour
- 1/3 cup of oats
- 1 small cauliflower

Directions:
1. Chop cauliflower in the pieces.
2. Preheat the Air Fryer to 380F.
3. Take the bowl and blend flour, coconut and oats.
4. Add salt and pepper.
5. Blend everything well.
6. Beat egg in another bowl.
7. Rub cauliflower with spices and herbs.
8. Place the pieces of cauliflower in beaten egg and after that in the oats.
9. Cook in the Air Fryer for 15 minutes at 380F.
10. Then put cauliflower and the other components. Cook for 5 minutes.

Nutrition:
- Calories: 69
- Fat: 8,6g
- Carbohydrates: 25.1g
- Protein: 15.2g

Veggie Burger

These burgers will be great snack for the picnic or if you wish to prepare something for your children, when they go to school.

Prep time: 25 minutes	Cooking time: 20 minutes	Servings: 4

Ingredients:

- 1/3 teaspoon of salt
- 1/3 teaspoon of pepper
- 1 tablespoon of mixed spices
- 2 teaspoons of parsley
- 2 teaspoons of thyme
- 1 teaspoon of mustard
- 2 cups of bread crumbs
- 1 egg
- 3 tablespoon of flour
- ½ cup of oats
- ¼ cup of coconut
- 1 tablespoons of garlic
- 3 tablespoons of oil
- 2 lbs of cauliflowers

Directions:

1. Wash and chop cauliflowers into small pieces.
2. Cook in the Air Fryer at 5 minutes at 350F.
3. Then add pepper, salt, mustard and garlic in the bowl.
4. Mix everything well. Then rub the pieces of cauliflowers with spices.
5. Then add the rest of ingredients, mix everything well.
6. After that, cook for 10 minutes at 380F.
7. Put the mixture on another side and cook for 10 minutes more.

Nutrition:

- Calories: 156
- Fat: 10,2g
- Carbohydrates: 22.1g
- Protein: 19.2g

Cauliflower Cheese Tots

The best meal you have ever prepared. These tots are easy in preparing and do not need a lot of efforts.

Prep time: 10 minutes	Cooking time: 26 minutes	Servings: 4

Ingredients:

- ¼ teaspoon of salt
- ¼ teaspoon of pepper
- 1 teaspoon of oregano
- 1 tablespoon of chives
- 1 tablespoon of parsley
- 1 teaspoon of garlic
- 2 oz of onion
- 1 large egg
- 1 oz of oats
- 1 teaspoon of coconut
- 1 cup of bread crumbs
- 6 oz of cheese
- 2 lbs of cauliflower

Directions:

1. Chop cauliflower in the small pieces and leave in the bowl with water for 20 minutes.
2. Put the bowl and mix bread crumbs, oats and coconut. Then add all spices.
3. Beat egg in another bowl.
4. After that put cauliflower in the Air Fryer, add cup of water and cook for 10 minutes.
5. Then add salt, pepper and garlic. Mix everything till you get the dough.
6. After that, create cutlets, put them in egg and in bread crumbs and cook them in Air Fryer at 370F for 6 minutes.
7. Put them on another side and cook for 10 minutes more.

Nutrition:

- Calories: 112
- Fat: 6,2g
- Carbohydrates: 20.1g
- Protein: 13.2g

Sweet Potato and Black Bean Taquitos

Just try to prepare this meal and you will be satisfied with the result. Delicious, tasty and healthy meal, which you can prepare for your family.

Prep time: 10 minutes | **Cooking time:** 42-43 minutes | **Servings:** 4

Ingredients:

- 1 tablespoon of oil
- 12 small flour or corn tortillas
- ¼ teaspoon of salt
- ¼ teaspoon of pepper

- ½ teaspoon of garlic
- ¾ teaspoon of onion powder
- 4 tablespoons of milk
- 1 oz of black beans

- 1 cup of cheese
- 2 big sweet potatoes

Directions:

1. Take potatoes, wash and clean them.
2. After that, cut in the pieces and put in the Air Fryer.
3. Cook for 35 minutes at 320F.
4. You can add also 1 cup of water.
5. When the potato is ready, leave it aside.
6. After that mix in the bowl with milk.
7. Then add beans, onion powder, salt, cheese, garlic powder, cumin, and pepper.
8. Mix everything well.
9. Put the mixture on tortillas.
10. Then put them in the Air Fryer and cook for 7-8 minutes.
11. When they are ready, you will be surprised, because you can have the complete dinner if you prepare them.

Nutrition:

- Calories: 212
- Fat: 13.1g

- Carbohydrates: 33.1g
- Protein: 27.2g

Peppery Zucchini with Sweetened Carrot

This recipe is exactly for you. When they try these vegetables, you will like them forever.

Prep time: 10 minutes | **Cooking time:** 42-43 min | **Servings:** 4

Ingredients:

- 1 tablespoon tarragon leaves
- ½ teaspoon of white pepper
- 1 teaspoon of salt
- 1 pound of yellow squash
- 1 pound zucchini
- 6 tablespoons of oil
- ½ pound of carrot

Directions:

1. Chop carrot in the pieces.
2. Mix carrot with 2 tablespoons of oil, pepper, salt and put in the frying basket.
3. Cook in the Air Fryer for 5 minutes at 390F.
4. Then put zucchini and squash in the bowl.
5. Cover them with the rest of oil and mix well.
6. Then add to the basket with carrot and cook for 30 minutes at the same temperature.
7. Shake vegetables 2-3 times while you are cooking them.

Nutrition:

- Calories: 109
- Fat: 8.1g
- Carbohydrates: 29.5g
- Protein: 19.3g

Healthy and Crispy Vegetables

Inexpensive and unassuming. These main factors can help you to get the pleasant and fantastic vegetables.

Prep time: 10 minutes | **Cooking time:** 25-29 min | **Servings:** 4

Ingredients:

- ¼ teaspoon of salt
- ½ teaspoon of pepper
- ½ cup of corn flour
- ½ tablespoons of rosemary
- ½ tablespoons of oil
- 4 big carrots
- 4 big parsnips
- 2 big sweet potatoes

Directions:

1. Preheat the Air Fryer to 350F.
2. Wash and clean all vegetables.
3. Cut them into pieces.
4. Put them in 3 separate bowls.
5. Sprinkle vegetables with all spices.
6. After that, put potatoes in the Air Fryer and cook for 6-9 minutes.
7. If you see, that it is crispy, put on the plate and mix with salt.
8. Then cook parsnips for 3-4 minutes and put on the plate.
9. Carrot should be cooked for 10-15 minutes.
10. Mix vegetables on the plate.

Nutrition:

- Calories: 67
- Fat: 5.8g
- Carbohydrates: 23.5g
- Protein: 16.8g

Scrumptious and Piquant Potatoes

It is uncomplicated and appetizing. Do not miss your chance.

| Prep time: 25-30 minutes | Cooking time: 10-15 minutes | Servings: 4 |

Ingredients:

- 1 tablespoon of oil
- 2 cups of maida
- ½ tablespoon of garam masala
- 1 teaspoon of coriander powder
- ½ tablespoon of red chili pepper
- 1 tablespoon of amchoor
- ½ teaspoon of salt
- ½ teaspoon of pepper
- 2 inch of ginger
- 3-4 green chili pepper
- 1 cup of green peas
- 6 big potatoes

Directions:

1. Cut potatoes in pieces and boil with the peas.
2. Mix in the bowl and add maida, salt and oil.
3. Leave it for 15-20 minutes.
4. Then mash potatoes, add ginger, chili, salt and pepper.
5. Blend the products well.
6. After that add garam masals, red chili pepper and blend the components.
7. Then create the small roles and cook them in the Air Fryer at 10-15 minutes at 380F.
8. Serve hot, with green and red chutney.

Nutrition:

- Calories: 139
- Fat: 11.1g
- Carbohydrates: 23.8g
- Protein: 10.3g

Cooked Peppers with Spices

You can make this scrumptious meal with all kinds of pepper. It is tasty, appetizing and wonderful.

Prep time: 10 minutes	**Cooking time:** 25 minutes	**Servings:** 4

Ingredients:
- 12 bell peppers
- 1 small onion
- 1/3 teaspoon of salt
- ½ teaspoon of pepper
- ½ teaspoon of oregano
- 1 teaspoon of chili
- ½ teaspoon of garlic powder
- 1 teaspoon of cumin

Directions:
1. Preheat the Air Fryer to 380F for 5 minutes.
2. Sprinkle the frying basket with oil.
3. Chop all peppers in small pieces.
4. Then chop onion and mix with pepper well.
5. Add salt, pepper, oregano, chili, garlic powder, cumin to vegetables and blend the components well.
6. Cook for 25 minutes at 380F.
7. Enjoy with the healthy and delicious pepper meal.
8. Decorate with sauces, basil or mint leaves.

Nutrition:
- Calories: 67
- Fat: 3,2g
- Carbohydrates: 9.5g
- Protein: 1.3g

Grilled Endive in Marinade

Something special and you will be interested in it. You can try the delicious and incredibly tasty vegetables in this recipe.

Prep time: 40 minutes	**Cooking time:** 10 minutes	**Servings:** 6

Ingredients:
- 3 tablespoons of lemon juice
- ½ teaspoon of black pepper powder
- ½ teaspoon of salt
- ½ teaspoon of curry powder
- 1 teaspoon of garlic powder
- ½ cup of plain yogurt
- 5 heads of Belgian endives

Directions:
1. Wash and clean the endives, cut them into the pieces and leave aside.
2. Rub them with lemon juice.
3. After that mix salt, pepper, curry powder, garlic together in the bowl.
4. Cover the endives with this mixture.
5. Then put them in yogurt and leave for 30 minutes.
6. Preheat the Air Fryer to 350F.
7. Cook the pieces of endives for 10 minutes,
8. Serve them hot or warm.
9. They can be eaten with bread. Just try!

Nutrition:
- Calories: 184
- Fat: 7.3g
- Carbohydrates: 18.8g
- Protein: 7.3g

Flavorsome Cooked Carrots

Everyone knows, that carrot is very healthy. However, it can be also delicious. Cook and try and you will see it.

Prep time: 10 minutes | **Cooking time:** 25 minutes | **Servings:** 4

Ingredients:
- 4 tablespoons of orange juice
- 2 tablespoons of oil
- ½ teaspoon of salt
- ½ teaspoon of pepper
- 1/3 tablespoon of paprika
- ¼ teaspoon of chili
- 1/3 teaspoon of cumin
- 1/3 teaspoon of garlic
- ½ teaspoon of mustard

Directions:
1. Wash and clean carrots.
2. Preheat the Air Fryer to 380F.
3. Sprinkle the frying basket with oil.
4. Mix salt, pepper, paprika, chili, cumin, mustard and garlic with carrot.
5. Then put everything in the Air Fryer.
6. Cook for 20 minutes at 380F.
7. Then sprinkle everything with the orange juice and cook for another 5 minutes.
8. Cook and enjoy.

Nutrition:
- Calories: 84
- Fat: 2,9g
- Carbohydrates: 8,6g
- Protein: 5,2g

Hot Fried Mushrooms

It is possible to prepare a lot of delicious meals from mushrooms, but it is the best and the healthier one.

Prep time: 10 minutes | **Cooking time:** 30 minutes | **Servings:** 4

Ingredients:
- 2 tablespoons if the white wine
- 2 teaspoons if mixed herbs
- ½ teaspoon of salt.
- ¼ teaspoon of pepper
- ½ teaspoon of chili
- ½ teaspoon of oregano
- ½ teaspoon of garlic
- 1/3 teaspoon of cumin

Directions:
1. Wash and clean mushrooms.
2. Mix the cumin, garlic, oregano, chili in the bowl.
3. After that, add pepper, salt and herbs.
4. Mix everything and shake a lot.
5. Put mushrooms in the wine and leave for 10 minutes.
6. Preheat the Air Fryer to 380F.
7. Rub mushrooms with spices.
8. Then put mushrooms in the Air Fryer basket and cook them for 25 minutes.
9. After that just shake them and cook for another 5 minutes.
10. You can serve them with potatoes and decorate with vegetables.

Nutrition:
- Calories: 92
- Fat: 3,9g
- Carbohydrates: 12,5g
- Protein: 6,9g

Roasted Parsnips

You will spend up to 1 hour of your time, but the result will exceed all your expectation. This meal is great for breakfast or supper. You will have a lot of energy after eating it.

Prep time: 10 minutes | **Cooking time:** 45 minutes | **Servings:** 4

Ingredients:
- 2 tablespoons of maple syrup
- 1 tablespoon of fry parsley
- 1 tablespoon of duck fat
- 2 pounds of parsnip
- ½ teaspoon of salt
- ½ tablespoon of pepper
- 1/3 tablespoon of garlic
- 1/3 tablespoon of mustard
- ½ teaspoon of ginger

Directions:
1. Preheat the Air Fryer to 380F.
2. Put the duck fat in the Air Fryer and melt it for 2 minutes.
3. Wash and clean the parsnip.
4. Chop in the pieces.
5. Mix parsley, salt, pepper, garlic, ginger and mustard in the bowl.
6. Then rub the pieces of parsnip with this mixture.
7. Put them in the Air Fryer and cook for 40 minutes.
8. Do not forget to shake them 2-3 times while you are preparing them.
9. After that add maple syrup, mustard and cook for 5 minutes more.

Nutrition:
- Calories: 162
- Fat: 2.9g
- Carbohydrates: 10,3g
- Protein: 6,2g

Grilled Beets with Sweaty Syrup of Maple

There is nothing simplier, that you can cook for the family. They will enjoy with healthy and at the same time delicious vegetables.

Prep time: 10 minutes | **Cooking time:** 50 minutes | **Servings:** 4

Ingredients:
- 4 tablespoons of maple syrup
- 1 tablespoon of oil or duck fat
- 3 lbs of beetroots
- 1 teaspoon of pepper
- ½ teaspoon of salt
- 2 cloves of garlic
- 1 teaspoon of paprika
- ½ teaspoon of cumin
- 1/3 teaspoon of ginger

Directions:
1. Wash the beetroots and clean them.
2. Chop them into the pieces.
3. They should not be too huge or tiny.
4. Preheat the Air Fryer to 370F.
5. Mix pepper, salt, garlic, cumin, ginger in the bowl and add there the beetroots.
6. Shake everything well.
7. After that put the beetroots in the Air Fryer.
8. Cook for 40 minutes.

Nutrition:
- Calories: 68
- Fat: 1,7g
- Carbohydrates: 8,3g
- Protein: 5,2g

Grilled Tomatoes

Tomatoes have a lot of different vitamins and because of it they are very healthy. Prepare them and you will discover the new meal for you and your family.

| **Prep time:** 5 minutes | **Cooking time:** 20 minutes | **Servings:** 2 |

Ingredients:
- 2 big tomatoes
- ½ teaspoon of salt
- 1 teaspoon of pepper
- 3 cloves of garlic
- ½ teaspoon of paprika
- ½ teaspoon of cumin
- ½ teaspoon of ginger

Directions:
1. Wash tomatoes and chop them in 2 pieces.
2. After that, sprinkle the Air Fryer with oil.
3. Mix pepper, salt, garlic, ginger, cumin and paprika together.
4. Rub the pieces of tomatoes with these spices.
5. After that, put tomatoes in the Air Fryer.
6. Cook them for 20 minutes at 370F.
7. Then put tomatoes on another side and cook for 5 minutes more.
8. Serve hot. You can decorate them with parsley.

Nutrition:
- Calories: 27
- Fat: 8g
- Carbohydrates: 8,3g
- Protein: 7.4g

Peppery Zucchini with Cheese

Delicious, flavorsome, inexpensive and it does not require a lot of your time. Cook and enjoy with it.

| **Prep time:** 10 minutes | **Cooking time:** 14 minutes | **Servings:** 4 |

Ingredients:
- 2 zucchinis
- 2 eggs
- ¼ teaspoon of cayenne pepper
- 1/3 teaspoon of black pepper
- ¼ teaspoon of oregano
- ¼ teaspoon of basil
- ¼ cup of cheese
- ½ cup of bread crumbs

Directions:
1. Mix pepper, oregano, black pepper, basil, then cheese and bread crumbs in the bowl.
2. Cut zucchinis in the small pieces.
3. After that, beat eggs in the bowl.
4. Rub zucchinis with spices and bread crumbs.
5. After that, place them in eggs and then again in bread crumbs.
6. Preheat the Air Fryer to 380F.
7. Cook them for 7 minutes.
8. Then put zucchinis on another side and cook for 7 minutes.
9. Serve hot with ketchup or mayo.

Nutrition:
- Calories: 76
- Fat: 2,3g
- Carbohydrates: 9,3g
- Protein: 6,8g

Appetizing Rhubab with Sweat Carrot

It is not the typical meal and because of this fact, it will be motivating for preparing and tasting. It is very scrumptious.

Prep time: 10 minutes | **Cooking time:** 25 minutes | **Servings:** 4

Ingredients:
- 1 big orange
- ½ cup of nuts
- ½ teaspoon of salt
- ½ teaspoon of pepper
- 1 pound of rhubab
- 1 pound of carrot
- 2 teaspoons of oil

Directions:
1. Wash and clean carrot.
2. Chop carrot in the pieces. They should not be too big or too small.
3. Then sprinkle the Air Fryer basket with oil and cook carrot for 20 minutes at 380F.
4. Then wash the rhubab and cut it in the small pieces.
5. Add the rhubab to carrot and cook for 5 minutes.
6. Then mix everything with salt, pepper, nuts and pieces of orange.
7. Serve it hot. Enjoy with tasty and unusual meal.

Nutrition:
- Calories: 182
- Fat: 10,5g
- Carbohydrates: 15,3g
- Protein: 16,1g

Yummy Eggplant

You will have a lot of energy after eating these eggplants. It is easy, unassuming and appetizing.

Prep time: 10 minutes | **Cooking time:** 25 minutes | **Servings:** 4

Ingredients:
- 1 teaspoon of oil
- ½ lemon
- 2 basil leaves
- 1 teaspoon of garlic powder
- 1 teaspoon of onion powder
- ½ teaspoon of salt
- ½ teaspoon of pepper
- ½ tablespoon of seasonings sauce
- 3 big eggplant

Directions:
1. Wash and clean eggplants.
2. Chop them in the medium pieces.
3. Take the deep bowl.
4. Blend salt, pepper and onion powder, then garlic powder, seasoning sauce in the bowl.
5. Then rub eggplants with this mixture.
6. Place eggplants in the Air Fryer.
7. Add the pieces of lemon and 2 basil leaves.
8. Cook for 20 minutes at 300F, then shake well and cook for 5 minutes more.
9. Place on the dish and serve hot. It will be the ideal meal if you are waiting for guests.

Nutrition:
- Calories: 63
- Fat: 3,4g
- Carbohydrates: 10,2g
- Protein: 6,4g

Sweat Potatoes

Do you like the appetizing potatoes? This potato meal is for dinner time or for the easy lunch.

| **Prep time:** 5 minutes | **Cooking time:** 30 minutes | **Servings:** 4 |

Ingredients:

- 2 lbs of sweet potatoes
- 2 tablespoons of oil
- ½ teaspoon of pepper
- ½ teaspoon of salt
- 1/3 teaspoon of red chili pepper
- ½ teaspoon of green chili pepper
- 3 cloves of garlic
- ½ teaspoon of cumin

Directions:

1. Wash and clean potatoes.
2. Cut into chips and put in the container.
3. Add 2 tablespoons of oil to potatoes in the container.
4. Shake potatoes, because they should be covered with oil completely.
5. Then add pepper, salt, red chili pepper, green chili pepper, chopped garlic and cumin.
6. Preheat the Air Fryer to 390F.
7. Place potatoes in the Air Fryer basket and cook it for 20 minutes at 380F.
8. Then shake potatoes and cook them again for 10 minutes more.

Nutrition:

- Calories: 269
- Fat: 3,1g
- Carbohydrates: 12,7g
- Protein: 8,8g

Appetizing and Crusty Chips with Potato

It seems that everyone likes chips. Prepare for your children these chips and they will be grateful to you for them.

| **Prep time:** 15 minutes | **Cooking time:** 50 minutes | **Servings:** 4 |

Ingredients:

- 2 lbs of potatoes
- 1 teaspoon of salt
- 1 teaspoon of pepper
- ½ teaspoon of paprika
- ½ teaspoon of green chili pepper
- ½ teaspoon of red chili pepper
- ½ tablespoon of dry herbs
- 5 tablespoons of oil

Directions:

1. Wash and clean potatoes.
2. Leave them in the bowl with water for 10 minutes.
3. Take another bowl and mix salt, pepper, paprika, red chili pepper, green chili pepper, dry herbs and 1 tablespoon of oil.
4. Cut potatoes in chips.
5. After that, cover chips with the mixture of spices.
6. Preheat the Air Fryer to 380F.
7. Put chips in the basket and cook for 20 minutes.
8. Shake them well and cook for 20 minutes again.
9. Then shake them and add the rest of oil.
10. Cook for another 10 minutes.

Nutrition:

- Calories: 201
- Fat: 3,5g
- Carbohydrates: 12,3g
- Protein: 8,5g

Zucchini with Cheese

This meal is so tasty, that you will prepare it a lot of times. You will have a lot of energy and power.

Prep time: 10 minutes | **Cooking time:** 35 minutes | **Servings:** 4

Ingredients:

- 3 zucchini
- ½ cup of eggs
- ½ teaspoon of black pepper
- ½ teaspoon of salt
- 1/3 teaspoon of oregano
- 1/5 cup of basil leaves
- ½ cup of cheese
- 1 cup of bread crumbs
- 3 tablespoons of oil

Directions:

1. Wash and cut zucchini in the pieces.
2. Put the bowl and mix pepper, salt and oregano.
3. Then put eggs in the plate.
4. Take bread crumbs and put them on the third plate.
5. Rub the pieces of zucchini with spices.
6. After that, put every piece of zucchini in bread crumbs, then in egg and again in bread crumbs.
7. Preheat the Air Fryer to 372F.
8. Sprinkle the basket with the rest of oil.
9. Put the pieces of zucchini in the basket and cook for 20 minutes.
10. Then put them on another side and cook for 15 minutes more.
11. Enjoy with the meal.

Nutrition:

- Calories: 76
- Fat: 1,8g
- Carbohydrates: 10,3g
- Protein: 5,5g

Spicy and Appetizing Potatoes with Fresh and Fried Vegetables

It is original and scrumptious potato meal. Just cook!

Prep time: 15 minutes | **Cooking time:** 40 minutes | **Servings:** 4

Ingredients:

- 8 oz of egg substitute
- 1 teaspoon of salt
- 1 teaspoon of pepper
- ½ teaspoon of thyme
- ½ tablespoon of herbs
- ½ green pepper
- 1 onion
- 2 tablespoons of oil
- 2 lbs of potatoes

Directions:

1. Clean and slice onion in the tiny pieces.
2. Clean the green pepper and chop it into pieces.
3. Place it in the Air Fryer and cook for 5 minutes at 380F.
4. Wash potatoes, clean and cook in the Air Fryer for 30 minutes.
5. After that, blend potatoes, pepper and onion in the bowl.
6. Add the herbs, thyme, pepper and salt with egg substitute in the bowl.
7. Blend the components well.
8. After that place all ingredients in the Air Fryer and for 5 minutes.
9. Serve it hot with tomatoes. It is really delicious.

Nutrition:

- Calories: 199
- Fat: 2,5g
- Carbohydrates: 11,2g
- Protein: 5,1g

Crusty and Scrumptious Chips

These chips are yummy and uncomplicated in preparing. Cook these flavorsome chips.

Prep time: 5 minutes | **Cooking time:** 30 minutes | **Servings:** 4

Ingredients:
- 2 lbs of potatoes
- 1 teaspoon of black pepper powder
- ½ teaspoon of salt
- ½ teaspoon of garlic
- ½ teaspoon of cumin
- ½ teaspoon of oregano
- 5 basil leaves
- 3 tablespoons of oil

Directions:
1. Wash and after then clean potatoes.
2. Chop vegetables in the slices.
3. Place the products in the deep bowl.
4. Then add salt, pepper and blend the components well
5. After that sprinkle the Air Fryer basket with oil and preheat it for 2 minutes at 380F.
6. Add garlic, cumin and oregano to the pieces of potatoes and blend flavors.
7. Then set chips in the Air Fryer. Cook for 15 minutes.
8. Place them on the other side. Then cook for 15 minutes more.
9. Chips should have golden color and be crispy.
10. Enjoy with peppery chips.
11. Decorate chips snack with basil leaves.

Nutrition:
- Calories: 231
- Fat: 4,5g
- Carbohydrates: 14,2g
- Protein: 9,7g

Garlic Flavorsome Potatoes

The meal with potato is for every event. Appetizing, easy and lovely.

Prep time: 15 minutes | **Cooking time:** 40 minutes | **Servings:** 4

Ingredients:
- 3 lbs of potatoes
- 3 cloves of garlic
- ½ teaspoon of salt
- ½ teaspoon of paprika
- 1/3 teaspoon of pepper
- ½ teaspoon of chili pepper
- 1/3 teaspoon of onion powder
- 3 tablespoons of oil

Directions:
1. Wash potatoes.
2. Clean it and leave in water for 10 minutes.
3. Then chop in the pieces.
4. They should be like chips.
5. Mix salt, pepper, paprika, chili and other flavors in the bowl.
6. Rub potatoes with these spices.
7. Preheat the Air Fryer for 5 minutes to 380F.
8. Place vegetables in the Air Fryer and cook for 20 minutes.
9. Then put potatoes on the other side. Cook for 20 minutes.
10. Serve with basil leaves and sauces.

Nutrition:
- Calories: 66
- Fat: 1,9g
- Carbohydrates: 12,1g
- Protein: 8,3g

Potatoes with Pepper

It is flavorsome and pleasant meal.

Prep time: 5 minutes | **Cooking time:** 40 minutes | **Servings:** 4

Ingredients:
- 1 big green pepper
- 2 lb of potatoes
- ½ teaspoon of salt
- ½ teaspoon of pepper
- ½ teaspoon of paprika
- 3-4 cloves of garlic
- 2 teaspoons of onion powder
- 3 tablespoons of oil

Directions:
1. Wash and clean potatoes.
2. Chop it in the middle pieces.
3. Chop pepper into the pieces.
4. Blend all spices and rub potatoes with them.
5. Place the pieces of pepper in the Air Fryer. After that cook them for 5 minutes at 380F.
6. Then place pepper in the bowl.
7. Cook potatoes for 20 minutes.
8. Then add pepper and blend all ingredients.
9. Cook for 15 minutes more.

Nutrition:
- Calories: 251
- Fat: 13g
- Carbohydrates: 18,9g
- Protein: 14,7g

Salad Pasta with Scrumptious Vegetables

Do you want to get delicious and healthy salad with vegetables? Then you are on the right way. Simple and flavorsome!

Prep time: 20 minutes | **Cooking time:** 25 minutes | **Servings:** 4

Ingredients:
- 2-5 leaves of basil
- ½ cup of oil
- 8 tablespoons of cheese
- 2 teaspoons of pepper
- 1 teaspoon of salt
- 1 cup of tomatoes
- 2 peppers
- 4 cups of pasta
- 4 medium tomatoes
- 1 tablespoon of oil
- 3 zucchinis
- 3 eggplant

Directions:
1. Preheat the Air Fryer to 380F.
2. Cook pasta with the cup of water for 5 minutes.
3. Then leave it aside.
4. Chop tomatoes in the pieces.
5. Clean eggplants and chop them in the medium pieces.
6. Cook in the Air Fryer for 10 minutes and then put them on the plate.
7. Mix in the bowl salt, pepper, chopped tomatoes, peppers, oil, zucchini and eggplants.
8. Put everything in the Air Fryer and cook for 10 minutes.
9. Then mix everything with pasta.

Nutrition:
- Calories: 121
- Fat: 1,3g
- Carbohydrates: 14,1g
- Protein: 12,2g

Fried Fiery Broccoli

Broccoli has a lot of minerals and vitamins. It is possible to prepare a lot of meals from it. Check one, which does not need a lot of your efforts.

Prep time: 10 minutes | **Cooking time:** 20 minutes | **Servings:** 4

Ingredients:

- 1 teaspoon of pepper
- ½ teaspoon of salt
- 1/3 teaspoon of paprika
- 2-4 cloves of garlic
- 3 tablespoons of oil
- ½ teaspoon of cumin
- ½ teaspoon of seasonings
- 1 teaspoon of dry herbs
- 1 tablespoon of sesame seeds
- ½ lemon
- 1 big head of broccoli

Directions:

1. Wash broccoli and cut in the medium pieces.
2. Then leave it for some time.
3. Chop garlic in the small pieces.
4. Preheat the Air Fryer to 390F.
5. Sprinkle the basket with oil, lemon juice and cook for 2 minutes.
6. Then mix the pieces of broccoli with salt, pepper, garlic, cumin, seasonings, herbs and seeds.
7. Put them in the Air Fryer and cook for 10 minutes.
8. Shake everything well and cook for another 10 minutes.

Nutrition:

- Calories: 96
- Fat: 4,6g
- Carbohydrates: 12,1g
- Protein: 10,2g

Crusty Potatoes with Appetizing Bread Rolls

You can prepare the best rolls in the world. They are scrumptious, with the crispy skin.

Prep time: 10 minutes | **Cooking time:** 20 minutes | **Servings:** 4

Ingredients:

- ½ teaspoon of salt
- ½ teaspoon of pepper
- 2 curry leaves
- ½ tablespoon of mustard seeds
- ½ tablespoon of turmeric
- 2 small onions
- 1 coriander
- 2 green chilies
- 8 slices of bread
- 5 big potatoes

Directions:

1. Wash and clean potatoes.
2. Chop them in the tiny pieces.
3. Add salt and pepper and mix everything.
4. Sprinkle the Air Fryer with oil and cook potatoes for 10 minutes at 380F.
5. Then put potatoes in the bowl.
6. Add mustard seeds, turmeric, chopped onion, coriander, chopped green chilies, slices of bread and mix them with potatoes.
7. Try to create the rolls and put them in the Air Fryer.
8. Cook for 5 minutes and after that put them on another side.
9. Then cook for 5 minutes again.

Nutrition:

- Calories: 164
- Fat: 9,8g
- Carbohydrates: 16,1g
- Protein: 12,3g

Buffalo Cauliflower

Tasty, easy and delicious. What is possible to say more? Only that it can be prepared in a short time.

Prep time: 10 minutes | **Cooking time:** 20 minutes | **Servings:** 4

Ingredients:

- 2 cloves of garlic
- ½ cup of sauce
- 2 tablespoons of oil
- ¼ teaspoon of chili
- 1 cup of soymilk
- 1 teaspoon of chili powder
- ¼ teaspoon of cayenne pepper
- 1 teaspoon of vegan bouillon
- 1 cup of flour
- 1 big cauliflower

Directions:

1. Wash and cut cauliflowers in the pieces.
2. Mix garlic, oil, chili, soymilk, chili powder, cayenne pepper, vegan bouillon and flour in the deep bowl.
3. You should get the dough.
4. Sprinkle the Air Fryer basket with oil and preheat for 10 minutes to 390F.
5. After that, put every piece of cauliflower in the mixture and after that in the Air Fryer.
6. Cook for 10 minutes and after that put them on the other side.
7. Cook also for 10 minutes more.

Nutrition:

- Calories: 133
- Fat: 5,8g
- Carbohydrates: 12,5g
- Protein: 12,8g

Crispy Veggie Fries

Tasty and delicious, these chips will be the dream of every child. Also, they are very easy in preparing and you will be delighted with this meal.

Prep time: 10 minutes | **Cooking time:** 20 minutes | **Servings:** 4

Ingredients:

- 2/3 cup of water
- ½ teaspoon of pepper
- ½ teaspoon of salt
- 1 cup of flour
- 1 cup of bread crumbs
- 2 tablespoons of yeast flakes
- 2 tablespoons of egg powder
- Vegetables, for example onion, green beans, squash, zucchini and so on.

Directions:

1. Put flour in the plate.
2. Take the second plate and put the flakes, vegan egg and 2/3 cup of water there.
3. Mix everything well.
4. On the 3rd plate mix salt and bread crumbs.
5. Cut vegetable you like into pieces and put in flour, after that in the vegan egg and in bread crumbs.
6. You should do it with every piece of vegetables.
7. Preheat the Air Fryer to 380F.
8. Cook them for 8 minutes at 380F, after that shake them and cook for 12-13 minutes again.

Nutrition:

- Calories: 139
- Fat: 12,6g
- Carbohydrates: 14,2g
- Protein: 13,5g

Roasted Corn

Easy snacks in a few minutes. Prepare and enjoy with the result.

Prep time: 10 minutes	**Cooking time:** 20 minutes	**Servings:** 4

Ingredients:
- ½ teaspoon of pepper
- ½ teaspoon of salt
- 4 corns
- 2-3 tablespoons of oil
- ½ teaspoon of herbs
- ½ teaspoon of paprika
- 1/3 teaspoon of oregano

Directions:
1. Wash and clean the corns.
2. If the corn is too big, cut it in the pieces.
3. Preheat the Air Fryer to 390F.
4. Sprinkle the Air Fryer basket with 2 tablespoons of oil.
5. Rub the corns with oil, salt, pepper, herbs, paprika and oregano.
6. The corns should be covered with spices.
7. After that put them in the Air Fryer.
8. Cook for 20 minutes.
9. But you should shake the corns every 5 minutes.
10. Enjoy with healthy and delicious corn. Your children will appreciate your efforts.

Nutrition:
- Calories: 36
- Fat: 2,1g
- Carbohydrates: 12,1g
- Protein: 10,3g

Appetizing and Peppery Baked Potatoes

This meal is very healthy, because backed potatoes have vitamins. If you wish to cook something unassuming, then this recipe is for you.

Prep time: 10 minutes	**Cooking time:** 35-40 minutes	**Servings:** 2

Ingredients:
- 1 tablespoon of pepper
- ½ teaspoon of salt
- 1 tablespoon of oil
- 2-3 backing potatoes

Directions:
1. Wash and clean potatoes.
2. Then cut every in 4-5 pieces.
3. Preheat the Air Fryer to 370F.
4. Then rub the pieces of potatoes with salt and pepper.
5. Leave them for 5 minutes.
6. Sprinkle the frying basket with oil.
7. Put potatoes in the basket and cook for 15 minutes.
8. After that put the pieces of the potato on the second side and cook for 15 minutes again.
9. Take out of Air Fryer and leave for 5 minutes.

Nutrition:
- Calories: 45
- Fat: 4,2g
- Carbohydrates: 13,1g
- Protein: 14,3g

Paneer and Cheese Cutlet

It is very simple and easy meal. It does not need too much of your time and efforts.

Prep time: 10 minutes | **Cooking time:** 15 minutes | **Servings:** 3

Ingredients:
- 1 tablespoon of butter
- ½ tablespoon of oregano
- ½ teaspoon of salt
- ½ teaspoon of pepper
- ½ teaspoon of chat masala
- ½ teaspoon of garlic
- 1 onion
- 1 cup of cheese
- 2 cups op parmesan

Directions:
1. Chop cheese in the small pieces in the bowl.
2. Add salt, pepper, chopped onion and mix everything.
3. After that, add butter and melt the mixture.
4. Then add garlic, chat masala and oregano.
5. Shale everything and mix well.
6. Preheat the Air Fryer to 380F.
7. Create cutlets from the mixture.
8. Sprinkle the frying basket for the Air Fryer with oil.
9. After that cook cutlets for 10 minutes at 370F,
10. Put them on another side and cook for 5 minutes more.

Nutrition:
- Calories: 95
- Fat: 7,2g
- Carbohydrates: 12,1g
- Protein: 15,2g

Yummy Cheese Balls with Crispy Potatoes

Do you want to prepare something with cheese? There is nothing easier then these cheese balls with potatoes.

Prep time: 10 minutes | **Cooking time:** 15 minutes | **Servings:** 3

Ingredients:
- ½ cup of cheese
- 1 cup of bread crumbs
- ½ teaspoon of salt
- ½ teaspoon of pepper
- ¼ teaspoon of oregano
- ½ teaspoon of chili pepper
- ½ teaspoon of garlic powder
- 3 tablespoons of corn flour
- 1 capsicum
- 2-3 boiled and mashed potatoes

Directions:
1. Put the boiled potatoes in the bowl.
2. Cut the capsicum in the small pieces.
3. Then add salt, pepper, oregano, chili pepper, flour, garlic and mix everything well.
4. Create the balls from this mixture.
5. Put these bowls in bread crumbs and after that put in the Air Fryer.
6. Cook them for 10 minutes at 390F.
7. Them shake them well, add chopped cheese and cook for 5 minutes more.

Nutrition:
- Calories: 178
- Fat: 10,5g
- Carbohydrates: 13,2g
- Protein: 11,5g

Crispy Chips with Sweat Banana

Do you think, that chips are only with the potato? Prepare the wonderful banana chips and you will see, that you will like it.

| Prep time: 10 minutes | Cooking time: 10 minutes | Servings: 3 |

Ingredients:
- 4 big bananas
- ½ teaspoon of salt
- ½ teaspoon of pepper
- ½ teaspoon of dry herbs
- 3 tablespoons of oil

Directions:
1. Wash and peel bananas.
2. Chop them in the thin pieces.
3. Mix salt and pepper in the bowl.
4. Rub every piece of banana with this mixture.
5. Also, sprinkle them with 2 tablespoons of oil.
6. Then sprinkle the cooking basket of the Air Fryer with oil.
7. Put chips in the basket.
8. Cook in the Air Fryer for 5 minutes at 380F.
9. Then put chips on another side, mix them again and cook for another 5 minutes.

Nutrition:
- Calories: 167
- Fat: 3,5g
- Carbohydrates: 8,2g
- Protein: 9,5g

Cheese Rice Balls

These balls will be your favorite snack. If you wait for your guests, you can prepare exactly these cheese rice balls.

| Prep time: 10 minutes | Cooking time: 15 minutes | Servings: 4 |

Ingredients:
- ½ teaspoon of salt
- ½ teaspoon of pepper
- ½ teaspoon of garlic powder
- 1 cup of bread crumbs
- 1 tablespoon of corn slurry
- 1 tablespoon of corn flour
- 2 tablespoons of sweet corn
- 1 green chili pepper
- ½ cup of cheese
- 2 tablespoons of carrot
- 1 cup of paneer
- 1 cup of boiled rice

Directions:
1. Put rice in the bowl.
2. Add paneer, salt, pepper, garlic and corn flour.
3. Mix everything well.
4. Put the second bowl and put there chopped carrot, pieces of cheese, corns and chili.
5. Mix everything again.
6. Create cheese balls and put every ball in the bowl with the paneer and other ingredients.
7. Cover it with the mixture and after that put in the Air Fryer.
8. Cook for 10 minutes at 350F,
9. After that out them on other side and cook for 5 minutes more.

Nutrition:
- Calories: 145
- Fat: 8,6g
- Carbohydrates: 15,2g
- Protein: 11,6g

Appetizing Cooked Falafel

If you want to cook something uncomplicated and delicious, then you can make this falafel. It is delicious meal. It can be great for breakfast.

Prep time: 12 hours 10 minutes

Cooking time: 15 minutes

Servings: 4

Ingredients:
- 1 cup of chic peas
- 1 onion
- ½ teaspoon of garlic
- 5 coriander leaves
- ½ teaspoon of salt
- ½ teaspoon of pepper
- 1 tablespoon of garam masala
- 2 teaspoons of baking powder
- 3 tablespoons of oil

Directions:
1. Put the peas in water for 12 hours.
2. After that put it in the bowl.
3. Cut onion and add it in the bowl.
4. Add garlic, coriander leaves, salt, pepper, garam masala, 1 tablespoon of oil and baking powder. Put everything in the food processor.
5. When the combination of the products is ready, create cutlets from it.
6. Sprinkle the Air Fryer basket with the rest of oil.
7. Put cutlets in the Air Fryer and cook them for 15 minutes at 370F.

Nutrition:
- Calories: 129
- Fat: 8,2g
- Carbohydrates: 14,2g
- Protein: 16,6g

Flavorsome Balls with Fresh Spinach and Cheese

These balls with cheese and with the piquant spinach are appetizing and easy for preparing.

Prep time: 10 minutes

Cooking time: 15 minutes

Servings: 4

Ingredients:
- 3 tablespoons of oil
- ½ teaspoon of salt
- ½ teaspoon of pepper
- 2 teaspoons of corn flour
- ½ teaspoon of paprika
- ½ teaspoon of garlic
- 2 teaspoons of red chili flakes
- ½ cup of cheese
- ½ cup of bread crumbs
- 9 oz of spinach
- 1 onion

Directions:
1. Mix the boiled and chopped spinach with salt and pepper.
2. Chop onion in the slices and add in the bowl with spinach.
3. After that put another bowl and blend the corn flour, paprika, red chili flakes, chopped cheese and bread crumbs. Create the small balls from spinach.
4. After that sprinkle the Air Fryer with oil.
5. Put the balls in the Air Fryer and cook for 10-15 minutes at 380F.
6. Then shake them and cook for 5 minutes more.

Nutrition:
- Calories: 187
- Fat: 12,3g
- Carbohydrates: 12,2g
- Protein: 13,6g

Crispy Veg Rolls

If you do not like meat – you can prepare these veg rolls. They will be the great decoration on your dinner table and your family will appreciate your efforts.

Prep time: 2 hours 10 minutes

Cooking time: 15 minutes

Servings: 4

Ingredients:

- 2 cups of maida
- ½ teaspoon of baking powder
- ½ teaspoon of salt
- ½ teaspoon of pepper
- ½ teaspoon of oregano
- 1 teaspoon of oil
- ½ cup of peas
- 2 potatoes
- ½ of capsicum
- ½ of carrot
- ½ teaspoon of coriander
- 2 teaspoons of butter
- 2 sweet corns
- 1 onion
- 1 teaspoon of masala powder
- 2 teaspoons of corn flour

Directions:

1. Create the dough and leave it for 2 hours. Take the bowl.
2. Put chopped potatoes, capsicum, carrot, corns, onion in the bowl and mix everything well.
3. Divide the dough into small pieces. Put vegetable mixture on the pieces of dough and roll them. Sprinkle the frying basket with oil.
4. Put the rolls in the Air Fryer and cook them for 15 minutes.

Nutrition:

- Calories: 156
- Fat: 9,5g
- Carbohydrates: 9,3g
- Protein: 10,2g

Delicious Snack with Onion

It is possible to prepare the appetizing meal, where onion is the main ingredient. Just try and you will be satisfied with the result.

Prep time: 10 minutes

Cooking time: 15-20 minutes

Servings: 2

Ingredients:

- 1 teaspoon of pepper
- ½ teaspoon of salt
- ½ teaspoon of roasted jeera powder
- 1 ajwain
- ½ teaspoon of coriander powder
- 3 big onions
- 1 cup of cheese
- 2 tablespoons of oil

Directions:

1. Take the bowl and put all ingredients in the bowl. Onion should be chopped into the small pieces.
2. Add a few teaspoons of water and mix the dough.
3. Sprinkle the Air Fryer with 2 tablespoons of oil.
4. Create cutlets from the dough and put them in the Air Fryer.
5. Cook for 380F for 10-15 minutes.
6. Then shake them and put on other side. Cook for 3-4 minutes more.

Nutrition:

- Calories: 123
- Fat: 4,5g
- Carbohydrates: 3,3g
- Protein: 2,2g

Bread Roles

You can try to prepare the great bread snake for your friends. The easiest and the most delicious snake will be always on your dinner tables.

Prep time: 10 minutes | **Cooking time:** 10 minutes | **Servings:** 4

Ingredients:

- ½ teaspoon of pepper
- ½ teaspoon of salt
- 2-3 tablespoons of coriander
- ½ teaspoon of masala
- ¼ teaspoon of cumin

- 1 green chili pepper
- ¼ teaspoon of red chili pepper
- ½ teaspoon of dry pomegranate seeds
- 2 big potatoes

- 2 tablespoons of oil
- 5-6 slices of bread

Directions:

1. Wash, clean and boil potatoes.
2. Put potatoes in the bowl and add pepper, salt, masala, cumin, red chili pepper, seeds and 1 tablespoon of oil.
3. Then chop the green pepper and add to the bowl.
4. Divide bread into the pieces.
5. Put these rolls in water and after that in the mixture.
6. Create cutlets from this mixture with bread.
7. Preheat the Air Fryer to 380F.
8. Sprinkle the basket with the rest of oil.
9. Put bread roles in the Air Fryer and cook for 10 minutes.
10. The ready bread roles will have crispy skin and golden color.
11. Enjoy with the different sauces or ketchup.

Nutrition:

- Calories: 185
- Fat: 2,6g

- Carbohydrates: 3,1g
- Protein: 1,2g

Spinach Kabab

This meal will help you if you do not have a lot of time to prepare something special. Simple, delicious and not expensive – this meal is for everyone.

Prep time: 15 minutes

Cooking time: 15-20 minutes

Servings: 4

Ingredients:

- 1-2 tablespoons of oil
- ½ teaspoon of salt
- ½ teaspoon of pepper
- 3 tablespoons of flour

- 1 tablespoon of ginger-garlic pasta
- 1 teaspoon of dry mango powder

- 1 teaspoon of chaat masala
- ¾ cup of peals
- 2 big potatoes
- 1 cups of spinach

Descriptions:

1. Wash and clean spinach in salt water. Then leave it for cold water.
2. Chop spinach and leave in the bowl.
3. Then mix oil, salt, pepper, flour, ginger-garlic pasta, mango powder, chaat masala in the bowl.
4. Boil the peas and potatoes.
5. Them nix everything together.
6. Create cutlets from this mixture.
7. Preheat the Air Fryer to 380F.
8. Cook cutlets for 10 minutes on one side.
9. Then cook them 5-10 minutes on the other side.
10. When they are ready, decorate them with basil leaves or parsley.

Nutrition:

- Calories: 45
- Fat: 4g

- Carbohydrates: 7,9g
- Protein: 3,5g

Flavorsome Cutlets with Fresh Vegetables

You can prepare these vegetable cutlets instead of meat ones. You will see, that they are very delicious and tasty.

Prep time: 2 hour 15 minutes

Cooking time: 10 minutes

Servings: 4

Ingredients:
- ½ teaspoon of salt
- ½ teaspoon of pepper
- 2 teaspoons of coriander
- 1 teaspoon of lemon juice
- 1-2 green chili pepper
- 1 teaspoon of ginger
- ¼ cup of flour
- 1 cup of boiled potato
- 2 teaspoons of oil
- ½ cup of sabudana

Directions:
1. Wash the sabudana and leave for 2 hours.
2. If there is the need, add some water to it.
3. Then mix the sabudana with salt, pepper, coriander, lemon juice, pepper, ginger, flour, potato and oil. Divide the dough in 12 pieces.
4. Create cutlets from this mixture.
5. Preheat the Air Fryer to 375F. Cook cutlets for 10 minutes.

Nutrition:
- Calories: 76
- Fat: 5,3g
- Carbohydrates: 7,2g
- Protein: 4,5g

Fried Rolls

If you wish to prepare something original for your family – that is exactly what you wanted to find. Vegetable rolls, which are healthy simple and tasty.

Prep time: 2 hour 15 minutes

Cooking time: 10 minutes

Servings: 4

Ingredients:
- ½ teaspoon of salt
- ½ teaspoon of pepper
- 2 teaspoons of oil
- 1 teaspoon of curry
- 1 teaspoon of coriander
- ½ teaspoon of dry herbs
- 2-3 green chilies
- ½ teaspoon of ginger
- 1 onion
- 1 teaspoon of flour
- ½ cup of chana dal

Directions:
1. Wash chana dal.
2. Then leave it in ½ cup of water for 2 hours.
3. Then put on the plate and leave for 20-30 minutes.
4. After that, chop onion with the green pepper and green leaves.
5. Chop onion and add to the bowl.
6. Put salt, pepper, oil, coriander, dry herbs, ginger and flour in the bowl.
7. Mix everything well.
8. Make the balls and put them in the Air Fryer.
9. Cook for 10 minutes at 300F.

Nutrition:
- Calories: 97
- Fat: 5,1g
- Carbohydrates: 7,5g
- Protein: 4,2g

Flavorsome and Crispy Fried Potato with Spices

This potato meal is delicious and very simple. Only a few minutes of your time and it is ready. Just try and you will be surprised.

Prep time: 15 minutes	**Cooking time:** 10 minutes	**Servings:** 3

Ingredients:

- 5 big potatoes
- ½ teaspoon of pepper
- ½ teaspoon of salt
- 1 teaspoon of dry herbs
- 3 tablespoons of oil
- 2 teaspoons of paprika

Directions:
1. Wash and clean potatoes.
2. Chop them into thin pieces.
3. Mix pepper, salt, dry herbs, 1 teaspoon of oil and paprika in the bowl.
4. Put chopped potatoes in this bowl and mix everything well.
5. Then sprinkle the Air Fryer basket with 2 teaspoons of oil.
6. Cook potatoes for 5 minutes at 390F.
7. Then shake potatoes well and cook for another 5 minutes.
8. Enjoy with tasty potatoes and also, you can cover them with sauce.

Nutrition:
- Calories: 181
- Fat: 5,5g
- Carbohydrates: 7,9g
- Protein: 4,5g

Cooked Vegetables with Spices

You will like to eat vegetables after reading this recipe. The delicious meal with different spices which you can prepare in the short time.

Prep time: 15 minutes	**Cooking time:** 10 minutes	**Servings:** 3

Ingredients:

- ½ teaspoon of pepper
- ½ teaspoon of salt
- 1 green pepper
- 1 red pepper
- 1 yellow pepper
- 3 eggs
- 2 middle tomatoes
- ½ teaspoon of dry herbs
- 1 small onion
- 4 tablespoons of oil
- 2 teaspoons of ketchup

Directions:
1. Chop peppers in the bowl.
2. Then chop tomatoes with onion and add to the bowl.
3. Mix pepper, salt, dry herbs and 2 tablespoons of oil.
4. Rub vegetables with spices.
5. Cook vegetables in the Air Fryer for 15 minutes at 380F.
6. Then add 2 tablespoons of oil, nix everything and add eggs.
7. Cook for 5 minutes more.
8. Serve hot with ketchup.

Nutrition:
- Calories: 195
- Fat: 9,5g
- Carbohydrates: 8,3g
- Protein: 9,6g

DESSERTS

Apricot and Blackberry Crumble

Minimum of products and the maximum of satisfaction. It is something incredible and tasty.

Prep time: 10 minutes | **Cooking time**: 20 minutes | **Servings**: 4

Ingredients:
- 2 oz of cold butter
- 3 oz of flour
- 1 tablespoon of lemon juice
- 3 oz of fresh blackberries
- 2 oz of sugar
- 7 oz of apricots
- 1 pinch of salt

Directions:
1. Preheat the Air Fryer to 390F.
2. Chop apricots into the pieces and mix them with sugar and lemon juice in the bowl.
3. Grease the cake tin and put fruits on it.
4. Mix flour with salt and butter and add water.
5. Put the mixture on the fruits.
6. After that put it in the frying basket and cook in the Air Fryer for 20 minutes.
7. Dessert should have warm golden color.
8. Serve with ice cream or jam.
9. Eat and enjoy with it.

Nutrition:
- Calories: 480
- Fat: 30,51g
- Carbohydrates: 46,11g
- Protein: 6,2g

Strawberry Cupcakes

Recipe for a very delicate and light dessert. You will see, that it is very delicious.

Prep time: 10 minutes | **Cooking time**: 8 minutes | **Servings**: 4

Ingredients:
- ¼ cup of fresh strawberries
- 1 tablespoon of whipped cream
- ½ tablespoon of pink food coloring
- 4 oz of butter
- ½ tablespoon of vanilla essence
- 3 oz of flour
- 2 eggs
- 3 oz of sugar
- 3 oz of butter

Directions:
1. Preheat the Air Fryer to 380F.
2. Mix butter and sugar in the bowl.
3. Then add vanilla essence and beat eggs one by one.
4. Then add some flour.
5. Create buns and cook them for 8 minutes in the Air Fryer at 350F.
6. Mix sugar, food coloring, whipped cream and strawberries well.
7. When the cupcakes are ready, decorate them with the mixture of cream.
8. Serve hot with tea or coffee.
9. You can be sure, that everyone will like them.

Nutrition:
- Calories: 630
- Fat: 45,5g
- Carbohydrates: 44,11g
- Protein: 6,1g

Tasty Profiteroles with Chocolate

It is tasty cake and dessert will be cooked easily. The products are affordable and inexpensive.

Prep time: 10 minutes	**Cooking time**: 10 minutes	**Servings**: 4

Ingredients:
- 2 oz of butter
- 2 tablespoons of whipped cream
- 3 oz of milk chocolate
- 2 tablespoons of sugar
- 2 tablespoons of vanilla essence
- 2 cups of water
- 6 eggs
- 6 oz of flour
- 3 oz of butter

Directions:
1. Beat eggs in the bowl.
2. Then mix them with flour.
3. After that, leave them aside.
4. Then create cream for dessert.
5. Mix vanilla essence, whipped cream and sugar together.
6. Put the dough in the Air Fryer and cook 10 minutes at 380F.
7. Melt chocolate and put it aside.
8. Decorate the ready cakes with cream and add chocolate above.
9. Enjoy with the tasty dessert.

Nutrition:
- Calories: 589
- Fat: 42,5g
- Carbohydrates: 43,11g
- Protein: 6,5g

British Sponge

Very tasty and easy dessert for tea. There is nothing easier to prepare. Try and you will like it forever.

Prep time: 15 minutes	**Cooking time**: 25 minutes	**Servings**: 8

Ingredients:
- 1 tablespoon of whipped cream
- 3 oz of icing sugar
- 2 oz of butter
- 2 tablespoons of strawberry jam
- 2 eggs
- 3 oz of sugar
- 3 oz of butter
- 3 oz of flour

Directions:
1. Preheat the Air Fryer to 350F.
2. Beat butter and sugar well.
3. Then beat eggs and add some flour.
4. Put the mixture in the Air Fryer and cook for 15 minutes at 350F and then 10 minutes at 340F.
5. Mix butter with the ice sugar and you will get creamy mixture.
6. Then cover dessert with jam and later with cream.
7. Enjoy with the delicious dessert and juice. All your friends will like this dessert because it is tasty.

Nutrition:
- Calories: 598
- Fat: 44,7g
- Carbohydrates: 41,4g
- Protein: 6,3g

Orange Chocolate Fondant

Very easy, tasty and delicious recipe, which you can prepare it always. You should not spend too much time for it.

| **Prep time**: 15 minutes | **Cooking time**: 22 minutes | **Servings**: 4 |

Ingredients:

- 2 eggs
- 1 orange
- 3 oz of butter
- 3 oz of dark chocolate
- 4 teaspoons of sugar
- 2 tablespoons of flour

Directions:
1. Preheat the Air Fryer to 390F.
2. Melt chocolate and butter.
3. Then whist sugar and eggs together.
4. After that, add chopped orange with egg and sugar in chocolate.
5. Then add flour and mix all ingredients.
6. Divide the mixture in 12 pieces and cook them for 12 minutes in the Air Fryer at 390F.
7. Put the cakes on the plate and wait for 10 minutes. They should not be hot.
8. Serve with cold and scrumptious ice cream and juice.
9. Cook and enjoy with this dessert.

Nutrition:
- Calories: 585
- Fat: 45,8g
- Carbohydrates: 42,4g
- Protein: 7,3g

Heart-Shaped Churros

It will be your favorite cake. This cake is very easy for cooking. Also, you will find it delicious.

| **Prep time**: 16-21 minutes | **Cooking time**: 6 minutes | **Servings**: 4 |

Ingredients:
- 1 cup of flour
- ½ cup of sugar
- ¼ teaspoon of salt
- ½ cup of better
- ½ cup of water

Directions:
1. Mix water with butter in the pan and melt it.
2. After that, put the mixture of butter and water in the bowl.
3. Then add flour and mix everything well. Create the dough.
4. Leave for 10-15 minutes.
5. After that, add egg, sugar and salt.
6. Mix everything well.
7. Then create the churros in the shape of heart.
8. Put them in the Air Fryer at 380F.
9. Cook them for 6 minutes.
10. Put the ready cakes on the plate.
11. You can combine them with different jams and enjoy with your friends.

Nutrition:
- Calories: 278
- Fat: 19,5g
- Carbohydrates: 29,4g
- Protein: 6,3g

Peanut Banana Butter Dessert Bites

Here you can find a lot of ingredients and because of it, this dessert is incredibly tasty. Just cook and you will see, that your family will eat this cake in 1 minute.

Prep time: 5-10 minutes | **Cooking time**: 6 minutes | **Servings**: 4

Ingredients:

- ¼ teaspoon of cinnamon
- M and M'S
- 3 tablespoons of raisins
- 3 tablespoons of chocolate chips
- 1 oil mister
- 2 teaspoons of oil
- ½ cup of peanut butter
- 1 large banana
- 1 teaspoon of lemon juice

Directions:
1. Chop the banana in the pieces and put in water with teaspoon of lemon.
2. After that, mix the cinnamon, M and M's, raisins, chocolate chips, peanut butter in the bowl.
3. Add the banana to this mixture. After that preheat the Air Fryer to 380F.
4. Divide the mixture in the pieces and create balls.
5. Sprinkle the Air Fryer basket with 2 teaspoons of oil.
6. Put the sweet balls in the Air Fryer. Cook for 6 minutes.

Nutrition:
- Calories: 235
- Fat: 12,6g
- Carbohydrates: 25,3g
- Protein: 8,3g

Sweet Potato Pie

Can you imagine the pie from potato? No? Just try and you will see, that it is the best pie you have ever tasted.

Prep time: 30 minutes | **Cooking time**: 60 minutes | **Servings**: 4

Ingredients:

- 1 cup of whipped cream
- 1/8 teaspoon of ground nutmeg
- ½ teaspoon of cinnamon
- ½ teaspoon of salt
- ¾ teaspoon of vanilla
- 1 teaspoon of oil
- 1 tablespoon of sugar
- 2 tablespoons of maple syrup
- ¼ cup of cream
- 1 prepared pie
- 1 teaspoon of oil
- 1 6oz of sweet potatoes

Directions:
1. Wash and clean the sweet potatoes.
2. Cut them into pieces.
3. Sprinkle the Air Fryer basket with oil and cook potatoes for 30 minutes at 380F.
4. Do not forget to shake it after 15 minutes of cooking.
5. Mix potatoes with the ground nutmeg, cinnamon, salt, vanilla, sugar, maple syrup and cream.
6. Then put this mixture on the pie. Cook in the Air Fryer at 320F for 30 minutes.
7. The pie should have golden brown color. When it is ready, leave for 20 minutes.

Nutrition:
- Calories: 467
- Fat: 19,2g
- Carbohydrates: 22,3g
- Protein: 7,3g

Cinnamon Sugar Donuts

This is one of the most delicious, tender, high and porous donut recipe you have ever made. Rich chocolate taste, simplicity of cooking and a set of products that every housewife has at home!

Prep time: 5 minutes | **Cooking time**: 4 minutes | **Servings**: 2

Ingredients:

- 2-3 tablespoons of water
- ¼ cup of confectionary sugar
- 4 teaspoons of cinnamon
- 8 buttermilk biscuits
- 1 piece of chocolate

Directions:
1. Put all biscuits on the plate.
2. Mix sugar with the cinnamon and water
3. Put this mixture on every biscuit.
4. Melt chocolate.
5. Put the biscuits in the Air Fryer and cook for 4 minutes at 300F.
6. Then put on the plate and pour with chocolate.
7. Serve warm and it is possible to prepare milk of coffee with these donuts.
8. Eat them and enjoy with the result.

Nutrition:
- Calories: 414
- Fat: 14,2g
- Carbohydrates: 22,5g
- Protein: 7,2g

Peanut Butter Banana Smoothie

There is nothing easier than to cook this peanut banana smoothie. You will like it. Cook and taste and enjoy with it.

Prep time: 5 minutes | **Cooking time**: 2-3 minutes | **Servings**: 2

Ingredients:

- 2 tablespoons of ground flaxseed
- ¾ cup of vanilla yogurt (or you can choose any other you like)
- ½ cup of almond milk
- 1 banana
- 1 tablespoon of honey
- 1 tablespoon of peanut butter

Directions:
1. Chop the banana in the pieces.
2. Mix with yogurt, milk, honey, peanut butter and ground flaxseed well in the bowl.
3. Add the banana to the mixture of ingredients.
4. Preheat the Air Fryer to 380F.
5. Put the ingredients in the Air Fryer and then cook for 2-3 minutes.
6. Serve hot with fruits.
7. Also, you can put some ice and drink cold. It will be also delicious.

Nutrition:
- Calories: 56
- Fat: 1,2g
- Carbohydrates: 5,9g
- Protein: 5,2g

New York Cheesecake

This is something extraordinary! It is an indispensable dessert for your guests. It does not need a lot of expenses, has a very airy texture and most importantly – it does not take too much of your time.

Prep time: 20 minutes | **Cooking time**: 30 minutes | **Servings**: 4

Ingredients:
- 1 tablespoon of vanilla
- 3 eggs
- 2 cups of sugar
- 2 lbs of soft cheese
- 2 oz of melted butter
- 3 oz of butter
- 3 oz of brown sugar
- 7 oz of flour

Directions:
1. Mix flour with sugar well in the bowl.
2. Create the biscuit forms and put in the Air Fryer.
3. Cook for 15 minutes at 370F.
4. When the biscuits are ready, chop them in the small pieces.
5. Then add cheese, butter and sugar and whish everything.
6. You should get creamy mixture.
7. Beat eggs in the bowl and add vanilla.
8. After that, mix everything.
9. Put the mixture in the Air Fryer.
10. Cook for 30 minutes at 380F.
11. Serve hot with juice, tea or coffee.

Nutrition:
- Calories: 389
- Fat: 10,7g
- Carbohydrates: 9,9g
- Protein: 7,2g

Lime Cheesecake

Do you like lime? Prepare this lime cheesecake! The result will be great.

Prep time: 25 minutes | **Cooking time**: 30 minutes | **Servings**: 4

Ingredients:
- 1 tablespoon of vanilla
- 2 tablespoons of yogurt
- 6 limes
- 1 tablespoon of honey
- 3 eggs
- 6 oz of sugar
- 1 lb of soft cheese
- 2 oz of butter
- 1 cup of digestive biscuits

Directions:
1. Preheat the Air Fryer to 380F.
2. Cut the biscuits in the bowl.
3. Mix sugar and cheese well.
4. Add honey, 3 beaten eggs and vanilla to sugar and cheese.
5. Add juice of 6 limes and mix everything with yogurt.
6. Cook up to 15 minutes at 380F.
7. Then change the temperature to 350F and cook for 10-15 minutes.
8. Serve hot and after that enjoy with the delicious cheesecake with your family.
9. Prepare tea, juice or coffee with it.

Nutrition:
- Calories: 412
- Fat: 11,3g
- Carbohydrates: 27,9g
- Protein: 22,2g

Blueberry Cheesecake

Do you want to prepare something for summer? Then this cheesecake will be the great choice, because it is very delicious and has a lot of vitamins.

Prep time: 20 minutes	**Cooking time**: 25 minutes	**Servings**: 4

Ingredients:
- 5 tablespoons of icing sugar
- 1 tablespoon of vanilla
- 2 tablespoons of yogurt
- 3 oz of fresh blueberries
- 4 eggs
- 3 cups of sugar
- 1,5 lb of soft cheese
- 6 digestives biscuits
- 2 oz of butter

Directions:
1. Preheat the Air Fryer to 380F.
2. Chop the biscuits in the pieces and mix with butter.
3. Mix cheese and sugar in the bowl.
4. Beat eggs and add them to cheese.
5. Put there vanilla and yogurt.
6. Take the blueberries and mix them with all ingredients.
7. Cook cheesecake in the Air Fryer for 15 minutes at 370F and after that at 350 for 10 minutes.
8. Serve hot with tea.

Nutrition:
- Calories: 446
- Fat: 14,3g
- Carbohydrates: 24,9g
- Protein: 22,7g

Cheesecake with Caramel

If you like the sweets, you will not be able to refuse from this cheesecake. He incredibly delicious and not too complicated in the preparing.

Prep time: 20 minutes	**Cooking time**: 30 minutes	**Servings**: 4

Ingredients:
- 1 tablespoon of melted chocolate
- 1 tablespoon of vanilla
- 4 big eggs
- 7 oz of sugar
- 1 lb of soft cheese
- 6 digestives biscuits
- ½ cup of caramel

Directions:
1. Preheat the Air Fryer to 380F.
2. Then crushed the biscuits in the bowl.
3. Beat eggs and mix with the biscuits.
4. Then mix cheese, sugar, vanilla in the bowl.
5. Put cheese and rest of ingredients in the same bowl and mix everything well.
6. After that you can add the caramel.
7. Put everything in the Air Fryer.
8. Cook for 15 minutes at 380F, then 10 minutes at 370F and the last 5 minutes at 350F.
9. Take cheesecake out of Air Fryer and leave for 5-10 minutes.
10. At that time melt chocolate and cover cheesecake with it.
11. Enjoy with the delicious cheesecake. Do not forget about juice!

Nutrition:
- Calories: 458
- Fat: 16,3g
- Carbohydrates: 27,9g
- Protein: 25,7g

Cheesecake for Birthday

Do you have birthday and do not know what to prepare for your guests? The answer is very simple – the delicious cheesecake.

Prep time: 20 minutes | **Cooking time**: 30 minutes | **Servings**: 4

Ingredients:
- 1 melted chocolate
- 1 tablespoon of vanilla
- 2 tablespoons of honey
- 6 eggs
- 4 tablespoons of cacao powder
- 1 lb of sugar
- 2 lbs of soft cheese
- 2 oz of butter
- 6 digestives biscuits

Directions:
1. Break the biscuits into the small pieces and mix them with butter.
2. Put the bowl and mix the soft cheese with sugar.
3. Then add 5 eggs, honey and vanilla.
4. Mix everything well.
5. Beat the last egg and mix it with the cacao powder.
6. Cover cheesecake with it and put in the Air Fryer.
7. Cook 20 minutes at 380F, then 10 minutes at 370F.
8. Put it on the plate and cover with the melted chocolate.
9. You can server it hot or put in the fridge and server cold.
10. Your guests will be delighted with this cheesecake.

Nutrition:
- Calories: 449
- Fat: 16,1g
- Carbohydrates: 26,9g
- Protein: 25,4g

Small Cherry Cheesecake

This fruit cheesecake will be the great decoration for your dinner table. It is very delicious and tasty. Just try!

Prep time: 40 minutes | **Cooking time:** 20 minutes | **Servings:** 2

Ingredients:
- 2 cups of warm cherries
- 1 tablespoon of vanilla
- 2 oz of butter
- 2 oz of flour
- 1 oz of coconut sugar
- 1 oz of sugar
- 4 oz of soft cheese

Directions:
1. Mix sugar, flour and coconut sugar in the bowl.
2. Divide the dough in 4 pieces and put in the form for cakes.
3. Cook 20 minutes in the Air Fryer at 380F.
4. Then put in the fridge and leave for 20 minutes.
5. Put the bowl and mix the soft cheese, vanilla and sugar there.
6. Then add yogurt and mix again.
7. Put this mixture on your cakes and leave in the fridge for 10 minutes.
8. Decorate with the cherries and enjoy with tasty cakes.

Nutrition:
- Calories: 389
- Fat: 13,8g
- Carbohydrates: 24,7g
- Protein: 25,6g

Cookies with Chocolate

They are delicious, simple, tasty and do not need a lot of time. Prepare and enjoy.

| **Prep time:** 20minutes | **Cooking time:** 15 minutes | **Servings:** 2 |

Ingredients:

- 3 chocolate chips
- 1 tablespoon of vanilla
- 1 tablespoon of cacao powder
- 3 tablespoons of milk
- 4 tablespoons of honey
- 5 oz of butter
- 1 oz of coconut
- 8 oz of flour
- 2 oz of sugar

Directions:
1. Preheat the Air Fryer to 380F.
2. Put butter and sugar in the bowl and mix together.
3. Then add honey, milk, flour, cacao powder and vanilla.
4. Mix everything well.
5. Crush chocolate chips with your hands.
6. Mix everything for few minutes.
7. Put the foil in the Air Fryer basket.
8. Put the mixture on the foil and cook for 15 minutes.
9. Serve hot and enjoy with incredible delicious dessert.

Nutrition:
- Calories: 239
- Fat: 10,1g
- Carbohydrates: 18,7g
- Protein: 21,6g

Soft Cookies with White Chocolate

You will love this dessert. It is unusual and very tasty. The process of cooking is simple enough and because of it, you will cook it very often.

| **Prep time:** 10 minutes | **Cooking time:** 9 minutes | **Servings:** 2 |

Ingredients:

- 1 tablespoon of milk
- 2 tablespoons of honey
- 3 oz of white chocolate
- 7 oz of flour
- 3 oz of sugar
- 3 oz of butter

Directions:
1. Preheat the Air Fryer to 380F.
2. Mix sugar and butter in the bowl.
3. Then add honey and flour and mix everything well.
4. Chop the white chocolate into small pieces. It is possible to take the dark one.
5. Add milk in the bowl.
6. Put in the Air Fryer and cook for 6 minutes at 380F.
7. Then change it to 350F and cook for 2-3 minutes more.
8. Serve dessert with different jams of juice.
9. Eat and enjoy with the great dessert.

Nutrition:
- Calories: 167
- Fat: 8,3g
- Carbohydrates: 13,6g
- Protein: 16,6g

Cookies in Shape of Heart

These delicious and nice cookies will be the great decoration for your dinner table. They are really soft, fresh and tasty.

| **Prep time:** 20 minutes | **Cooking time:** 10 minutes | **Servings:** 3 |

Ingredients:
- Chocolate buttons
- 1 tablespoon of vanilla
- 6 oz of butter
- 8 oz of flour
- 2 tablespoons of oil.

Directions:
1. Preheat the Air Fryer to 380F.
2. Mix flour, butter and vanilla in the bowl.
3. Then you will get the sweet dough.
4. Leave this dough aside for 10 minutes
5. Then make the rolls from this dough.
6. After that make the heart shape for every roll.
7. Sprinkle the basket for Air Fryer with oil.
8. Then cook cookies for 10 minutes at 380F.
9. Serve hot with the marshmallows or something you like. It is possible to prepare some tea, coffee or juice with them.

Nutrition:
- Calories: 121
- Fat: 5,2g
- Carbohydrates: 12,4g
- Protein: 12,1g

Biscuits with Chocolate

These sweets will be great gift for Christmas. Prepare and check - the biscuit is interesting and soft.

| **Prep time:** 10 minutes | **Cooking time:** 15 minutes | **Servings:** 8 |

Ingredients:
- 8 pieces of dark chocolate
- 2,6 tablespoons of vanilla
- 2,3 tablespoons of cocoa powder
- 1 big egg
- 1 orange
- 3 oz of sugar
- 6 oz of flour
- 3 oz of butter
- 2 teaspoons of oil

Directions:
1. Preheat the Air Fryer to 380F.
2. Mix flour with the melted butter in the bowl.
3. After that add cacao powder, then vanilla, sugar and orange juice. Mix everything well.
4. Create the rolls from this mixture, then flatten these balls and put small piece of chocolate and roll the piece of dough.
5. Sprinkle the basket of the Air Fryer with oil.
6. Cook for 15 minutes at 380F.
7. Your relatives will be glad to eat.

Nutrition:
- Calories: 115
- Fat: 5,3g
- Carbohydrates: 12,2g
- Protein: 12,2g

White Chocolate Cookies

If you like the white chocolate, then this meal is for you. These cookies are really tasty.

Prep time: 10 minutes	**Cooking time:** 18 minutes	**Servings:** 8

Ingredients:

- 1 oz of milk
- 1 oz of honey
- 2 oz of white chocolate
- 2 os of sugar
- 3 oz of butter
- 6 oz of flour

Directions:

1. Beat butter until it is soft.
2. After that add sugar to butter and mix well.
3. After that add milk, flour, honey and white chocolate.
4. Mix everything well.
5. Preheat the Air Fryer to 390F.
6. Sprinkle the frying basket with oil.
7. Cook cookies for 18 minutes at 370F.
8. When they are ready, put them on the plate and serve warm.
9. It is possible to cover them with your favorite jam.
10. Enjoy with these cookies at the birthday, holiday or just at the usual day.
11. This dessert is very flavorsome.

Nutrition:

- Calories: 113
- Fat: 5,7g
- Carbohydrates: 12,3g
- Protein: 12,8g

Biscuits with One Chocolate Part

These cookies are tasty and unusual. If you eat chocolate too much, this dessert will be exactly for you.

Prep time: 1 hour 5 minutes	**Cooking time:** 18-19 minutes	**Servings:** 4

Ingredients:

- 1 tablespoon of vanilla
- 1 egg
- 2 oz of milk chocolate
- 3 oz of butter
- 3 oz of sugar
- 7 oz of flour

Directions:

1. Put flour, sugar and butter in the bowl.
2. Mix everything well.
3. Add vanilla and beaten egg.
4. Mix everything again.
5. Make the balls like a nut and put them in the Air Fryer.
6. Cook them for 15 minutes at 370F.
7. Then put cookies on the plate.
8. Ad that time, put chocolate in the Air Fryer.
9. Melt it for 3-4 minutes at 350F.
10. Put the half of every cookie in chocolate, then put in the plate and leave in the fridge for 1 hour.

Nutrition:

- Calories: 136
- Fat: 7,8g
- Carbohydrates: 12,9g
- Protein: 12,6g

Oat Sandwich Biscuits

These cookies are very healthy and delicious. If you wish to prepare something for dessert, this recipe will be your best choice.

Prep time: 15 minutes | **Cooking time:** 18 minutes | **Servings:** 4

Ingredients:
- 2 tablespoons of vanilla
- ½ tablespoon of lemon juice
- 2 oz of butter
- 3 oz of sugar
- 1 oz of white chocolate
- ½ cup of oats
- ¼ cup of dry coconut
- 1 egg
- 2 oz of white sugar
- 3 oz of butter
- 5 oz of flour

Directions:
1. Mix butter and sugar together.
2. Then add chocolate, beaten egg, coconut and 1 tablespoon of vanilla.
3. After that add flour and mix everything well.
4. Create the small biscuits and after that cover them with the oats.
5. Cook in the Air Fryer at 380F for 18 minutes.
6. Leave them on the plate.
7. Mix the white sugar with butter, add vanilla and lemon juice.
8. Then take one cookie, put the mixture on it and put another cookie on this mixture.
9. You will have small sandwiches.

Nutrition:
- Calories: 143
- Fat: 6,8g
- Carbohydrates: 12,5g
- Protein: 13,6g

Smartie Cookies

All: children or adults will like the smartie cookies. The sweets are easy and simple in preparing. Cook and see.

Prep time: 15 minutes | **Cooking time:** 10 minutes | **Servings:** 4

Ingredients:
- 2 oz of white chocolate
- 1/3 tube of smarties
- 3 tablespoons of cacao
- 1 tablespoon of vanilla
- 7 oz of flour
- 3 oz of butter
- 3 oz of sugar
- 5 tablespoons of milk
- 2 teaspoons of oil

Directions:
1. Preheat the Air Fryer to 380F.
2. Mix sugar, flour and cacao in the bowl.
3. Then add vanilla essence and mix everything well.
4. Crush the white chocolate into small pieces.
5. After that add chocolate and milk and mix everything well.
6. Sprinkle the Air Fryer basket with 2 teaspoons of oil.
7. Cook them for 10 minutes at 380F.
8. Serve hot with marshmallows. Your children will like these cookies.

Nutrition:
- Calories: 121
- Fat: 4,9g
- Carbohydrates: 11,5g
- Protein: 12,2g

Lemon Biscuits

Have you never eaten the delicious lemon biscuits? You should cook them right now, because they are too tasty and original.

Prep time: 15 minutes | **Cooking time:** 5 minutes | **Servings:** 4

Ingredients:
- 1 tablespoon of vanilla
- 1 egg
- 1 lemon
- 7 oz of flour
- 3 oz of sugar
- 3 oz of butter
- 2 teaspoons of oil

Directions:
1. Preheat the Air Fryer to 380F.
2. Mix butter and flour in the bowl.
3. Then add sugar and mix well.
4. Chop lemon in the tiny pieces and add to the bowl.
5. After that mix everything. You should get the dough.
6. Then sprinkle the frying basket for the Air Fryer with 2 teaspoons of oil.
7. Create cookies.
8. They should not be too big or too small.
9. After that cook them in the Air Fryer for 5 minutes at 380F.
10. Serve warm.
11. You will like it with tea of strong coffee.

Nutrition:
- Calories: 103
- Fat: 4,3g
- Carbohydrates: 11,2g
- Protein: 12g

Cookies with Coconut

These cookies are soft, simple and unusual. Just cook them and enjoy with the result.

Prep time: 15 minutes | **Cooking time:** 12 minutes | **Servings:** 4

Ingredients:
- 1 tablespoon of vanilla
- 3 tablespoons of dry coconut
- 2 oz of white chocolate
- 1 egg
- 5 oz of flour
- 2 oz of sugar
- 3 oz of butter

Directions:
1. Preheat the Air Fryer to 380F.
2. Put sugar and butter in the bowl and mix them well.
3. Beat egg and add in the bowl.
4. Put vanilla and mix everything.
5. Cut white chocolate in small pieces.
6. Then mix chocolate with flour.
7. Add them to the ingredients in the bowl and mix everything again.
8. Create the small balls and put them in the coconut.
9. They should be completely covered with the coconut.
10. Cook 8 minutes at 380F, then shake them well and cook for 4 minutes at 350F.

Nutrition:
- Calories: 115
- Fat: 4,6g
- Carbohydrates: 11,3g
- Protein: 11,9g

Chocolate Orange Muffins

Here you can find the instructions how to prepare the delicious and soft orange muffins. This dessert will be your favorite one.

Prep time: 15 minutes | **Cooking time:** 12 minutes | **Servings:** 4

Ingredients:
- 2 oz of orange juice.
- 3 oz of icing sugar
- 2 oz of butter
- 2 oz of milk
- 2 eggs
- 1 tablespoon of vanilla
- 1 tablespoon of honey
- 1 big orange
- 1 tablespoon of cocoa nibs
- 1 oz of cacao powder
- 2 oz of butter
- 3 oz of sugar
- 2 oz of butter
- 4 oz of caster sugar
- 3 oz of flour

Directions:
1. Mix 2 oz of butter, flour and sugar in the bowl.
2. Then add cacao, honey, vanilla and chopped orange in the mixture.
3. Mix all ingredients well.
4. Beat egg in another bowl and mix with milk.
5. Then add egg with milk in the bowl to the rest of ingredients and mix them.
6. You will get the dough for your muffins.
7. Divide into pieces and cook for 12 minutes at 370F.
8. Put butter, and icing sugar together.
9. Decorate the ready muffins with it.
10. Serve and enjoy with the incredibly delicious muffins.

Nutrition:
- Calories: 138
- Fat: 6,6g
- Carbohydrates: 13,3g
- Protein: 8,9g

Chocolate Muffins

Just prepare these muffins, this recipe is priceless. Sweet chocolate and biscuit will be your favorite dessert for the long time.

Prep time: 15 minutes | **Cooking time:** 15 minutes | **Servings:** 4

Ingredients:
- ½ tablespoon of vanilla
- 1/3 cup of water
- 5 tablespoons of milk
- 2 eggs
- 3 oz of butter
- 3 oz of milk chocolate
- 1 oz of cacao powder
- 6 oz of flour

Directions:
1. Preheat the Air Fryer to 380F.
2. Mix sugar, flour and cacao in the deep bowl.
3. Then add butter and mix everything well.
4. Beat eggs and add them and milk in the bowl with other ingredients.
5. Then add vanilla and if there is the need, add some water.
6. Chop chocolate in the small pieces and add to the products.
7. Then mix everything and divide into small bowls.
8. Put them in the Air Fryer and cook 9 minutes at 380F and then 6 minutes at 350F.

Nutrition:
- Calories: 145
- Fat: 8,6g
- Carbohydrates: 15,3g
- Protein: 8,3g

Cheesecake Cupcakes

Do you want to prepare something original but at the same time simple?
Just try and you will get the delicious, soft and tasty cupcakes.

Prep time: 30 minutes | **Cooking time:** 20 minutes | **Servings:** 4

Ingredients:

- 3 teaspoons of chocolate chips
- Red food coloring
- 4 tablespoons of honey
- 2 teaspoons of vanilla

- 2 tablespoons of yogurt
- 6 tablespoons of milk
- 1 lb of soft cheese
- 2 eggs
- 1 lemon

- 1 oz of cacao
- 3 oz of butter
- 7 oz of sugar
- 7 oz of flour

Directions:

1. Preheat the Air Fryer to 380F.
2. Mix butter with flour.
3. Then add sugar, 2 beaten eggs, cacao, vanilla and lemon juice.
4. Then add milk and mix everything well.
5. After that add red food coloring.
6. Put everything in the Air Fryer and cook for 20 minutes at 370F.
7. Then put the soft cheese and honey in the bowl and mix them.
8. After that add yogurt and mix everything again.
9. Put this mixture in the fridge for 10 minutes.
10. When the cupcakes are ready, leave them on the plate for 10 minutes.
11. Then take the mixture from the fridge and decorate the cupcakes.
12. You can decorate them with strawberries or jam.
13. Do not forget about coffee! Enjoy!

Nutrition:

- Calories: 151
- Fat: 8,9g

- Carbohydrates: 15,2g
- Protein: 8,5g

Lemon Cupcakes

The interesting combination lemon and sugar in these cupcakes.
Your guests will like the cupcakes with lemon.

Prep time: 20 minutes	**Cooking time:** 20 minutes	**Servings:** 4

Ingredients:

- 1 red coloring
- 1 blue coloring
- 2 tablespoons of vanilla
- 4 tablespoons of milk

- 1 tablespoon of yogurt
- 1 lb of soft cheese
- 3 lemons
- 2 eggs

- 2 oz of butter
- 5 oz of sugar
- 4 oz of flour

Directions:

1. Take the bowl and put milk, lemon, butter, sugar, flour and beaten eggs.
2. Put the mixture into 3 bowls.
3. Put the red coloring in one bowl and mix the ingredients well.
4. Then put the blue coloring in the second bowl and mix everything.
5. Take some dough from first bowl and some dough from another one.
6. Then add the dough from the third one and you will get the cupcake from 3 parts.
7. Create the cupcakes and put them in the Air Fryer.
8. Cook for 20 minutes at 360F.

Nutrition:

- Calories: 148
- Fat: 8,8g

- Carbohydrates: 15,3g
- Protein: 7,5g

Cupcakes with Strawberries

The cupcakes are very delicious and healthy. They have some vitamins and the children will like them a lot.

Prep time: 20 minutes	**Cooking time:** 8 minutes	**Servings:** 4

Ingredients:

- ¼ cup of fresh strawberries
- 1 tablespoon of whipped cream

- ½ teaspoon of pink coloring
- 3 oz of icing sugar
- 2 oz of butter
- ½ tablespoon of vanilla

- 3 oz of flour
- 2 eggs
- 3 oz of sugar
- 3 oz of butter

Directions:

1. Preheat the Air Fryer to 340F.
2. Mix butter and sugar in the bowl.
3. Then beat eggs and add vanilla.
4. Mix everything butter and sugar.
5. Make the cupcakes and put them in the Air Fryer.
6. Cook for 8 minutes at 380F.
7. Then take butter and mix it with icing sugar.
8. Add strawberries, food coloring and cream.
9. Mix everything well.

Nutrition:

- Calories: 290
- Fat: 15,6g

- Carbohydrates: 16,7g
- Protein: 7,6g

Lemon Buns

This dessert will be great choice for the birthday or some holiday. Easy in preparing and at the same time delicious, it will not take too much of your time.

Prep time: 20 minutes	**Cooking time:** 6 minutes	**Servings:** 4

Ingredients:

- ½ lemon
- 3 oz of icing sugar
- 2 oz butter

- 1 tablespoon of cherries
- ½ tablespoon of vanilla
- 3 oz of flour

- 2 eggs
- 3 oz of casted sugar
- 3 oz of butter

Directions:

1. Preheat the Air Fryer to 380F.
2. Mix butter with sugar in the bowl.
3. Then add vanilla.
4. Mix everything well.
5. Beat eggs and add one by one in the mixture.
6. Then add flour.
7. Make buns and put them in the Air Fryer.
8. Cook for 6 minutes at 380F.
9. Mix butter with the icing sugar.
10. Then add chopped lemon and mix everything well.
11. Chop the ready buns in 2 pieces and decorate with butter and sugar.
12. Then add cherries on the top of be buns.

Nutrition:

- Calories: 287
- Fat: 15,8g

- Carbohydrates: 16,5g
- Protein: 7,3g

Flourless Cupcakes

Are you interested in preparing dessert without flour? Then try to do it and you will be delighted with the result.

Prep time: 10 minutes	**Cooking time:** 20 minutes	**Servings:** 6

Ingredients:

- 2 limes (juice)
- ¼ cup of caster sugar
- 1 tablespoon of vanilla
- 1 big egg (yolk)
- 2 eggs
- 6 oz of soft cheese
- 8 oz of yogurt

Directions:

1. Mix yogurt with cheese in the bowl.
2. Then add eggs and mix everything again.
3. Add lime juice, vanilla and sugar and mix everything again.
4. Create 6 cakes and coo them for 10 minutes at 380F.
5. Then put them on another side and cook for 10 minutes more at the same temperature.
6. Put the cakes on the plate and decorate with your favorite fruits.
7. It is possible to use some jam and cover the cakes with this jam.
8. Enjoy!

Nutrition:

- Calories: 187
- Fat: 15,2g
- Carbohydrates: 13,9g
- Protein: 7,5g

Pineapple Cake

This dessert will be great choice for summer, because you can find a lot of fruits. If you wish, you can replace the pineapple with any other fruit – the result as tasty and delicious cake.

Prep time: 10 minutes	**Cooking time:** 40 minutes	**Servings:** 4

Ingredients:

- 2 tablespoons of milk
- 1 egg
- 2 oz of dark chocolate
- 3 oz of pineapple juice
- 3 oz of caster sugar
- 3 oz of butter
- 7 oz of flour

Directions:

1. Sprinkle the Air Fryer with oil and preheat to 380F.
2. Mix butter with flour in the bowl.
3. Add the pineapple juice and sugar.
4. Mix everything in the bowl.
5. Then chop chocolate in the small pieces.
6. Leave it aside.
7. Mix milk with egg in the second bowl.
8. Then add it to the first bowl and mix everything well.
9. Cook for 40 minutes at 380F.
10. Leave for 10 minutes and serve.
11. You can decorate it with cream or some fruits.

Nutrition:

- Calories: 197
- Fat: 15,8g
- Carbohydrates: 13,7g
- Protein: 7,8g

Flourless Chocolate Cake

You can prepare the delicious and tasty cake. It is not expensive and does not need too much of your time.

Prep time: 10 minutes | **Cooking time:** 40 minutes | **Servings:** 4

Ingredients:
- 1 avocado
- 8 eggs
- 4 tablespoons of honey
- 10 teaspoons of cacao
- 10 bananas

Directions:
1. Preheat the Air Fryer to 380F.
2. Beat eggs one by one and mix them.
3. Then add honey and cacao.
4. Chop bananas into the pieces and add them to the rest ingredients.
5. Put everything in the food processor and mix.
6. Take the half of the mixture and divide in 2 parts.
7. Cook them in the Air Fryer for 15 minutes every of them.
8. Then take the rest of the mixture and add chopped avocado there.
9. Put this mixture between 2 pieces of dough and cook for 10 minutes.
10. Then leave if for e few minutes.
11. Serve warm.

Nutrition:
- Calories: 186
- Fat: 14,5g
- Carbohydrates: 13,2g
- Protein: 7,4g

Carrot Cake

Do you want to get not only delicious cake, but also the healthier one? Then prepare this carrot cake, because it has a lot of vitamins.

Prep time: 15 minutes | **Cooking time:** 10 minutes | **Servings:** 4

Ingredients:
- 1/3 cup of water
- 7 oz of icing sugar
- 2 tablespoons of milk
- 3 oz of butter
- 4 oz of olive oil
- 2 eggs
- 2 bit carrots
- 1 tablespoon of dry herbs
- 4 oz of dark sugar
- 7 oz of flour

Directions:
1. Preheat the Air Fryer to 380F for 10 minutes.
2. Chop and cut carrots, add flour, sugar and dry herbs in the bowl.
3. Mix everything well.
4. Then add eggs, oil and milk to them.
5. Mix all ingredients.
6. Cook in the Air Fryer for 5 minutes at 380F and after that at 350F for 5 minutes more.
7. Beat butter with the icing sugar and decorate carrot cake.
8. Enjoy with delicious cake with your family.

Nutrition:
- Calories: 145
- Fat: 11,5g
- Carbohydrates: 10,2g
- Protein: 7,2g

Fruit Cake

Do you like fruits? This recipe will give you the treat opportunity to prepare the fruit cake, which is delicious and fantastic.

Prep time: 15 minutes | **Cooking time:** 15 minutes | **Servings:** 4

Ingredients:
- 1 tablespoon of honey
- ¼ cup of blueberries
- 1 peach
- 1 pear
- 1 apple
- 4 plumps
- 1 oz of sugar
- 1 oz of oats
- 2 oz of butter
- 4 oz of flour

Directions:
1. Preheat the Air Fryer to 350F.
2. Wash and clean the fruits.
3. Then chop the peach, apple, plumps and pear into small pieces.
4. Cover them with sugar and honey and mix well.
5. Mix flour, butter together and then add oats.
6. Put it on the top of cake.
7. Sprinkle the Air Fryer basket with oil.
8. Cook the cake for 10 minutes at 350F and then 5 minutes at 330F.
9. Serve warm and you will be glad with the perfect result.

Nutrition:
- Calories: 139
- Fat: 11,2g
- Carbohydrates: 10,3g
- Protein: 7,4g

Mug Cakes with Chocolate

It is incredibly tasty and delicious. The nice chocolate cakes are easy for preparing.

Prep time: 2 minutes | **Cooking time:** 10 minutes | **Servings:** 2

Ingredients:
- 3 tablespoons of coconut oil
- 3 tablespoons of milk
- 1 tablespoon of cacao
- 5 tablespoons of sugar
- ¼ cup of flour

Directions:
1. Take the bowl.
2. Mix coconut oil, milk, cacao, flour and sugar together.
3. Sprinkle the Air Fryer basket with oil.
4. Put the mixture in the Air Fryer.
5. Cook for 5 minutes at 380F.
6. Then put it in other side and cook 5 minutes more at 370F.
7. Take it out of Air Fryer and leave for 10 or 15 minutes.
8. Serve them warm.
9. It is possible to cover with jam.
10. Do not forget about tea or juice.
11. Enjoy with appetizing cakes with your friends or relatives.

Nutrition:
- Calories: 147
- Fat: 11,3g
- Carbohydrates: 10,6g
- Protein: 7,1g

Lemon Tarts

These tarts are very easy in preparing. You even cannot imagine how delicious they are. They are incredibly tasty.

Prep time: 15 minutes | **Cooking time:** 15 minutes | **Servings:** 2

Ingredients:

- ½ teaspoon of nutmeg
- 4 tablespoons of lemon cheese
- 2 big lemon
- 1 oz of sugar
- 7 oz of flour
- 3 oz of butter

Directions:

1. Take the huge bowl.
2. Put butter, sugar and flour there.
3. Mix everything well.
4. Chop lemon in the pieces and add to the mixture.
5. Add some water and nutmeg.
6. Mix everything well.
7. Create the cupcakes and cook them for 15 minutes at 370F.
8. Then take the cupcakes out of Air Fryer and leave for 10 minutes.
9. Chop the second lemon into small spices and decorate the cakes.
10. Serve warm and drink sweet juice, like apple or strawberry or even tea.

Nutrition:

- Calories: 126
- Fat: 10,3g
- Carbohydrates: 11,2g
- Protein: 7,6g

Orange Chocolate Cake

Your children will appreciate your efforts, because this cake will be great. It is sweet and soft and you can be sure, that it will be eaten immediately.

Prep time: 15 minutes | **Cooking time:** 24 minutes | **Servings:** 4

Ingredients:

- 2 eggs
- 1 orange
- 5 oz of dark chocolate
- 5 oz of butter
- 2 tablespoons of flour
- 2 tablespoons of oil.

Directions:

1. Preheat the Air Fryer to 380F.
2. Then melt chocolate and butter together.
3. Mix them well.
4. Beat eggs and add sugar there.
5. Add flour and mix all ingredients.
6. Sprinkle the frying Air Fryer basket with oil.
7. Cook for 12 minutes at 380F in the Air Fryer.
8. Then put in the other side and cook for 12 minutes more at the same temperature.
9. Serve warm.
10. Also, it is possible to serve with caramel or ice cream.

Nutrition:

- Calories: 118
- Fat: 10,34g
- Carbohydrates: 11,3g
- Protein: 7,5g

Cakes with Strawberry Jam

This cake will be always on your dinner table. Easy, simple and very delicious. Just try and see.

Prep time: 8 minutes | **Cooking time:** 10 minutes | **Servings:** 2

Ingredients:

- 1/3 cup of water
- ¼ cup of strawberry jam
- 1 oz of sugar
- 7 oz of flour
- 2 tablespoons of oil

Directions:
1. Preheat the Air Fryer to 380F.
2. Take the deep bowl and put butter, sugar and flour in the bowl.
3. Mix everything well.
4. Add 1/3 cup of water and even more if you need, it depends on the dough.
5. You should get the dough for the cake.
6. Add there the strawberries and mix everything again.
7. Sprinkle the frying basket with oil
8. Make the cakes and put them in the Air Fryer.
9. Cook for 10 minutes at 380F.

Nutrition:
- Calories: 121
- Fat: 10,6g
- Carbohydrates: 11,1g
- Protein: 6,9g

Mini Apple Pie

The apple in this pie has the incredible delicious note and when you eat this cake, you will be very satisfied. This pie with the apple is easy for preparing.

Prep time: 5 minutes | **Cooking time:** 18 minutes | **Servings:** 2

Ingredients:
- 1 teaspoon of sugar
- 1 teaspoon of cinnamon
- 2 apple
- ¼ cup of water
- 1 oz of caster sugar
- 1 oz of butter
- 2 oz of butter

Directions:
1. Put flour and butter in the bowl.
2. Mix them there.
3. Then add sugar and mix well.
4. Add water and create the dough.
5. After that wash and clean apples.
6. Chop them into pieces.
7. Mix them with sugar and cinnamon.
8. Add apples to the dough and put them on the top.
9. Preheat the Air Fryer to 380F.
10. Then cook the cake for 18 minutes at 380F.

Nutrition:
- Calories: 110
- Fat: 7,6g
- Carbohydrates: 9,1g

Pumpkin Pies

This pie from pumpkin is not only healthy, but very delicious. It is sweet and very soft.

Prep time: 12 minutes | **Cooking time:** 50 minutes | **Servings:** 4

Ingredients:
- ¼ cup of water
- 1 oz of caster sugar
- 1 oz of butter
- 2 oz of flour
- 1 pumpkin pie filling
- 2 tablespoons of oil

Directions:
1. Preheat the Air Fryer to 380F.
2. Put butter and flour in the bowl and mix everything well.
3. Then add sugar and mix the ingredients again.
4. Then add water. Just see how many cups of water you need, because it depends on flour.
5. The dough should not be too thick or too thin. It is up to you.
6. Sprinkle the Air Fryer basket with oil.
7. Put the dough in the Air Fryer.
8. Then put pumpkin filling on the pie.
9. Cook for 15 minutes at 380F.
10. Serve this warm dessert with the orange juice.

Nutrition:
- Calories: 102
- Fat: 4,6g
- Carbohydrates: 8,1g
- Protein: 6,3g

Cake with Sugar and Coconut

It is very sweet and very delicious cake. It is prepared very simple and easy. Just 15 minutes and the cake is ready.

Prep time: 15 minutes | **Cooking time:** 15 minutes | **Servings:** 4

Ingredients:
- ½ tablespoons of vanilla
- 7 oz of butter
- 2 oz of coconut sugar
- 7 oz of flour
- 1 condensed milk
- 2 tablespoons of oil

Directions:
1. Add water in the Air Fryer and put condensed milk there.
2. Preheat the Air Fryer to 320F.
3. Cook milk for 30-40 minutes.
4. Take the bowl and put flour, sugar and butter there.
5. Then add vanilla and mix everything well.
6. Sprinkle the Air Fryer basket with oil.
7. Cook bread in the Air Fryer for 10 minutes at 350F.
8. Chop bread into slices, put milk between 2 slices of bread and leave.
9. Serve warm.
10. Your children will like it.

Nutrition:
- Calories: 269
- Fat:12,8g
- Carbohydrates: 10,8g
- Protein: 6,9g

Sponge Cake with Chocolate

This cake is full of chocolate and everyone likes it. You will not spend a lot of your time to prepare this cake. Simple and delicious.

| **Prep time:** 10 minutes | **Cooking time:** 10 minutes | **Servings:** 4 |

Ingredients:

- ½ teaspoon of nutmeg
- ½ tablespoon of vanilla
- 1 oz of dark chocolate
- 1 oz of cacao powder
- 2 oz of milk chocolate
- 1 tablespoon of honey
- 2 oz of coconut sugar
- 2 oz of flour
- 2 eggs

Directions:

1. Take the bowl and beat eggs there.
2. Then add sugar and mix everything well.
3. After that add vanilla, honey and cacao powder.
4. Sprinkle the Air Fryer basket with oil.
5. Put the dough in the Air Fryer.
6. Cook for 10 minutes at 345F.
7. Then melt chocolate and add coconut and nutmeg there.
8. Cover the dough with chocolate.
9. Serve hot with coffee or tea.

Nutrition:

- Calories: 237
- Fat: 12,8g
- Carbohydrates: 13,8g
- Protein: 10,9g

Brownie Cake with Chocolate

If your children like cakes, cook chocolate cake for them. Delicious and easy, not expensive and tasty.

| **Prep time:** 5 minutes | **Cooking time:** 10 minutes | **Servings:** 4 |

Ingredients:

- 1 tablespoon of vanilla
- 2 eggs
- 1 tablespoon of cacao powder
- 3 oz of dark chocolate
- 3 oz of butter
- 6 oz of coconut sugar
- 3 oz of flour

Directions:

1. Melt chocolate with butter.
2. Beat eggs one by one and add to chocolate and butter.
3. Mix everything well.
4. Then add vanillas, sugar and cacao powder to the products.
5. Mix everything in the bowl very well.
6. Then sprinkle the Air Fryer basket with oil.
7. Put the mixture of the products in the Air Fryer.
8. Cook for 10 minutes at 370F.
9. Serve hot and you can decorate it with the fruits.
10. After it enjoy with your dessert.

Nutrition:

- Calories: 245
- Fat: 12,3g
- Carbohydrates: 13,2g
- Protein: 10,5g

Cranberry Scone Bread

This type of bread is too delicious and sweet. It is very simple for preparing. You will be satisfied to eat this dessert. It is soft and also healthy.

| **Prep time:** 10 minutes | **Cooking time:** 25 minutes | **Servings:** 4 |

Ingredients:
- 1 tablespoon of milk
- ¼ cup of cranberries
- 2 tablespoons of honey
- 2 oz of butter
- 9 oz of flour
- 2 eggs
- 2 oz of coconut sugar

Directions:
1. Preheat the Air Fryer to 340F.
2. Put butter, sugar and flour in the bowl.
3. Mix the products very well.
4. Then beat eggs one by one and add to the mixture.
5. Add milk in the bowl with the ingredients.
6. When the mixture is ready, add the cranberries to it and mix well.
7. Put the mixture in the Air Fryer and cook for 20minutes at 340F.
8. Then change the temperature to 320F and cook 5 minutes.
9. Serve warm end enjoy with it.

Nutrition:
- Calories: 198
- Fat:12,6g
- Carbohydrates: 13,2g
- Protein: 10,2g

Blackberries Bars

If you are looking for something new and delicious – pay your attention to this recipe. You have never tried these tasty and fantastic bars.

| **Prep time:** 5 minutes | **Cooking time:** 20 minutes | **Servings:** 4 |

Ingredients:
- 1 tablespoon of cinnamon
- 1 tablespoon of vanilla
- 2 tablespoons of honey
- 3 oz of soft cheese
- 6 oz of sugar
- 8 oz of flour
- 7 oz of butter

Directions:
1. Preheat the Air Fryer to 380F.
2. Mix flour, butter and sugar in the bowl.
3. Then add the honey and cinnamon and mix again all ingredients in the bowl.
4. Cook the dough in the Air Fryer for 15 minutes at 310F.
5. Then take another bowl and put cheese, vanilla, eggs and honey there.
6. Mix everything well.
7. After that put cheese mixture on the dough and cook for 5 minutes more at 330F.
8. You will get the delicious and great cake.
9. Enjoy with it.

Nutrition:
- Calories: 189
- Fat:11,8g
- Carbohydrates: 12,2g
- Protein: 10,6g

Mince Pies

This cake is very simple, but you should not create something new. If you have some guests, you can prepare it in the short time.

Prep time: 10 minutes	**Cooking time:** 17 minutes	**Servings:** 4

Ingredients:

- 1 egg
- 3 oz of mince meat
- 1 oz of sugar
- 2 tablespoons of oil
- 3 oz of butter
- 7 oz of flour

Directions:

1. Preheat the Air Fryer to 320F.
2. Mix flour and butter in the bowl together.
3. Then add sugar and mix the ingredients again.
4. You can add warm water to have better dough.
5. Divide the dough into pieces.
6. Then put meat on every piece and roll it.
7. Sprinkle the Air Fryer with oil.
8. Put the cakes in the Air Fryer and cook them for 12 minutes at 320F.
9. Then put them on other side and cook for additional 5 minutes.
10. Serve hot with parsley or basil leaves. It is up to you what to choose.

Nutrition:

- Calories: 350
- Fat:17,4g
- Carbohydrates: 11,2g
- Protein: 15,6g

Creamy Chocolate Cookie

It is the best recipe for people that cannot live without chocolate. Prepare and enjoy, because it is plenty of chocolate.

Prep time: 5 minutes	**Cooking time:** 20 minutes	**Servings:** 4

Ingredients:

- 1 tablespoon of milk
- 4 tablespoons of honey
- 3 oz of chocolate
- 5 oz of flour
- 3 oz of drown sugar
- 3 oz of butter

Directions:

1. Preheat the Air Fryer for 10 minutes to 290F.
2. Put sugar and butter in the bowl and mix them together.
3. After that mix the honey with flour.
4. Chop chocolate in small pieces.
5. Then put chocolate to rest ingredients and mix with milk.
6. Divide the dough in the pieces and put in the Air Fryer.
7. Cook for 10 minutes and then put on the other side and cook for 10 minutes more.
8. Enjoy with these delicious cookies. Serve with ice cream.

Nutrition:

- Calories: 313
- Fat:16,4g
- Carbohydrates: 10,2g
- Protein: 9,6g

Fluffy Shortbread with Cream

This dish is simple and easy in cooking. All people will like it and you will have a lot of guests. You will get the delicious cakes.

Prep time: 15 minutes	**Cooking time:** 12 minutes	**Servings:** 4

Ingredients:

- 1 lemon
- 2 oz of butter
- 3 oz of icing sugar
- 1 tablespoon of vanilla
- 6 oz of butter
- 3 oz of sugar
- 8 oz of flour
- 2 teaspoon of oil

Directions:

1. Preheat the Air Fryer to 340F.
2. Mix butter and sugar in the bowl.
3. Then add vanilla and create the dough.
4. Sprinkle the Air Fryer with oil.
5. Make cookies and put them in the Air Fryer.
6. Cook for 12 minutes at 340F.
7. Then put the icing sugar, butter and chopped lemon in the bowl.
8. Mix everything well.
9. When cookies are ready, decorate them with this mixture.
10. Serve warm with tea.

Nutrition:

- Calories: 198
- Fat:13,2g
- Carbohydrates: 10,7g
- Protein: 5,6g

Fruit Crumble

It is very interesting and delicious recipe, where you can prepare your favorite fruits. Your friend or relatives will like it.

Prep time: 15 minutes	**Cooking time:** 15 minutes	**Servings:** 4

Ingredients:

- 1 tablespoon of cinnamon
- 2 oz of frozen berries
- 4 medium plums
- 1 apple
- 1 oz of butter
- 1 oz of sugar
- 2 oz of flour
- 2 tablespoons of oil

Directions:

1. Preheat the Air Fryer to 350F.
2. Wash and clean all fruits.
3. Put them in the food processor. They should be chopped in small pieces.
4. Take the bowl and mix butter with flour well.
5. Mix the fruits with this mixture and put in the Air Fryer.
6. Do not forget to sprinkle the Air Fryer basket with oil.
7. Cook for 15 minutes at 350F.
8. Take them out of Air Fryer and put on the plate.
9. It is possible to serve with cream.

Nutrition:

- Calories: 220
- Fat:11,2g
- Carbohydrates: 13,7g
- Protein: 5,4g

Shortbread Fingers

This recipe is amazing and delicious. Also, you need only a few minutes to prepare and to cook it. You will like the result.

Prep time: 4 minutes | **Cooking time:** 12 minutes | **Servings:** 4

Ingredients:
- 8 oz of flour
- 2 tablespoons of oil
- 2 oz of sugar
- 5 oz of butter

Directions:
1. Preheat the Air Fryer to 350F.
2. Take the deep bowl
3. Put flour and butter in the bowl.
4. Mix them there.
5. Then add sugar and mix all ingredients well.
6. Create cookies and put them on the plate.
7. Sprinkle the Air Fryer basket with oil.
8. Then cook them for 6 minutes at 350F.
9. After that put them on the other side and cook for 6 minutes more.
10. When they are ready, take them off,
11. It is possible to serve them with jam, milk, ice cream or whatever you like.

Nutrition:
- Calories: 136
- Fat:7,2g
- Carbohydrates: 9,7g
- Protein: 3,4g

Chocolate Balls

If you wish to prepare something unusual for dessert, you can try these chocolate balls. Simple and delicious and everyone will like them.

Prep time: 4 minutes | **Cooking time:** 13 minutes | **Servings:** 4

Ingredients:
- 2 tablespoons of cacao
- 9 chocolate chunks
- 1 tablespoon of vanilla
- 8 oz of flour
- 3 oz of sugar
- 5 oz of butter

Directions:
1. Preheat the Air Fryer to 340F.
2. Mix flour, sugar and butter together in the bowl.
3. Make the rolls from this dough.
4. Chop chocolate in small pieces.
5. Put the piece of chocolate in the middle of every roll.
6. Then sprinkle the Air Fryer with oil.
7. Put the rolls in the Air Fryer and cook them for 8 minutes at 340F and then 5 minutes at 290F.
8. Serve warm with juice. It is possible to decorate them with the fruits.

Nutrition:
- Calories: 145
- Fat:7,9g
- Carbohydrates: 9,4g
- Protein: 3,2g

Chocolate Brownies with Caramel Sauce

It is very tasty and sweaty brownies. Just cook and try!

Prep time: 18 minutes | **Cooking time:** 15 minutes | **Servings:** 4

Ingredients:
- 2 tablespoons of vanilla
- 3 oz of flour
- 2 eggs
- 6 oz of sugar
- 2 oz of chocolate
- 4 oz of butter
- ½ cup of milk
- ½ cup of water
- 3 oz of caster sugar

Directions:
1. Preheat the Air Fryer to 340F.
2. Melt butter and chocolate together.
3. Add sugar, eggs and vanilla.
4. Then add flour to the bowl with the ingredients and mix everything well.
5. Sprinkle the Air Fryer basket with oil.
6. Put the mixture there and cook for 15 minutes at 340F.
7. Mix sugar and water and boil it. Then add milk and you will get the caramel sauce.
8. Cover cookies with this sauce.
9. Serve warm.
10. The best addition to these cookies will be fruits like orange or lemon.

Nutrition:
- Calories: 189
- Fat:9,1g
- Carbohydrates: 9,8g
- Protein: 4,2g

Chocolate Eclairs

You need to prepare them, because you will miss the chance to try these tasty and delicious eclairs.

Prep time: 15 minutes | **Cooking time:** 16 minutes | **Servings:** 4

Ingredients:
- 1 oz of butter
- 1 tablespoon of whipped cream
- 2 oz of milk chocolate
- 5 oz of whipped cream
- 1 tablespoon of icing sugar
- 1 tablespoon of vanilla
- 1/3 cup of water
- 3 oz of flour
- 2 oz of butter
- 3 eggs

Directions:
1. Preheat the Air Fryer to 300F.
2. Mix flour with 2 oz of butter.
3. Then add sugar.
4. Beat eggs one by one and mix everything well in the bowl.
5. Cook for 10 minutes at 300F and then 6 minutes at 280F.
6. Then mix whipped cream, vanilla and icing sugar in the bowl.
7. After that cover the eclairs with cream.
8. Serve warm.
9. You can add the fruits. Your family will like them.

Nutrition:
- Calories: 197
- Fat:9,5g
- Carbohydrates: 9,3g
- Protein: 4,5g

Dark Profiteroles

Simple, delicious and cheap. Just prepare and enjoy with delicious cakes.

Prep time: 15 minutes | **Cooking time:** 10 minutes | **Servings:** 4

Ingredients:
- 2 oz of butter
- 1 tablespoon of whipped cream
- 3 oz of milk chocolate
- 9 oz of whipped cream
- 2 tablespoons of vanilla
- 2 tablespoons of icing sugar
- ½ cup of water
- 6 eggs
- 6 oz of flour
- 3 oz of butter

Directions:
1. Preheat the Air Fryer to 350F.
2. Mix butter with flour in the bowl.
3. After that add beaten eggs step by step.
4. Sprinkle the Air Fryer with oil
5. Put the dough in the Air Fryer and cook for 10 minutes at 350F.
6. Mix cream with vanilla and icing sugar in the second bowl.
7. After that decorate the dough with this cream.
8. Melt chocolate and cover the eclairs with it.

Nutrition:
- Calories: 236
- Fat:10,3g
- Carbohydrates: 9,5g
- Protein: 4,1g

Doughnuts

They are really easy and tasty. Also, they are very delicious. You should try.

Prep time: 10 minutes | **Cooking time:** 15 minutes | **Servings:** 4

Ingredients:
- ¼ cup of strawberries
- 1 tablespoon of whipped cream
- ½ tablespoon of pink coloring
- 3 oz of icing sugar
- 2 oz of butter
- 1 egg
- 2 tablespoons of butter
- 1/3 cup of milk
- 2 oz of sugar
- 2 oz of caster sugar
- 7 oz of flour

Directions:
1. Preheat the Air Fryer to 300F.
2. Mix butter, flour, sugar and caster sugar in the bowl.
3. Take the second bowl and mix egg, butter and milk there.
4. Then mix everything from 2 bowls in the same one.
5. Sprinkle the Air Fryer with oil.
6. Cook for 15 minutes at 300F.
7. Then put them on the plate.
8. After that mix the coloring with the icing sugar, strawberries, cream.

Nutrition:
- Calories: 247
- Fat:12,3g
- Carbohydrates: 9,9g
- Protein: 4,2g

Egg Buns

You will be able to see, that they are delicious, not expensive and tasty. You need to cook them.

Prep time: 10 minutes | **Cooking time:** 20 minutes | **Servings:** 4

Ingredients:
- Mini eggs
- 9 oz of soft cheese
- 3 oz of icing sugar
- 1 tablespoon of vanilla
- 2 tablespoons of honey
- 2 eggs
- 3 oz of butter
- 3 oz of sugar
- 3 oz of flour

Directions:
1. Mix sugar with butter in the bowl.
2. After that beat eggs one by one and mix in the bowl with sugar and butter together.
3. Then add vanilla and honey.
4. After that add flour and mix everything well.
5. Put in the Air Fryer and cook for 20-25 minutes at 300F.
6. Mix cheese with the icing sugar together.
7. Decorate buns with this mixture.
8. Then add the mini eggs.
9. Enjoy with these buns with your friends and relatives.
10. You will get the perfect dessert for your family.

Nutrition:
- Calories: 378
- Fat:15,3g
- Carbohydrates: 12,3g
- Protein: 5,6g

Apple Pie

Cook this dessert for your guests. All of them will like it and the result of your efforts will be great.

Prep time: 10 minutes | **Cooking time:** 15 minutes | **Servings:** 4

Ingredients:
- 1 lb of apples
- 1 tablespoon of vanilla
- 3 eggs
- 1 teaspoon of coriander
- ½ teaspoon of salt
- 1 cup of flour
- ½ cup of sugar

Directions:
1. Wash and clean apples.
2. Chop them in the pieces.
3. After that mix the coriander, vanilla and salt.
4. Take the bowl and beat all 3 eggs.
5. Then mix then with flour and sugar.
6. Put the slices to apples and mix everything well.
7. Put the dough on apples.
8. After that sprinkle the Air Fryer basket with oil.
9. Put the pie in the Air Fryer and cook for 10 minutes at 380F.
10. Then change the temperature to 250F and cook for 5 minutes.

Nutrition:
- Calories: 170
- Fat:7,3g
- Carbohydrates: 10,3g
- Protein: 5,1g

GIFT

Dear Friend!

Please follow this link to GET your GIFT Cookbook with 365 Great Recipes:

https://goo.gl/pr9F1U

(No registration or subscription required)